SAFETY OF COMPUTER CONTROL SYSTEMS 1985 (SAFECOMP '85)
Achieving Safe Real Time Computer Systems

Proceedings of the Fourth IFAC Workshop
Como, Italy, 1–3 October 1985

Edited by

W. J. QUIRK

Computer Science & Systems Division,
Atomic Energy Research Establishment, Harwell, U.K.

Published for the

INTERNATIONAL FEDERATION OF AUTOMATIC CONTROL

by

PERGAMON PRESS

OXFORD · NEW YORK · TORONTO · SYDNEY · FRANKFURT

U.K.	Pergamon Press Ltd., Headington Hill Hall, Oxford OX3 0BW, England
U.S.A.	Pergamon Press Inc., Maxwell House, Fairview Park, Elmsford, New York 10523, U.S.A.
CANADA	Pergamon Press Canada Ltd., Suite 104, 150 Consumers Road, Willowdale, Ontario M2J 1P9, Canada
AUSTRALIA	Pergamon Press (Aust.) Pty. Ltd., P.O. Box 544, Potts Point, N.S.W. 2011, Australia
FEDERAL REPUBLIC OF GERMANY	Pergamon Press GmbH, Hammerweg 6, D-6242 Kronberg-Taunus, Federal Republic of Germany

First edition 1985

Library of Congress Cataloging in Publication Data
IFAC Workshop (4th : 1985 : Como, Italy)
Safety of computer control systems 1985
(SAFECOMP '85)
1. Automatic control — Reliability — Congresses.
2. Computers — Reliability — Congresses.   3. Industrial safety — Congresses.
I. Quirk, William J.   II. International Federation of Automatic Control. III. Title
TJ212.2.I338   1985   629.8'95   85–19088

British Library Cataloguing in Publication Data
SAFECOMP '85 *(Conference : Como)*
Safety of Computer Control Systems 1985 : (SAFECOMP '85) : achieving safe real time
computer systems : proceedings of the fourth IFAC workshop, Como, Italy, 1–3 October 1985.
1. Control theory — Data processing   I. Title   II. Quirk, W. J.   III. International Federation of
Automatic Control   IV. Series
629.8'312   QA402.3
ISBN 0–08–032570–X

These proceedings were reproduced by means of the photo-offset process using the manuscripts supplied by the authors of the different papers. The manuscripts have been typed using different typewriters and typefaces. The lay-out, figures and tables of some papers did not agree completely with the standard requirements; consequently the reproduction does not display complete uniformity. To ensure rapid publication this discrepancy could not be changed; nor could the English be checked completely. Therefore, the readers are asked to excuse any deficiencies of this publication which may be due to the above mentioned reasons.

The Editor

Printed in Great Britain by A. Wheaton & Co. Ltd., Exeter

FOURTH IFAC WORKSHOP ON SAFETY OF COMPUTER CONTROL SYSTEMS (SAFECOMP '85)
Achieving Safe Real Time Computer Systems

Organized by
The Associazione Nazionale Italiana per l'Automazione (ANIPLA)

Sponsored by
The International Federation of Automatic Control (IFAC) through
Comitato Nazionale per la Ricerca e per lo Sviluppo dell'Energia Nucleare e delle
    Energie Alternative (ENEA)
Raggruppamento Ansaldo S.p.A.
Centro Studi ed Applicazioni in Tecnologie Avanzate (CSATA)

International Programme Committee

E. de Agostino *(Chairman)* (Italy)
T. Anderson (U.K.)
S. Bologna (Italy)
Don Bristol (U.S.A.)
P. Ciompi (Italy)
G. Dahll (Norway)
B. K. Daniels (U.K.)
J. Dobbins (U.S.A.)
W. Ehrenberger (Germany)
H. Frey (Switzerland)
R. Genser (Austria)
E. Johnson (U.K.)

Th. Lalive d'Epinay (Switzerland)
R. Lauber (Germany)
A. Mariotto (Italy)
V. Massari (Italy)
P. G. Mirandola (Italy)
W. J. Quirk (U.K.)
J. M. Rata (France)
I. C. Smith (U.K.)
B. J. Sterner (Sweden)
U. Voges (Germany)
R. W. Yunker (U.S.A.)
R. Zoppoli (Italy)

National Organizing Committee

S. Bologna (ENEA) *(Chairman)*
S. Anderloni (ENEL)
E. de Agostino (ENEA)

PREFACE

Computers continue to be used in more and more areas. Once the province of high technology industry, they now pervade the electronics controlling everything from space vehicles to domestic appliances. Further, they are expected not only to control and monitor, but also to provide speedy and accurate information concerning the state of their environment; not only at the superficial level of their raw input data, but increasingly in terms of the likely fundamental causes of that data. Many research projects are already underway on the use of artificial intelligence to aid operator in plant control rooms. The robot, not so long ago firmly in the world of science fiction, is now an industrial reality. No doubt it will soon be a domestic reality too. Not only must such a device act safely despite its programmer, it must also act safely despite the baby, the dog and the precious antiques.

Since the first SAFECOMP, held in 1979 in Stuttgart FDR, much has been learned concerning the successful implementation of computer systems where safety is a primary concern. The operational benefits to be gained from using computers, in terms of the enhanced control and safety capabilities which can be implemented, are readily acknowledged. Subsequent SAFECOMPs in 1982 at West Lafayette USA and in 1983 at Cambridge UK have reported the continuing progress in achieving and demonstrating these benefits.

The initiative and impetus for these events continues to be TC 7, the 'System Safety and Security' technical committee of the European Workshop on Industrial Computer Systems. TC 7 is a body of experts concerned with all aspects of safety and security arising from the use of computers in potentially hazardous situations. It addresses the problems of protecting human wellbeing, the environment and the plant itself against hazards arising from failures in computer control or safety systems however these may occur. The objectives of TC 7 include the determination and dissemination of procedures to construct, document, test and verify the safe performance of such systems. The 'Call for Papers' for the present SAFECOMP'85 reaffirmed the continuing interest and activity in this area: many more replies were received than could possibly be accommodated in a workshop. Contributions were proffered from 15 different nations, of which 14 are represented in this volume.

These papers cover a wide range of topics; both hardware and software receive attention, as do theoretical and practical aspects both experimental and real life. The systems of interest range from direct process control through robotics to operator assistance, with safety aspects being central in each case. Construction techniques, including diversity, are balanced against reliability assessment techniques.

The programme committee wish to record their thanks to the sponsoring organisations: the International Federation of Automatic Control (IFAC), the Associazione Nazionale Italiana per l'Automazione (ANIPLA), the Comitato Nazionale per la Ricerca e per lo Sviluppo dell'Energia Nucleare e delle Energie Alternative (ENEA), the Raggruppamento Ansaldo S.p.A., and the Centro Studi ed Applicazioni in Tecnologie Avanzate (CSATA); also to the National Organising Committee and ENEA for their administrative efforts, to TC 7, particularly to the past and present chairmen W.D. Ehrenberger and J.-M.A. Rata whose enthusiasm has kept the committee united through financially troubled times, and to the Safety and Reliability Society of Great Britain for their supportive efforts. The editor is grateful for the assistance of the staff of the IFAC Publisher Pergamon Press and of Mrs. W.A. James of Harwell in the preparation of these proceedings. It is hoped that this event continues the fine tradition of previous SAFECOMPs and will lead to many more in the future.

W.J. Quirk
AERE Harwell

CONTENTS

STRUCTURING PROCESSES AS A SEQUENCE OF NESTED ATOMIC ACTIONS

F. Baiardi and M. Vanneschi

Dipartimento di Informatica, Universita di Pisa, Corso Italia, 40, 56100 Pisa, Italy

Abstract. Implementation of atomic actions by means of concurrent programming constructs is discussed. It is shown that several trade-offs between performance and reliability may be obtained when an atomic action is defined through the composition of constructs and not as an elementary one.

Several alternative implementations are then discussed with reference to the ECSP concurrent language.

Emphasis is placed on process structuring, parallel activation and termination.

Keywords. Atomic action; Concurrent programming; Distributed system; Reliability; Performance.

INTRODUCTION

It is by now widely recognized that the notion of distributed atomic action is essential for the development of reliable distributed software (Liskov, 83; Randell, 78; Lomet, 77).

A computation can be easily structured into a sequence of steps, each implemented by an atomic action. Because of the "all or nothing" property of atomic actions, a failed step does not modify its input data and hence can be easily recovered. Furthermore, the ability of nesting atomic actions supports high granularity for both error detection and recovery.

As a counterpart of these advantages, usually atomic actions constrain the degree of concurrency and of asynchronicity of a computation since, as an example, the components of the action are forced to enter and to leave the action simultaneously (Gray, 78). This condition is not necessary for an action to be atomic, but is imposed to guarantee atomicity independently from the semantics of the computation of each component (Jensen, 83). Several advantages, in terms of efficiency, are possible if the previous constraint is relaxed provided that it is allowed by the action semantics. This can be done when the notion of atomic action is not primitive in the adopted programming language. Instead, atomic actions should be defined in terms of the composition of constructs for error recovery and synchronization. In this way the degree of synchronization and the amount of data to be saved may depend upon the particular computation that is made atomic.

In this paper we describe the implementation of distributed atomic actions in terms of the constructs of ECSP, a message passing concurrent language defined by a set of extensions to the CSP model (Hoare, 82). The extensions allow the programmer to define, among others, a continuation on the occurrence of a command failure. ECSP has been designed to be able to support fault-tolerance policies based upon cooperation among autonomous partners with the same authority.

Process cooperation is based not only upon communication but also upon process structuring and process termination handling. Termination handling is the fundamental mechanism for error detection and confinement, as well as the basis for forward and backward error recovery. Forward recovery is possible by establishing alternative communications with processes that are functionally equivalent to those that are supposed to be faulty. Backward recovery is instead based upon the ability of preventing the update on the state of a process when one of its commands fails.

ECSP is briefly reviewed in sect. 2, where we also discuss the failure model we assume, as well as some assumptions on ECSP implementation in a distributed system. The implementation of atomic actions in ECSP is discussed in sect. 3. In sect. 4 we show some solutions to a problem of stream manipulation. Each solution is based upon the notion of atomic action, but it offers a different trade-off between efficiency and reliability.

COOPERATION AND ERROR RECOVERY IN ECSP

We give here a short introduction to the main constructs of ECSP (Baiardi, 81, 84a, 84b). The sequential part of the language, which is Pascal-like, and some concurrent constructs not relevant here will not be described. Furthermore, some familiarity with the CSP model is assumed.

Communication and nondeterminism Control

Processes of an ECSP program can exchange values through the execution of input/output (i/o) commands. The result of the joint execution of an output command A!c(expr) and of an input command B?c(y) in processes B and A respectively, is the assignment to y of the value of expr. The communication has place through typed channels, each one individuated by the triple (source process, destination process, message type). The message type is a pair (constructor, type of value) where the constructor is an identifier that may be absent. As an example, the two previous i/o commands exploit a channel (A, B, (c, type of y)).

In ECSP communications can be asynchronous and each channel contains a constant amount of buffers implementing a FIFO queue. A synchronous communication with rendez-vous may be obtained as a particular case by not declaring any buffers for a given channel.

ECSP channels are not shared objects, instead they are considered as data structures local to the receiver process. As an example, the declarations of the amount of buffers appear in the receiver process only. Because of the absence of shared objects, we can avoid the introduction of protection mechanisms distinct from those for communications (Baiardi, 84c).

Both dynamic and static channels may be defined. A dynamic channel is exploited when the partner name in an i/o command is given by the value of a processname variable. The range of values of a processname X declared in a process P is given by the names of processes that can be referred by P and the undefined value ∅. The following operations are defined on X (they can be executed only by P):

a) connect(X,name), connect(X,Y): the constant value "name" or the value of the processname Y is assigned to X. All the commands using X refer now to a process distinct from the one referred by the previous value of X;

b) detach(X): the undefined value ∅ is assigned to X. All the i/o commands using X do no longer refer to any process;

c) is(X) : this is a boolean functions that returns true only when the value of X is different from ∅;

d) eq(X, name), eq(X,Y) : this is a boolean function that returns true when the value of X is "name" or is equal to that of Y.

Dynamic channels are the main ECSP mechanism to implement protection and reconfiguration of communication channels. They support the implementation of policies based upon the "minimum privilege" principle (Denning,76), since a process can create a dynamic channnel to communicate with another one and destroy the channel as soon as it decides that the communication is terminated.

Taking into account dynamic channnnels, we can define the termination conditions of an i/o command as follows:

a) with successs: for an output command this means that the message value has been either copied into a channel buffer or assigned to a variable in the receiver. In the case of an input command this means that a value has been assigned to the target variable;

b) with failure because of the partner termination;

c) with failure because the (dynamic) channel has been disconnected: this failure signals that the partner has uptated (or has not yet updated) the value of a processname variable and hence no communication is possible on the channel individuated by the command;

d) with failure because of the unability to communicate with the node where the partner is allocated; this outcome models decisions of the diagnostic procedures in the communication protocol of the language run time support.

The failure of an i/o command may be handled by the onfail clause

    i/o command   onfail
                  terminated : CL1
              disconnected : CL2
                    failed : CL3

After a failure, the appropriate command list, if present, is executed and then the execution goes on as if the command were successful; an unhandled failure results in the process termination with failure.

To control and express nondeterminism, ECSP adopts the alternative and repetitive commands with input guards of CSP. Each guard may be associated an integer variable to express the priority of the corresponding alternative. This allows the programmer to express directly scheduling policies and real-time decisions.

The termination conditions of guarded commands are similar to those of CSP. The failure of an alternative command may be handled by the onfail clause.

Process Structuring

ECSP supports nesting of parallel commands. Therefore each program has a hierarchical-parallel structure to support the implementation of the required degree of modularity and parallelism. As an example, a process P can activate processes P1 and P2 by the parallel command

    out(X,Y,Z)
    [P1 :: in(X,Z); ...; out(T)
    ||P2 :: in(X,Y); ...; out(Z)]
    in(T,Z);

This causes the simultaneous activation of P1 and P2, and suspends the execution of P until the command is terminated, i.e. until both P1 and P2 are terminated. A process terminate by the execution of the command terminate(succ) or terminate(fail). A paralllel command terminates successfully only when all the activated processes terminate successfully.

The nested structure of processes induces a visibility rule for process names. Let PR(Pi) be the set of process that can be referred to by Pi. If Pi has been activated by process P through a command including processes P1, ..., Pn then PR(Pi)=PR(P)U(P1, ...,Pi-1, Pi+1, ..., Pn). In the previous example, PR(P1)=PR(P)U(P2), PR(P2)=PR(P)U(P1). This implies that a process Q that can refer to P cannot refer to P1 or to P2, while P1 and P2 inherit from P the knowledge of the name Q. Hence P1 and P2 can send/receive messages to/from Q, while Q cannot detect whether the partner of a communication is P or P1 or P2. Implementation of nested parallel commands is discussed in (Baiardi, 84a, b).

Communication among P and P1 and P2 is implemented through import/export (I/E) lists. The clause out(list of variables) in P specifies the export list, i.e. the variables whose values are to be transmitted to P1 and P2. The clause in(list of variables) in P specifies the variables that will be assigned the values received from P1 and P2. P1 and P2 include, in turns, an import and an export list to specify the variables that receive a value from, and those whose values are to be transmitted to, P. The value of a variable in an export list is assigned to the variable with the same name in the corresponding import list. To avoid ambiguities, the export list of P1 and P2 have to be disjoint. In the given example, on the execution of the parallel command, the values of X, Z are assigned to variables in P1 while the values of X, Y are assigned to variables in P2. When the parallel command ends, the values of T in P1 and of Z in P2 are transmitted to P and assigned to the corresponding variables.

According to the ECSP semantics, the assignements to variables in the input list of P are executed only if the parallel commands terminates successfully. This is the ECSP mechanism for backward recovery policies as well as the basis for the definition of atomic actions.

The failure of a parallel command may be handled by the onfail clause, where a distinct recovery action may be executed for each distinct subset of failed processes.

Failure Model and Language Implementation

In the following we assume that any fault in the system corresponds to an inconsistent behaviour of a set of processes. By inconsistent behaviour we mean, for example, a process unexpected termination or an erroneous communication attempt.

The language run time support should include mechanisms that transform an error into an inconsistent behaviour. As an example, the support transforms the crash of a processor into the termination with failure of all the the processes (Pi) allocated to the processor. In turn, this induces the termination with failure (kind b) of any i/o command referring to a Pi. When, instead, a Pi is executing a parallel command, its anomalous termination has to be masked until the parallel command terminates. Hence a proper implementation has to be adopted to prevent the crash from affecting the processes of the parallel command not allocated to the crashed processor.

Another essential hypothesis is that, even when physical communication media are unreliable, the diagnostic mechanisms at the communication level are reliable. This corresponds to say that the termination conditions of an i/o command are uniquely distinguishable. The mechanisms to grant the non ambiguity condition about the kinds of a command termination are implemented:
a) in a way that strongly depends upon language constructs for the cases a),b),c) of sect. 2.1;
b) by implementing mechanisms as diagnostic procedures in the run time support for the case d).

IMPLEMENTATION OF ATOMIC ACTIONS IN ECSP

The basic mechanism to implement atomic actions is the parallel command with I/E lists. In this section we introduce some sufficient conditions to guarantee that a set of parallel commands is an atomic action.

Let us consider, at first, a single command

```
out(LO)
[ P1:: in(LO1); ... ; out(LI1)
||        .
          .
          .
||Pn:: in(LOn); ... ; out(LIn)]
in(LI) onfail ....
```

If the following conditions are verified, the command is an atomic action:
c1) each Pi can communicate only with processes belonging to the command;
c2) the output of the command are the values to be assigned to LI and they depend only upon the values transmitted by LO.

The two conditions guarantee, respectively, idempotency and restartability of the command. Condition c1 can be relaxed: consider the case when a Pj invokes a server process Q to execute a function f on a value X. If X is not stored into Q's state after computing f(X), the communication between Pj and Q does not violate atomicity. Condition c2 guarantees that the outputs of the action can be made persistent, e.g. stored on an external device, only after the termination of the action.

It is worth discussing now some noticeable characteristics of the implementation of atomic action in terms of ECSP parallel commands.

Consider the case when a Pj fails. After this failure, it is known that the work executed by the other processes is useless, since the command will fail anyway and hence no results will be transmitted to the process executing the parallel command. Thus, in this case, all the other processes of the parallel command could be aborted. In ECSP, instead, the other processes terminate only when they detect that the failure of Pj prevent them from accomplishing their tasks. This choice preserves the autonomy of each process whose behaviour cannot be affected by other processes. In particular, a process cannot be forced either to terminate or to take part in an interaction.

The abandonement of the autonomy principle, though it could increase the efficiency of some computations, may introduce "privileged" system components that could strongly reduce the overall reliability and, furthermore, would make it very difficult to express forward recovery policies. Anyway, since a process is informed of the failure of a Pj through the failure of its i/o commands referring to Pj, it is very simple to stop a computation by propagating process termination.

Consider now a set S of parallel commands (PC1, ..., PCn), where each PCi activates processes (Pij, 1≤j ≤ mi) that receive values in LOi and returns values in LIi. S is an atomic action if we can guarantee that:
c3) a Pij activated by PCi can communicate only with a process Pkl activated by PCk;
c4) communications between processes not belonging to the same parallel command exploit dynamic channels that are connected before executing the parallel command and detached when a failure occurs;
c5) all the parallel commands end in the same way.

Condition c3 corresponds to c1 since it guarantees that no intermediate result is visible outside the action. Condition c4 is instead related to the scope rule for process names. Since two processes Pij and Pkl activated by distinct parallel commands of S cannot refer to each other directly, an anomalous termination of Pij cannot be detected by Pkl. When the communication is implemented by dynamic channels, these channels can be detached by the process activating Pij and thus the i/o commands of Pkl will return a failure of kind "disconnected channel". Furthermore, since the state of a dynamic channel is reinitialized when the channel is detached or connected to a new partner, c4 guarantees idempotency with respect to communications.

By structuring an atomic action into several parallel commands it is possible to increase the amount of concurrency among components.

As illustrated in the following, conditions c3 and c4 can also be relaxed depending upon the semantics of the action.

ALTERNATIVE IMPLEMENTATIONS OF ATOMIC ACTIONS

To show alternative implementations of atomic actions we will refer to the following problem: given two data streams, S1 and S2, produced from data structures IS1 and IS2 respectively, compute the stream S3 defined as follows:

$S3_j=g(h(S1_j),S2_j)$ if $j \leq L1$, $j \leq L2$; $S3_j=h(S2_j)$ if $L1 \leq j \leq L2$;
$S3_J=k(S1_j)$ if $L2 < j \leq L1$
where Li is the length of Si and Sij is the j-th element of Si.

The solutions we present are all structured as follows. The program is partitioned into two sets of processes: processes in the first one receive IS1 and IS2 from processes in the other and return to them the whole stream S3. The second partition will be modelled by a single process called Other: this is not a limitation since parallelism inner to Other may be expressed by nested processes.

Let us consider a first simple solution that does not take into account reliability or robustness.

Prog::[P1||P2||P3||P4||Other]

P1 and P2 receive IS1 and IS2 from Other, and produce S1 and S2, respectively. As soon as an element of the stream is produced, P1 sends it to P3 and P2 to P4. P1 and P2 end when the last element of the corresponding stream has been produced.

The programs of P3 and P4 are:

```
P3::<declarations>
    begin
      *[P1?new ⟶ P4!h(new)];
      terminate(succ);
    end
P4::<declarations>
    begin
    *[P2?x1 ⟶ rec:=false;
      * [ not(rec), P3?x2 ⟶ rec:=true;
    R1                      append(S3,g(x2,x1))
       ]  ;
          if not(rec) then begin
                            append(S3, k(x1));
                *[ P2?x1 ⟶ append(S3, k(x1))]
                             end
     ☐ P3?x2  ⟶ rec:=false;
             * [ not(rec), P2?x1 ⟶ rec:=true;
    R2                          append(S3, g(x2,x1))
              ];
            if not(rec) then begin
                              append(S3, x2);
              *[ P3?x2 ⟶ append(S3, x2) ]
                            end
    ];
        terminate(succ)
    end
```

Process P3 applies function h to all elements of S1. The termination of P1 will produce the failure of the guard and the successfull termination of P3. P4 waits for a pair of elements, one from P2 and the other from P3. When both producers end, the repetitive command ends successfully. If one stream is longer than the other, then either R1 or R2 will end because of the failure of the input guard. In this case, P4 will wait only for elements of the longer stream. Notice that P3 and P4 assume that the communication from the producer fails iff the stream is terminated.

To transform the computation of P1-P4 into an atomic action, we can nest the processes into another one that receives IS1 and IS2 and returns S3. the corresponding program is :

Program::[Rstream||Other]

```
Rstream::<declarations>
        begin
          Other?IS1;
          Other?IS2;
          done:=true;
          nret:=0;
          repeat
             out(IS1,IS2)
              [ P1||P2||P3||P4 ]
             in(S3) onfail begin
                            nret:=nret+1;
                            done:=false
                            end;
          until done or (nret>max);
          if done then Other!S3 else ...;
          terminate(succ)
        end
```

In this solution, P1 and P2 receive their inputs by I/E lists and P4 returns S3 to Rstream in the same way. If any Pi fails, this will prevent the assignement to S3 and the parallel command will be executed again. If we do not modify the program of P4, it will not detect the anomalous termination of P2 or P3 and thus it will append to S3 the elements received from the other producer. This can be avoided by forcing P3 and P2 to communicate explicitly their termination and by replacing the repetitive command in P4 by the following repeat command:

```
repeat
  if not(end1) then [ P2?x1 ——► skip
                     □ P2?end() ——► end1:=true
                     ] ;
  if not(end2) then [P3?x2 ——► skip
                     □P3?end() ——► end2:=true
                     ] ;
  case end1, end2 of
    begin
      false, false : append(S3, g(x1,x2))
      true,  false : append(S3, x2)
      false, true  : append(S3, k(x1))
      true,  true  : skip
    end;
until end1 and end2
```

If neither a value nor the message end() is received from a producer, then P4 will fail immediately, thus inducing the termination of the other producer. Notice that this solution is much more synchronous that the previous one since both IS1 and IS2 have to be received before the parallel command is executed. Other synchronization are introduced to stop the computation on the failure of a producer.

Let us consider now a solution where the atomic action is implemented by a pair of parallel commands.

```
Program::[Rstream1 || Rstream2 || Other ]

Rstream1:: ...
    Other?IS1;
    repeat
      connect(sink, Rstream2);
      Rstream2?ready();
      out(IS1,sink)
      [P1||P3] onfail begin
                      (P1, P3) :<processsor recovery>
                          (P3) : done:=false;
                                 nret:=nret+1;
                                 detach(sink);
                                 Rstream2?detect();
                              end;
    until done or (nret>max);
    ...
Rstream2 :: ...
    Other?IS2
    repeat
      connect(source,Rstream1);
      Rstream2!ready();
      out(IS2,source);
      [P2||P4] in(S3) onfail begin
                      (P2, P4) :<processor recovery>
                          (P4) : done:=false;
                                 nret:=nret+1;
                                 detach(source);
                                 Rstream1!detect();
                              end
    until done or (nret>max);
```

The dynamic channnels corresponding to the processname variables sink and source implement the communications among processes of the two parallel commands. To assure that these channels have been properly connected, Rstream1 and Rstream2 are synchronized by the message ready().

In the programs of Rstream1 and Rstream2, we have assumed that a failure of P3 or of P4 is due to a line fault. In this case the recovery action consists in a new execution of the parallel command in both processes. As an example, after the failure of P3, Rstream1 will detach the processname variable sink thus inducing a failure in P4 and the termination of the parallel command in Rstream2. Then Rstream1 and Rstream2 will exchange the message detect() and connect sink and source before executing again the parallel command.

It is possible that P3 (P4) is affected by a fault after having sent (received) the last message to (from) P4 (P3). In this case the disconnection of the dynamic channel has no effect on the partner: this is a consequence of the "uncertainity principle" (Gray, 78) and it will be considered as a "disaster" similar to that induced by a crash during the "commit" phase of a distributed atomic action.

The programs of Rstream1 and Rstream2 assume that the failure of the process working on the input sequence is due to a processor crash. An appropriate recovery action may be, in this case, the execution of a parallel command activating processes with the same input/output behaviour of the failed ones. As an example, in Rstream1

```
< processor recovery>= detach(sink);
                       Rstream2?detect();
                       connect(sink, Rstream2);
                       Rstream2?ready();
                       out(IS1, sink)
                       [P1'||P3']
```

where Pi' may be a copy of Pi allocated to a distinct processor.

The programs of P1, P3, P4 in this solution may be the following:

```
P1:: in(IS1)
     begin
       while IS1≠0 do
         begin
           produce new;
           P3!new onfail terminate(succ);
         end;
       P3!end()
     end
P3:: in(sink)
     begin
     [P1?el——► sink!h(el)
     □ P1?end() ——► sink!end()
     ] ;
     terminate(succ)
     end;
P4:: in(source)
     begin
       end1:=end2:=false;
       repeat
         ...
       until end1 and end2;
       terminate(succ);
     end
```

The program of P2 is similar to that of P1. Notice that the failure of the output command is transformed into the termination with success of P1 or P2.

The implementation of the distributed atomic action by a pair of parallel commands supports a larger degree of concurrency. As a matter of fact, we have that:

i) IS1 and IS2 are received concurrently by distinct processes;

ii) as soon as S1 has been produced, Rstream1 may continue its execution without waiting for the termination of the parallel command in Rstream2. This increase in concurrency is paid in terms of reliability: as previously discussed, a fault in P2 or P4 cannot be recovered when the parallel command of Rstream1 is already terminated.

Another trade-off between performance and reliability can be achieved if we require that the two parallel commands are initiated asynchronously, i. e. the message ready is eliminated. In this case, the input command of P4 and the output command in P3, using respectively sink and source, could fail since the other process has not yet connected its processname variable. Since in ECSP this kind of failure can be distinguished, the process can recover the failure and attempt later the communication.

This behaviour can be described, in the case of P3, by the following program:

```
P3:: in(sink)
     end:=false;
     repeat
     [ P1?el ──→ if empty(S') then x:=el
                                  else append(S', el);
              done:=true;
              sink!el onfail
                      disconnected : done:=false
      ☐ P1?end() ──→ end:=true
     ];
     until end or done;
     if end then begin
        Timer!delta;
     *[ not(done), Timer?delta ──→
               sink!x onfail
                      disconnected : done:=false
      ] ;
        Timer!stop();
              end;
     while not(empty(S')) do
           begin
             x:=first(S');
             sink!x;
           end;
     if not(end) then ⟨previous program for P4⟩;
```

We have assumed that S1 is not empty. Timer is a process that, after receiving a time interval delta, sends a signal each delta units of time, until it receives a message stop(). The loss of reliability is due to the fact that P3 can detect that the dynamic channel has been disconnected only after it has succeded in sending at least one message. When instead, P4 fails before receiving the first message, P3 will assume that the channel has still to be connected and hence will go on attempting the communication.

Other trade-offs are possible, but it is important to notice that in the same program we can have several distinct implementations of atomic actions, even nested one into the other. Furthermore, the ability of nesting parallel commands, and hence atomic actions, makes it possible to recover some faults not detected by inner actions.

CONCLUSION

We have shown how it is possible to define nested atomic actions using a small set of programming constructs. These constructs support several trade-offs between reliability and efficiency, thus allowing to exploit information about the semantics of the action to be implemented.

As far as concern the implementation of these constructs, it can be shown that no efficiency is lost by obtaining atomic actions through the composition of constructs (Baiardi, 81, 84b).

REFERENCES

Baiardi, F. and others, (1981). Mechanisms for a robust multiprocessing environment in the MuTEAM kernel. Proc. of 11th Fault Tolerant Computing Symp., Portland, June 1981, pp.20-24.

Baiardi, F., Ricci, L. and Vanneschi, M. (1984a). Static checking of interprocess communications in ECSP. ACM SIGPLAN Symp. on Compiler Construction, Montreal, June 1984.

Baiardi, F. and others, (1984b). Distibuted implementation of nested communicating processes and termination. 13th Int. Conf. on Parallel Processing, Aug. 1984.

Baiardi, F. and others, (1984c). Structuring processes for a cooperative approach to fault tolerant distributed software. Proc. of 4th Symp. on Reliability in Distributed Software and Database Systems, Silver Spring, Oct. 1984, pp. 218-231.

Denning, P.J. (1976). Fault tolerant operating systems. ACM Computing Surveys; 8,4, pp.359-389Gray, J.N. (1978). Notes on database operating systems. in Operating systems - An advanced course, Lect. Notes in Comp. Science, Springer & Verlang, Berlin.

Hoare, C.A.R. (1982). A calculus of total correctness for communicating processes. Science of Computer Programming; 1,1, pp.49-72.

Jensen, E.D., and others, (1983). Distributed cooperating processes and transactions. ACM SIGCOMM Symposium, Oct. 1983, pp.98-105.

Liskov, B. and Scheifler, R. (1983). Guardians and actions: linguistic support for robust, distributed programming. ACM TOPLAS; 5, 3, pp. 381-404

Lomet, D.B. (1977). Process structuring, synchronization and recovery using atomic transactions. ACM SIGPLAN Notices, 12, 3.

Randell, B. Lee, P.A. and Treleaven, P.C. (1978). Reliability issues in computer system design. ACM Computing Surveys; 10, 2, pp. 123-165.

A DYNAMIC SYSTEM ARCHITECTURE FOR SAFETY RELATED SYSTEMS

W. J. Quirk

Atomic Energy Research Establishment, Harwell, Oxfordshire, UK

Abstract. Safety related applications usually demand the provision of redundant resources within the system and some method of reconfiguration when a failure is detected. One problem with such an approach is that it has proved to be very difficult to design, implement and test adequately this reconfigurability. A dynamic system architecture is described which obviates some of these difficulties. This architecture takes advantage of the fact that the processing associated with any set of inputs and at any instant of time is of finite duration. By arranging for sufficient parallel redundancy to be available so that the system is not compromised by a single process instance failure, system error recovery becomes almost trivial. There is no need to recover the single instance failure (because of the available redundancy) and future processing will be initiated by normal process initiation. Little error-recovery specific procedure is necessary other than producing an effective fail-stop processor. The efficient implementation of such a system depends crucially on a number of issues. These include a novel, fully distributed scheduling procedure and the topology and functionality of the underlying communication system. The implications of such an architecture for overall system safety include the effects and benefits of software diversity and the possibility of producing systems which are to some extent proof against their own design errors.

Keywords. Architecture, diversity, fault tolerance.

INTRODUCTION

Safety related applications usually demand the provision of redundant resources within the system and some method of reconfiguration when a failure is detected. However, one major problem with such an approach is that it has proved to be very difficult to design, implement and test adequately this reconfigurability. Much useful work has been done on this problem, but most approaches rely on the assumption that the software is fully functional when an error occurs /LaSh82/, /Lomb84/ and that all errors are due to the hardware. Published figures reveal that a sizeable proportion of complete system failures are brought about by a failure to reconfigure correctly while attempting to recover from what was intended to be a recoverable error /Toy78/. The assumption that the software is totally error free seems hardly justified in most cases and the safety implications of such failures can be extremely serious.

This paper describes the basis of a dynamic system architecture which obviates some of these difficulties. The architecture takes advantage of the fact that the processing associated with any set of inputs and at any instant of time is of finite duration. The fact that the processing procedure may be repeated a potentially unlimited number of times does not mean that a process implementing this procedure need

have a potentially unlimited life. Rather, new processes can be initiated when required and can terminate when they have completed a particular processing sequence.

By arranging for sufficient parallel redundancy to be available so that the system is not compromised by a single process instance failure, system error recovery becomes almost trivial. There is no need to recover the single instance failure (because of the available redundancy) and future processing will be continued by normal process initiation. No error-recovery specific procedure is necessary other than producing an effective fail-stop processor, a topic already addressed by a number of workers /CrFu78/, /ScSc83/, /Kenw84/, /Schn84/.

The efficient implementation of such a system depends crucially on a number of issues. These include a novel, fully distributed scheduling procedure and the topology and functionality of the underlying communication system. Such an architecture has several interesting implications for overall system safety. Of particular interest are the effects and benefits of software diversity to overcome problems of common-mode failure and the possibility of producing systems which are to some extent proof against their own design errors.

FUNCTIONAL REDUNDANCY

In a previous paper /GiQu79/, the basis of functional redundancy was described. The provision of redundant input data is of course a standard requirement for safety systems and the provision of redundant data processing, usually by identical replication, is also well established. But within single computing systems, the provision of such redundancy needs careful design. Otherwise, reliability 'bottlenecks' may occur, where the benefits of redundancy in one part of the system are lost because of potential common mode failures in another. The aim of functional redundancy is to achieve a uniform level of coverage throughout the system, taking into account any inbuilt redundancy available due to replication of input sensors or output actuators available. The approach taken is to trace the data flow through the system and to ensure that independent processing paths are followed so that a failure on one path does not affect other redundant data. Not only must there be separate physical data paths through the system, but, in order to obviate common mode failures, separate software must be utilised on the different data paths.

This previous paper also observed that redundancy in the input data was provided so that failures in the input sensors did not compromise the integrity of the system. This implies that the system can tolerate a limited amount of faulty input data and, in particular, a number of transient input errors. But there is no difference between a faulty input and a failure within the system along the path followed by that input, providing the failure is isolated to just that path. Thus, with the provision of suitable internal redundancy, it is possible for the system to be essentially unaffected by isolated transient failures. Indeed, if the normal output range of a process is augmented with a recognisable 'failed' value, then subsequent processes using that process output can take appropriate safe action. This can be achieved even without the augmentation, but it is easier to implement and demonstrate if it is done. With proper design, system safety can be maintained through single isolated failures.

The problem then is to design the system so that all failures are are transient and isolated. Clearly no system can be made proof against total failure; the architecture proposed below will be demonstrated to be proof against single internal failures which are sufficiently separated in time. The precise definition of this sufficient separation will be derived later.

The first step in rendering all failures transient is to note that there is no requirement to dedicate physical resources to functional units on a long-term or near-permanent basis. The 'standard' architecture for repetitive functionality has the form shown in figure 1. The WAIT interval is often omitted, with the program cycling as often as possible. However, the system requirement, properly assessed, will yield the required repeat interval. This fragment is then equivalent to that shown in figure 2.

```
REPEAT FOREVER
    [
    WAIT REQUIRED TIME INTERVAL
    READ INPUTS
    DO CALCULATION
    WRITE OUTPUTS
    ]
```

Fig   1. Static Scheduling Fragment.

```
    WAIT REQUIRED TIME INTERVAL
    RESCHEDULE NEW COPY OF SELF
    READ INPUTS
    DO CALCULATION
    WRITE OUTPUTS
    EXIT
```

Fig   2. Dynamic Scheduling Fragment.

Practically all the system components can be implemented in this second fashion. System 'long term' memory can be implemented as overlapping finite duration 'data server' processes. Only the system peripherals cannot be made dynamic, but these must be replicated in any case to provide a suitable level of fault tolerance and safety. Thus implementing the system in this manner hinges on the rescheduling procedure and the rest of this paper considers only the messages associated with this procedure.

In order to render the former fragment fault tolerant, some other part of the system needs to oversee its performance and, when a failure is detected, attempt to allocate the fragment to an alternative resource. This is precisely the operation in the second line of the latter fragment. The difference is that this operation is used only rarely in the former architecture (and then only at a time of stress for the system), whilst it is regularly used in the latter. Thus the procedure is extremely thoroughly tested and great confidence placed in it.

One should also notice that the characteristics of failures change subtly as systems are made more and more reliable and fault tolerant. Because there are less failures observed, they tend to be more complex than the 'simple', 'common' failures observed in less reliable systems. The difference between transient hardware failures and software failures also becomes blurred. The software is likely to function properly for all but a very small range of rarely-occuring special circumstances. Consequently, a failure on one cycle is unlikely to imply a failure in a subsequent cycle (providing that no code or data has been corrupted by the failure). This is just the same as the observed effects of a hardware transient; after a suitable reset, the device will resume normal operational characteristics. Thus, the latter architecture is inherently more resilient to these failures. It is this observation coupled with the confidence in the scheduling procedure which justify the assumption that failures will appear transient and isolated in time.

DYNAMIC SCHEDULING & FAULT TOLERANCE

The fundamental scheduling design is shown in
figure 3. This mirrors the fragment in figure 2.
However, some extra messages have to be added. First,
the initial action of the process is to signal its
grandparent. Second, after completing its normal
processing, it waits another scheduling interval,
and listens for the signal from its grandchild. In
normal circumstances, this final signal arives as
expected and the grandparent exits. If it fails to
arrive, it could mean a number of possible errors
have occured: that the child failed before scheduling
the grandchild, that the grandchild failed before
signaling the grandparent, or that the message was
sent but not delivered. The corrective action in all
cases is for the grandparent to attempt to schedule
a grandchild directly. However, if the error was
delivery failure, this would lead to two copies of
the grandchild being activated. To prevent this, the
initial action of each process is not to signal the
grandparent first, but rather to try to signal any
copy of itself. It expects no reply from its own
generation, because there should not be such another
copy. In order to prevent two copies killing each
other, a priority scheme has to be included. This
too can be made dynamic: by adding the process
instance number to the physical processor
identification and reducing the result modulo the
total number of processors. This yields a number
which is unique for any particular process instance.
If processes only exits in response to a higher
priority message from the same generation, then only
the highest priority process will not be killed.

There are further failure possibilities in this
system. Having scheduled its child, the grandparent
may fail. If it merely dies quietly, there is no
effect on the system. If it erroneously tries to
schedule a grandchild when one is already successfully
scheduled, then the mechanism described above will
resolve the situation. But in all message sending
situations, there is the possibility, at least in
principle, of the sender going into a tight loop
sending repeat messages. This poses two different
problems. One is to ensure that the communications
subsystem does not saturate, locking out all other
processes. The other is to ensure that the system
can effectively ignore the erroneous messages. In
the case of process initiation, it is required to
allow one process to run, rather than for an infinite
sequence of processes to be initiated and almost
immediately die. Support for this is based on the
priority structure already discussed. This determines
an unique processor to continue from any pair trying
to perform the same process. Once this one has been
established, any other can be killed by the working
one. In order to limit the initial number to two,
some support from the communications subsystem is
proposed, as described below. Indeed, if process
creations are sequenced by the communications system,
the priority system could be replaced by a simple
'first-started continues' approach. But sequencing
is difficult to enforce if the communications
subsystem is itself replicated.

The ability to kill a process might initially seem
to be a great problem; the possibility of a rogue
processor killing the whole system must be made
negligible. However, the power to kill used here is
very restricted. A process is killed only by asking
to be killed, and it can check the validity of that
reply. When a process requests to be killed, it
broadcasts only its name, not its instance number.
Each process of the same name can reply with a kill
for their own instance number. Thus only one
generation can be killed by any single process. It
is worth noting that the system will still recover
if two processes of the same generation survive, or
if they both die. In the former case, only one of
their offspring should survive after the next
reschedule; in the latter the normal reschedule
procedure will restart the next generation. This is
because the architecture is, in fact, resilient to
many, but not all, twin failures too. This fact can
be used to enforce a harder regime; that a whole
generation should die if two or more identical
processes appear. By allowing a process to continue
only if at least one of its grandfather or father
reply to its 'check' broadcast, one can remove any
possibility of the system being·compromised by an
infinite reschedule loop. Such a system is still
proof against a single failure, but it becomes
vulnerable to more twin failures than would otherwise
be the case.

GRAND
FATHER   FATHER   SON

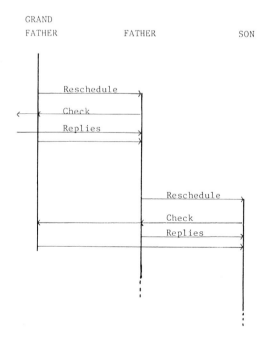

Fig 3. Principle Scheduling Transactions.

The formal verification that the above scheme is indeed single error tolerant is too long to include here. A number of important points can be made however. The proof is essentially a fault tree analysis of the failure modes for the proposed architecture. It involves taking the failure of each inter-process message pass and analysing its consequences. It hinges crucially on the single error 'at one time' criteria, so that, for example, if the failure is caused by the sender process, then the would-be receive process is working normally. The credible failures for the system include an unspecified process failure causing no further communication - essentially a HALT, an infinite loop of a repeating message sequence, and the loss or false generation of a single message. One has to assume that some conceivable faults are in fact incredible. This class includes the kill process mechanism discussed in some detail above; it is held incredible that any single process can generate randomly the correct sequence of instance numbers to kill more than one generation of any particular process. The 'at one time' can now be seen within the time spanning the activities shown in figure 3. All that is required is that failures will not affect two successive generations. Although the failure criteria are stated in terms of a single failure in the time interval, this is in fact overly conservative, as failures in other scheduling sequences can be accommodated analogously and at the same time, subject only to their being sufficient working processors left available.

COMMUNICATIONS

In order for an architecture such as the one proposed to be viable, an efficient and reliable inter-processor communication system is necessary. To schedule a process, it must be possible to locate an idle processor. There are a number of ways to do this. One is that each processor keeps a table of the availability of every other processor in the system. This means that whenever a processor changes state, it has to broadcast that change to all the others. A second way is to have a 'free processor server' which is called upon as required. This removes the necessity to broadcast, but is clearly an extremely sensitive part of the system in terms of reliability and availability. Both involve keeping a data-base intact through failures in the system, and seem to pose more problems than they prevent. For example, since a processor which dies cannot be relied upon to announce that fact to anyone, let alone to the data-base manager, some extra functionality would have to be built in to the system to allow the manager to interrogate each processor. An alternative approach is to seek an idle processor as and when a schedule request is to be made. This essentially involves a 'who is free?' broadcast from the scheduler. This has its own problems however: a lot of replies may be generated although only one is required, in a fault situation one processor might always be the first to claim it was available, and because there are multiple schedulers there are

problems with synchronising requests and time outs. One way around these problems is to place some of the arbitration logic required in the design of the communications subsystem.

The normal behaviour of the communications system is to pass messages between known pairs of processors. For broadcasts, a modified behaviour is introduced. Using a priority scheme as described above, the communications system reserves time after the broadcast for any reply. The time for reply is controlled by the priority. Thus the first reply will be from the highest priority free processor. Knowing that this is a broadcast reply all lower priority replies can be blocked by the network interfaces. The successful replier will know locally that he was successful because his reply message will be accepted and therefore he knows he is no longer idle. The reply blocked processors will know locally because their reply attempt is rejected and that therefore they are still idle. In normal situations, there is only one reply message. This idea is similar to that used by the HYPERchannel system, a product of Network Systems Corporation. In this, every message reserves a reply time for the addressee, followed by a statically allocated priority based time for next use by another address on the HYPERchannel /FrHe84/. Although this discussion shows that a modified ETHERNET-type communications system is appropriate, this is not mandatory. Other architectures could provide the functionality required.

As mentioned above, there needs to be some protection against jamming the communications subsystem, especially in a fault condition. One way to help achieve this is to enforce a time delay between consecutive transmissions without any intervening reception. This effectively limits the bandwidth that any single process can utilize and thus prevent jamming. It should be noted that if it is credible for the communication system to jam or fail under internal fault conditions, then the whole communication subsystem must be replicated. Indeed, the whole of this architecture assumes a secure communications subsystem.

Data communication must also be supported between the processors. This too can be provided rather easily with broadcast facilities as data can be passed to a process by its name rather than by its physical address on a network. It is maybe worth observing that this use of broadcast to process by name obviates some conceivable error modes, such as misrouting, in more conventional physically addressed systems.

DISCUSSION

Since the scheme described above is more complicated and needs more resources than a more conventional statically allocated architecture, it is worthwhile examining the advantages of the proposed system. The first advantage, indeed the key reason for following the approach, is the elimination of nearly all the error specific recovery mechanism. This means that all the code in the system can be uniformly well tested and greater confidence established in its ability to tolerate errors. A second advantage is that availability and reliability are effectively separated by this approach. The design fits very naturally on a processor pool machine. Although such machines have been proposed previously for process control applications, either they have not been scheduled dynamically or else they have been very closely coupled /KiKa84/. With such an architecture, the system availability is determined solely by the total number of processors still working in the system. If on-line replacement is possible, then the availability can be made as high as one wishes (at least under the single failure at a time hypothesis). A third advantage is that the scheme also handles many software errors and internal design failures. Assuming that reasonable care has been taken over the software, as would befit any safety-related project, it is reasonable to suppose that failures will be relatively rare. Such a failure will appear to the system just as a transient hardware failure, so that if the software error is indeed an isolated one, the system will suffer only transitorily. In general, an 'idle' processor would be running some diagnosis program so that a real hardware failure would be detected eventually and the processor halted.

Diversity can also be considered in this context. We have argued that the proposed system is proof against any single failure in the scheduling procedure. Although the functional behaviour of each generation of scheduler is identical, they could be implemented diversely if it was thought that the complexity of their internal structure merited it. In this case, three different implementations could be used cyclically, again making the assumption that a failure of more than one implementation in any small time interval is sufficiently unlikely that it can be considered incredible. Similarly, the data transformation software could be cyclically initiated diverse versions. This sequential diversity is in contrast to the more common parallel diversity in that its benefits are obtained without having to double or treble the physical resources in the system.

The number of messages that the system generated and has to handle Might at first sight appear to be quite large. However, this is not really the case. In normal circumastances, each reschedule generates four messages (1 reschedule broadcast, 1 check broadcast and 2 replies). These would have to be augmented with any necessary data transfers, but would be unlikely to exceed ten in total. The bandwidth of standard local area networks are already quite high (10Mbit for ETHERNET, for example), and this can easily support a thousand messages per second each of a hundred bytes. This implies that one hundred reschedules per second could be supported, a figure which seems more than ample. In any case, the scheme proposed can be modified to reduce the

number, though only at a cost to the reliability. We have proposed a new process instance for each new calculation required. This could be weakened to a new process instance for each batch of N calculations required for some finite N, as shown in figure 4.

```
WAIT REQUIRED TIME INTERVAL * N
RESCHEDULE NEW COPY OF SELF
REPEAT N TIMES
    [
    WAIT REQUIRED TIME INTERVAL
    READ INPUTS
    DO CALCULATION
    WRITE OUTPUTS
    ]
EXIT
```

Fig 4. Modified Dynamic Scheduling Fragment.

The cost is that the system would then have to be able to tolerate not single isolated calculation failures but batches of N consecutive failed calculations. Notice that this need not compromise safety, however, as the failure would be revealed. It is possible that a hybrid scheme could be devised in which a new process instance is created after N calculations or after a failure, whichever comes first. However, the added complexity of such a scheme has so far prevented a proof of being single failure tolerant.

Finally, complexity of proof also makes it difficult to establish an extension of the scheme to 2 or more 'simultaneous' failures. The proof of single error tolerance draws heavily on the single failure at a time assumption so that, for example, it can be assumed that the procedure for recovering from a real error will itself execute correctly. The validity of the assumption itself rests on the non error specific nature of the scheduling procedure and on the lack of any common mode failure. In any case, such an extended system would require significantly more physical resources in the system, and it may be more effective to implement a second, single failure tolerant system.

CONCLUSION

The architecture proposed and discussed above offers the basis for a highly reliable and highly available system. Although it needs more resources and is apparently more complex than static systems during normal operation, its operation is much simpler in error situations. The assumptions and conditions under which it can survive errors can be made quite explicit, allowing its performance and reliability to be assessed relatively easily. It can incorporate diversity if required to strengthen the necessary single failure criterion and is very suitable for multi-microprocessor implementation on an ETHERNET type local area network.

REFERENCES

/CrFu78/   A.H. Cribbens, M.J. Furniss, H.A. Ryland
"An Experimental Application of Microprocessors to
Railway Signalling". Electronics & Power, March 1978.

/Toy78/   W.N. Toy "Fault-Tolerant Design of Local
ESS Processors". Proc IEEE, Vol 66 No 10, October 1978.

/GiQu79/   M.H. Gilbert, W.J. Quirk "Functional
Redundancy to Achieve High Reliability". SAFECOMP'79,
Stuttgart FRG, 16-18 May 1979.

/LaSh82/   L. Lamport, R. Shostak, M. Pease "The
Byzantine Generals Problem". ACM Trans Prog Lang
Sys, Vol 4 No 3, July 1982.

/ScSc83/   R.D. Schlichting, F.B. Schneider "Fail-Stop
Processors: An Approach to Designing Fault-Tolerant
Computer Systems". ACM Trans Comp Sys, Vol 1 No 3,
Aug 1983.

/FrHe84/   W.R. Franta, J.R. Heath "Measurement and
Analysis of HYPERchannel Networks". IEEE Trans
Computers, Vol C-33 No 3, March 1984.

/Kenw84/   C.J. Kenward "A Microprocessor Based
Safety System". UKAEA Harwell Research Report
AERE-R 11235, July 1984.

/KiKa84/   H.D. Kirrmann, F. Kaufmann "Poolpo - A
Pool of Processors for Process Control Applications".
IEEE Trans Computers, Vol C-33 No 10, October 1984.

/Lomb84/   F. Lombardi "Reconfiguration in
Microprocessor Schemes". Microprocessors &
Microprogramming, Vol 13 No 5, May 1984.

/Schn84/   F.B. Schneider "Byzantine Generals in
Action: Implementing Fail-Stop Processors". ACM
Trans Comp Sys, Vol 2 No 2, May 1984.

SAFETY INTEGRITY ASSESSMENT OF ROBOT SYSTEMS

K. Khodabandehloo, R. S. Sayles and T. M. Husband

Department of Mechanical Engineering, Imperial College of Science and Technology, Exhibition Road, London SW7 2BX, UK

Abstract. The safe performance of an industrial robot system relies on many factors, which include the integrity of the robot's hardware and software, the way it communicates with sensory and other production equipment and the integrity of the safety features present. This paper examines the issues involved in the safe performance of an industrial robot cell from the design viewpoint. Fault tree analysis (FTA) and Event Tree Analysis (ETA) are presented for this cell, illustrating how the integrity of the robot system hardware and software can be assessed. The robot's hardware is examined with the consideration of the modules that control its operation and its safety integrity is quantified in terms of the probability of undesirable motion due to failures. Particular attention is paid to the interactions of the robots software with other system hardware such as external actuators and production equipment, identifying the critical and safety related parameters. The role of design features that can improve the safety integrity of the system are discussed.

Keywords. Industrial Robots, Safety Integrity, Reliability, Fault Tree Analysis, Event Tree Analysis, Hardware and Software Interactions.

INTRODUCTION

Safety integrity is a feature that any carefully engineered system should possess. Our understanding of the circumstances under which a robot system could fail to perform its intended task can be improved by formal analysis during its design and development. This is crucial as the erratic behaviour of the robot, caused by failures in the hardware and errors in the software, could have safety implications for personnel as well as the equipment. Several techniques may be applied to a robot system to examine the integrity of the system hardware and software.

Analysis Techniques

Fault Tree Analysis (FTA) and Event Tree Analysis (ETA) may be applied at various levels for examining the errors and failures in the system software and hardware. FTA is a top-down technique for assessing the way in which several failures can cause a single outcome or a system failure (termed the top event). Standard logic gates (AND, OR, etc) are used to combine several failures taking into account their logical interactions. ETA is a forward technique which may be used to examine the propagation of an initiating event (or failure) with the presence of a number of other events, failures, faults or conditions. MacCormick (1981) has presented a detailed account of Fault and Event Tree construction.

Industrial Robots

The definition of an industrial robot as defined by the British Robot Association is:

"An industrial robot is a reprogrammable device designed to both manipulate and transport parts, tools, or specialised implements through variable programmed motions for the performance of specific manufacturing tasks".

The important preconditions that distinguish an industrial robot from other machine tools and transfer devices are:

(a) It can be reprogrammed to perform a different task.
(b) It is the motion of the arm that may be programmed.

Hartley (1983) describes the design and configuration of a number of industrial robots and their applications.

In this study the PUMA 560 robot is used to perform a loading and gauging task within an integrated cell to be presented later. A brief description of this robot is given, but for more details refer to the PUMA manual (1980).

THE PUMA ROBOT

The Puma 560 robot is a six axis multi-jointed, microprocessor controlled robot. Each joint is driven by a d.c. electric motor through gears and rods. The motors, gears and rod are coupled by rigid and flexible couplings as appropriate. Fig. 1 shows the configuration of the mechanical arm. The joints are controlled by a number of distributed microprocessors, one per joint, in a digital control loop (Fig. 2). A supervisory control computer system, based around the DEC PDP11 computer hardware with special software allows complex arm movements to take place under user software. Each joint consists of a digital servo card, an analogue servo card, a servo power amplifier, a d.c. motor with a tacho-encoder feedback transducer. The feedback electronics and the special function circuitry are shared by the six joints. A servo interface card is used for the required communication between the control computer and the microprocessors of the joints. The robot is of a continuous path type which provides straight line motion in addition to joint interpolation. Joint interpolation is used wher the path taken by the tool is not critical. For operations such as part insertion and part picking straight line motion is essential.

VAL PROGRAMMING LANGUAGE

VAL (Variable Assembly Language) is a sophisticated high level robot language. The VAL user guide (PUMA Manual 1980) describes in detail the way in which the Puma robot may be programmed. A selection of VAL instructions are presented here which are used in the application software to be discussed later.

MOVE <location>
Moves the robot from the current position to the location and tool orientation specified by the variable <location>. Joint interpolation is performed within this instruction.

MOVES <location>
Same as MOVE but straight line motion is produced with smooth re-orientation to the final location.

APPRO <location> , <distance>
Moves the tool or gripper to the position and orientation defined by the variable <location> at an offset along the tool z axis of the distance given (see Fig. 1). A positive distance sets the tool back from the specified location. Joint interpolation is used in the motion.

APPROS <location> , <distance>
Same as APPRO but straight line motion is produced from the current position to the final location.

DEPART <distance>
Moves the tool by joint interpolated motion the distance given along the z axis of the tool from the current position.

DEPARTS <distance>
Same as DEPART except straight line interpolation motion is produced.

OPENI
Opens the gripper

CLOSEI
Closes the gripper

SIGNAL <channel> , <channel> , (channel) , etc
Activates or deactivates the output relays specified by the channels. A positive channel number activates the relay and a negative channel number deactivates the relay (d.c. solid state relays are used).

REACTI <channel> , <programme> ALWAYS
This instruction initiates a continuous monitoring of the external signal to an input relay specified by the channel number. When a high value is detected the current instruction is aborted immediately and the programme specified will be executed.

IGNORE <channel> ALWAYS
This will disable the REACTI instruction for the channel specified.

IFSIG <ch>, <ch>, <ch>, <ch> THEN <label>
If the state(s) of the indicated external input signals exactly match the channel states specified, the programme branches to the instruction identified by the given label. That is, if any mismatch is detected the next programme step is executed. A positive channel number looks for a high input signal and a negative number for a low signal.

ROBOT MACHINING AND GAUGING CELL

A Puma robot is arrange in a cell with the configuration shown in Fig. 3. It is programmed to transfer a parts from the pallet to a CNC lathe where it will be machined. It is then transfered to a turn around station for the robot to re-hold it with the correct orientation before loading it onto the gauging station. The part is released when loaded in the gauging station and its diameter measured. If the machining tolerances are acceptable after the gauging process, the part is returned to the pallet via the turn-around station. An unacceptable part is rejected and dropped into a bin. The flow diagram of Fig. 4 shows the sequence of operation of each device with the robot acting as the system supervisor.

Robot Teaching

The robot is taught several points at the appropriate locations needed for programming the movements. These include the part locations on the pallet (PART), a convenient intermediate point (INTEM) to be used for movements that require clearance from the rest of the equipment, the load/unload points of the CNC lathe (CHUCK) and the positions for the turn around and gauging stations. The process of teaching involves the manipulation of the robot arm to the appropriate location with the required orientation using the teach pendant. The locations are taught by storing them under different names. These are used in a VAL programme to produce the required part manipulation for the task.

VAL SOFTWARE ERRORS

There are many ways in which errors could be introduced into a robot programme. Although VAL is used as an example the problems that are mentioned below are equally relevant for any other robot programming language similar in structure. A classification of errors in VAL with likely consequences is attempted here.

Syntax Error

The VAL editor which is used for creating the robot programmes is capable of recognising the more obvious syntax errors including spelling and positional errors that could occur in typing the codes. Certain faults that could be classified under this category include the following:-

- MOVE   used in place of MOVES
- APPRO   used in place of APPROS
- DEPART used in place of DEPARTS
- Incorrect sign used in the channel numbers of SIGNAL, IFSIG statements
- Incorrect sign used for the distances specified in DEPART, DEPARTS, APPRO and APPROS instructions

Damage due to collision is likely in the above cases, especially when the robot path is effected.

Logic Errors

It is essential to place the instructions in the correct order. In programmes where no controlling function is performed the order of the instructions will merely result in the calculation of a wrong answer or programme halt. A robot programme must be constructed with carefully postioned instructions. A collision will result if the robot moves to a particular location at the wrong time. The logic involved in conditional branching of IFSIG instructions can also cause this. An analysis of the sequence of actions can identify such problems and is presented later. Omission of statements also affects the logic of the sequence of movements and can be dangerous.

Parametric Errors

Errors in defining the locations for the instructions MOVE, MOVES, APPRO and APPROS can cause severe damage to the robot and other equipment. Parameters such as the distances in the APPRO(S), DEPART(S); channel numbers in SIGNAL, IFSIG, IGNORE and REACTI; the programme names in the REACTI and other subroutine call instructions, and the addresses in IFSIG and other conditional/unconditional branching instructions are also examples.

ANALYSIS OF SOFTWARE/HARDWARE INTERACTIONS

It is imperative that any software written in a robot language for a particular application is assessed for safety integrity during its development. This will ensure that the kind of errors mentioned are revealed early during design and implementation. Further more the interactions of the software with the hardware should be examined, as failures in the system hardware can often cause the robot software to behave correctly, but erratically. Identification of the possible problem areas, using systematic analysis techniques such as FTA and ETA, will serve in taking preventative measures during development of systems.

The fault tree in Fig. 5 considers the top event of "undesirable robot movement causing likely damage or harm". There are two separate causes of this which could be inter-related but are examined in isolation here: Robot Control Hardware Failures, and Robot Application Software Related Failures. The embedded software which includes the VAL operating system as well as the firmware that controls the movements of each joint are assumed fully operational. This is valid in so far as the application software for performing the task contains no errors and has been executed satisfactorily for one complete cycle via all possible routes under all likely operational conditions. To illustrate how the robot cell can be analysed for integrity two specific subprogrammes, representative of a number of programme modules for the robot cell are chosen.

Analysis of Part Picking Routine

The part picking routine requires the robot to move to a pallet position, where a part is present, grab the part and remove it from the pallet. The robot then moves to the intermediate position ready to load the part onto the CNC lathe (Fig. 3). The subprogramme that would perform the part picking task is as follows:

```
1.   APPRO PART, 50.00
2.   OPENI
3.   MOVES PART
4.   CLOSEI 0.00
5.   DELAY 0.5
6.   DEPARTS 100
7.   MOVE INTEM
```

The event tree shown in Fig. 6 examines the possible errors that could cause the top event of the fault tree in Fig. 5. The initiating event considered is "part picking routine started". The likely parametric errors in the approach instruction (Step 1) are considered with the consequences stated. The next event examines the states of the gripper. If the gripper fails to open (Step 2) the movement that follows (Step 3) will result in gripper-part collison. With the gripper open, the correct execution of the MOVES instruction will be a safe one unless the location

specified is incorrect. Step 4 closes the gripper to grab the part. The delay of 0.5 seconds is included to ensure that the gripper pneumatic drive system has sufficient time to act. The possible errors that could have safety implications are examined in the event tree with the consequences stated for Steps 4 and 5. If the delay is too short the robot may move (i.e. depart from the part location) before the part is gripped. This would cause the part to be held in a different postion which could result in a collision during the operations that follow. The DEPARTS instruction produces a motion in a straight line, retracting the part from the pallet hole. If the distance specified is too small the part will remain partially inserted in the hole leading to a part-pallet collision when the next step (MOVE INTEM) is executed. The safe way of defining the depart distance is to have it slightly greater than the length of the part. A distance of 100mm was adequate in this case, with the consideration of the physical constraints of the cell.

Analysis of the Lathe Loading Routine

This procedure follows after the part picking routine with the robot at the intermediate location (INTEM). To load the part onto the lathe the position named CHUCK is used. This is the required location where the part will be held for machining. The programming steps corresponding to the operations flow diagram of Fig. 4 are as follows.

```
8.        APPRO CHUCK , 100
9.        MOVES CHUCK
10.       SIGNAL 1,,,,,,,
11.       OPENI
12.       DELAY 0.5
13.       DEPARTS 100
14.       MOVE INTEM
15.       SIGNAL 3,,,,,,,
16.       DELAY 0.5
17.       SIGNAL -3,,,,,,,
18.  100  IFSIG -4,,, THEN 100
19.       APPRO CHUCK , 100
20.       MOVES CHUCK
21.       CLOSESI
22.       SIGNAL -1,,,,,,,
23.       DELAY 0.5
24.       DEPARTS 100
25.       MOVE INTEM
```

The event tree in Fig. 7 is constructed for examining the possible outcomes of errors or failures in this piece of software - Steps 8 and 9 produce the required motion for placing the part in the chuck. The chuck must be open before Step 9 is executed (it is assumed that an initialisation routine opens the chuck at the start of the operation). As the state between events 8 and 9 in the tree indicates (Fig. 7a), a collision involving the part, the gripper, and the chuck, will result if the chuck jaws are closed. This could be caused by an incorrect signal or failure in the chuck actuation system. Step 10 enables a signal for closing the chuck assuming the previous steps are successfully executed. The consequences of errors for Step 10 are shown in the event tree. Having placed the part into the chuck and successfully released it (Step 11) the robot should move away before machining can start. Steps 13 and 14 move the arm safely to the intermediate point. The consequences of errors in these two instructions are presented by the appropriate branches of the tree.

Output channel 3 of the robot is used to signal the CNC lathe to start machining. It is however imperative that this signal is active for only a short period of time to allow its recognition by the CNC lathe (Steps 15, 16 and 17). Omission of

Step 17 or failure to set channel 3 back to its inactive state can have severe consequences. Failures or faults that cause channel 3 to remain active will result in CNC cutting tool-robot collision as well as part-gripper damage because machining will start as soon as the chuck is closed. (It has been assumed that the chuck must be closed before machining is possible.) This occurs immediately after step 10 and the event related to the channel 3 state in the event tree examines the outcome.

When machining is complete (see Fig. 3) a signal from the CNC lathe via the robot's input channel 4 informs it to remove the part from the chuck. Step 18 enables the robot to accept this signal and act accordingly. A failure causing this signal to be activated at the wrong time can lead to unsafe consequences, including robot-CNC lathe collision. The event tree (Fig. 7) presents the possibilities. Steps 19 through to 23 move the robot to the chuck location to remove the part. The possibilities of errors in these instructions and their consequences are given by the appropriate branches of the event tree (Fig. 7c). It is important to hold the part, i.e. close the gripper, before opening the chuck by deactivating the signal on channel 1 (Step 22). If a fault occurs causing the chuck to remain closed then damage will occur when the robot tries to remove the part. Step 23 produces the required delay for pneumatic actuators before the part is removed at Step 24. The robot once again returns to the intermediate location before the turn around operation is initiated. The remaining parts of the programme are not presented here, nevertheless the routines described represent the majority of the safety related problems characteristic of this kind of software.

SOME SAFETY INTEGRITY IMPROVEMENTS POSSIBLE

It is possible to include certain features in these programmes which would overcome some of the problems mentioned, or at least, reduce their likelihood. Perhaps the more representative of the difficulties highlighted by this analysis are failures in the gripper system. Two switches, which indicate the opened and closed states of the gripper jaws respectively, connected to input channels 5 and 6, can allow detection of gripper system failure during operation. The VAL instruction REACTI (presented earlier) may be used in combination with IGNORE to continuously monitor these switches and take necessary action. Steps 1 to 13 are re-organised to illustrate this concept. The pattern shown can be repeated throughout the programme and is as follows:-

```
1.   APPRO  PART,50
2.   OPENI
     REACTI 5, ALRAM ALWAYS
3.   MOVES PART
     IGNORE 5 ALWAYS
4.   CLOSE I
5.   DELAY 0.5
     REACT I 6, ALARM ALWAYS
6.   DEPARTS 100
7.   MOVE INTEM
8.   APPRO CHUCK, 100
9.   MOVES CHUCK
10.  SIGNAL 1,,,,,,,
     IGNORE 6 ALWAYS
11.  OPENI
12.  DELAY 0.5
     REACTI 5,ALARM ALWAYS
13.  DEPARTS 100
     etc
```

(The programme carries on with continuous monitoring of channel 5 until just before the gripper is closed again, and so on).

The programme named ALARM can typically consist of the following instructions:-

```
1.   REMARK PROGRAMME ALARM FOR GRIPPER FAULTS
2.   REMARK SIGNAL ALARM LIGHT
3.   SIGNAL 7,,,,,,,
4.   REMARK HALT WITH MESSAGE
5.   HALT GRIPPER PROBLEM
```

This will activate output channel 7, which could be enabling an alarm for the operator, and halts the programme displaying the message GRIPPER PROBLEM on the screen.

In a similar manner other failures such as the chuck failure or faults in the turn-around station, could be detected and corrective actions taken in real-time. The limiting factors are however, the number of input/output channels available and the level of sophistication required of the robot programming language for perfoming fault tolerant tasks such as this. It is essential that some of these requirements are foreseen if a robot with the necessary specifications is to be employed for a particular application. Indeed, as it has been demonstrated, analyses of this kind are perhaps the only means of identifying safety related problems for which practical solutions can be found.

ROBOT HARDWARE SAFETY INTEGRITY

Branch 1 of tne fault tree in Fig. 5 relates to the failures within the robot control hardware. A similar fault tree for a typical electric robot which considers undesirable robot motion has been constructed by Khodabandehloo et al (1984). The way numerical assessment for such a tree can be performed in terms of component and sub module failure rates is also presented.

It is not often possible to fully examine the exact way in which failures can cause undesirable robot movement. This is mainly due to the lack of detailed design description made available by the manufacturers. The fault tree branch of Fig. 8 gives the major sources of failures that can cause undesirable motion. This fault tree applies to any six-axis electric robot with a similar control configuration as shown in Fig. 2. Two states are examined. The first considers the failures that can cause robot movement with the arm power on, and the second examines this with the arm power off. When power to the electric motors of the robot are disabled the brakes are automatically activated on three major joints (1, 2 and 3) to stop motion due to the stored energy in the arm. When servo power is on, the movements of the robot are controlled by the control system. In this situation a failure in any one joint or in the control system supervisory computer hardware can cause aberrant arm movement. This is indicated by the OR combination of all the failures within the modules. Brake failures can cause problems if the failure activates the braking system whilst servo power is on. A gripper failure is also a contributory factor to undesirable movement of the robot as illustrated by the event tree analysis of the software. Rigid and flexible couplings play an important role as their failure can result in a joint becoming free to move.

Further breakdown of the basic faults has not been attempted and it has been assumed that any failure in the modules causes the top event. This assumption will produce an over-estimation in the failure probability to be calculated since not all the failures will affect the motion of the arm.

This assumption is acceptable for the following reasons:

(a) The correct motion of the robot arm requires the simultaneous operation of all joints. A failure in any one joint can cause erratic motion in that joint or cause it not to move at all. Either case will result in an overall aberrant behaviour of the robot arm.

(b) The majority of the electronics hardware consists of large and medium scale integrated circuits. The failure modes of such circuits are impossible to identify under all conditions of use. Such circuits usually perform a critical function and any failure irrespective of the mode will inevitably cause a system failure. This is particularly the case for microprocessor and control computer hardware.

Furthermore a detailed understanding of the embedded software for the programmable devices is needed to consider the conditions under which failure modes influence operation.

NUMERICAL ANALYSIS OF ROBOT FAILURE PROBABILITY

Failures occuring in the electronics, mechanical, or electromechanical components can be a major cause of undesirable movements. Failures could occur because of systematic design errors or random failures. Systematic faults can be detected during the design process by formal computer analysis techniques and testing under the conditions specified for the unit. There remain random failures that could occur during normal operation. The MIL 217D handbook (1982), the System Reliability Service (SRS) Data Bank (1984), and the NPRD-2 handbook (1981) provide reliability data for a large selection of components. These may be used for predicting the likely probability of undesirable movement over a particular period of time.

Table 1 presents the failure rate estimates of typical modules that influence the motion of the arm.

TABLE 1   Failure Rates for the Robot Modules (see Fig. 2)

No	Item	Quantity	Failure Rate Faults/Million Hours			Source
----	------	----------	@10°C	@30°C	@50°C	--------
1	Digital Servo Card	6	33.0	62.6	154.5	A
2	Analogue Servo Card	6	12.6	21.4	64.9	A
3	Servo Amplifier	6	13.9	17.9	25.0	A
4	Servo Interface	1	23.4	27.1	38.2	A
5	Special Function and Feedback Electronics	1	20.1	27.8	42.8	A
6	D.C. Motor and Tacho-Encoder	6	20.0	20.0	20.0	B
7	Brakes (motor)	3	4.3	4.3	4.3	C
8	Flexible Coupling	6	17.0	17.0	17.0	B
9	Rigid Coupling	6	1.2	1.2	1.2	B
10	Gripper System	1	114.0	114.0	114.0	A
11	Supervisory Processor, Interface and Memory	1	487.0	487.0	487.0	D

The sources used are:-

(A) MIL 217D (1982) models used for the components of each board
(B) SRS data bank (1984)
(C) NPRD-2 (1981)
(D) Daniels (1979) - Field reported

The failure probability of branch 1 may be estimated using the failure rates given in Table 1 and the relationship

$$P_j = 1 - \exp(-f_j t) \qquad (1)$$

for each element, together with

$$P_{TOT} = 1 - \prod_{j=1}^{n} (1-P_j)$$

$$= 1 - (1-p_1)(1-p_2)(1-p_3)...(1-p_n) \qquad (2)$$

where P_j is the failure probability of the jth module with failure rate f_j over time period t and P_{TOT} is the failure probability for branch 1.

Table 2 gives the total failure probabilities over 1000 hours at three different case temperatures for the electronic modules. A computer programme has been used for predicting the failure probabilities.

TABLE 2   Failure Probability of Branch 1(t=1000 hours): Robot Control Hardware Failures Causing Undesirable Motion

	10°C	30°C	50°C
Failure Probability Over 1000 hrs	0.712 (71.2%)	0.779 (77.9%)	0.908 (90.8%)

This suggests that a failure probability of about 78% is to be expected over 1000 hours of operation at 30°C. The operating case temperature of electronic components can make a considerable difference. It should be emphasised that the elements in this robot are representative of almost every industrial robot of this type and complexity, and that the failure rates used are for typical modules.

PREVENTATIVE MEASURES THROUGH HARDWARE DESIGN

Electronic component failures are the major cause of erratic motion in the robot. The main reasons for this are:

(a) Electronic components perform complex controlling tasks and the majority of components have a critical role to play.
(b) They constitute the greatest proportion of the elements in a robot.

Temperature can influence the operation of digital and analogue circuitry. The MIL-217D (1981) models indicate that a rise in operating temperature increases the failure rate of the electronic components. This is illustrated in Table 1. Reduction in temperature within the electronic modules is one way to reduce failures. Altering the stress condition by using over-rated components is another way to achieve this (Khodabandehloo et al 1984).

It is also possible to have monitoring circuitry present which compare the required motion or position with the actual movements and position being performed or maintained; taking corrective action if a deviation is detected. This can be done by utilising the signals from the encoders and the movement demand signals from the supervisory controller to each joint. A separate feedback transducer may also be incorporated but this effects the weight of the arm and may not be feasible.

In view of the financial investment in software and hardware, it is cost effective to have an overall microprocessor based monitoring unit. The only disadvantage is that this technology is software based and there are no defined rules that indicate this is legally acceptable. However using the techniques illustrated one could prevent errors in software development if the programmes are of a manageable size. Testing the overall design for operation by introduction of actual faults could also be a means of further proving the integrity of any safety software and hardware. There remains however one important point to be considered which relates to the level of improvement achieved. Assuming the microprocessor based monitoring system has a failure rate equal to that of a system similar in complexity to the digital servo card (no. 1, Table 1), both the robot control system <u>and</u> the monitoring system must fail for the robot to produce an undesirable motion. This reduces the previous failure probability to

$$P_N = P_{TOT} \cdot (1-\exp(-62.6E-6\times1000)) \quad (3)$$
$$= 0.047 \text{ (or } 4.7\%)$$

where P_N is the new failure probability at $30^{o}C$, which clearly demonstrates improved safety integrity for the hardware.

DISCUSSION AND CONCLUSION

An industrial robot cell has been presented and the software for performing part of the loading and gauging tasks are given. The VAL programming language is described briefly to demonstrate typical software errors that are likely and the way they may be classified. These include errors in syntax, logic and parameters such as locations and distances that define robot movements. The structure of programme routines for part picking and lathe loading machinery are presented and Fault and Event Tree Analysis performed to show hardware and software interactions.

Software in a robot can easily be influenced by external hardware faults with severe consequences. Inclusion of safety features in both hardware and software can reduce the likelihood of failures producing aberrant behaviour. This often demands specific software requirements of the robot programming language and should therefore be a major factor in deciding what robot to use for a particular application. Assessment of the integrity of the software as part of its development procedure has an important role to play in ensuring overall safety and must be formally undertaken.

Robot hardware must also perform satisfactorily. Any hardware fault that affects the motion of the robot arm has safety implications for the equipment and the personnel regardless of the state of software. Fault tree analysis can once again be applied, but this time in addition to identification of critical failure interactions, a numerical assessment can be performed. This is demonstrated in terms of erratic movement, which is quantified in terms of the probability of failure over a particular period of time. For the example of a typical six-axis electric robot, we have estimated a failure probability of about 0.78 per 1000 hours at $30^{o}C$.

Every undesirable motion will not necessarily lead to a collision or an accident. It is the enviromental interactions of the arm and its relative position to the rest of the equipment, in addition to the distances involved that govern this. Methods for reducing such occurences due to robot hardware failures are presented suggesting

that it is impossible to eliminate undesirable movement. Nevertheless preventative measures can be taken through design, by using high quality components, improving the enviromental conditions of electronic components, and adding monitoring electronics to the design to reduce the likely occurrence of erratic robot movement in any mode of operation.

It should be noted that similar analysis can be performed for any robot, and infact the numerical assessments apply equally to any other electric robot with the same complexity. System assessment during the design and development phase is the best method of achieving safe and effective production. Advances in vision, sensory equipment and artificial intelligence, and their integration with robotics and automation systems, will be the major growth areas of technology. Analyses of the kind demonstrated can have a substantial role to play in ensuring inherent safety integrity in such systems.

ACKNOWLEDGEMENTS

The autors would like to thank the Science and Engineering Research Council, U.K., for the funding of this research.

REFERENCES

Daniels, B.K. (1979). <u>Reliability and protection against failure in computer systems</u>, NCSR R17, The National Centre of Systems Reliability, UKAEA.

Hartley, J. (1983). <u>Robots at work: a practical guide for engineers and managers</u>, IFS (Publication) Ltd.

Khodabandehloo, K., Duggan, F. and Husband, T.M. (1984). <u>Reliability assessment of industrial robots</u>, 14th ISIR Conference Proceedings.

MacCormick, N.J. (1981). <u>Reliability and risk analysis: methods and nuclear power applications</u>, Academic Press.

MIL-217D. (1982). <u>Reliability prediction of electronic equipment</u>, US Military Handbook.

NPRD-2. (1981). <u>Nonelectric parts reliability data</u>, Reliability Analysis Center, Rome Air Development Centre.

PUMA Technical Mannual. (1980). <u>Unimation (Europe) Ltd.</u> UK.

SRS data bank. (1984). <u>Systems Reliability Service</u>, UKAEA, Wigshaw Lane, Culcheth, Warrington, UK.

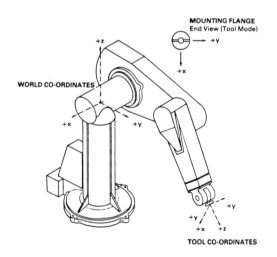

Fig. 1   Puma Robot Configuration with Tool Co-ordinates Defined

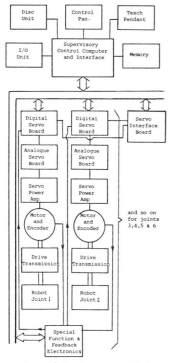

Fig. 2 Schematics of Robot Control Hardware Configuration

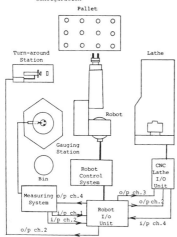

Fig. 3 Schematics of Robot Loading, Machining and Gauging Cell

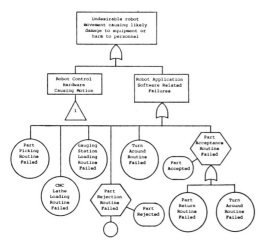

Fig. 5 Fault Tree for the Top-Event of Undesirable Robot Motion

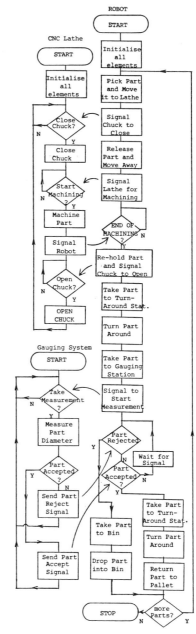

Fig. 4 Flow Diagram for the Robot Cell Operation

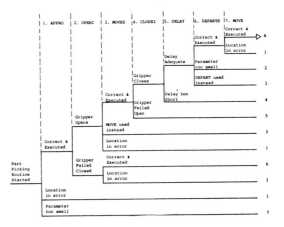

Fig. 6 Event Tree for the Part Picking Routine (See List of Outcomes)

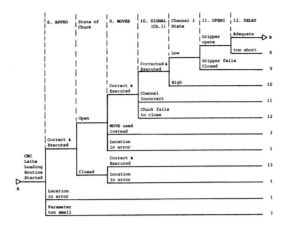

(a)   Continuation of branch A, Fig. 6

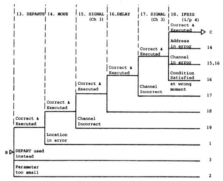

(b)   Continuation of branch B

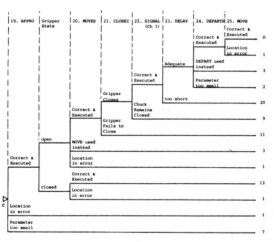

(c)   Continuation of branch C

Fig. 7   Event Tree for CNC Loading Routine

Event tree outcomes

1. Robot moves to a wrong location. High level of hazard due to likely collision between robot and other equipment. Potential hazard for any person present in the robot envelope.
2. Part will remain partially inserted in the gripper, the chuck or the pallet hole. Collision will occur when the following instruction is executed. Severe damage likely.
3. Joint interpolation will be used instead of straight line for the motion. Collision will occur between one of the following: Part-Chuck, Part-Pallet, Part-Gripper or Robot-CNC lathe as appropriate.
4. Part may not be gripped correctly leading to collision between part and pallet. Damage to robot, pallet or part is likely.
5. Part will not be held. No production possible.
6. Gripper-Part collision will occur leading to severe robot and part damage due to the gripper being closed before the PART location is reached.
7. Potential hazard due to likely collision between robot and other equipment. Workpiece may also be damaged _if_ it is held by the robot.
8. Part may not be released before robot motion occurs. Damage to gripper or the workpiece is likely.

9. Part will not be released. Severe damage to gripper, robot, the chuck or the workpiece is likely.
10. Severe damage will occur as the CNC lathe will start machining when the chuck closes. Robot, CNC Lathe, chuck and/or workpiece will be damaged.
11. Channel 1 will not be activated due to fault in software. Part will be released in the CNC lathe. Damage to workpiece is likely.
12. Chuck closure will not occur and workpiece will be released when gripper opens. Damage to workpiece is likely.
13. Severe damage will result due to robot, workpiece and chuck collision.
14. Branching to the wrong step likely if the incorrectly specified label is present in the programme. Severe damage is likely due to Robot-Lathe collision as the sequence of arm movements will be altered.
15. Condition may not be satisfied at all, in which case robot will simply fail to continue the task and will be halted at Step 18.
16. Condition may be satisfied at wrong moment. Robot-CNC Lathe collision will occur. Severe damage likely.
17. Signal for machining cycle to start will remain active and the Lathe will start machining as soon as the chuck is closed, this will result in severe part, robot, CNC Lathe and workpiece damage. (Steps 10-11, Fig. 7a)
18. Incorrect delay will have two effects: either the signal to CNC Lathe to start machining cycle will not be recognised hence the operation will halt, or production process will be delayed if the delay is too long.
19. Machining will not occur. Programme will halt at Step 18 waiting for signal from Lathe.
20. Part may not be gripped or released correctly leading to possible damage as a result of collision between part and chuck.

A. Part Picking Routine performed correctly, Proceed from A
B. Proceed from B
C. Proceed from C
D. CNC Lathe loading and machining performed correctly. Branch terminated here, but could be similarly continued for the rest of the programme.

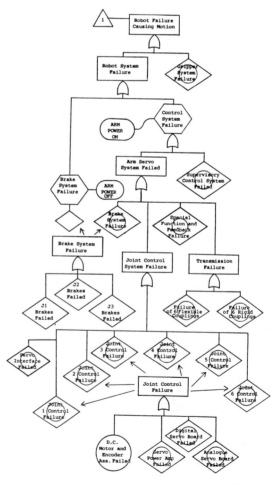

Fig. 8   Branch 1: Fault Tree for the Robot Failures Causing Motion

RELIABILITY AND INTEGRITY OF COMPUTER ASSISTED DECISION MAKING PROCESS

M. Hashim

Burroughs Machines Ltd., Cumbernauld, Scotland, UK

Abstract.

Computer Assisted Decision Making (CADM) is finding its use more and more both in engineering and service industries. In our daily life real intelligence is being rapidly replaced by artificial intelligence (AI).

This explosion of AI demands a heavy emphasis on meeting the expectations and requirements of all four components of CADM process i.e. hardware, software, man and society. The crucial part played by software in transporting the "thinking, judging and deciding" mechanism from human brain to computer brain (memory or logic) cannot be over emphasised. The nature of this role is no longer a purely technical matter, it must be now seen in more realistic i.e. Socio-technical context due to unique features of CADM process. Designing into a software the reliability and integrity depends very much on learning the behaviour of software through model based on Socio-technical considerations e.g. complexity. One such model is presented in this paper. This work suggests that CADMP is a Socio-technical entity which is going to influence each and every aspect of our society and, therefore, should be dealt with accordingly. The error prediction model based on complexity can be used as a step forward towards this understanding of AI explosion.

Keywords.

Computer Assisted Decision, Reliability Models, Software Complexity, Socio-Technical Nature of AI, Human Machine.

INTRODUCTION

The bewildering rapid advances of our computer age have brought us to a cross road of physical and intellectual illusions where 'real intelligence' (human brain) is being replaced by 'artificial intelligence' and in future may see real people replaced by artificial people (robotics). We also see the wizardly machines called computers not only assisting us in our decision making process in our daily life but often making actual decisions for us even if we don't like them and have no option to change them either. The noble, refined and joyful experience of listening, pondering, thinking, judging and then deciding upon to do or say something seems to have been taken over by concepts such as expert systems, AI etc.

One of the most important elements of Computer Assisted Decision Making Process (CADMP) is the set of those unseen commands and instructions to the machines that do the so called magic work and what we term as software. The software forms the core of all Artificial Intelligence (AI) activity with unique requirements. Though substantial efforts are being spent on developing the heaps of hardware and piles of software for CADMP, little attention seems to have been paid to the fundamental requirement of integrity and reliability of software particularly used in decision making process. The impact of integrity and reliability of software on the society has not yet been fully appreciated.

This paper discusses the important elements of CADMP in terms of its socio-technical behaviour with emphasis on software. It also proposes a reliability prediction model based on complexity particularly applicable to CADMP and similar software. The paper also highlights the unique features of computer assisted decision making process and compares it with the conventional (manual) decision making process.

COMPUTER ASSISTED DECISION MAKING PROCESS

Figure 1 shows a conventional decision making process without the use of computer where the know-how resides in the human brain. If this know-how (the body of knowledge as the experts call it) is transferred from the human brain to a computer memory, the process of thinking also transfers from one location (brain) to another (memory). This sounds simple and we want to leave it to such simplicity for the purpose of our understanding.

Figure 2 shows the above mentioned location - transfer of know-how where apparently nothing else seems to have changed except that the human brain is now behaving like a robot. Unfortunately what seems simple is not what it is. The fundamental concept behind AI is the reproduction of 'thinking' mechanism which in spite of being

imperfect in may respects, is still able to
perform at least as good as a human being in at
least one isolated area of knowledge. Computer
Assisted Decision Making (CADM) is a complex
process of :

i.   presentation of a body of knowledge and
        rules and guidelines to use it appropriately

ii.   the retrieval of this knowledge when called
        upon to do so with full reliability.

iii.   stepwise and logical scanning through the
        whole body of knowledge (information) and

iv.   most difficult of all to make a decision,
        give a verdict or provide a sensible and
        authorised answer to the problem posed by
        the user.

These decisions may be, for example, if a person
is suffering from a heart disease (medicine);
why a large sum (say £50K) should be spent on
the construction of a warehouse (engineering);
is Mr XYZ a criminal? (law) and so on.

NATURE AND ELEMENTS OF CADMP

Computer assisted decision making is finding its
use more and more both in engineering and service
industries. Its' particular use is seen recently
in the diagnosis of medical ailments from symptoms
If we look at the entire process of CADM, we find
it very democratic. It starts with people writing
the intelligent software for other people to use
it, where the former utilise their 'thinking and
intelligence' to spare the latter from using their
'thinking and intelligence'.

Hardware or the machines only play a mere mechanical
role in this whole process. That is why concepts
like artificial intelligence and expert systems
cannot be regarded as purely technical in nature.
When Aleksander (1) wrote a book on Artificial
Intelligence, he named it 'The Human Machine' and
very appropriately so.

The CADMP has four basic elements namely: Hardware,
Software, Man (as user and as well as manufacturer)
and his environment or society. The hardware has
already taken a giant step forward in the
reliability field. Man as user is being asked to
keep his real intelligence away from the process
so he is behaving just like robotics in the expert
system or AI environment. The society is receiving
the impact of CADMP in the form of ripe fruit and
is not directly involved in the actual process of
computer assisted decision making. We must,
however, remember that man as a manufacturer of
CADMP is very much involved. The fourth component,
the software is the most crucial of all and results
from the efforts and interaction of the other three
elements to the maximum, as it is established that
CADMP would become an impossible task without
software explosion (2).

The reliability and integrity of each of the above
mentioned four components is not merely a technical
concept or a known mathematical number. It is on
the contrary a state of confidence and
trustworthiness of each component that adds up to
give the overall integrity and reliability of
CADMP.

THE UNIQUE FEATURES OF COMPUTER ASSISTED DICISION PROCESS

It seems appropriate to highlight some of the
unique features of CADMP before discussing the
integrity and relaiability of this concept.
These features are summarised as follows :

a.   In a conventional decision making process
(Figure 1) man is always on-line with the problem
solving system and his environment. In CADMP man
as a user is not directly involved to the high
degree of thinking.

b.   CADMP can only house a limited amount of
information (no matter how large computer storage
is) from a body of knowledge which is very
commonly available and used in practice but may
not possess such rules and information that may be
of critical importance under special circumstances
or in the solution of boundary line cases.
Decisions in these cases are almost always urgent
requiring high degree of integrity and accuracy
as the balance lies in the fact that a small piece
of information is present or not. Man in
conventional process has a ready access to such
information or is known to him, computer can't
think what it requires to fill the gap or what is
missing at the first place.

c.   Rational behaviour, constraints, prejudices,
sympathy, considerations, change of mind etc. all
play important parts in the overall process. These
factors, however, cannot be programmed into a
computerised decision process hence lacks the
integrity and reliability of decision to be of
immense use to those concerned and affected by the
decision.

d.   Before a man makes a final decision he is at
liberty to iterate and re-iterate his findings in
view of social, economical and behavioural aspects
going in favour or against his decision. This
gives him the freedom and opportunity to judge the
overall impact of the decision. He is not reluctant
to change if need be. During the process of
thinking and deciding a man gathers more and more
information, wisdom, screening logic and balance
between emotions and needs. These factors
contribute immensely to the integrity and
reliability of decision. A 'computer brain' is,
unfortunately unaware of these scenarios and
cannot, therefore, be relied upon completely with
decisions made by it.

e.   There is always a small sub-set of correct
decisions to a problem out of a universal solution
set. Man is capable of and has access to this
sub-set in entirety. Computer is bonded and can
reach only a part of the above mentioned sub-set.
This limitation is one of the greatest sources of
unreliability and lack of integrity of computer
assisted decision process.

f.   CADMP exhibits a lack of freedom of thought
thus reducing the integrity of the process of
decision making. The above features clearly
indicate the need for each element (particularly
software being the major component of CADMP) to be
designed to revoke these limitations and intentional
efforts to be made to achieve the desired
reliability and integrity of the whole system.
Without this the due benefits of CADMP cannot be
appreciated.

INTEGRITY AND RELIABILITY OF CADMP

Let us go back to the fundamental question of
defining the terms 'integrity' and 'reliability'
when used in relation to computer assisted
decision making processes and its components.

Integrity of CADMP

Literary meaning of word 'integrity' is the state
of being entire; wholeness; honesty and uprightness
But I think it is more than that. In terms of CADM
it means providing a decision which is 'timely'

with respect to nature, type and requirement of the problem. (Functioning timely in physical time frame is called reliability/availability).

Let us illustrate this by a well known example. A six minute alert in a USA nuclear base following a fault in the system software that almost took the world at the doorsteps of a third world war may be absolutely reliable from technical or operational view but it certainly had no integrity and respect attached to it. It was indeed not an honest manufestation of computer assisted decision making process.

Integrity also means to respond quickly and strongly to the wrong input to the process thus avoiding unwanted or undesired decisions. The bulk of the responsibility to inculcate the integrity into the computer assisted decision process falls upon the decision process designers i.e. software expertise.

Reliability of CADMP

Reliability is often thought in technical terms, a number associated to the system confidence or trustworthiness. It should, however, be looked into broader framework of social and environmental scenarios too. The high mathematical probability that a system will 'decide' rightly to stop functioning if there occurs a malfunction in one of the sub-systems and components withouth causing a fault or a failure is considered to be the reliability of the decision process. This becomes a crucial parameter if such a decision has to be taken under a correct function and time frame at the same time. A fault in the system hardware or software could be more deadly and fatal than input or data induced faults. This in turn throws the whole burden on designing in the reliability in the system components like software and hardware.

The total effectiveness of CADMP is therefore a function of socio-technical reliability component of each element. In very simple notation it can be expressed as follows :

$$R_p = r_h + r_s + r_m + r_e, \quad \text{where}$$

R_p, r_n, r_s, r_m, r_e are the reliabilities of the decision process, hardware, software, man and environment. With the advances in technology the values of most of these parameters have already been achieved as high as possible. The software, however, has not yet achieved the required reliability. This is the component that shares most of the burden of unreliability and disrespect. One of the reasons for this is the lack of suitable models that take into consideration the true nature of software development in relation to its socio-technical behaviour particularly in the design phase. We shall now try to concentrate on this component.

THE CADMP 'BUG' : THE SOFTWARE

Complexity plays a very significant part in the reliability and integrity of a software specially if the software is eventually to be used in complex and strategic decision making situations. Many works exist in the literature that provide models of one type or the other for software reliability but few take the social and technical complexity look together. One such work for prediction of software reliability is decribed in (3) and provides a suitable working model.

It is summarised in APPENDIX A along with the model equations and uses a complexity factor 'C' in predicting the number of errors remaining at various stages of software life cycle and development phases.

This allows the management to foresee the trend and thus to mobilise the various resources to the best use accordingly.

The above model has been applied to data obtained from many large modular software developments in telecommunication, medical diagnosis software and from real time programmes developed for the flexible manufacturing systems (FMS). The results on one of the software modules are shown in Figure 3.

CONCLUSIONS

The overall objectives of computer assisted decision making is to provide accuracy, efficiency speed and reliability of decision. The efficiency in terms of nano-seconds may be surely achieved through hardware but other parameters mentioned above and the integrity cannot be hammered into as it depends on the software of CADMP that resides inside the machine as a human brain with limited memory. The professionals in the field have a heavy responsibility on their shoulders to make the software as reliable and respectful as possible within the human limits. The manufacturer user and environment of CADMP is all socio-technical and its impact in case of failure to provide a right decision can be enormous and catastrophic. This component of CADMP is most critical and needs most attention. This paper has suggested a complexity based error prediction model for the software during its various phases of development (including early phases) for the management and designers alike.

REFERENCES

1.   Aleksander, I (1977), The Human Machine, Georgia Publishing Company, USA.

2.   Hayes, J.E. and Michie, D. (1983), Intelligent Systems, The Unprecedented Opportunity, Ellis Howard Ltd., U.K.

3.   Hashim, M (1984), 'A Socio-technical Model for the Planning and Prediction of Software', National Conference on Quality (NCQR-'84) Bombay, India.

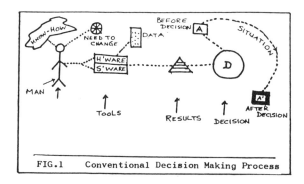

FIG.1   Conventional Decision Making Process

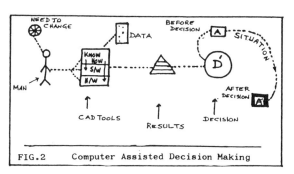

FIG.2   Computer Assisted Decision Making

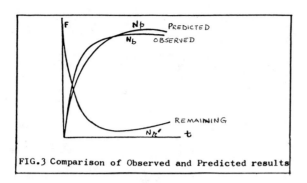

FIG.3 Comparison of Observed and Predicted results

APPENDIX A

Symbols:

Q_o ,Estimated initial faults
N_f ,Faults found to time t
N_r ,Faults removed in j
N_m ,Maintenance induced faults
N_R ,Total faults removed
N_p ,Faults remaining at t
C ,Complexity factor
K ,Residual factor
L ,Programme(S/W) size
T_o ,Mean time to failure
f ,Fix factor
Z ,Complexity shadow
p ,Patching factor
P ,Programmability factor
s ,Team profile index
m ,S/W modularity
U ,Utility factor
E_d ,Error density
V .Severity factor
j ,Maintenance number
$MTTR$,Mean time to repair

Model Equations

$$C = \frac{U \times E_d \times MTTR}{P \times s \times m} \qquad 1$$

$$Z = \sqrt{C / Q_o} \qquad 2$$

$$f = \sqrt{1-C} \qquad 3$$

$$p = 2\sqrt{C} \qquad 4$$

$$K = \left[Log((L \times N_f)/(T_o \times \eta)) \right]^{-1} \qquad 5$$

$$Q_o = N_f \times K \qquad 6$$

$$V = j^2 \qquad 7$$

$$N_r = (N_f \times f) \qquad 8$$

$$N_m = (N_r \times V)^p \qquad 9$$

$$N_p = Q_o - N_r + N_m \qquad 10$$

A SOFT CONTROL DESK FOR POWER GENERATION

D. M. Usher

Scientific Services Department, South West Region, Central Electricity Generating Board, UK

Abstract. Modern computers make it economic to extend the automatic
supervision of power generation to the point at which the whole plant,
including its operators, can be regarded as a single, highly interactive
system. The problem of providing an adequate interface for the operator
within this context has been addressed directly for the Central Control Room
refurbishment project at Didcot Power Station, Oxfordshire UK.

We have developed a control desk consisting of six consoles each with a
dedicated computer and two touch-screens. The user can move through a
plant-based information structure by touching what he requires. A high
level of security is ensured by the complete flexibility of the consoles.
We discuss types of displays, methods of touch-registration and alarm handling
strategies, as well as ways of continuously monitoring the 'health' of the
touch-screens themselves.

The project has been concerned with achieving reliable and safe operation
through good human factors, and the provision of comprehensive back-up
facilities.

Keywords. Man-machine systems; computer control; human factors; computer
graphics

INTRODUCTION

The efficiency of power generation has been
steadily increased in recent years, particularly
through improvements in the control of plant. The
use of digital computers enables plant to be more
closely and continuously monitored than under
manual supervision. It can be brought into and out
of service more quickly and safely, and optimum
running conditions can be maintained more
tenaciously. The recent requirement for
'two-shifting' - generation only on two out of
three shifts - increases the advantages of
computer control, because control actions are
taken more frequently than when running
continuously.

Where a large proportion of the plant is
computerised, such as is increasingly the case in
CEGB stations, the control-room operator can be
seen as one part of a single highly-interactive
system with many hundreds of input and output
signals. The interface between the operator and
the rest of the system must be reassessed in this
light, because the traditional control-room
hardware - over 100 square metres of hard-wired
knobs, lamps and switches - is likely to be too
bulky and inflexible.

This paper describes the principles and techniques
of the improved Man-Machine Interface (MMI) for
the new control-desk under development at the 4 x
500 MW coal-fired Power Station at Didcot,
Oxfordshire. The formidable problems attaching to
the other main interface, that between the
computer and the plant, lie outside the scope of
the paper. At the time of writing, only a pilot
project on one of the four generating Units has
been implemented at Didcot; completion of the full
scheme is proposed for 1986.

PRINCIPLES OF IMPLEMENTATION

Perhaps the most fundamental principle of the work
is to ensure that the highest priority is given to
the needs and preferences of the operators
themselves. All too often, the use of particular
computer techniques begs MMI design questions; we
feel that the computer should be transparent to
its users. Also, we have resisted as far as
possible the temptation to pre-empt, in the
software, control decisions which might seem
inevitable in the prevailing circumstances. To
deprive the operator of certain options or
information, because of the computer's view of the
situation, would be to deny him his role in the
system: to be the resource of skill, intuition,
training and experience. The need for automatic
decision-making ('expert systems') is reduced if
the MMI makes it possible for the experts
themselves to be in full control.

In the South West Region of the CEGB, we have for
some time favoured distributed mini-computer
control systems because of their resilience and
ease of maintenance. We recognise the
impossibility of completely preventing computer
failure, and see the key to reliability in the
provision of sufficient flexibility and redundancy
to permit a diminished operation during the
recovery period.

Of course, another important principle arises out
of these. It is that during the trial period the
staff must be consulted fully and there must be
sufficient flexibility to adopt their suggestions
for improvements.

SYSTEM ARCHITECTURE

Figure 1 shows schematically the hardware of the
desk and the flows of information within the whole

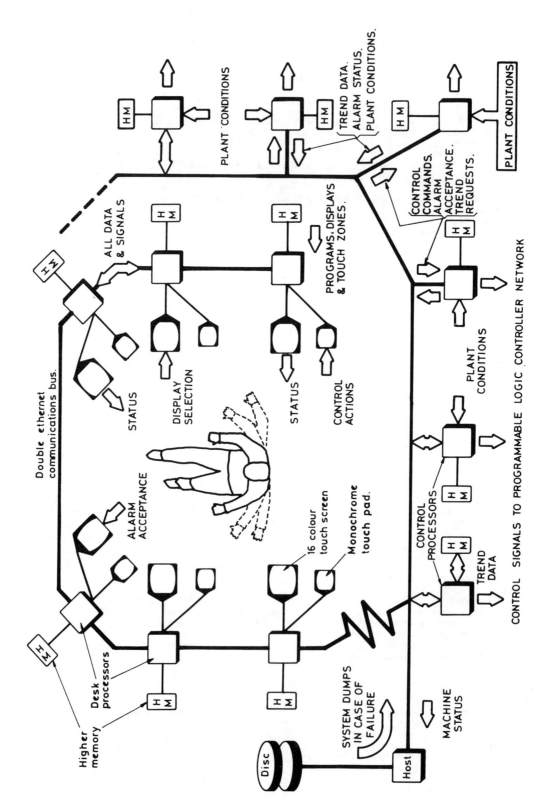

Fig. 1. The system hardware and its information flows.

system. DEC LSI 11/73 minicomputers are used throughout, each with 256 kbytes of file structured RAM, known as Higher Memory (HM). They are all linked through two independent Ethernet communications lines, giving data transmission at up to 10 MBaud. The processors are divided between control and desk functions; the control machines are linked to the programmable logic controller network by three RS232C serial lines, and the desk machines each have two serial line touch-screens, to be described below.

There is a single 'host' machine, whose task is limited but vital: to reload from disc any processor found to have crashed. · In this way, the entire system can recover from a total power failure without manual intervention. The host processor is also used, of course, for on-line access to any of the 'slave' machines. Variables representing the status of a particular part of the plant are logged by (and stored within) the control machine dedicated to that part. There is thus no special 'database' structure; the data and the statuses of control loops and alarms are distributed over the whole system within the pertinent machines.

THE MAN-MACHINE INTERFACE

The MMI consists of the hardware comprising the desk, the software running within it, the operators' mental model of the plant and the structure of the information. Any of these parts could be taken as the starting point of a description of the MMI, as they could for the design process itself. We shall begin with the information structure, and show how the desk design follows. The Unit is divided into the six principal areas of plant shown in Fig. 2: Draught, Mills A-D, Mills E-H, Boiler, Turbine and Feed. The seventh is treated differently as it covers

the computer system itself. We have found that a display can be created for each of these areas which contains enough information for the operators' routine monitoring purposes. These are the 'Root' displays, each of which indicates broadly the status of the plant in its area, showing the principal data and alarms. Hence, the whole Unit (when in a quiescent state) can be successfully displayed on six colour touch-screens.

To obtain more detail, the operator must descend the hierarchy to the 'Branch' level. For instance, Mill A must be chosen from the four Branches of the A-D Mill Root display (shown in Fig. 3) to access its control loops or data not shown on the Root display. Taken together, the Branch displays and their associated Sub-branches show all the data within the system. Below these lies the 'Control' level, the only one from which plant status can be altered. The Control displays appear on a separate monochrome screen, an arrangement which ensures that the other information on the display – the status of closely associated plant – is presented to the operator throughout the period of his control action.

The MMI, then, is based upon an information hierarchy whose nodes are associated with physical plant, rather than with procedures or types of information. We feel that this coincides closely with the operator's mental model of his task.

Operation

The operator moves through the structure of displays and controls by touching the screens. To focus on a particular Root, Branch, Sub-branch or Item, he simply touches the part of the screen dedicated to it, and the hierarchical level below is obtained. Sibling displays are accessed through

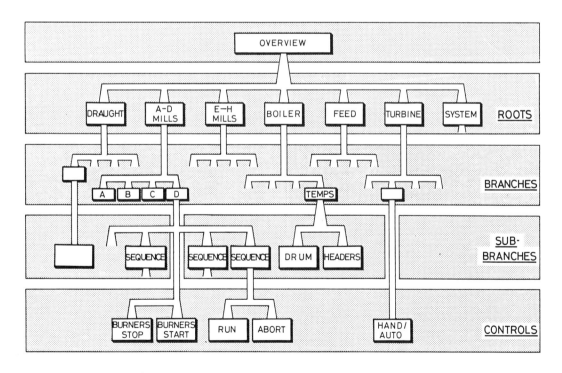

Fig. 2.   The hierarchical information structure of the Man-Machine Interface

soft keys at the top of the screen, and upward movement to antecedent displays is achieved by touching the key whose legend has been replaced by an up-arrow. Above the Roots lies an Overview, which shows important data from every part of the system, and allows access to any additional subsidiary Roots which may be included, but which are not associated directly with plant.

It is implicit in this general description, of course, that any Root can be accessed from any of the touch-screens comprising the desk. Such flexibility allows the operator conveniently to assemble plant areas on which he wishes to concentrate. It also provides a very high level of redundancy, as processor failure results merely in a reduction in the amount of information that can be presented to the operator simultaneously. Another result of this flexibility is that it is possible, if more than one screen is devoted to the same Root, that there will be hidden Roots, whose data are nowhere displayed on the desk. This is true of the System Root unless it has been specially selected, since it has no default screen.   However, as we describe below, the alarm handling procedures serve to warn the operators of developments in hidden Roots.

Whenever the screen is touched, a white circle surrounds the finger, providing immediate visual feedback. If the touch is within a meaningful zone (such as one of the four large rectangles in Fig. 3) a line to the centre of the zone, a second circle and an audible tone indicate to the user which of the possible options he has registered. The touch-screen user is thereby amply compensated for the lack of tactile feedback given by a keyboard. If the touch is outside all the zones, the first circle simply serves to reassure the user that the screen is operational.

If a user touches the numerical value of variable, as it appears on a touch-screen display, a 'trend display' appears on the pad, fetched from the memory of the control processor which scans the variable. The operator may alter the scale of either axis, so as more closely to analyse the variable's recent history, and a second variable may simultaneously be trended in order to discover the correlation between them.

Of the control displays on the pad, the interface with the control loops, (the 'Hand/Auto station') is the most challenging in human factors terms. Each loop may be in one of four statuses: HAND, meaning hard-wired control; MANUAL, in which the actuators are moved by the operator sending commands through the computer system; AUTOMATIC, in which the commands are sent by the computer in furtherance of maintaining a variable at its set-point; and SUPERVISORY, where the set-point of the variable is itself derived from a computer algorithm. The Hand/Auto display must therefore indicate clearly: the present loop status, the availability of the three other statuses, the tentative set-point as it is injected by the user, the set-point itself, the set-point as modified by the control algorithms, the measured value of the variable, the actuator position, and the target actuator position, as well as alarm limits and the possible inhibition of certain control actions. On the input side, the operator must be able to change the control mode, and to enter new values for set-points or actuator positions either incrementally or numerically. We have contrived a single display with all these functions, except that during number entry some of the data are temporarily replaced by the keys.

All the displays selected on the pad are automatically replaced, after a period of inactivity, by a display giving single-touch

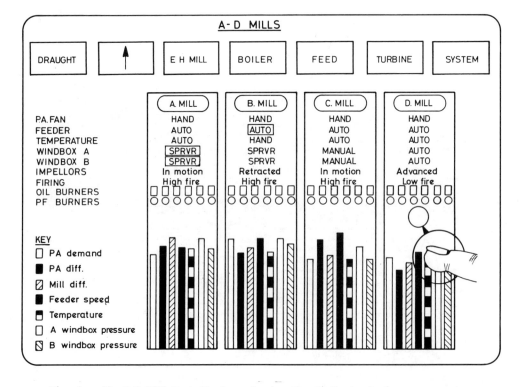

Fig. 3.   The A-D Mill Root display, showing the feedback circles consequent
on touching a sensitive zone. The D Mill Branch will be obtained.

access to certain of the sequence shut-down routines, for use in emergencies.

Alarm handling

When a plant item enters an alarm state that alarm is 'owned' by the Branch which contains the variable. The ownership of the alarm is then propagated upwards in the hierarchy, and the operator is guided to the display containing the item by red backgrounds to the owner Root and Branch keys. The alarm is cleared when the variable itself is touched, and the operators' understanding of recent developments is reinforced by the trend display which appears as usual. When the alarm has been accepted, the red background to the variable is replaced by a red box surrounding it, which remains until the plant item leaves the alarm state.

There may be rare occasions when no screen is showing the Root keys at time of the occurrence of the alarm. For example, if they are all at Branch level or below, and the alarm is in a hidden Root. For this reason the Root keys are are permanently reproduced on the Pad, and flash when an alarm occurs. Touching a Root key on the pad has exactly the effect it does when on the screen: it brings up the Root display.

Particularly serious events such as loop trips are accompanied by audible warnings, and in future, voice output may serve as a better guide for the operators. There is considerable further work needed to accomodate the many binary alarms not so far scanned by the system.

Desk hardware

The touch-screens stand on specially designed consoles, inside which are the desk computers and the touch-pads. The consoles are arranged in the U-shape shown in Fig. 4 so as to minimise the operators' viewing distances. The two central portions of the desk are to be used for mounting telephones and emergency switchgear. Whereas provision has been made for a comfortable sitting posture, the height of the consoles has at present been set for standing operation. This allows the operators either to stand or to sit on stools - a choice which they would be without if the consoles were lower.

The colour displays on the screens are generated by Gresham-Lion PPL's Single Board Display device. It provides two pages of 768 x 574 resolution in 16 colours, non-interlaced. A 30 kHz line-rate monitor is needed, and we are using the Cotron's 14" 'Arrow', available as a touch-screen from Mellordata Ltd. These screens give a pleasantly steady and clear display, with a very black background. The pad displays are monochrome, and of lower resolution, so that a standard line-rate monitor is sufficient. We are at present using PPL's Univisor (512 x 256) and a specially developed 9" touch-pad from Mellordata.

The touch sensitivity of both the screen and the pad is achieved through the interruption by the finger of one or more of the infra-red beams covering the surface of the screen. Both devices incorporate a microprocessor running a CEGB program, developed so as to bring their performance up to the standards of reliability necessary to the control-room. Permanently obscured or faulty beams are accomodated, as described in the following section, and there are many enhancements of operation and communication over commercially available products. The accumulation of dust, which can greatly reduce the reliability of touch-screens of this type, has been specifically reduced in both devices.

Desk software

The computer language used for the whole project is SWEPSPEED, a multi-task language developed in the South West Region of the CEGB, running under its own executive. SWEPSPEED code can be very clear, so that if care is taken with variable names, and comments are provided prodigally, the software listings themselves can be largely self-documenting. This is important for operational safety, since the power-station staff must be able to understand and maintain programs of whatever provenance.

Each touch-screen display has four distinct components: (i) a background picture-file, stored on higher memory (HM), which creates permanent features such as mimics or tables, (ii) a foreground job, running regularly, which reads new data from the control machines (via Ethernet) and writes them to the screen, (iii) a touch-zone file, stored on HM, which contains the positions and sizes of the various touch-sensitive zones attaching to the picture, and (iv) a

Fig. 4.   The consoles, each with a touch-screen and touch-pad, surrounding the operator. The desk processors are mounted within the consoles. Emergency switchgear and telecommunications equipment are fitted to the central pair.

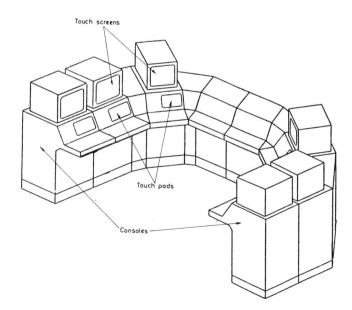

'touch-interpreter' job which runs when the screen is touched within a zone, and makes appropriate changes to global variables. These globals are monitored by a resident program which retrieves the necessary display jobs from HM, and overlays them into their job slots. Displays for the pad are produced in the same way, except that picture files for the Univisor are not supported, and the backgrounds must be drawn by code execution. Displays for both pad and screen can be drawn in about one second.

The touch-coordinate data, sent by the screens in terms of their grid of IR beams, are immediately converted to the coordinate system of the graphics generator, through a linear mapping. When a new touch-screen is connected, this mapping is defined by prompting the user to touch various parts of the display. Eschewing the beam grid in this way means that touch-screens of different sizes and types can be readily interchanged. Also, any inaccuracies of touch registration can be reduced by continually updating the mapping to compensate for systematic errors caused by changes in picture size, or different angles of approach. This reduces the possibility of touches being wrongly interpreted.

The touch-screens and pads are each serviced by a resident 'touch-register' job, similar in both cases. There may be as many as forty rectangular touch-zones per display, which can overlap or be completely contained within one another. The touch-registers report the numbers of the zones which have been touched to the touch-interpreters, but they also continuously monitor the 'health' of the touch-screens. Every ten seconds, the screens report whether they possess either permanently obscured beams, or ones which have just recovered from obscuration, or both. In each of these cases, a command is sent to the touch screen which allows any broken beams to be eliminated from future scans. Lines are then drawn through the display to indicate the faulty beams, making use of the beam-to-graphics mapping described above. Treating the broken beams in this way not only allows touch-screens to continue in service with degraded components, but also, of course, greatly assists in their swift renovation.

During the development of each display, the touch-zones are defined by an interactive on-screen zone-file editor. To minimise errors caused by inaccurate touches, the sensitive zones should be both as large and as well-spaced as possible. The zone editor obviates the need for the display designer ever to specify explicitly the actual coordinates and sizes of the zones; they are simply painted on the screen surrounding the display feature with which they are to be associated. The very creation of the zones, then, ensures that they are touchable.

SAFETY FEATURES

In this final section, we shall draw together those features of the desk system which particularly enhance its safety. There are many strategies used in the control software and hardware for ensuring safety and reliability, but they are beyond the scope of this paper.
(i) A good MMI is an important component of a safe system. If the staff can monitor and understand the plant status without strain, they will be more likely to anticipate operational problems, and be able to correct them quickly.
(ii) The operators are always involved. No attempt has been made to encode any operating strategy, so as deliberately to encourage the vigilance of the operators and preserve their role as 'prime movers' in the system.

(iii) High levels of redundancy and flexibility are maintained throughout the hardware and software. We have discussed in some detail the interchangeability of the desk processors and touch-screens. The control machines are paired, so that if necessary, a neighbouring machine can take over the manual control of the actuators. This is another example of limiting the effect of a fault to a downgrading of performance. All Ethernet communications are switched automatically between the two lines after a number of consecutive failures; there is enough redundant capacity on both lines for the transmission of all of the data.
(iv) CEGB touch-screen firmware is used. The touch-screens are loaded with an obscuration width above which touches are not accepted. This means that the screens may be cleaned with a cloth or by hand without fear of affecting the plant. Simultaneous separated touches also inhibit the sending of coordinates, and there is a 'depth' parameter which can be used to set a minimum duration for each touch. An important feature is that the touch-screens are always prompted for touch-coordinates rather than being allowed to send them indiscriminately, so that data are not corrupted by being sent before the receiver is ready.
(v) All machines and programs are continually checked. The host computer's program (which runs immediately on power-up and thereafter) can detect failure and reload any system from disc. Also, every control program has 'watchdog' flags to warn of stoppages.
(vi) Code is included specifically to ensure that new control displays are compatible with the current Root and Branch. This prevents the danger of confusion which may occur if, for example, a job has run incorrectly, despite the setting of the appropriate flags.
(vii) Changes in plant status cannot be initiated by a single touch.

CONCLUSION

We have described part of a large new control project at Didcot Power Station: a control desk design which gives greater priority to human factors. The desk is to a large extent based upon the structure of the information, which is one part of the Man-Machine Interface. The use of touch-screens and dot-addressable graphics provides a desk which is inherently flexible and can be modified and enhanced without compromising its safety.

ACKNOWLEDGEMENTS

Thanks are gladly given to Jon Gething, project leader, and to Norman Holland Station Manager, Didcot. This paper is published with the permission of the Director-General South West Region CEGB.

DESIGN VERIFICATION FOR (SAFETY-RELATED) SOFTWARE SYSTEMS

P. Baur and R. Lauber

*Institute for Control Engineering and Process Automation, University of Stuttgart,
Federal Republic of Germany*

Abstract: Currently, the verification procedures applied to safety related software are time-consuming, and they require highly skilled assessors. Therefore, computer aided verification methods and, eventually, an automation of the verification process is strongly advocated.
While there are some techniques already available to realize the formal verification of programs by computer means, only very few results are known to solve the problem of computer-aided verification of the software design. The paper to be presented proposes a two-step procedure to solve this problem:

- Use a computer-aided development-support system (including specification languages, analysis tools, documentation tools) for the software development. This results in a considerable improvement of reliability due to the various powerful features of fault-avoidance and fault-removal incorporated in the methods and tools of such a system.
  Unfortunately this does not guarantee the achievement of an error-free system nor is it a substitute for a verification of safety. But it is the prerequisite for the second step.

- Use an automatic verification tool for the symbolic execution of the software design specification based on design-assertions. The underlying verification procedure goes hand-in-hand with the development of a hierarchically structured software design and includes the following steps:

  . Identification of the system states/state sequences (of the technical process to be controlled) which are required/forbidden for the correct system function.

  . Based on this, generation and formulation of the corresponding design-assertions. This is assisted by so-called track-charts documenting the system part to be verified by showing the different controlflow-pathes and their influences in reaching the desired system states.

  . The computer-aided symbolic execution of the software design specification. Thereby it is determined which system states will be reached during operation and whether they are in compliance with the desired system states.

Keywords: Design verification, safety-related software, development environment, computer-aided development-support systems, verification specification, verification language, design-assertions, requirements specification, design specification, symbolic execution.

INTRODUCTION

Safety- related systems have to be in an error-free condition before starting operation. Therefore several attempts have been made to solve the problem of program verification by providing appropriate methods and tools [1, 2, 3].
Hitherto only few sucessful results have been reported and it seems to be still a matter of research.
Especially the support of verification activities by computerised means is restricted to special application with low complexity and size.
The reason for this may be the fact, that program verification is not seen in the right context.

Program verification is only one activity among others in the software development process and furthermore it is only one out of a series of verification activities (fig.1) [4].

The following evident facts should always be kept in mind:
- verification is the comparison between the output of successive stages of the software life cycle to determine that there is a faithful translation of one stage into the next one.
That means, verification always evaluates the output of work which just has been completed.
So program verification does not help if things have already gone wrong.

To cope this problem the verification should be done in steps as small as possible (after each intermediate development stage), and it is absolutely necessary to put as much effort as possible in the avoidance and detection of errors prior to verification.

- the feasibility of a verification depends on the previous development steps.
  Like a certain programming style is enabling testability, there are development strategies which are prerequisites for a successful verification.

This leads to the conclusion, that we have

- at first to apply methods and tools, which may support the development of an error-free system [5, 6]

- to do the verification in parallel to the development (especially to avoid solutions which can not be verified).

- to recognize that design verification is the most important verification activity, because design errors are very critical and costly and because all the following development and verification depend on their results.

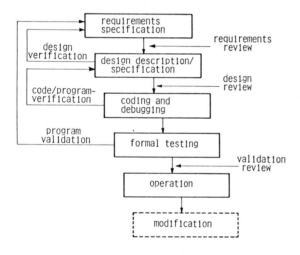

Fig.1: Programm Development Process indicating the V&V-Activities

PREREQUISITES FOR A SUCCESSFUL DESIGN VERIFICATION

The concepts for design verification, explained in the following chapters, are an extention of the development environment EPOS (Engineering and Project Oriented Support System) Therefore some of its features, wich are relevant or fundamental for the proposed design verification strategies shall be briefly explained.

All together the EPOS-system includes seven components: three specification languages, three softwaretool systems and a communication system [7, 8].

The specification languages are

- **-EPOS-R** to define the requirements in the customers needs and system requirements document
- **-EPOS-S** to describe system design including the possibility of automatic code generation
- **-EPOS-P** to describe the information related to project management and configuration management

The softwaretool systems

- **-EPOS-A** for early detection of specification and design errors and for producing test and result reports
- **-EPOS-D** for producing the entire documentation (texts, lists, graphical representations) according to the information entered by means of **EPOS-R, EPOS-S** and **EPOS-P**.
- **-EPOS-M** which offers computer support for management activities and configuration management.

The communication system **EPOS-C** is used to facilitate user-oriented communication between the user and the EPOS work station.

Concerning a successful design verification the following features of EPOS are used:

Fault avoidance

- by substituting human error-prone methods by automated ones (e.g. automatic documentation).

- by reducing the occurance of human errors during the system development (e.g. enhancing perceivibility by enforcing structured design and stepwise refinement).

Fault detection & removal

by static and dynamic analysis of the requirements- and design specification.

(Design)-Verification support

- by means of identifying and categorizing requirements
- by formal checks whether all elements of the requirements specification have been referenced during design in order to ensure mutual consistency
- by listing all elements of the requirements specification indicating their references to the corresponding parts of the design specification
- by providing a complete, precise and unified (standardized) documentation and
- by automatic updating of documents after changes.

THE NEED FOR A VERIFICATION SPECIFICATION

The purpose of the design verification is to ensure, that the program design is a correct representation of the requirements.
The verification effort requires a formal design description, which is provided by the design specification language EPOS-S.
Unfortunately a computer-aided design verification also requires a formal definition of the software requirements.
But this stands in contradiction to the nature of a requirements specification as a basis for the communication among the different kind of people (qualification, experience etc.) involved in this early development phase.
The specification language EPOS-R therefore mostly uses semi-formal description means to ensure on the one hand readability and understandability and on the other hand to avoid interpretation errors.
Supplementary it provides the possibility to formalize the requirements by specifying decision-tables and state-graphs.
This imposes the question how to solve this conflict meaning how to formalize an informal description, which can be used as axiomatic basis for design verification.

The proposed solution to this problem is the extention of the design language EPOS-S by a verification language.
This verification language can be used to define the relevant requirements (-selected out of the requirement specification) in a formal notation and attach them to the design specification (fig. 2).

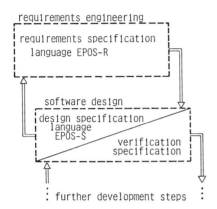

Fig 2: Integrated design- and verification specification

The advantages of this concept are, that

-the present notation of the requirements specification can be retained
-the relevant requirements can be explicitly selected
-the formalization of the verification language can be adapted to the notation of the design language
-the computer-aided verification is facilitated because all the information can be retrieved out of one database.

GENERATION OF DESIGN-ASSERTION

It is assumed that the requirements specification contains all the information needed as basis for the design verification.
Now this information has to be selected and specified by the verification language.
But caused by the lack of restrictions concerning the structure of the requirements specification and by the special needs of the different applications the specifications may strongly vary.
Therefore it is necessary to have a model which enables the selection, structuring and formalizing of the requirements.

The proposed model considers the technical process (to be controlled) as a generalized state process.
Thereby the first step is to identify the (finite) set of states (state sequences) which are required or forbidden for correct system function.
These states can be described by terms of the information the automation system gets from or puts to the technical process via the process-input/output. So each state can be defined by a logical expression containing the relevant input-/output-variables, their history and selected internal data.
After this set of states is defined one has to identify the required transitions between the states (if this information is available.).
Each transition consists of its causes (events, conditions) and the actions which will be executed to realize the transition.
For a safety-related application that can mean to identify the dangerous system states.

Figure 3 shows an example part of a state graph with two states and a transition in between.

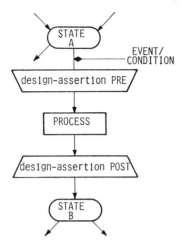

Fig.3: Part of a state graph

The technical process modelled by fig.3 may be in state A. Triggered by a EVENT or for a true CONDITION the PROCESS has to be executed. After that the technical process has to be in state B.
Thereby PROCESS shall be a design-object which represents a modul, function or procedure to be implemented later in the automation system.

According to this view two relations between the automation system and the technical process can be seen:

-PRE: the required state of the technical process' before and
-POST:the required state of the technical process after the execution of PROCESS

Hereby it is to be recognized, that these PRE- and POST-states are not directly derivable from state A and B. They refer only the cut-set of state-variables belonging to the individual transistions e.g. from state A to state C, D, ... which all should have especial PRE-states.
Now these PRE- and POST-states provide the possibility to attach the information concerning the required process-states to the design specification (design objects). Therefore the PRE-and POST-states have to be formally defined by the verification language coming up to so-called design-assertions. (see next chapter).

So far we have not set up any restrictions concerning the formalization of the requirements specification and therefore it may be sometimes difficult to formally specify the requirements according this model.
On the other hand there exists a great class of (safety-related) applications for which the requirements can be formally specified by means of decision-tables and state-graphs (e.g. machine tools, interlocking).
Assuming this class of applications with such a formalized requirements specification, their formal elements can be easily translated into design-assertions.
A decision-table defines rules each of which contains a conditional expression and a set of actions. These rules are indicating which action (sequence of actions) has to be executed if a condition (conditional expression) is true.
Therefore the conditional expression can be transformed into a PRE-assertion and assigned to this action (realized by a design object).

THE RELATION BETWEEN THE VERIFICATION AND THE DESIGN LANGUAGE

As just mentioned above there is a relation between the design-objects and the design-assertions. To understand this relation some features of the design language EPOS-S shall be roughly explained.

In order to describe the different levels of the design, so-called design-objects are defined. These design objects are of the types ACTION, MODULE, DATA, INTERFACE, EVENT, CONDITION, EXECUTION UNIT. Between these objects a series of interactions are possible including control- and dataflow. All these objects can be hierarchically decomposed according a stepwise refinement of the design using a entity-relationship-model.

Figure 4 shows the very general structure of an EPOS-S design-object ACTION.

```
ACTION                        Name of the design object
Description-Part              (mandatory)
Decomposition-Part            (optional)
                              Definition of the hierarchical
                              refinement combined with the
                              definition of the controlflow
                              between sub-actions
Relation to other objects     (optional)
Assertion-part                Definition of the design-
                              assertions
ACTIONEND
```

Fig.4: General structure of a design-object ACTION

According to figure 4 the specification of the design assertions is done in a sub-part of an action. This sub-part contains the PRE-/POST-/ PRE-POST-assertions, which describe the (program-) system states required for correct operation before/after/intermediate to the program-execution represented by this action.

An example of the specification of such a design-object containing design and verification information is shown in fig. 5.

```
ACTION LOCAL-ROUTE-SETTING

DESCRIPTION:
   PURPOSE:"..."
DESCRIPTIONEND.

INPUT: ROUTE1, ROUTE2.
OUTPUT: SWITCH, SIGNAL1, SIGNAL2, SIGNAL3.

DECOMPOSITION:
   IF ROUTE1-OR-ROUTE2-FREE
      THEN IF ROUTE1
         THEN SET-ROUTE1
         ELSE IF ROUTE2-FREE
            THEN SET-ROUTE2
            FI
      FI
      ELSE LOCK-ROUTES
   FI.

ASSERTIONS: <TOP> TYPE VERIFY
     PRE  :  TRUE
     POST :  SWITCH="STRAIGHT"IMPLIES SIGNAL2="RED"AND
             SWITCH= "CURVE"  IMPLIES SIGNAL1="RED".
ASSERTIONSEND.

ACTIONEND.
```

Fig.5:   Specification   of   the   design-object
          LOCAL-ROUTE-SETTING

SUPPORTING THE SPECIFICATION OF DESIGN-ASSERTIONS

The handicraft way to come to the specification of a design-assertion may be sometimes difficult and error-prone.
Therefore an evaluation program is available which supports the generation and hierarchical transformation of the assertions by

- automatic generation of a graphical representation of a selected part of the design specification for which assertions have to be assigned. This is provided by the so-called track-charts (fig.6) which are a combination of control- and dataflowgraphs, showing each controlflow-path separately.
  Thereby each path can be easily evaluated, starting either with the POST-or the PRE-Assertion.
- evaluating the relations between the design-specification and the already specified assertions and documenting them in the track-charts.

For example it is shown

. which of the input-/output-data and the conditional controlflow-elements are referenced in the assertions
. which sub-paths are not concerned by the assertions, etc.

If there are requirements formally defined by means of decision-tables and state-graphs they will be automatically transformed into aquivalent design-assertions or a document is generated containing a proposal for the transformation.

CONSISTENCY & COMPLETENESS OF THE DESIGN/VERIFICATION SPECIFICATION

In order to detect specification errors as soon as possible the design specification can be analyzed for unambiguities, completeness etc. by EPOS-A.
Now the extension by design-assertions enforces to add further analyzing facilities.
These analyzing tools have to ensure that the combined design/verification specification is complete and statically consistent.

The concerning analysis tools can be devided into three parts:

- Self-consistency of the design-assertions
- Hierarchical completeness of the design-assertions (meaning that they have to be completely transformed according the hierarchical refinement of the design)
- Structured consistency of the design-assertions (meaning that they have to be consistent according the functional properties of the design specification).

SYMBOLIC EXECUTION OF THE DESIGN/VERIFICATION SPECIFICATION

The hierarchical structure of a design specified by EPOS-S is decomposed into design-levels with corresponding hierarchically related sub-systems (so-called "level-i-systems") whereby the sub-actions are related by controlflow (see fig. 7, 8). The resulting top-down-structure of these abstract level-i-systems enables a top-down-verification.

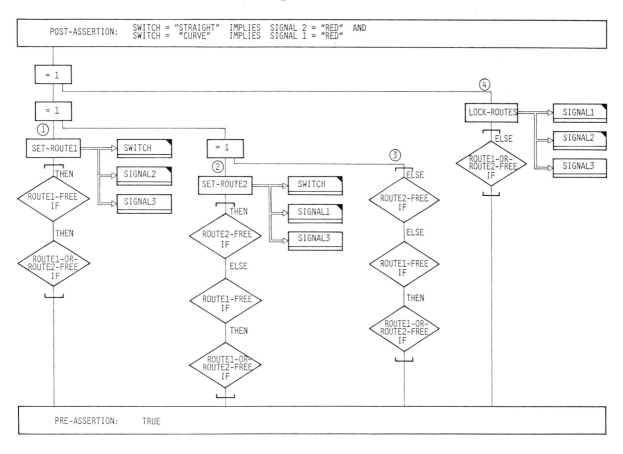

Fig. 6: Track-Chart of the level-i-system LOCAL-ROUTE-SETTING

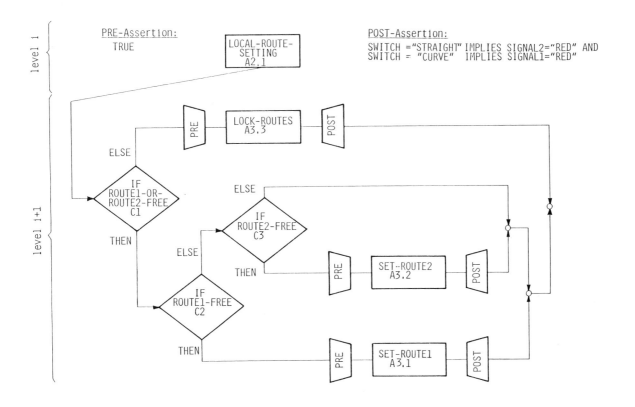

Fig. 7: Controlflow of a level-i-system (LOCAL-ROUTE-SETTING)

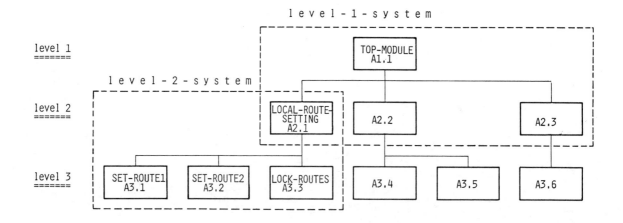

Fig. 8: Design-hierarchy indicating level-i-systems

So it is possible
- to partition the complex verification of the
  complete design/verification specification into
  small and manageable sub-system with less complexity
- to do the verification in parallel to the design
  process ensuring an early detection of defficen-
  cies.

The scope of the symbolic execution of the
level-i-system is to proof, that the execution of
all possible control-flow pathes leads to results
which are consistent with the design-assertions of
the level i.

Thereby for the actual verification of a
level-i-system the assertions of the design-objects
at level i+1 are assumpted to be correct.
Fig. 7 shows an example of a level-i-system with
its controlflow-pathes and the design-assertions at
level i+1.
The symbolic execution of a single path consists of
the following steps:
First of all it is determined which variables/data
are used or changed by the path.
Then these variables will be arranged in a special
data pool, by which the execution can be recorded.
This provides a representation of all system states
(defined by the variables) which may be influenced
by the path execution.

The explicit symbolic execution starts with the
initialization of the data pool according to the
definitions in the PRE-assertion of the level-
i-system.

Then each controlflow-element (according the con-
trolflow-sequence) is treated by two evaluations:

I) consistency-analysis
    A consistency-analysis is carried out, if the
    execution comes to a PRE-assertion (at level
    i+1) or a conditional control-flow-element.
    Thereby it is to check, whether the actual
    pool-status is constistent with the actual
    PRE-assertion (at level i+1) or with the
    value of the condition required by the actual
    path execution.

II) pool-actualisation
    An actualisation is done for each POST-asser-
    tion by transforming its definitions into the
    pool representation.

If the assertions contain conditional or alternative definitions for which the validity can not be
determined, this is registrated in the pool and the
execution is repeated for all possible alternatives.
(Thereby the amount of necessary runs may increase
considerably. This is an important reason for devi-
ding the verification according to the
level-i-systems.)

The execution is terminated with an error-report if
a
    . consistency error is detected
      or a
    . conditional branching is found, which is in
      contradiction to the execution of the consi-
      dered path.

If consistency can not be explicitly stated,
caused by incomplete assertions, the execution is
continued after reporting a warning.

After all controlflow-elements have been gone
through the actual pool-status represents the result of the path-execution.

Now the final step is to proof the consistency
between the pool status and the POST-assertion of
the level-i-system.

This procedure is carried out for all the
level-i-systems until the level of non-refined
design-objects is reached.
These objects are those to be translated into a
program-realization.
Their verification can be done either manually or
by computer-aided means if the coding realization
is additionally specified.

A third possibility, which brigdes the gap between
design and implementation is the automatic translation of the assertions (of the terminal objects)
into executable program-code.
So their validity can be checked during real program execution.
This is especially interesting, because EPOS allows
an .automatic program-generation from the design
specification.
The resulting runtime-assertions can be either used
during the test-phase or in case of highly critical
functions embedded in the final application
program.

CONCLUSION

By the use of the computer-aided development support system EPOS a first step towards the achievement of an error-free and verifyable program-system
is done.
Despite that it is necessary to enhance its features
e.g. concerning the support of the various verification activities.
Therefore the following concepts have been proposed:

- Provide a model and appropriate tools which support the selection and structuring of the requirements
- Provide notational tools for formally specifying
  requirements and assigning them to the design
  specification.
- Make it possible to do the verification in parallel to the development
- Provide software tools to automate the verification activities.

References:

[1]   Software Validation, Verification and
      Testing Technique and Tool Reference Guide.
      NBS Special Publication 500-93.
      U.S. Departement of Commerce 1982

[2]   Software Validation, Inspection - Testing -
      Verification - Alternatives.
      Proc. of Symposium of Software Validation
      Darmstadt, FRG, Sept. 83 (Ed. Hansen)
      North Holland Publ. Co. 1984

[3]   Techniques for Verification and Validation
      of Safety-Related Software
      EWICS Position Paper No. 5, January 1985

[4]   Standard for Software Quality Assurance
      Plans, ANSI/IEEE STD 730-1981

[5]   Fault-Avoidance and Fault-Removal Features
      of the Computer-Aided Development Support
      System EPOS
      Proc. 3rd IFAC/IFIP Workshop SAFECOMP `83
      Cambridge, U.K., Sept. 83, Pergamon Press,
      pp 103-110

[6]   Lauber, R.: Impact of Computer-Aided
      Development Support System on Software
      Quality and Reliability.
      Proc. 6th Int. Computer
      Software & Application Conf. COMPSAC 82,
      Chicago, Nov. 1982. IEEE Comp. Soc. Press,
      Los Angeles 1982, pp 248-256

[7]   Biewald, J., Göhner, P., Lauber, R.,
      Schelling, H.: EPOS - a Specification and
      Design Technique for Computer Controlled
      Real-Time Automation Systems.
      Proc. 4th Int. Conf. Software Engineering,
      München 1979, IEEE Comp. Soc. Los Alamitos,
      Cal., 1979, pp 245-250

[8]   Lauber, R.: Development Support Systems
      IEEE Computer 15(1982), May, pp 36-46

VERIFICATION AND VALIDATION PROGRAM FOR A DISTRIBUTED COMPUTER SYSTEM FOR SAFETY APPLICATION

D. M. Rao* and S. Bologna**

*Westinghouse-Nuclear WRD/NSID, Pittsburgh, Pennsylvania, USA
**ENEA CRE-Casaccia, Rome, Italy

Abstract: The importance of a Verification & Validation (V&V) program, to affirm the reliable operation of computer systems in real time safety applications, is widely recognized. To ensure consistent, traceable, and auditable high performance of the individuals involved in the V&V program, several pragmatic issues such as quality of documentation, details and staging of activities, etc., should be resolved prior to the practical application of the V&V program.

This paper presents the V&V program established for the development of 16-bit, microprocessor-based distributed safety systems, for application to the safety of nuclear power plants and especially tailored for the Italian plants. The development project, which is under the responsibility of Westinghouse, has the participation of various Italian organizations, each contributing in different areas of expertise.

Keywords: Safety Systems; Computer Software; Software Testing; Design and Development process; Documentation Standards; Verification and Validation.

Acknowledgments: Major contributors to this reported V&V program development were G. P. Gajdzik, D. V. Gennaro, and G. W. Remley.

1. INTRODUCTION

Gallagher (1983) reported on the role, and the resulting application, of well-developed principles of design, testing, and documentation of software in an earlier Westinghouse digital-based Integrated Protection System (IPS) development program. Based on such accrued experiences in developing Instrumentation and Control (I&C) systems, the approach at Westinghouse WRD is to consider the verification and validation process of digital-based I&C systems as an integral part of System Development and Implementation Process (SYSDIP), as depicted in Figure 1.

The verification and validation process for I&C safety systems is used during the life cycle of the system product to confirm that the system design has met the system design objectives. The V&V process is a set of technical activities that permits the examination of the system design and implementation by viewing its functional behavior as well as the system's specific operational characteristics.

1.1 V&V Plan Required

Like for any other systematic process, a plan must be created to describe the V&V process in detail. This is required in order to have a ready reference that the V&V team can follow. The V&V Plan describes the V&V approach and methods of performance, specifies reports, specifies the level of detail, and establishes the degree of rigor to be imposed in accordance with the level of importance to safety.

The I&C V&V program details the V&V process, applicable V&V principles, concepts, and methods directing V&V activities during various stages, and provides a checklist for detection of potential defects/errors appropriate to the stage. As a part of this document, the testing process is detailed, and various test tools and techniques were described in order to permit judicious deployment of combination of test methods. The following excerpts are taken from the developed V&V program to illustrate some key aspects considered in the formulation of the program.

2. ROLE OF V&V IN THE SYSTEM DEVELOPMENT PROCESS

2.1 Overview

Basically, the approach taken at Westinghouse WRD in the development of new I&C systems is that the design is conducted from the "top down," while the V&V tests are conducted "bottom up." This philosophy was instilled in the SYSDIP documentation structure (Figure 1), where specific sets of documentation are prepared for the various phases of development, implementation, and operation, as well as for the various stages of V&V within the phases.

SCCS-D

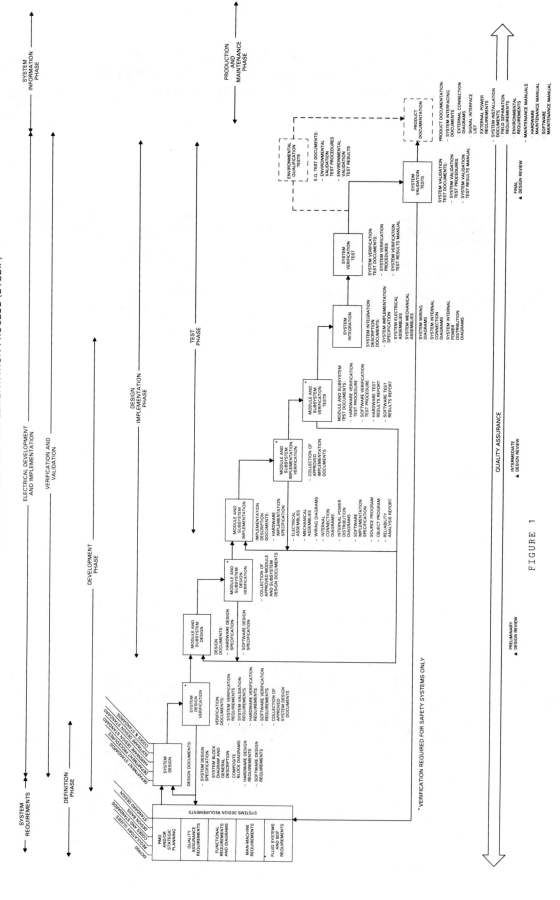

SYSTEM DEVELOPMENT/IMPLEMENTATION PROCESS (SYSDIP)

FIGURE 1

The relationship of the SYSDIP documentation structure and the V&V program becomes readily evident in the ensuing description of the V&V process and activities.

2.2 Requirements Verification

The top-down design decomposition process begins with the development of the system design requirements documents in establishing the overall system design. Input information for the system design is provided by the functional requirements document, that defines the system functional operations. Accompanying input documents would involve quality assurance requirements, and if applicable, man-machine, fluid systems, balance of plant requirements, and system design requirements. Although formal design reviews, which can be used as part of the V&V process, may occur earlier in SYSDIP, the initial V&V stage conducted by the V&V team is done after the system design documents are completed. These documents include the system design specifications, the hardware, and software, design requirements. The system design documents are verified back to the system design requirements document as the major reference document.

2.3 Design Verification

The progression of the system design decomposition proceeds with the hardware and software module/subsystem designs. During this phase of development, the hardware, and software, design specification documents are produced. Until this step in the development phase, the SYSDIP documents are primarily requirements, or to simplify further, they designate "what" is required of the design. The specification documents provide the particulars and details "how" the design is to materialize. A second stage of verification follows the establishment of the design specifications, whereby the design specifications are verified back to the preceding system design step and the system design requirements documents.

The module and subsystem implementation documents which provide the descriptions of the hardware and software are produced during the next step of the development and implementation process. Specifications, in the form of electrical and mechanical assembly drawings, rack and cabinet internal wiring diagrams, and internal power distribution diagrams furnish the descriptions for the system hardware implementation.

In the same regard, specifications for the system software implementation are provided by the source program and object program documents. A third stage of verification follows, which involves the subsystem and module implementation verification by reviewing the implementation description documents and by also the actual physical testing of the subsystems and modules. Hardware verification test procedures and software test procedures are provided by the verification process, again totally independent of the design team. All verification testing of the system software and hardware modules/subsystems is conducted by the V&V team. A report of the hardware test results and the software test results are provided after this stage of verification. These reports in conjunction with the hardware, software, and system design specifications, and the verification test procedures, must contain enough information to enable a third party to repeat any of the tests and understand the test results.

2.4 Integrated System Verification & Validation

The system integration is performed during the next step of SYSDIP. The system implementation specifications provides the as-built description of the total integrated system. This document is a composite of various system electrical and mechanical specifications that forms the manufacturing standard drawing package. Included is information such as the system description, bill of materials, schematics, and production test procedures. Other implementation type documents such as the system electrical and mechanical assemblies, and wiring diagrams are compiled as part this document. The system integration verification and validation stage follows this final step of the system development and implementation process. The writing of documents to perform the system validation tests, and the conductance of the tests is under the control of the verification team. However, participation in these efforts by the design team members is permitted, as long as the designer was not directly responsible for the portion of the system to be tested. Any environmental validation tests would be conducted at the end of this V&V stage if the tests are required. A test results manual is compiled at the conclusion of the tests. Summaries of these test results and the summaries of the test results compiled after the module and subsystem verification tests are submitted for review as part of the licensing process. It is understood that any portion of the V&V process may be audited by internal or external auditors in the licensing process.

3.   VERIFICATION & VALIDATION (V&V) CONCEPTS

This section describes a number of concepts associated with the V&V process. In general, they cover the V&V activities during the system development and implementation process and will affect one or more stages of the system development/implementation as shown in Figure 1 (SYSDIP structure).

3.1 System Design Requirements Mandatory

The system design requirements form the basis of all the system design and verification efforts, and are used throughout the rest of product life cycle. System Design Requirements are the bases against which all the validation activities are performed.

3.2 Checklists in Testing Process

Since the definition and implementation of the testing process is one of the most important aspects in the overall Verification and Validation process, it is helpful to have a checklist against which the verification test procedure and the test results report can be checked to ensure that all aspects have been considered.

3.3 Organization of Independent Teams

The independent V&V team concept extends to all aspects of the hardware, software, and system designs. This approach necessitates the existence of sufficient and unambiguous documentation of the system. The verification team has the freedom to raise pertinent questions and report errors; however, they do not resolve the errors. The latter is the function of the design team.

3.4 Verification Team Organizational Responsibilities

For safety systems, full independent testing is performed without evaluating or using the developer's test set-up, test cases, and test results. The documentation of the V&V test plan, test bed, test results, and discrepancies is provided for review by the Quality Assurance Department, or any other third party.

3.5 Systematic Development Methods Required

Differences in the quality of software are directly related to the degree of a systematic development methodology that was used. An orderly approach to system development, supported by clear, concise documentation, reduces the verification costs.

3.6 Cannot Be Done Using Only One Technique

Traditionally, testing has been the only technique of software verification. However, a single technique of verification cannot provide sufficient substantiation of the correctness and reliability of the software.

3.7 Configuration Management Necessary for Effective Verification

A Configuration Management (CM) system is required, which identifies and controls approved and implemented changes. The determination whether a change requires re-verification is made by the chief verifier.

3.8 Library Required for Effective Maintenance

The use of a library allows for the orderly development, release, and maintenance of the system, hardware, and software. When the verification team is satisfied that the software item has met specifications, the item is released to the library as acceptable for use. All revisions must be approved by the chief verifier.

3.9 Costs Can Be Reduced By Using Automated Tools

Part of the V&V planning process is the selection of appropriate tools for a given project.

3.10 Accurate Records of V&V Activities

There are many documents that should be generated during the system life cycle which record the V&V activities. Audits shall be used as a design control method to assure compliance to all aspects of the WRD Quality Assurance programs.

4.   V&V PROGRAM IMPLEMENTATION HIGHLIGHTS

4.1 V&V Organization

V&V for a safety system requires that those individuals who do verification do not participate in the design or implementation.

4.2 Documentation

Systematic and formalized review of documentation is of paramount importance in successful implementation of the V&V Program. The documentation structure of SYSDIP presents a traceable, step-by-step approach to the development of a system and its application.

4.3 V&V Review & Analysis Process

Two of the V&V activities, a) the design requirements review, and b) design specification and implementation review, are based on the reviews and analysis of the documentation prepared as part of normal project activities. The other V&V activities that this document details involve testing of the completed system, design implementation testing of modules and subsystems, and the integrated system acceptance tests.

4.4 V&V Test Classification

The V&V test classification for a particular system in nuclear applications is dependent on the potential impact on safety and public protection. The determining factors normally place a system into one of the three following categories: safety, safety related, or non-safety. This classification is of major significance to a system V&V plan because it prescribes the program test strategy and ensuing activities. Examples of the test methods may be full independent testing, independent supplemental testing, or technical consultancy. It should also be noted that a particular test method may vary in depth dependent on how stringent the safety classification. The software associated with actuation of reactor trip and engineered safeguards (IEEE-279-1971) must receive the highest level of verification identified. As such, all software at the unit level must be structurally tested to ensure that all lines of the unit indeed meet the intended design specification.

4.5 Test of Data Base

It is not sufficient to test only the algorithm to verify the correctness of a safety related program. It is also necessary to establish the correctness of the data base used by that program by considering data accuracy, data completeness, data structure, and data accessibility.

4.6 Production Systems

Once a system design and implementation has been verified and validated, any succeeding systems manufactured with the same design need only be certified by standard manufacturing test procedures. Many of the tests used by manufacturing may be the same or equivalent to those used in the system V&V process. The equivalent of the system validation tests should be performed, as a minimum, on every successive system of the same design that has been previously verified and validated.

4.7 Testing Process

The testing process, used as part of the V&V plan, defines a set of steps necessary for the generation and utilization of verification test procedures.

These steps cover the areas of test features selection, test case design, test development, and processing of test data. This section includes hardware, software, and system testing considerations. The verification test procedure includes designing of test cases and their bases, step-by step instructions for executing the tests, expected results, and the analysis of actual monitored and collected test results.

The verification test results document, as defined in the SYSDIP document, is comprised of the final results of the verification testing activities. The verification test procedures documents are linked to the verification test results documents and to the other documents of the total verification activities, as outlined in Figure 2.

SYSDIP PLAN

The System Development/ Implementation Process (SYSDIP) was established as a means to conduct the operations of a design/manufacturing program in the Instrumentation and Control Systems Department. The SYSDIP documentation structure was developed to facilitate the verification and validation (V&V) activities that may be required for the program. The terms used in the definition of the documents were selected to be consistent with Westinghouse and industrial standards and terms already established by in-house licensing practices.

5. SYSTEM DESIGN REQUIREMENTS DOCUMENTS

5.1 System Design Requirements

This document defines the requirements for the system design and system integration. The document includes the performance requirements for access control, data security, and external interfaces, as well as for interfacing the system hardware and software elements including the accuracy, time response, and noise levels. Also included in the document are requirements for definitions of system functions such as direct memory access, programmed input/output, interrupt driven input/output, serial communications between processors, and direct communication between processors over a common bus. The following two documents are also part of the system design requirements.

System Block Diagram and General Description

The system block diagram represents a top level depiction of the system architecture and its interconnections. A general description of the subsystems is provided to further define the functions and interactions required of the subsystems at a system level. The document also provides a description of the system architecture.

Composite Block Diagrams

These drawings depict the implementation of the system functional requirements, functional diagrams, flow diagrams, channel lists, and other key documents in both hardware and software. All system protection and control functions are identified in these drawings.

5.2 Hardware Design Requirements Document

The document defines the requirements for the system hardware. The document includes the general system and technical requirements, the environmental requirements, field termination requirements, and system interface requirements.

5.3 Software Design Requirements Document

This document defines the essential requirements, including the functions, performance, design constraints, and attributes, of the overall system software and external interfaces. The requirements specifically include process inputs/outputs including ranges, accuracy, sampling intervals, functional algorithms, flow charts, configurations, external interfaces (operator, software, and communications), in-service test features, response to detected failures, timing requirements, requirements for common and individual functions, and other performance requirements.

5.4 System Verification Requirements Document

These requirements provide the basis in which the system conforms to the system design requirements. The objectives are to make evident that the subsystems are properly interfaced and that the system interfaces properly with the external environment. Additional objectives are that all interfaces between the functional units are correct and that the data flow and control flow between different software modules works correctly.

5.5 System Validation Requirements Document

This document defines the functional operations of the integrated system. This document includes a description of the validation principles applicable by testing, that the system functional operations are correct, and that the system software is capable of operating in the integrated system hardware environment. The system validation shall exercise all module/subsystem

interfaces. Test cases should be developed to include various transients that may occur during plant operations.

5.6 Hardware/Software Verification Requirements Documents

Defines the process of demonstrating that the hardware/software design requirements are met. These verification requirements are applicable for the system hardware/software at the module and subsystem level. These documents contribute to the establishment of their respective verification test procedures document.

6. MODULE AND SUBSYSTEM DESIGN DOCUMENTS

6.1 System Design Specifications

This document provides the detailed specifications for the system design and integration of the modules and/or subsystems to meet the system design requirements. It describes the purpose of the system, the system structure, system operations (including any constraints, error recovery mechanisms, resource contention between modules and/or subsystems), and the detailed system performance characteristics to meet the system design requirements. This document contributes to the establishment of the system verification test procedures documents.

6.2 Hardware Design Specification

This document provides the details for the hardware design at the module and/or subsystem level to meet the hardware design requirements. It defines the purpose of the hardware, the physical structure, any interface constraints, and the hardware ratings and characteristics. It further describes the functional operation, its inputs/outputs, power requirements, and any special features that may be required.

6.3 Software Design Specification

This document provides the details for the software design at the module and/or subsystem level to meet the software design requirements. It includes software language, the logical structure, variable names, information flow, logical processing steps, and the data structure of software programs to meet the software design requirements. It also describes the functions performed, support software, the storage and execution limitations, interface constraints, error conditions/detection/actions, and details of the software operation in the hardware environment.

7. MODULE & SUBSYSTEM IMPLEMENTATION DESCRIPTION DOCUMENTS

7.1 Hardware Implementation Specification

This document represents the description of the hardware design as its implemented (the 'as-built') documentation. The document includes a manufacturing standard drawing package, which includes information such as the hardware description, the bill of materials, printed circuit artwork, drill plans, schematics, production test procedures, and a revision control sheet which is provided for each hardware module. Other implementation type documents such as the electrical and mechanical assemblies and the various wiring diagrams (which are also used as stand alone documents) are compiled as part of this document.

7.2 Software Implementation Specification

This document represents the description of the software design as its implemented (the 'as-coded') documentation and includes the source program listings and object programs. This document, along with the software design specification document, contributes to the basis for the software verification test procedures document.

7.3 Reliability Analysis Report

The reliability analysis report provides an analysis of the systems availability.

8. MODULE AND SUBSYSTEM VERIFICATION TESTS DOCUMENTS

8.1 Hardware Verification Test Procedure

Defines the tests to be performed, the test methodology, test environment, expected results, and the acceptance criteria. Each test procedure covers a specific functional item such as a printed circuit board, data link, etc. These test procedures contain step-by-step test procedures for performing the specific test(s). Included are tests such as voltage limits, throughput, response times, and limited environmental exposure.

8.2 Software Verification Test Procedures

This document defines the software verification tests. It defines the tests to be performed, test methodology, test environment, expected results, and the acceptance criteria. This document contains details of the input test-bed, how the expected results and the acceptance criteria are determined, and the revision status of the system software under test.

8.3 Hardware/Software Test Results Report

These test results reports present a summary of the hardware/software verification tests results, the errors found, and resolution of discrepancies. These documents, in conjunction with the design specification and verification test procedure documents, must contain enough information to a enable a third party to repeat the tests and understand the results impact.

9. SYSTEM INTEGRATION DESCRIPTION DOCUMENTS

9.1 System Implementation Specification

This document represents the description of the system design as it is implemented, or more commonly in terms of document control, the 'as-built' documentation. The document includes a manufacturing standard drawing package, which includes information such as the system description, the bill of materials, schematics, production test procedures, and revision status. A manufacturing standard drawing package is provided for each system. Other system implementation type documents, such as the system electrical and system mechanical assemblies, and the various system wiring diagrams which are also used as stand alone documents, are compiled as part of this document.

10. SYSTEM VERIFICATION & VALIDATION TESTS DOCUMENTS

10.1 System Verification Test Procedures

This document defines the procedures used to perform the integrated system verification test. It defines the tests to be performed, test methods, and acceptance criteria to achieve system verification. Test cases are typically a series of systematic overlapping static and/or dynamic tests which progress from detailed performance checks of module and subsystems to more expanded performance checks of the overall system. Test cases and test results information is compiled with the system validation test information to establish system test results manual.

10.2 System Validation Test Procedures

This document defines the procedures used to perform integrated system validation tests. It details the stages and progression routes to accomplish the functional tests for the total system. This document defines test cases and acceptance criteria required to achieve the validation of the system functional operations. The test cases should simulate real-life plant conditions and should include tests such as static and dynamic calibration and operational tests, functional logic tests including system interactions, signal interface tests, variable, and ramp input tests. The test cases and test results information are compiled with the system verification test information to establish the system test results manual.

11. TEST RESULTS MANUAL

A summary of test results information from the following documents are used in the licensing process for the system.

11.1 System Verification Test Results

The system verification test results are the actual performance test results compiled during integrated system verification tests of the system's physical ratings and characteristics. These performance test results cover items such as response times, accuracy and power margins, noise levels, and overload and recovery characteristics.

11.2 System Validation Test Results

The system validation test results are the actual functional test results compiled during integrated system validation tests of the system functional operations. These functional tests results includes items such as external stimulus verses output results, the interaction between subsystems, and the transporting of information.

CONCLUSIONS

Developing a good V&V program requires the application of sound technical and management principles. A systematically planned V&V program, in conjunction with the documentation structure as reported, facilitates consistently good and auditable contribution by the V&V team to system quality.

DEFINITION OF KEY TERMS USED

Verification is the comparison of the stage-by-stage system development to determine that there is a faithful translation of one stage (such as design) into the next stage (such as implementation).

Validation is the process of determining the level of conformance between the operational system and the system requirements, under simulated plant operational conditions.

Testing is the process of exercising the system in order to determine whether the results it produces are correct.

REFERENCES

Gallagher, J. M., (1983) Software for Computers in Safety Systems of Nuclear Power Plants. Proceedings of the Third IFAC/IFIP Workshop (SAFECOMP '83), pp. 159 - 165.

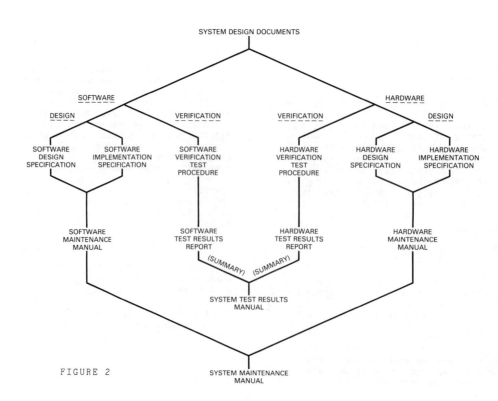

FIGURE 2

VALIDATION OF A COMPUTERIZED
OPERATOR SUPPORT SYSTEM

S. Fukutomi*, S. Yoshimura,* Y. Takizawa,* J. Itoh* and
N. Mori**

*Nippon Atomic Industry Group Co., Ltd., Kawasaki, Japan
**Isogo Engineering Center, Toshiba Corporation, Yokohama, Japan

Abstract. This paper presents the experimental validation of a computerized operator support system (COSS) for BWR (Boiling Water Reactor) power plants. To assess the effects of the COSS on operator performance, a realistic experimental control room and a full scope BWR plant simulator were developed. The control room includes a main and two auxiliary control panels equipped with color cathode-ray tubes (CRT's), control switches, annunciators and paging devices. A supervisory console with CRT's is also installed in the control room. Test transients were selected by taking account of their severity, complexity, generality, duration time and relevance to the functions of the COSS. Experimental data of the operating crew's performance and the plant status during simulated transients were collected on-line by using computers and audio/video tape recorders. The data were processed and transformed into summarized forms to facilitate analysis. Questionnaires and interviews were performed to collect subjective data for analyzing and decision making process of the operators. The results of the experiment show the usefulness of the COSS as an operator aid, especially in diagnosing the causes of disturbances and in establishing counteractive strategies.

Keywords. Verification and validation; operator support system; nuclear power plant; man-machine systems; computer application; guidance system.

INTRODUCTION

The importance of a well-designed man-machine system to safe operation of a nuclear power plant has been recognized since the TMI (Three Mile Island)- 2 incident.

An advanced control room was developed to improve man-machine interface with the use of color cathode-ray tubes (CRT's) and computers (Tomizawa, 1983). To further enhance the monitoring and diagnosing capabilities of the advanced control room, a computerized operator support system (COSS) was developed for BWR (boiling water reactor) power plants (Monta, 1983a, 1983b, 1984 and Sano, 1984).

The objective of the COSS is to enhance operational safety, reliability and availability by aiding the operators in coping with disturbed plant conditions.

The COSS comprises the following five major functions : operational margin monitoring, control rod operational guidance, standby system management, disturbance analysis and post trip operational guidance.

Before its application to actual plants, the COSS must be validated to assure its effectiveness as an operator aid, especially in adverse plant situations.

Validation experiments of similar types had been conducted by the OECD Halden Reactor Project (Hollnagel, 1983) and by the Electric Power Research Institute (Woods, 1982). In the above two experiments, only one or two CRT's had been related to the system to be validated, whereas in the COSS experiment, twelve CRT's were used to validate the system.

Emphasis was placed on establishing realistic test

conditions including an experimental control room, a plant simulator, participation of experienced operators, appropriate training and selection of test transients.

In the following sections ,operator's cognitive tasks and the COSS functions are described first to clarify the significance of the experiment from the cognitive viewpoint. Then the test conditions are described together with the experimental design and procedure. An outline of data collection and analysis is also described. Results of the experiment are presented and discussed in the later sections followed by concluding remarks.

EXPERIMENTAL VALIDATION

Operators Cognitive Tasks and the COSS

Tasks of the operator in man-machine systems such as nuclear power plants are generally divided into two categories : controlling and problem solving. Problem solving is an internal process on a higher cognitive level. It is an important task especially in abnormal plant situations. To prevent a disturbance from spreading and to mitigate the consequences, operators are expected to manage the failure and plan adequate strategies in a limited time. From the cognitive viewpoint, the main objective of the COSS is to support this operator's cognitive task.

The COSS was designed on the basis of a model of the operator's cognitive process consisting of the following steps:

- detection of a deviation from normal status,
- identification of present plant status,
- interpretation of situation,
- planning the task strategy,

- execution of the procedure based on the strategy,
- monitoring the consequence of the execution.

The functions of the COSS were designed so as to aid the operator in his cognitive process.

The disturbance analysis system (DAS) of the COSS helps the operator in detecting plant disturbances at an early stage and in diagnosing the cause of the disturbance. The operator is also assisted by the DAS in prediction of the propagation of the disturbance, in planning of the counteractive strategy, and in the execution of the selected procedure.

The post trip operational guidance system (PTOG) of the COSS helps the operator in identifying the plant status, in formulating the strategy and in executing the procedure.

In monitoring of the plant status, the operator is also assisted by the COSS.

Man Machine Interface of the COSS

The information from the COSS is presented to the operator through the man-machine interface. The color CRT's are the major devices for displaying information. The number of CRT's used by the COSS is twelve in all including a large screen CRT. Touch sensitive screen are attached on most CRT's to facilitate selection of desired displays. The voice annunciation system (VAS) is also a means of presenting information by the COSS. The VAS mainly assists the operator in detection.

CRT Displays of the COSS

To help the operator in his cognitive process, the COSS provides a hierarchy of CRT displays. The top level display informs the operator of the overall status of the plant. The second level displays show the diagnoses and operational guidance of the COSS. More detailed information can be obtained through the third level displays.

One of the second level displays is the COSS information summary consisting of four windows. The four windows relate to plant status, causes of malfunctions, operational guides and trends of main plant parameters. The plant status display window assists the operator in data collection and identification of the plant status. The window informing the causes of malfunctions increases the operator's confidence in his interpretation of the plant status. The operational guide window supports the operator in planning the strategy and procedures to achieve the goal status of the plant. The consequence of the procedure execution is verified through the change in the color of the message in the operational guide window.

So far the functions of the COSS have been described from the cognitive viewpoint.

The objective of the experiment is to evaluate the effects of the COSS on the operator's cognitive performance.

The following are the details of the experiment.

Control Room and Crew Structure

One of the key factors in carrying out a successful validation of the operator aid is to provide a realistic control room.

The experimental control room for the COSS validation was modeled after the advanced control room mentioned in the introduction of this paper.

The experimental control room consisted of the main console, the emergency core cooling system (ECCS) console, the balance of plant (BOP) console and the supervisor console. Since each console was designed to be operated or supervised by one person, an experimental operating crew was organized by four operators. Each of the crew members received information from the COSS through CRT's on his console.

Simulator

To generate realistic plant conditions, a full scope BWR simulator was developed. The simulator was modeled after an actual 1100 MWe BWR plant. The simulator employed a three-dimensional core model to realistically simulate the nuclear instrumentation system. Plant interlocks were simulated on the level of component relays to generate detailed plant malfunctions.

The simulator has additional functions such as replay, fast simulation and back tracking to facilitate the experiment.

The fidelity of the simulator is ensured in that it satisfies an ANSI/ANS standard (ANSI/ANS, 1981).

Experimental Operating Crews

With the co-operation of utilities, experienced operators took part in the COSS validation. They formed nine crews, each of which consisted of a shift supervisor, a main console operator, a BOP (Balance of Plant) console operator and an ECCS (Emergency Core Cooling System) console operator.

In addition, two in-house crews including novice operators (with technical plant background but no operating experience) participated in the early stage of the experiment.

Training

Although most operating crews consisted of experienced operators, it was necessary to have time for familiarizing them with the COSS and the test environment. Time was spent on getting accustomed to the operation of the consoles without the use of the COSS and on becoming familiar with the COSS.

Before and during this training period, explanations were made of how to access CRT displays and how to use additional equipment in the control room like the paging devices.

Explanations were also made of the content of displays, characteristics of the simulated BWR plant, and of how to apply the COSS information and the display hierarchy to cognitive tasks of the operators.

Test Transients

The following factors were considered when designing test transients : the effects on the plant, difficulty to cope with, independence on the plant types and relevance to the COSS functions.

Three scram avoidable and three scram inevitable

transients were selected for the experiment.

Data Collection

Both objective and subjective data were collected for eleven crews against the six test transients. Data on operator control actions, plant status, alarm logs and CRT display accesses were recorded by the use of computers. Audio and video devices were employed to record operator movements and communications for some crews. Observer checklists were used to identify the differences between the predetermined operator reference performance and the actual one. The reasons for these discrepancies were investigated in the interview after each transient session.

Along with the interviews, the operators were requested to complete three groups of questionnaires. The first group was concerned with the operability of the control panels and display access devices. The second group was related to the recognizability of the information presented by the COSS. The third group was connected with the effectiveness of the COSS in the decision making process of the operators and with the adequacy of the test conditions.

Experimental Design

The experiment was designed so as to assess the effects of the COSS on the cognitive process of an operating crew.

Since it was expected that the performance would vary from crew to crew, a within-group design was utilized as a basis of the experiment.

Every crew was supposed to follow the schedule presented below:

1. Training in the operation of the experimental consoles without the use of the COSS.
2. Base-line performance test.
   In this test, a scram avoidable and a scram inevitable transients were used to assess the performance of the crew without the aid of the COSS.
3. Training in the use of the COSS.
   Explanations were made of the usage of the COSS. Several transients including the ones used in step 2 were applied to attain the crew's proficiency in using the COSS.
4. Test transients with the use of the COSS.
   As actual test transients , a scram avoidable and a scram inevitable transients were used to assess the usefulness of the COSS. Although the transients differed from the ones in step 2, they were designed to be comparable in their effects on the crew's performance.
5. Questionnaires and interviews.
   Each time after steps 2,3 and 4, the questionnaire was filled out and the interview was performed to collect information on the cognitive process of the operating crew.

EXperimental Procedure

For each crew, the experiment was carried out for three days.

On the first day, explanations were made of the purpose of the experiment and of the experimental control room. Training was then carried out in the use of the control room without the aid of the COSS.

On the second day, the base-line performance test was performed. The questionnaire was filled out and the interview was conducted. After this, the COSS functions were presented. This was followed by the training in the use of the COSS. The questionnaire and the interview were performed.

On the third day, test transients were carried out with the use of COSS. This was followed by the questionnaire and the interview sessions.

A summary discussion concluded the three-day experiment.

Data Analysis Methodology

The data analysis was performed by generating timeline descriptions and cognitive process diagrams for each of the test trials. A summary of the important decision-making points was made from the timeline descriptions. Cognitive process diagrams were then developed with this summary timeline. The usefulness of the COSS was evaluated from these diagrams. The results from interviews and the summaries of questionnaires were also taken into account. Figure 1 shows this data integration and analysis process for the COSS validation.

RESULTS AND DISCUSSIONS

Results from a Test Transient

Results are presented for a test transient performed by six crews with the use of the COSS. The transient includes three malfunctions . The first one is a valve failure in the steam jet air ejector and the second one is a valve malfunction in the condenser, which is accompanied by the third malfunction of a control logic failure for the primary loop recirculation system. In this transient, the reactor will scram, if no corrective actions are taken in due course.

To analyze operator performance, the cognitive process of the operator is considered to include the five major stages of detection, interpretation of the situation, goal state selection, procedure formulation and procedure execution. Examples of the reference and the actual cognitive processes are shown in table 1 and in Fig. 2, respectively. By comparing these two cognitive processes, the following points are obtained:

- The guides of the COSS were utilized by all the six crews to cope with the transient.
- The time between the presentation of the guide and the actual initiation of the operation varied significantly with the crews.
- Only one crew caused reactor scram. The crew did not see the guide for corrective actions against the third malfunction.

Findings from Other Transients

In addition to the above results, findings from other test transients are summarized below.

- Omission errors can be reduced by referring to the operational guides provided by the COSS.
- The time needed to recover the plant after scram may be reduced with the help of the COSS.

Subjective Evaluation by the Operators

As to the subjective evaluation of the COSS by the operators, summarized answers to the questionnaire on the validity of the COSS are presented below.

- The diagnoses and operational guides provided by the COSS are adequate and they facilitate the understanding of the plant situation. They were in agreement with the operators decisions in most situations.
- The installation of the COSS into actual plants is considered to be useful.

Additional comments by the operators on the COSS are as follows:

- The COSS is useful in helping the operator's decisions in an emergency.
- In the case of multiple failures, the COSS is a useful decision aid.
- There might be a possibility that the operator becomes too dependent on the COSS.
- The guide of the COSS makes the operator more confident in his decision.

Table 1 Reference Cognitive Process

Mis-Closure of CHT Inlet Valve and
Subsequent Failure of PLR Automatic Runback

Category	Content
Detection of Transient	Alarm of low water level in condenser secondary hotwell.
Cognition of Event	Due to closure of CHT inlet valve, feedwater flow to condenser secondary hotwell is small, only through bypass flow line. PLR automatic runback should be initiated by low water level of condenser secondary hotwell, but fails to be initiated. Condensate pumps will soon trip and it leads to loss of feedwater to reactor.
Operational Goal	Restoration of condenser secondary hotwell water level in order to avoid condensate pump trip.
Operation Strategy	Manual runback of PLR which is inoperable in automatic mode to rapidly decrease reactor power, and subsequently to decrease feedwater flow rate from condenser to reactor. Water level of secondary hotwell of condenser will restore its normal level.
Action	Manual runback of PLR pumps.

CHT : Condensate Head Tank
PLR : Primary Loop Recirculation System

Discussions

To assure the validity of the experiment, it should be clarified whether the experimental results obtained above can be extrapolated into real-life situations. In other words, it should be checked whether the experimental conditions really correspond to real-life conditions.

The adequacy of the following factors will be discussed:

- the experimental control room
- the experimental simulator
- the operators of the COSS
- the test transients

The experimental control room is modeled after an actual advanced control room and it includes the main and auxiliary control panels and the supervisory console. The panels are equipped with color CRT's with annunciators and control switches. The experimental control room well represents an actual control room.

The simulator used for the experiment is a full-scope BWR simulator modeled after an actual 1100 MWe plant. The fidelity of the simulator is assured by the fact that it satisfies an ANSI/ANS standard (ANSI/ANS, 1981).

The operators of the COSS in the experiment were mostly experienced operators having more than five years of actual operating experience. The fact ensures the adequacy of the experimental condition of operator selection .

The test transients employed in the experiment were selected by taking account of their severity, complexity, generality and relevance to the functions of the COSS. The results of the questionnaires support the adequacy of the test transients.

To summarize, the above four major experimental conditions well correspond to real-life conditions.

CONCLUSIONS

The validation experiment of the COSS for BWR power plants was conducted.

To assure the validity of the experiment, realistic test conditions were established, including a sufficiently equipped control room, a full-scope BWR plant simulator, participation of experienced operating crews, adequate training and well designed test transients. The experiment was conducted for eleven crews, most of whom were experienced utility operators.

Data were collected by means of computers and audio/video devices. Questionnaires and interviews were also performed.

Qualitative analysis of the test results shows the usefulness of the COSS as an operator aid, especially in diagnosing the causes of adverse events and in formulating counteractive strategies.

ACKNOWLEDGEMENT

The authors would like to express their thanks to the operators from the utilities for their co-operative participation in the COSS validation.

REFERENCES

ANSI/ANS (1981). Nuclear Power Plant Simulators for Use in Operator Training. ANSI/ANS-3.5-1981.
Hollnagel, E., G. Hunt, and E. Marshall (1983). The Experimental Validation of the Critical Function Monitoring System Preliminary Results of Analysis

Project, May 1983.

Monta, K., N. Naito, M. Sugawara, N. Sato, N. Mori, I. Tai, A. Fukumoto, and M. Tsuchida (1983a). A computerized operator support system with a new man-machine interface for BWR power plant. Proceedings of an International Symposium on Operational Safety of Nuclear Power Plants, vol. 1, Marseilles, France, 2-6 May 1983, 333-347, IAEA-SM- 268/11.

Monta, K., N. Sato, S. Tsunoyama, K. Sekimizu, and N. Mori (1983b). A computerized operator support system for BWR power plant during normal and abnormal conditions. IAEA Specialists Meeting on Systems and Methods for Aiding Nuclear Power Plant Operators During Normal and Abnormal Conditions, Balatonaliga, Hungary, 4-6 October, 1983, 259-272.

Monta, K., K. Sekimizu, T. Araki, and N. Mori (1984). Development of a computerized operator support system for BWR power plant. IAEA Seminar on Diagnosis of and Response to Abnormal Occurrences at Nuclear Power Plants, Dresden, GDR, 12-15 June 1984, IAEA-SR-105/7.

Sano, Y., A. Fukumoto, E. Seki, I. Tai, N. Mori, M. Tsuchida, and N. Sato (1984). Man-machine communication based on the computerized operator support system. IAEA Seminar on Diagnosis of and Response to Abnormal Occurrences at Nuclear Power Plants, Dresden, GDR, 12-15 June 1984, IAEA-SR-105/10.

Tomizawa, A., A. Fukumoto, T. Neda, and Y. Takizawa (1983). Enhanced operational safety of BWRs by advanced computer technology and human engineering. Proceedings of an International Symposium on Operational Safety of Nuclear Power Plants, vol. 1, Marseilles, France, 2-6 May 1983, 349-370, IAEA-SM-268/17.

Woods, d.d., J.A. Wise, and L.F. Hanes (1982). Evaluation of Safety Parameter Display Concepts. EPRI NP-2239, vol. 1 and 2, Electric Power Research Institute, Palo Alto, Calif. February 1982.

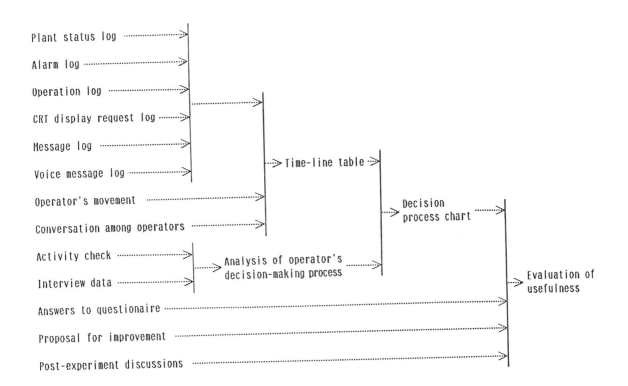

Fig.1 Process of Validation Data Analysis

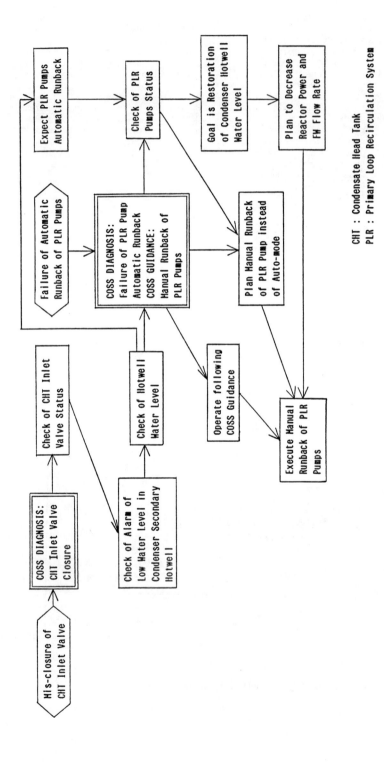

Fig.2 Cognitive Process for Avoiding Reactor Scram
—— Mis-closure of CHT Inlet valve and Subsequent Failure of PLR Automatic Runback ——

A TOOL FOR SPECIFICATION ANALYSIS: "COMPLETE" DECISION TABLES

A. M. Traverso

ESACONTROL S.p.A.*, via Hermada, 6, Genova, Italy

Abstract. An experience and its theoretical background are proposed, relating to verification of functional specification for a railway transportation system with high reliability requirements.

A formalism, called "complete" decision tables, was defined which uses the key idea of decision tables, suitably modified and enhanced to meet the goals of analysis coherence and exhaustivity and of verification degree measurement.

The same formalism was the basis for the construction of testcases and gave also an ongoing measure of the testing activity in progress.

Keywords. Computer testing; quality control; formal method; software life cycle; functional specification.

* This work was partially sponsored by Italian National Research Council (C.N.R.)

INTRODUCTION

This paper deals with the formalisation work undertaken by the Verification and Validation group (V&V) over a software functional specification with two main goals:
- to verify the internal coherence and exhaustivity of SW functional specs,
- to provide a ground for test design and for test quality quantitative assessment.

A third result was obtained in terms of a basis for communication between project and test groups, and between manufacturer and user.

The basic idea we started from is decision tables, as described in the literature. Soon the need was felt to enrich the formalism according to the characteristics of the application; the resulting formalism, i.e. "complete" decision tables, may have some general value.

The application was the project of a railway station signalling and control system; the SW functional specs were originally written by project team in natural language, and were rewritten by V&V team by complete decision tables.

The formalism suitable application field will be that of high reliability requirements systems, where it is especially important to achieve a high confidence degree about the system correctness.

The actuality of these topics is witnessed by their presence in international research projects, like for instance the REQUEST project (REliability and QUality for European Software Technology) sponsored by the CEC in the ESPRIT context.

Static and dynamic descriptions of 'complete' tables will follow, and then a discussion of the use of this tool for V&V purposes.

STATIC DESCRIPTION

A table is made of four sections graphically divided by couples of horizontal lines and each section is composed of one or more entries separated by single lines. The first part, at the top, carries the reference to functional specs document and the table entry condition, in terms of the current state of the operation (synchronous processing) or of an external action, such as a received command from the operator (asynchronous processing).

In this last case the operation current state specification will be found in the second part of the table: the decision condition part.

In the decision condition section each entry describes a condition, and the easiest case is that of an entry splitted on two lines, the first assessing the condition is true, and the second that is false.

There are also more complex situations, for example a two light railway signal may assume one of a number of valid expected aspects or, for a device failure, its aspect may be unknown to the processing system: it is necessary to distinguish among these alternatives and it is important that the analysis does not omit any possible issue, so great care is put in defining a complete and muntually exclusive set of values for each condition. Of course for a certain processing purpose some values may be grouped together to form a subset, but in any case the set of values has to be divided in equivalence classes and each class has to receive an esplicit treatment. Moreover all the conditions have to be indipendent from each other.

These two rules, exhaustiveness and indipendency, have a very benefic impact in the validation of the original specs contents, because the analysis of the inputs must become, if it wasn't yet, absolutely complete and not contradictory.

In the third part of the table, which eventually does not exist, are listed the output actions to be done. If several action are relative to the same item, for example if they are commands to one signal, and they are thereafter mutually exclusive, they are grouped in "families", separated by one horizontal line.

The fourth and last part of the table concerns the declaration of the new state the operation will assume.

Like in any decision table, on the right of the table, sections 2,3 and 4 are marked. Signs corresponding to condition lines mean that this value of the condition is true and those corresponding to event lines mean that this action will be undertaken.

In our implementation of decision tables there are important rules to respect: for each family of conditions just one mark can exist in a vertical line, and the same for each familiy of output events and for the next entry status part. When facing the functional specification to fill the corresponding table with these rules in mind, several remarks arise, because the incompleteness and ambiguities of natural language are focused.

Moreover there is an algorithmic procedure to establish if all the possible and meaningfull combinations of conditions have been considerated. In fact the number of the conbinations is just the product of the condition families cardinalities. For example for two conditions having respectively two and three possible values, the combinations are two times three equal six.

DYNAMIC DESCRIPTION

The entry state condition part of a table and the fourth one constitue the links between this table and the logically following ones.

The tables and their links relating to an operation may be considered as a network, which is not very different from the state diagram description of the operation; however, it is easier to verify the deadloch and unreacheable state absence properties using this notation.

In fact having the input conditions explicity stated, it is quite straightforward to detect inconsistencies.

In addition a series of verifications can be made, more directly relating to the semantic or meaning instead that to the synthaxis or formal aspect of the tables. For instance it is possible to point out and compare analogous situations (i.a. input configurations) in two tables (or in one)and the relative processing (i.e. output configuration).

USE FOR V&V PURPOSES

The specs representation by complete decision tables provides a complete picture of the input domain and of the expected outputs, so it is conceptually easy to design testcases in correspondence to each vertical combination of input, to execute the tests, and then to observe whether real outputs match with expected ones.

Counting the input combinations and the corresponding testcases we have a sensible estimation of the functional coverage degree of our tests.

The pratic big problem is the combinatorial explosion of the input possible combinations.
In fact, for example, in order to exhaustively specify the output of an operation with six two values input conditions and four three values input condition, it would be necessary to consider $2^6 * 3^4 = 5184$ possible input configurations, i.e. 5184 test cases. In most cases, however, several configurations, or vertical lines of marks, may be unified because their treatment is identic.

So it is important to preliminarily verify with code inspections if the SW implementation actually realizes this treatment identification for groups of input combinations, as it follows from functional specs. Then it is rigorous enough to build just one input combination test case choosing one among such a group.

Analogously, in some cases for a number of input condition families it is only important to distinguish between the condition values combinations that correspond to an 'OK' situation and those which correspond to an error situation, and then it is sufficient to pick one OK input data combination and one not OK.

It is quite simple to determine four figures which give fine estimators of the test effort quality.

The first one is the total number of possible input data combinations for all the tables.

The second is the reduced number obtained identifying input data groups with the same treatment, as said before.

The third is the actual quantity of the test cases that it seems reasonable to really provide, depending on cost/benefit considerations and on specific reliability and safety application requirements.

The last number is the amount of test cases already produced at a certain date.

CONCLUSION

A formalism derived from decision tables has been presented. it provides a very complete and rigorous form to express the functional description of a program. Some remarks have been presented arising from an experience of application to a high reliability project, in the railway transportation field. We believe that it would be interesting to develop an authomated tool for helping in the editing of the tables and for performing certain algorithmic checks, but at present this work is still on progress.

1st part

Reference to functional specs

Entry condition to the table (operation state or asynch. event)

...

2nd part

ith family of decision conditions   value 1 ...
value n

...

3rd part ...

jth output action family

...

4th part ...

Kth new operation state

...

...

fig.2   Description of a complete decision table structure (left section)

condition 1	T	F	T
...	T	T	F
condition n	F	T	F
event 1	X		X
...		X	
event m			X

fig.1   Example of a classic decision table structure

```
chapter n paragraph m
_____
received command of preparing   the ith
non stop path for a train through the
station
_____
the path is free        x x x
  "    "  "   reserved         x x x
  "    "  "   engaged               x x x
_____
the signal ligh is
              green     x     x     x
  "     "   "     is
              red         x     x     x
  "     "   "     is
         undeterminated     x     x     x
_____
switch the signal
to red                  x   x     x x   x
_____
notify an anormality
to operator                 x     x x   x
_____
notify the command is
accepted                x
notify the command is
refused                   x x x x x x x x
_____
reserve the path        x
_____
command accepted        x
_____
command refused           x x x x x   x x
_____
error recovery state              x
```

Fig. 3 Simplified example of table

REFERENCES

- Myers, G.J. (1976) Software Reliability.Wiles & Sons,NY
- Myers, G.J. (1979) The art of SW Testing. Wiles & Sons, NY
- Goodenough, J.B. and S.L. Gerhart Toward a theory of test data selection.IEE Trans. on Software engineering SE1-3 (June 1975)
- Halstead, M.H. (1977) Elements of Software Science.Elsevier, North-Holland, NY.
- Littlewood, B. How to measure software reliability and how not to ... IEEE Trans. Reliability, Vol. R-28 (June 1979).

SOFTWARE TOOLS AS AN AID FOR HARDWARE AND SOFTWARE RELIABILITY ANALYSIS

R. Benejean*, J. C. Michon** and J. P. Signoret***

*E.D.F., 1, avenue du Général de Gaulle, 92141 Clamart, France
**Italtest via Pordoi 8, I20019 Settimo Milanese, Italy, and Contrôle et Prévention,
34, rue Rennequin, 75017 Paris, France
***SNEA(P), Chémin Vignancour, 64018 Pau Cédex, France

Keywords : Reliability, computer aided design

Modern complex system reliability has to take into account more and more programmed system reliability. This raises two kinds of problems:

- Software reliability: i.e. software quality assurance, specifications, development methods, languages, programming, test policies,...

- Hardware reliability at three levels: input, processors, output.

A method among others enabling to modelize software and hardware behaviour from the reliability point of view is the stochastic Markov process method.

First, the principles of the method will be given and advantages will be pointed out in comparison with other more classical methods for reliability analysis.

In the second part of the paper, software tools to solve this kind of problems will be described and in the final part of the presentation an example of successful use of these computer codes will be given.

I - STATE DIAGRAMS

The state diagram method:

- enables a global analysis of the evolution of a system states,

- is based on a synthesis of deductive methods for a sharper analysis of transitions between these states, for instance by considering transition from one state to another as the top event of a fault tree.

Therefore, one way for representing a complex functioning is to study the system possible states and the transition possibilities from one state to another.

Such states can be characterized as: normal state, degraded functioning states, failure states, some among degraded functioning or failure states being possibly critical states with regard to the risks under study.

The transition from one state to another occurs through transient or permanent error, or on the contrary through repair, take-over, reconfiguration. (In the first case, the system passes to a worsening state, in the second case to an improving one).

Let us consider a system with N possible states. Thus, the system functioning may be represented by a N node diagram (from A to N) and as many arrows as possible transitions between states.

The description of the system evolution will be made by probabilities P_A (t), P_B (t) ... P_N (t) for the system to be in states A, B, ...N at time t. (Of course, $P_A + P_B + ...P_N = 1$ at any time).

Therefore, such a method can lead to the successive evaluation of the following parameters:

. probabilities for each state to be the system state at time t,

. cumulated mean sojourn times in each state,

. system mean availability over a given period for a given mission,

. system efficiency over a given period, a state efficiency being defined as a measure of the service performed by this state with reference to the perfect functioning state. This notion of efficiency is very often equivalent to this of productivity and is a generalization of the mean availability,

. system limit efficiency and generalized MTBF.

This method can even be applied, when a particularly efficient computing tool is available, to multi-phased systems, which considerably increases its application and investigation field.

II - MARK COMPUTING CODES (licence SNEA(P) - TOTAL/CFP - IFP)

MARK is a specialized computing code for processing Markov diagrams, i.e. state diagrams with constant transition rates.

MARK uses an original algorithm, based on a matrix direct exponentiation, which gives it higher performances than these of usual codes: it is faster, enables to process a higher number of states and to obtain more detailed results.

Data input is conversational and they can be stored on files of mass storage devices and retrieved to be re-used with or without modifications.

MARK outputs include:

. the probabilities of the different states at time t,

. the mean value (expected value) of the cumulated sojourn times spent in the various states.

In addition, introducing the efficiency notion enables to estimate the productivity of production systems.

Efficiency of a given state is defined as a value, between 0 and 1, measuring the service done by this state with reference to the perfect functioning state (equal to 1). Then, a failure state has an efficiency of 0 an a state which is not perfect but not completely failed has an efficiency between 0 and 1.

Then we may obtain, over a given period, the system mean efficiency or its efficient functioning duration: functioning duration in the perfect state which would do the same service as this ensured by all the system states (perfect or degraded).

Moreover, the asymptotic values can be calculated: limit efficiency, mean sojourn times before absorption (when absorbing states are existing in the diagram) and generalized MTBF (sum of mean sojourn times before absorption, balanced by each state efficiency).

At last, a second version of MARK, called MARK SMP, enables to process multi-phased systems. Here, the system behaviour is defined as a chronological succession of several phases. Each phase is described as above by a particular matrix corresponding to a Markov process.

Then, transitions from one phase to another are described by establishing connections between the states of one phase and the states of the following phase: the probabilities of the states at the end of phase n° i are used to initialize phase n° i + 1.

The results obtained are of the same type as those given by the standard version but can integrate a whole exploitation or production period.

In the often acceptable hypothesis where the transition rates between states are independent from time, the state diagram is said to be a Markovian one and the calculation at every time of probabilities for the system to be in one of the states is made by means of a set of differential linear equations.
Obviously, this rapidly implies, as soo, as there is a high number of states, the use of computing means such as the MARK EXD and MARK SMP codes (1) described above.

Compared to the more classically used methods such as fault trees (2) or causes-consequences diagrams (3), the state diagram method offers the main following advantages, which make it interesting for analyzing systems involving programmed equipments:

- taking into account the evolutive, sequential, even recursive phenomena;

- taking into account reconfigurations, especially monitoring, detection, back-up, repair;

- pointing out in a same diagram intermediate states between perfect functioning state and complete failure state, possibility to calculate the corresponding probabilities, associating to each state a degradation degree in the form of an efficiency coefficient.

III - EXAMPLE OF USE OF THE METHODOLOGY

The high power concentrations that are generated in nuclear power plants, relative to other means of power generation, have necessitated the development of a more advanced means of regulating and controlling the alternators used in the production of electrical power. A microprocessor-based control system using analog/digital technology was designed to meet these new requirements. While this new control technology has proved satisfactory, it was important for Electricité de France to know how reliable the control systems were.

The first part of the following study presents the theoretical methods used to predict the reliability of the microprocessor-based control technology as well as the results, of the analysis. In the second part of the study, the assumptions and predictions made in the analysis are compared to operational results and to the method of physical simulation of faults (1).

III.1. Objectives

One characteristic of electricity-generating systems is their stability; that is, the ability to return to equilibrium conditions after perturbations of a stationary state (static stability) or of a transient state (transient stability).

Recent studies have shown that through the evolution of network use, new requirements for stability have been imposed. In particular, studies on the dynamic behaviour of future electrical power conduction networks have shown that there are problems with the maintenance of power stability. These problems are mainly due to the development of power imbalances among the various units within the power network. The resulting static instability is primarily due to two factors. First, a more rapid power surge in the various units may occur relative to the short-circuit capabilities of the network as a whole. Second, the nuclear power plants may be located far from utilization centers.

The presence of static instability in nuclear power generating systems led to the design of more sophisticated alternator control systems. The "4-loop" control system was found to be sufficient to insure the stability of the network system (3, 4). While former control systems used only one or two parameters to control the turboalternator, the "4-loop" system regulates the stator of the alternator through the excitation voltage by measuring four parameters of the turboalternator. The system studied consists of two "4-loop" analog controllers, one of which serves as a back-up in case of failure of the other one. The controller in use is monitored by a microprocessor which is designed to detect system control failure; under which conditions the back-up control system and alarm system are activated. In the current study, the analog system was evaluated by means of classical methods including qualitative analysis with FMEA (Failure Modes and Effects Analysis) and fault trees (4) and quantitative analysis by means of CNET (Centre National d'Etudes des Télécommunications) data.

The analysis in this study is, however, new in that it was applied to every component of every card. Furthermore, computation of "down time" of the system is based on the occurence probability of each of four possible undesirable events (as described below) the causes of which have been systematically assessed using very detailed fault trees.

The purpose of this detailed study is twofold:
1. to be exhaustive
2. to eliminate the errors usually encountered when the failure rate of the system is simply arithmetically determined from the failure rates of its components.

III.2. Reliability prediction methods

A. Analog control unit

The analog controller consists of a series of electronic cards which perform the various functions involved in the control chain. To simplify the FMEA analysis, macrocomponents of each card were analyzed separately. For example, a given card might be disassembled into amplifier, integrator and parity units. The failure mode of each component could be analyzed and used to define the failure mode of the macrocomponents, which in turn could define the failure mode of each electronic card. Finally, the effects of the failures of each card could be defined at the system level.

From this analysis, four possible undesirable events were predicted which could cause the control system to fail:

1. Operation of the alternator at low frequency (45 Hz)
2. Operation of the alternator at maximum frequency (55 Hz)
3. Loss of inducer voltage
4. Saturation of inducer voltage

The failure rates of each of the four undesirable events were computed in two steps with the help of computer codes as follows:

1. Determination of Boolean function from the fault trees by means of DEFAIL (5)
2. Computation of failure rate by means of FIAB (6).

B. Whole system

The whole system, including both control units and the microprocessor, was simulated by means of a MARKOV diagram (8). Two assumptions were made in the analysis:

1. Software errors in the microprocessor unit are non-existant
2. "Watch-dog" function detects 80% of the microprocessor failures.

The first assumption is justified by quality assurance during software design (9), by the relative simplicity of the program and by debugging techniques. The second assumption is justified by the physical simulation of faults as described below.
The results show the importance of the assumptions made, particularly with regard to assumption 2, concerning the "watch-dog".

III.3. Operational results

Data on control system reliability from currently functioning plants along with results of physical simulation studies were compared to the results obtained in the present study.

A. Data from currently functioning plants

Data from a single control unit installed in currently functioning plants were studied initially (11). Prototype control units were installed in the second and fifth reactors of the Bugey nuclear plant (900 MWe P.W.R.) and in the Aramon power plant (a fossil fuel plant of 700 MWe).

The results obtained using the operational data were similar to those obtained using the predictive method. Therefore, the validity of the reliability prediction method was confirmed.

B. Physical simulation of faults

Physical simulation of faults (1,12) was conducted on the microprocessor components which monitored the control units. Through this simulation, the assumption of an 80% efficiency of the "watch-dog" was tested. The reliability of the system as a whole (as shown above) depends heavily on this assumption. Simulation of faults of the monitoring system was necessary in order to determine whether or not the control system failure was detected by the "watch-dog".

Physical simulation of faults is a non-destructive test of a system. The component output signal is replaced by another predetermined signal. The system, in its different configurations, is monitored for its reaction to the erroneous signal. Five erroneous signals were used to replace the output signals of the tested components:

1. 0 V as binary 0
2. 5 V binary 1
3. uncertain signal (infinite impedance)
4. short-circuit between component tested and previous component
5. short-circuit between component tested and next component

The steps involved in reliability testing of the microprocessor are as follows:

1. simulated failure of the monitoring microprocessor components by physical simulation of faults
2. recording of failure detection (or absence of detection) by the monitor
3. simulated failure of the analog unit (in presence of simulated monitor failure)
4. recording of switch (or its absence) to back-up control unit

The following equipment was used in the implementation of these tests:

1. Hewlett-Packard HP 9825 A
2. Hewlett-Packard interfaces
3. Test box developed by EDF in order to simulate system failures.

Physical simulation of faults of the whole system was possible and would have been interesting. However, it was more practical and cost-effective to limit the number of components tested. The results of the reliability prediction study made it possible to test only those components which were qualitatively and quantitatively important.

The results of this study show that the assumption of an 80% monitoring by the "watch-dog" is not necessarily required in order for the system to work according to specifications. Moreover, a new precise specification for the "watch-dog" was made from this study.

III.4. Conclusions of the case study

The reliability prediction analysis was shown to be an accurate and powerful method for evaluating the performance of the new control systems currently used in nuclear power plants. The agreement between the results obtained from operational data and from the reliability prediction data lends validity to the technique of reliability analysis. Techniques involved in reliability analysis are detailed, precise and systematic. Although reliability studies are generally long and costly, the benefits derived from these studies can far outweigh the cost incurred. If, as a result of the present studies, one day of "down time" in one reactor is avoided, EDF stands to save: 24 x 1.300 x 1000 x 0.13[*] FF = 4 000 000 FF, i.e. 400 000 US dollars.

IV - GENERAL CONCLUSIONS[.]

Up to this date, the state of knowledge and present experience do not allow to accurately appraise a software reliability. However, the joint use of classical methods such as fault trees and more efficient methods such as MARKOV diagrams enables to evaluate in certain cases and under certain conditions the reliability of a system including programmed parts. Some powerful computing tools are available and represent an interesting aid for these studies. The confrontation of the previsional results obtained to the operational experience enables to provide the main recommendations regarding hardware as well as software parts, and validates the efficiency of the methods and calculation tools used.

REFERENCES

(1) Italtest (Italy) - Controle et Prevention (France)
MARK EXD - MARK SMP - SNEA(P) - TOTAL - CFP - IFP licence; author: JP SIGNORET

(2) JF BARBET
Les arbres de défaillance - Bulletin de la Direction des Etudes et Recherches d'Electricité De France : nucléaire, électricité, thermique ; n° 2, 82, série A.

(3) PS NIELSEN
The cause-consequence diagram method as a basis for quantitative accident analysis - Danish Atomic Energy Commission - Risö: M1374, May 1971

(4) HUGOUD-NEGOESCO-BENEJEAN-IRVING-BARRET-BLANCHET-MONVILLE-HEROUARD-MEYER
Amélioration de la stabilité du réseau de transport par réglage de l'excitation des groupes de production.
Revue Générale d'Electricité-Spécial CIGRE - Juillet 80 p. 64 à 92.

(5) R. BENEJEAN, E. CHANVRY, M. RENAUD
Alternateurs du palier 1.300 MWe : description du fonctionnement du régulateur de tension.
Note E.D.F. -HI 13800-02-Mars 81 -HT 13/35/81

(6) DEFAIL (EDF/CEP) Logiciel de traitement qualitatif des arbres de défaillance - Notice Contrôle et Prévention - Italtest - Service Systèmes 1984.

(7) FIAB (EDF/CEP) Logiciel de traitement quantitatif des arbres de défaillance - Notice Contrôle et Prévention - Italtest - Service Systèmes 1984.

(8) JP BARBET, M. RENAUD
Alternateurs du palier 1300 MWe - Etude de fiabilité d'une des chaînes de régulation de tension.
Note EDF - HT 13/57/81 - Septembre 81.

(9) A. PAGES, M. GOUDRAN
Fiabilité des Systèmes - Eyrolles 1980.

(10) J. RATA
Contrôle des logiciels des équipements programmés Note EDF : HI/3721-02 Mars 81

(11) JP BARBET - R. BENEJEAN - P. DALME - A. DOCHY
Alternateurs du palier 1300 MWe : étude de la fiabilité de la surveillance à microprocesseur.
Note EDF HT-13/19/83 - HI-44-80-02 Avril 83

(12) JP BARBET - P. DAIME - A. DOCHY
Alternateurs du palier 1300 MWe.
Comparaison entre la fiabilité prévisionnelle et la fiabilité opérationnelle du régulateur analogique à quatre boucles
Note EDF HT-13/21/82 Mars 83

(13) JC MICHON - P. COLOMBO - C. LEPEUTREC
Fiabilité d'un système de régulation à microprocesseur
Etude SERAM - Ecole Nationale d'Arts et Métiers de PARIS 1983

[*] cost at time of study of nuclear kWh.

ON SOME NEW RELIABILITY IMPORTANCE
MEASURES

B. Bergman

Division of Quality Technology, Linköping Institute of Technology, Linköping,
Sweden

Abstract. In this paper some new reliability importance measures are suggested. These measures, which have been developed from ideas presented in Bergman (1985) and by Natvig (1985a), are suitable for the evaluation of component reliability importance of a time dependent system.

Keywords. Reliability theory; system analysis; component reliability importance measures.

1. INTRODUCTION

In order to support the designer during the design process of a system the reliability analyst shall not only investigate the reliability structure of the system and present reliability figures but- and this is often the most important objective - he has to point out weak points of the design and suggest where to allocate resources for reliability improvements. Helpful tools for this latter duty of the reliability analyst are different kinds of reliability importance measures.

Birnbaum (1969) suggested two importance measures, one purely structural and the other probabilistic. Using the usual reliability theory notation, let $\phi_t = \phi(\underline{x}(t))$ denote the binary state of the system at time t as a function of the n-dimensional binary state vector $\underline{x}$ representing the states of the n components of the system where in all cases the state 1 denotes "functioning" and the state 0 denotes "nonfunctioning". As usual we assume that, for fixed t, ϕ_t is a structure function of a coherent system, see Barlow and Proschan (1981). However important, we shall often in the following suppress the reference to time t. A component i is critical with respect to the state vector $\underline{x}$ of component states if $\phi(1_i,\underline{x}) - \phi(0_i,\underline{x}) = 1$; here and in the following we use for any vector $\underline{z}$ the notation $(\cdot_i, \underline{z}) = (z_1, z_2, \ldots, z_{i-1}, \cdot, z_{i+1}, \ldots, z_n)$. For each component we can determine 2^{n-1} different state vectors $(1_i, \underline{x})$ and the Birnbaum (1969) structural importance measure is the relative number of these for which the i:th component is critical.

Assuming a random state vector $\underline{X}(t)$ the Birnbaum (1969) reliability importance measure of the i:th component, taking into account the randomness of $\underline{X}(t)$, is the probability that the i:th component is critical, i.e.

$$I_B^{(i)}(t) = P(\phi(1_i, \underline{X}(t)) - \phi(0_i, \underline{X}(t)) = 1),$$

here $\underline{X}(t)$ denotes the time dependent random state vector of the components. If $X_i(t)$, i=1,...,n, are independent with $R_i(t) = P(X_i(t)=1)$, then it is easily seen that (see Barlow and Proschan, 1981),

$$I_B^{(i)}(t) = \frac{\partial}{\partial R_i} h(\underline{R}(t));$$

here $h(\underline{R}(t)) = E(\phi(\underline{x}(t)))$. This means that the

Birnbaum reliability importance measure of the i:th component at time t may be interpreted as the "system reliability improvement per component i reliability improvement at time t". An obvious difficulty with this measure is its time dependence. Obviously a designer may be interested in the reliability over a lot of different points in time. Several authors have suggested time independent measures of component reliability importance, see e.g. Barlow and Proschan (1975), and Natvig (1979, 1982, 1985a). Here we shall consider some further possibilities. We restrict ourselves to coherent systems (for a definition see e.g. Barlow and Proschan, 1981) with nonrepairable components. If not explicitly stated otherwise we assume in the following that component states are independent. For an interesting discussion on a model for dependence between component states we refer to Arjas in a discussion of Bergman (1985).

Before suggesting alternative importance measures we shall in the next section investigate the use of importance measures in the design process and its dependence on different system reliability objectives. Especially, we shall focus our attention on expected system life length. A basic result will be given in Section 3, where also a general class of importance measures is introduced. In Section 4 we shall study a certain subclass of this general class and, finally, in Section 5 some further generalizations are indicated.

2. RELIABILITY PERFORMANCE MEASURES

As indicated in the introduction the objective of a reliability importance measure is to advice the analyst on weak points in the design and possibly where to allocate reliability improvement efforts Thus an importance measure has to be closely connected with the system reliability objective. If we are interested in the reliability of the system at a fixed point t in time, then the Birnbaum reliability importance measure may be adequate, but if we are interested in a long expected life of the system we should probably look for another importance measure.

Let τ_ϕ be the random life of the system. Listed below we give some different reliability measures of the system with respect to which it may be adequate to measure the reliability performance of a non-repairable system in different situations:

(a) Survival probability at t_0, $P(t_\phi > t_0)$. This reliability performance measure is suitable if we want to assure that the system is functioning during

61

a critical time interval (0,t). This measure may be generalized to $P(\tau_\phi > t_2 | \tau_\phi > t_1)$, if the critical interval is (t_1, t_2).

(b) <u>Expected life</u>, $E(\tau_\phi)$. This is the natural measure if we want a long life of the system rather than a high survival probability during a certain time interval. (This or similar measures may also be useful for repairable systems when availability performance is of interest).

(c) <u>Expected restricted life</u>, $E(\min(\tau_\phi, T))$. This measure may be of interest in the same type of cases as the one above, but a finite time horizon T exists after which the reliability of the system is of no interest e.g. because of obsolence due to economic or technical reasons.

(d) <u>Discounted expected life</u>, $E(1-e^{-\alpha\tau}\phi)/\alpha$. Sometimes a failure late in the life of the system is not judged as critical as if the failure occurs early. This may be an effect of obsolence.

(e) <u>Expected yield</u>, $E(Y(\tau_\phi))$. Assuming $Y(\cdot)$ to be an increasing random process - the accumulated yield of the system - the expected yield during the system life time is a natural performance measure in many situations. Obviously, the above system performance measures (a), (b) and (d) are special cases of this general performance measure.

Certainly also other types of reliability performance may be adequate. For repairable systems different types of availability performance measures are suitable. Observe, however, that in this paper only non-repairable systems are considered. In this paper we shall in the following mainly study the performance measure (b), expected life.

When the first type, (a), of reliability performance measures above is applicable, it seems very suitable to use the Birnbaum reliability importance measure. Generally, a reasonable requirement on an importance measure is, that it indicates how important the components are with respect to the chosen system reliability performance measure. It is natural to assume that component most important, for which a small improvement in reliability performance gives the best system reliability performance improvement. To make the comparison valid we have to make "the same" improvement to each of the components - we have a problem to define this small component reliability improvement. Natvig (1982) discusses this problem. He found that a possible interpretation for components with proportional hazard rates could be an infinitesimal reduction in these. However, he did not find this interpretation satisfactory. In the following sections we shall give some different suggestions.

While studying importance measures and, especially when comparing different importance measures, it is natural to make a normalization so that the component reliability importances sum up to one.

3. A BASIC RESULT

Let $\tau_1, \ldots, \tau_n$ denote the random lives of the n components of the system and let $F_1, \ldots, F_n$ be the corresponding life distributions, which we assume to be continuous. As usual we write $\bar{F}=1-F$ for any life distribution F. Now, assume that the i:th component is replaced by a component with life

distribution G_i instead of F_i. Let $\tau_{\phi,i}$ be the life length corresponding to the new system. The difference in expected life length is

$$\Delta_i = E(\tau_{\phi,i}) - E(\tau_\phi) = \int_0^\infty (\bar{G}_i(t) - \bar{F}_i(t)) I_B^{(i)}(t) dt;$$

here we have used that the expected system life may be written as

$$E(\tau_\phi) = \int_0^\infty P(\tau_\phi > t) dt = \int_0^\infty E(\phi(\underline{X}(t))) dt$$

$$= \int_0^\infty \bar{F}_i(t) I_B^{(i)}(t) dt + \int_0^\infty E(\phi(0_i, \underline{X}(t)) dt,$$

together with the independence assumption.

Now, representing the "small component reliability improvement" by the replacing life distribution G_i, a natural importance measure is $\Delta_i / (\Sigma_{j=1}^n \Delta_j)$. We only have to decide on which improvements $G_i, i=1, \ldots, n$, to consider.

Natvig (1985a) assumes that upon failure of the i:th component it is replaced by an unfailed component of the same age or, equivalently, that it is restored to the same state as immediately before the failure. After a second failure the component is not repaired. This means that F_i is replaced by G_i, where

$$\bar{G}_i(t) = \bar{F}_i(t) - \bar{F}_i(t)\ln(\bar{F}_i(t));$$

observe that this is the survival function of the time to the second event in a non-homogeneous Poisson process with mean value function equal to $\ln(\bar{F}_i(t))$. The obtained importance measure is the same as $I_{N_1}^{(i)}$ suggested by Natvig (1979).

Another approach would be to replace $F_i(t)$ by $G_i(t) = F_i(t-c)$ for some small positive shift c common to all components. In this case it is natural to assume c infinitesmal and we obtain

$$\frac{\partial \Delta_i}{\partial c} = \frac{\partial}{\partial c} \int_0^\infty [F_i(t-c) - F_i(t)] I_B^{(i)}(t) dt$$

$$= \int_0^\infty I_B^{(i)}(t) dF_i(t) = I_{B-P}^{(i)};$$

here $I_{B-P}^{(i)}$ is the component reliability importance measure suggested by Barlow and Proschan (1975). The quantity $I_{B-P}^{(i)}$ may also be interpreted as the probability that system failure is caused by the i:th component, see Barlow and Proschan (1975). We have obtained a new interpretation of the Barlow and Proschan (1975) reliability importance measure. (Observe that in this case there is no need for a further normalization).

In the next section we shall suggest the study of infinitesimal scale changes.

4. INFINITESIMAL SCALE CHANGES

For the designer the most natural type of reliability improvements is the decrease in relative stress of the component, which may be effectuated either by protecting the component or increasing its strength. In both cases it is natural to assume that a scale change of the component failure distribution is obtained. Almost all published models relating life distributions on several stress levels to each other are of this type.

Generally, a function $a(S_2,S_1;t), t\geq 0$, is called an acceleration function if

$$F_{S_2}(t)=F_{S_1}(a(S_2,S_1;t)), \quad t\geq 0,$$

where F_{S_i} is the life distribution on stress level $S_i, i=1,2$. Most models, like the power-law, the Arrhenius and Eyre models, assume a linear acceleration function, i.e.

$$a(S_2,S_1;t)=\alpha(S_2,S_1)t, \quad t\geq 0,$$

for some constant $\alpha(S_2,S_1)$. Hence, a change in stress level is assumed to give a scale change in the corresponding life distribution. For some interesting discussions on acceleration functions we refere to Viertl (1980, 1983) and Viertl and Strelec (1982) and references cited there.

Thus, in the following we represent the improvement by $G_i(t)=F_i(t/c)$ for some $c>1$. As in the last section it is natural to make only small changes, which means that c should be close to one, and that the same changes are performed on all components. Making the scale changes infinitesimal it is natural to consider

$$\lim_{c\searrow 1}\frac{\Delta_i}{c-1} = \lim_{c\searrow 1}\int_0^\infty \frac{1}{c-1}(\bar{F}_i(t/c)-\bar{F}_i(t))I_B^{(i)}(t)dt$$

$$= \int_0^\infty t\, I_B^{(i)}(t)dF_i(t).$$

After normalization we call this component reliability importance measure $I_E^{(i)}$; here E stands for expectation since it is, in our opinion, the relevant importance measure when the system reliability performance measure is the expected system life length:

$$I_E^{(i)}=\frac{\int_0^\infty t\, I_B^{(i)}(t)dF_i(t)}{\sum_{j=1}^n \int_0^\infty t\, I_B^{(i)}(t)dF_j(t)}.$$

In a special case, when all life distributions are Weibull with the same shape parameter, it is easily shown (Natvig, private communication) that this importance measure coincides with $I_{N_1}^{(i)}$ suggested by Natvig (1979). If the life distributions are exponential with failure rates $\lambda_1,\ldots,\lambda_n$ and the system is a series system it is easily shown that $I_E^{(i)}$ is proportional to

$$\lambda_i/(\sum_{j=1}^n \lambda_j)^2,$$

and if the system is a parallell structure $I_E^{(i)}$ is proportional to

$$\int_0^\infty t\, \prod_{j\neq i}(1-\exp[-\lambda_j t])\lambda_i\exp[-\lambda_i t]dt$$

$$= \lambda_i[\lambda_i^{-2}- \sum_{j\neq i}(\lambda_i+\lambda_j)^{-2}$$

$$+ \sum_{\substack{k\neq j\neq i\\k\neq i}}(\lambda_i+\lambda_j+\lambda_k)^{-2}+ \ldots+(-1)^{n-1}(\lambda_1+\ldots+\lambda_n)^{-2}].$$

In general, we have to rely on numerical approximations to find our component reliability importance measures. However, computer programs for fault tree analysis often contain some component reliability importance measure calculations; usually $I_B^{(i)}(t)$ is calculated. Based on these calculations also the suggested importance measures may be derived.

5. DISCUSSION

It would be tempting to take into consideration even more information, as e.g. cost figures. Of course, this should be done before deciding on a specific reliability improvement. But cost information usually is rather hard (and costly) to find and therefore it is unnecessary to gather such information for all components. Only for those components, which have a high component reliability importance measure, it seems worthwhile to look for costs of improvements balanced against the improvement in system reliability, in order to make final decisions on the allocation of resources to reliability improvements. At this stage also other reliability improvement considerations, as e.g. changes in the reliability structure, has to be taken into account.

Observe, that even if in this paper we have restricted ourselves to the study of coherent non-repairable systems with independent components, the ideas presented may be applied to more general systems without any but computational problems.

A more general class of component reliability importance measures is based on the general system reliability performance measure "expected yield", see (e) ebove. A further generalization is obtained if multistate components are considered. In Natvig (1985b) such generalizations of some of the earlier suggested importance measures are given.

A further discussion on the merits of different types of importance measures and cost considerations will be given in a forthcoming paper authored together with Bent Natvig and his coworkers at University of Oslo.

Acknowledgement

I wish to thank Bent Natvig and his coworkers at University of Oslo for stimulating discussions on reliability importance measures.

REFERENCES

Barlow, R.E. and F. Proschan (1975). Importance of
    system components and fault tree events. Stoch.
    Proc. Appl. 3, 153-173.
Barlow, R.E. and F. Proschan (1981). Statistical
    theory of reliability and life testing. Probabil-
    ity models. To Begin With, Silver Springs, Mary-
    land.
Bergman, B. (1985). On reliability theory and its
    applications (with discussion). Scand. J. Statist.,
    12. (to appear).
Birnbaum, Z.W. (1969). On the importance of different
    components in a multicomponent system. In Multi-
    variate analysis-II, ed. P.R. Krishnaiah.
    Academic Press, New York, 581-592.
Fussel, J.B. (2975). How to hand-calculate system
    reliability and safety characteristics, IEEE Trans.
    Reliability, 24, 169-174.
Natvig, B. (1979). A suggestion of a new measure of
    importance of system components. Stoch. Proc.
    Appl. 9, 319-330.
Natvig. B. (1982). On the reduction in remaining
    system lifetime due to the failure of a specific
    component. J. Appl. Prob. 19, 642-652. Correction
    J. Appl. Prob. 20, 713.
Natvig, B. (1985a). New light on measures of im-
    portance of system components. Scand. J. Statist.,
    12 (to appear).
Natvig, B. (1985b). Recent developments in multi-
    state reliability theory, in Probabilistic methods
    in the mechanics of solids and structures, Springer
    Verlag, Berlin.
Viertl, R. (1980). Acceleration functions in
    reliability theory, Methods of Operations Research,
    36, 321-326.
Viertl, R. (1983). Nonlinear acceleration functions
    in life testing, Methods of Operations Research,
    47, 115-122.
Viertl, R. and H. Strelec (1982). Estimation of ac-
    celeration functions in reliability theory under
    multicomponent stress, in Progess in Cybernetics
    and Systems Research, vol 10, Hemisphere Publ.
    Comp.

RELIABILITY EVALUATION OF A SAFETY RELATED OPERATING SYSTEM

W. Ehrenberger*, J. Märtz**, G. Glöe*** and E.-U. Mainka***

*Fachhochschule Fulda
**Gesellschaft für Reaktorsicherheit Garching
***Technischer Oberwachungsvere in Norddeutschland, Hamburg,
Federal Republic of Germany

Abstract. The operating system of the control rod motion computers of the German boiling water reactor plants was investigated. The computers have a limited safety relevance: the worst accident they might cause in case of failure could hurt the reactor core.
Two approaches have been tried: an analytic verification and a probabilistic one. The analytic approach quickly revealed a very tricky structure. Some system parts, however, proved to be accessible by analysis. These parts were peripheral. The central part of the real time executive on the other hand resisted to all analytical efforts. The analysis showed that the protection against improper system call was very weak.
The probabilistic approach used Bayesian statistics. It took its data from a questionaire that had been answered by some long term users of this computer both from the nuclear and the non nuclear field. More than 80 years of operating experience were available. Computer failures had been mainly observed due to hardware defects. The few operating system errors that had been detected had occured quite early and have been removed. On the basis of that experiece it could be shown that the system quality was sufficient for the intended use.

Keywords. Software reliability; operating system; program analysis; Bayesian statistics; control rod motion computer;

INTRODUCTION

At the previous SAFECOMP in Cambridge the contribution /1/, presented by O. Nordland gave an overview on a project about the verification of the software of a control rod motion computer. Such computers have been installed in all German nuclear power stations with boiling water reactors. The computer has a limited safety relevance. In case of computer failure together with other unpleasant circumstances the reactor core might be hurt. Any more severe consequences are prevented by the protection system of the plant, which acts completely independently.

The computer hardware had been investigated earlier and equiped with a self supervision program. The aim of the now completed project was to retrospectively verify the software or rather show whether or not it qualified for its purpose from the reliability point of view. During earlier discussions it had been stated that computers of the safety relevance of the investigated one should have an availability in the order of magnitude of $<10^{-4}$. The expectation of the probability of safety related failure should be one order of magnitude less. So the values for one part of the system such as the operating system should be evens smaller.

THE METHOD OF PROGRAM ANALYSIS

Program analysis starts from the source code or the machine code. The source code may be used, if the translator employed works correctly with reasonable confidence. The analysis tries to reveal the program functions by making obvious:

- the control flow and
- the data flow

of the investigated program. The verification of freedom from errors can be done in essentially in two ways, namely by

- comparison of the revealed functions with the functional specification of the software, or by
- execution of test cases that perform a complete test of the software and comparison of the test results with the specification.

A third way might consist in a mixture of the two above. In the second case the anaylsis must be directed to specify exhaustive test runs; in the first case it should lead to a representation of the functions programmed that is as close as possible to the formalism used in the original functional specification. In both cases a clear and complete functional specification is indispensible.

The analysis method must be easy to understand to allow people from outside to check the results gained. The basis may be graphic or mnemonic.

Since the user programs, i.e. the control rod motion programs of the computer were not too complex, the following approach lead to results:

- The individual instructions were transferred into a representation where the assignment function to each operand becomes obvious.
- From this representation all memory operands, i/o operands, CPU registers used, flags, subroutine calls, branching goals and the related addresses were listed.
- The sequentially working parts were identified. For these sequences the operands and operators were put together, thus forming a higher order representation of the function programmed. The influence of the input operands of the sequence to the other operands present were represented by a correspondence matrix.
- The sequences were grouped to modules through consideration of their own series of occurring

65

The project reported on herein was sponsored by the German Federal Minister of Home Affairs.
The authors express their thanks for the sponsorship.

and the branching instructions between them.
The well known constructs IF ... THEN ... ELSE,
WHILE ... DO etc were employed thereby. For one
such module the correspondence matrices were
put together as well. They did now contain
conditional correspondences.
- Subroutines were freated before main modules
  and their results inserted into the calling
  sequences. The process of forming modules was
  repeated iteratively, thus leading to higher
  and higher representations of the programmed
  functions.

This process has been carried out successfully with
the main parts of the user programms. It lead to
representations of the code that could be compared
with the software functional specifications at the
end.

During analysis the following difficulties arise:

- Since the data to be processed are not known
  at the time of performing the analysis, data
  dependency cannot be treated adequately in all
  cases, e.g. if a computed goto is employed.
- For the same reason any dynamically evaluated
  array boundary causes difficulties.
- The same applies for dynamically changed
  instructions, such as executes.
- The method is only applicable, if the functions
  programmed are not too complex and if the
  investigated code is reasonably well structured.

ANALYSIS ATTEMPTS OF THE OPERATING SYSTEM

The version of the operating system used comprised
about 153 pages of code. It took 8k computer words
of core memory. 22 from the pages were investigated
in detail. The selection was made according to the
different tasks of that system:

- system entry from the user program
- executive control program part
- quasi instructions
- i/o drivers.

The aim of the investigations was not an analysis in
itself, but to find out, whether or not more detailed
efforts would lead to test cases within a forseeable
amount of time. Such test cases should lead to a
complete test of the relevant system part, in the
sense that all properties of that part would be revealed by that test.

The entry to the operating system from the user
programs prooved to be quite tricky. Lots of shifts
were made in order to put certain bits of the information of the call in certain positions and to
branch upon the result. The instructions used, however, revealed that each bit from the call was used
either separately or together with some of its
neighbours only. Arbitrary combinations of such bits
did not have any influence on further processing. A
complete test would have consisted in changing the
calling bit separately, one after the next. It
turned out as well that such a test would have revealed a clear shortcomming of the system: The check
against user errors was incomplete. Many of the
feasible calls are meaningless and even failure
prone.

This statement applied also for the entry to the
quasi instructions. The purpose of these instructions was to simulate a larger machine on the small
one. Only fife such instructions existed in the
investigated system. Error check for not implemented
instructions did not exist. The available instructions on the other hand proved to be implemented by
simple code sequences that would be testable exhaustively without too much effort.

Among the i/o drivers those for digital input and
output were investigated in more detail, because
of their importance at the application in the power
plant. They turned out to be quite simple, with
two loops only, using nearly no arrays and comprising only fife pages of code. Complete analysis and
exhaustive test seemed feasible.

The executive control program (ECP) is the central
part of the operating system. It decides which user
program is the next to run. It can be called from
several parts of the operating system, among others
from the console type writer driver, the interrupt
handling part and the time handling part. Figure 1
shows the control flow graph and the tables employed. The table TVLKET stores the calling cues.
One of the tricks used was to load an index register
with a load instruction and to address a table by
emloying an execute instruction on that index register. The advantage was to change the address
within the table via an index register instruction
and to thereby safe few instructions per addressing.

As figure 1 shows, many entries to that program part
exist. The sequence of executions is not well
structured. This makes it extremely difficult to
attribute meanings to the sequences of operations.
In addition to that the tables have a quite tricky
structure as well. Although a good documentation
was available, no possibility was found to understand that program part or to derive any meaningful
test run.

As already mentioned, not all parts of the operating
system were investigated in detail. From the existing documentation, however, it could be concluded
that the major portion of the not considered parts
was tricky as well. Such tricky parts did in particular deal with

- interrupt handling
- time supervision
- console type writer.

It was therefore decided not to spend the enormous
amount of time that would have been necessary to do
all the detailed investigations and to rely on
probabilistic investigations instead.

BAYESIAN STATISTICS AND QUESTIONAIRE

At the beginning of the project it was quite clear
that the effort necessary to carry out a statistical
test, the required amount of test time would be
too long! and therefore infeasible. For this reason
not only operating experience from power plants but
from non nuclear applications as well was to be considered. In so doing the assessment of the system
was put on a broader basis. Bayesian statistics had
been chosen because it allows to integrate further
information through using an a priori distribution.
In our case the failure rate λ was considered to be
the parameter of interest and consequently a priori
distribution was surched for λ. The underlying
mathematical background has been described already
in /1/. In order to be as complete as possible in
this paper, it is reproduced again in appendix 1.

A questionaire was derived which addressed the
questions that were considered to be important for
taking into account the existing experience. It is
reproduced in appendix 2. It was mailed to users of
the same computer and a similar operating system
version. All users were approached by telephone be-
forehand and all were very open with their information. Not one refused to contribute. Whether or not
the operating system considered was comparable to
the nuclear installations could be judged on the
answeres to question 1.

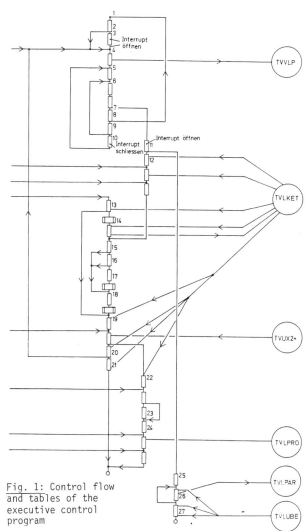

Fig. 1: Control flow and tables of the executive control program

MAKING USE OF THE OPERATING EXPERIENCE

The evaluation of the questionaires was done in two steps: first single forms were considered, second the overall experience was evaluated. The operating experience from each site was used as input to a progam that calculated the probability density functions of the failure rate λ and the distribution function of λ for each installation individually. For those applications, where an operating system error had been removed during the observation time, one way of considering this would have been to disregard the experience that was prior to that error removal and to take the experience after error removal only. This would have lead to lower failure rate results as the last columns of table 1 show. Therefore the whole operating experience of the related installations was burdened with the observed errors for the derivation of the priori distribution. The system change for error correction made during the operation can be accepted at the derivation of this priori distribution.

The overall evaluation was made as follows: Since software does not have any wear out, it was decided that it was allowed to add both the operating experience and the connected errors. Another question was whether or not the experience comming from the non nuclear applications could be considered as representative for the nuclear installations as well i.e. whether it could be used directly without any change as a prior distribution for the nuclear applications. Otherwise a malus would have to be considered. The opinion followed was that there was no meaningful difference in the use of an operating system in a nuclear computer and in any other type of use. This was backed by the investigation /3/, which showed that the use of compilers for commercial programs and for scientific programs was about the same.

The graphical results are shown in figures 2 and 3, both from the report /2/. The figures make clear, how the accumulation of the operating experience lead to more and more precise results. The dotted line that represents the experience from the nuclear stations has a different shape to the others due to the lack of any failure observation. The related installations in the nuclear power plants were made after the errors in the non nuclear applications had occurred and had been corrected.

The most important data and results are given in a compact form in the tables 1, 2 and 3. Table 1 is about the non nuclear applications only, table 2 deals with the nuclear ones and table 3 gives the synopsis. As the results show, the operating system failure rate is

$$\lambda < 1.27 \cdot 10^{-5}$$

at a level of confidence of 95%. The expectation
$$E(\lambda) = 0.69 \cdot 10^{-5}.$$

These figures are in the order of magnitude of the initially requred ones. The system qualifies for its use.

CONCLUSION

The operating system of the control rod motion computer was subject to both systematic and probabilistic investigations. The systematic investigations revealed a very tricky system structure and some weakness of protection against improper use. The main parts resisted to any systematic verification approach, because they were too complex. Due to the long use of the computer, operating experience existed at various sites. This experence was gathered by questionaires. The results were evaluated by means of Bayesian statistics . It came out that the system reliability was adequate for the intended use. The method employed can easily be used in connection with other application as well.

It were questions 4 and 5 that lead to quantitative results: question 4 dealt with operating experience and question 5 with expert opinion. Both were aiming at a priori distribution. The expert opinion question was put, because we were not sure whether suitably documentable operating experience would be available at all. The question on expert opinion lead to some unforseen problems, because in most cases only the interval $2 \cdot 10^{-4} \leqslant MTBF < \infty$ was marked with probability 1. From this it is not possible to define an unambiguous gamma distribution. Nevertheless the expert opinions were quite in line with the operating experience from question 4. See also last lines of tables 1 to 3. In case of any new action one would prefer to put the question in a different way. One would fix the probabilities (e.g. 20%, 60%, 20%) and ask to attribute the most likely MTBF intervals to them.

The final evaluation was based on the operating experience only, because it was available in quantitative form. There was no necessity to rely on expert opinion.

Questionaires came back from:

- nuclear power plants,
- a radio transmitter station
- a steel tube manufacturer
- a rolling mill
- a blast furnace plant

In some cases two computers had been used in parallel with identical tasks. Then only one computer was counted.

Table 1: Characteristic values for the failure rate of an operating system due to experience outside of nuclear power plants

		A 1	A 2	A 3	A 4	A 5	A 6	A 7	Characteristic values for the changed versions, values after error removal: A 1, A 2, A 3 after error removal	A 5 after error removal
	time of operating experience [h]	92000	92000	92000	50000	90290	85000	69000	74500	77290
	obseved errors	1	1	1	0	1	0	0	0	0
gamma distribution of the failure rate λ [1/h]	95% Quant. $[10^{-5}]$	5,16	5,16	5,16	5,99	5,26	3,53	4,35	4,02	3,88
	expectation $[10^{-5}]$	2,17	2,17	2,17	2,00	2,22	1,18	1,45	1,34	1,30
	Median $[10^{-5}]$	1,82	1,82	1,82	1,39	1,86	0,82	1,00	0,93	0,90
	modal value $[10^{-5}]$	1,09	1,09	1,09	0	1,11	0	0	0	0
	variance $[10^{-10}]$	2,36	2,36	2,36	4,00	2,45	1,38	2,10	1,80	1,67
probabilities for MTBF intervals	$0 \le MTBF < 10^4$	0	0	0	0,01	0 ¦ 1/3	0	0	0	0
	$10^4 \le MTBF < 2 \cdot 10^4$	0,06	0,06	0,06	0,08	0,07 ¦ 1/3	0,02	0,03	0,03	0,02
	$2 \cdot 10^4 \le MTBF < \infty$	0,94	0,94	0,94	0,91	0,93 ¦ 1/3	0,98	0,97	0,97	0,98

Table 2: Characteristic values for the failure rate of an operating system due to experience in nuclear power plants

		SSFR 1	SSFR 2	SSFR 3	SSFR 4
	time of operating experience [h]	31000	25000	33600	63000
	observed errors	0	0	0	0
gamma distribution of the failure rate λ [1/h]	95 % Quantil $[10^{-5}]$	9,67	11,99	8,92	4,76
	expectation $[10^{-5}]$	3,23	4,00	2,98	1,59
	Median $[10^{-5}]$	2,24	2,77	2,06	1,10
	modal value $[10^{-5}]$	0	0	0	0
	variance $[10^{-10}]$	10,41	16,00	8,86	2,52
probabilities for MTBF intervals	$0 \le MTBF < 10^4$	0,05	0,08	0,03	0 ¦ 0,1
	$10^4 \le MTBF < 2 \cdot 10^4$	0,17	0,21	0,16	0,05 ¦ 0,8
	$2 \cdot 10^4 \le MTBF < \infty$	0,78	0,71	0,81	0,95 ¦ 0,1

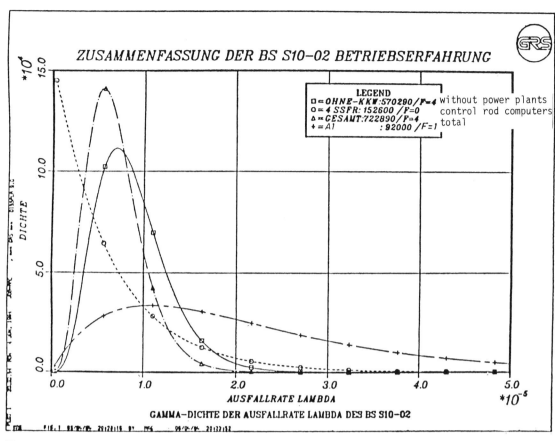

Figure 2: Gamma density of the failure rate of the operating system

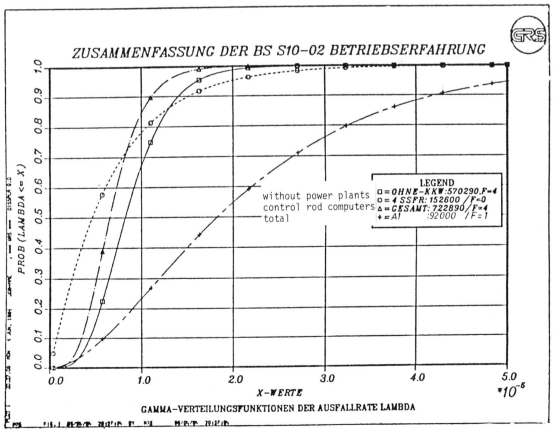

Figure 3: Gamma distribution functions of the failure rate

Table 3:   Characteristic values for the failure rate of an
           operating system , combination of the experiences

		BS S 10-02 not in power plants	BS S 10-02 in power plants	BS S 10-02 total
	time of operating experience **[h]**	570290	152600	722890
	observed errors	4	0	4
gamma distribution of the failure rate λ [1/h]	95 % Quantil [10^{-5}]	1,61	1,96	1,27
	expectation [10^{-5}]	0,88	0,66	0,69
	Median [10^{-5}]	0,82	0,45	0,65
	modal value [10^{-5}]	0,70	0	0,55
	variance 10^{-10}]	0,15	0,43	0,10
probabilities for MTBF intervals	$0 \leq MTBF < 10^4$	0	0	0
	$10^4 \leq MTBF < 2 \cdot 10^4$	0	0	0
	$2 \cdot 10^4 \leq MTBF < \infty$	1	1	1

REFERENCES

/1/ G.Glöe, E.-U.Mainka, O.Nordland, G. Rauch,
    U.Schmeil and J. Märtz
    SAFETY ASSESSMENT OF THE SOFTWARE OF A CONTROL
    ROD MOTION COMPUTER
    IFAC Safecomp 83, Cambridge, UK, 1983

/2/ W.Ehrenberger, G.Glöe, E.-U.Mainka, O.Nordland,
    G.Rauch, U.Schmeil and J.Märtz
    SICHERHEITSANALYSE DER PROGRAMME DER STEUERSTAB-
    FAHRRECHNER, ABSCHLUSSBERICHT
    Bericht des TÜV Norddeutschland, Hamburg,
    Dezember 1984

/3/ G. Hommel
    ÜBERSETZUNGSEFFIZIENZ VON COMPILERN
    Dissertation an der TU-Berlin, 1978

/4/ Kurt Stange
    BAYES VERFAHREN
    Springer Verlag, 1977

Appendix 1: Bayesian statistics

The operating system of a computer is a continuous task code, continuously controlling the activities of the computer and its user software. In order to determine the reliability of a continuous task code the point of interest is the time T until the next failure occurs or the probability of m failures within a given space of time. The probability of T being the time to the next failure is described by the exponential distribution:

$$P (T < t) = 1 - e^{-\lambda t}$$

The probability that the number of failures X within a certain space t of time will be m is described by the Poisson-distribution:

$$P(t; X = m) = \frac{(\lambda t)^m}{m!} e^{-\lambda t}$$

In both cases, λ is the (unknown) failure rate, which has to be determined by the statistical examination. It is not the aim of our statistical examination to determine the most likely value of λ, but rather to determine a limiting value which will not exceed with, say, 95% probability. This requires tests. In order to demonstrate a high degree of reliability, classical statistical methods require a very long or even prohibitively long testing time. Using Bayes' methods the amount of testing can be considerably reduced, when a sufficiently large amount of positive experience is available. Due to the AEG 60-10's large number of implementations, there is a large amount of experience available and we can apply

Bayes' methods. With classical statistics, before testing each value the failure rate λ can assume, has the same probability. When within a testing time of duration t the occurrence of k failures was observed, this test result (t,k) can be used to compute a confidence interval, within which the true value of λ will lie with a probability of for example 95%.

Bayes' statistics, however, takes advantage of previous knowledge on the behaviour of the system being examined: the possible values that λ can assume are given a probability, which produces a prior distribution $F_0(\lambda)$ for λ. To make the previous knowledge on λ more precise, a test is performed. Applying Bayes' theorem, the previous knowledge $F_0(\lambda)$ is combined with the additional knowledge of the test result (t,k) to produce the more precise knowledge $F_1(\lambda)$, termed the posterior distribution. The 95% quantile of $F_1(\lambda)$ corresponds to the 95% confidence interval of classical statistics. Furthermore, Bayes' method can be applied iteratively, because each posterior distribution can be used as a new prior distribution for the next test.

The type of distribution to be applied to the failure rate is the Gamma-distribution:

$$\text{Gamma}(b,p) = \frac{b^p}{\Gamma(p)} e^{-bx} x^{p-1}$$

The Gamma-distribution is determined by the parameters b and p which are easy to interpret: the parameter b corresponds to the duration of tests t, and the parameter p corresponds basically to the number of failures k. Some examples of Gamma-distributions are shown in the figure.

One of the great advantages of the Gamma-distribution lies in the ease with which the transformation from prior to posterior distribution can be performed. If Gamma (b,p) is a prior distribution for the failure rate λ, then the test result (t,k) leads to a posterior distribution Gamma (b+t, p+k). In other words, by adding the duration t of the test to the parameter b, and the number of observed failures to the parameter p, the results of a test can very simply be used to compute the posterior distribution.

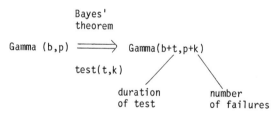

The main advantage, however, of applying Bayesian methods to the statistical examination lies in the considerable reduction of the amount of testing necessary to demonstrate a given reliability, when a large amount of positive experience is available and reflected in a corresponding prior distribution. There are various ways of deriving an initial prior distribution. Obviously the worst is to make an "intelligent" guess. A better founded distribution can be obtained by collecting expert opinion, though this also contains a large degree of subjectivity. Finally, already existing data, based on for example log books or similar records, can be collected and used to derive a prior distribution. This gives the best founded prior distribution.

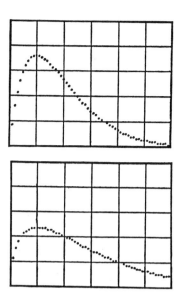

Fig.   Gamma-distributions for b=1,p=2 (top and b=½,p=³⁄₂ (bottom)

Appendix 2:   Questionnaire

1. Company, Institution
   Address
   Person to ask, if questions arise
   Date
   Version of system used

2. During which period has the system been used? Has any log book been employed?

3. For what purpose has the computer been used?

4. During ... operating hours ... failures have been observed. From these failures were
         ... hardware failures
         ... operating system failures
         ... user program failures
         ... of unknown origin.
   Were there any operating system failures of outstanding effects?
   Have the errors been removed?
   Did you use your memory, the log book or both to answer the questions?

5. The mean time between failures (MTBF) is given in operating hours. Please attribute a probability to each of the three intervals given below. Probability means your personal degree of being sure that the correct value of the MTBF lies between the limits of the interval. The sum of the probabilities must be 1. Intervals:

$0 \leqslant \text{MTBF} < 10^{-4}$, $10^{-4} \leqslant \text{MTBF} < 2.10^{-4}$,

$2.10^{-4} \leqslant \text{MTBF} < \infty$

COMPUTER AIDED DESIGN FOR RELIABILITY ASSESSMENT, A PACKAGE SPECIFICATION

A. M. Featherstone* and B. K. Daniels**

Department of Electrical and Electronic Engineering, Aston University, Birmingham, UK
**Systems Reliability Service, UKAEA, Culcheth, Warrington, UK*

Abstract Computers have been used by the reliability analyst for the past decade or more. Computers are able to increase the efficiency and capability of the analyst because of their numerical and graphical abilities. There is great debate about the use of new algorithms to solve problems of varying type and complexity, but there has been less work done on co-ordinating these algorithms into a cohesive, "user-friendly" package.

This paper is concerned primarily with the ways of building up a Computer Aided Design (CAD) package for reliability assessment. It reviews what work has been carried out in this area to date, surveying and assessing features that have been implemented in CAD packages.

The paper examines the required features of a CAD package for reliability assessment and the methods of implementation. The three primary requirements of such a package are:-

(1)   The package enhances the capability of the reliability analyst.
(2)   The package improves the efficiency of the reliability analyst.
(3)   The package is usable i.e. "user-friendly".

To achieve these requirements a given sequence of implementation is necessary and this paper details the sequence and argues for the order and control of the proposed package.

The paper concludes by examining some of the hardware requirements of such a package, advising on the choice of a given configuration.

1.   INTRODUCTION

In reference (1), the authors specified the need for a computer aided design package for reliability assessment (CAD-RA). In this paper we are specifying the requirements of a "user-friendly" package for CAD-RA. Computer package designers have been attempting to generate user friendly packages over many years, as early as 1977 Kogen et al. (2) identified a growing trend to "user-friendly systems". There are numerous definitions of "user-friendly systems" e.g. The Dictionary of New Information Technology by Meadows, Garden and Singleton, published in 1982[3], defines user friendly as, "a system with which relatively untrained users can interact easily. This normally implies the use of a high level programming language and often of graphical representation". This definition, like many others, has features within it with which we agree we would add the need for other facilities e.g. menus, however our meaning of the term user-friendly will be explained in greater detail in Section 2. It should be noted that Section 2 follows more closely the ideas put forward by Stevens[4] where the definition is expressed in terms of system requirements.

Recently many computer packages such as FTAP[5], ALMONA[6], PREP-KITT[7], PROSIM[8] etc. and simulators such as ERMA[9], ESCAF[10] and START1[11] have been developed as tools in reliability assessment work. All these packages are tried and tested and in regular use for analysing and solving reliability assessment problems. However, without fail, all these mentioned and other packages and systems we are aware of, require the user to be both an expert reliability technologist and an expert in computer usage, and are therefore, using the above definition, NOT "user-friendly". They also suffer from incompatibles in the input/output and representation of the system being assessed. They do not form a cohesive reliability assessment package.

This paper sets out to define the requirements by combining the ideas of "user-friendly systems" with the ideas inherent in the reliability assessment packages and simulators available. By combining those ideas it is envisaged that a suitable CAD-RA package can be defined which is of benefit to the reliability analyst as well as being "usable".

2.   USER-FRIENDLY FEATURES

Project reliability assessment is generally a task which requires 50-60% of the analyst's time spent on researching the project definitions and interactions, 20-25% of the time spent on qualitative assessment, 10-15% of the time on quantitative assessment and 10-15% on report presentation. (Footnote 1). It is interesting to

---

1.   Results of survey taken of the project reliability assessment analysts within NCSR (Feb. 1983).

note that the packages dealing with reliability assessment have been generally aimed at the 10-15% of time spent on quantitative assessment. It is however noted that RIKKE[12] is different in that it is aimed at the qualitative assessment with the capacity to extend into quantitative assessment. CAD-RA has a role to play in all facets of reliability assessment. If the four stages of reliability assessment are examined with respect to computer requirements the following picture emerges. The problem definition stage has a primary requirement for access to design, operational and maintenance data. It requires access to, and interaction with, a variety of databanks. Qualitative assessment has a primary requirement for computer graphics to construct, display and manipulate diagrams, text and results, and to access failure mode parts of data bases in an efficient manner. Quantitative assessment, conversely, has a primary requirement for arithmetic facilities and access to the failure and repair models and parameter sections of reliability databanks. (Footnote 2). Finally, the report writing stage has two requirements; (i) word processing facilities and (ii) computer graphics. These requirements can thus be categorised:

ASSESSMENT STAGE	COMPUTER REQUIREMENTS			
	Access to a variety of Databanks	Graphics Facilities	Arithmetic Facilities	Word Processor
Problem Definition	*	*		*
Qualitative Assessment	*	*		*
Quantitative Assessment	*		*	
Report Writing		*		*

Following the recommendation in Reference (4) the above specifies the requirements of the system. The hardware and software aspects of fulfilling these requirements are dealt with in Sections 3 and 4, however in this section the requirements will be related, in turn, to available "user-friendly" facilities.

The first requirement is the ability to access relevant databanks. This requirement is best met if the computer to be used has good communications facilities, e.g. part of a network. The arithmetic requirement is implicitly achieved by all computers since this is their primary function. Graphics and word processing facilities require appropriate hardware facilities, i.e. good quality screen and appropriate hardcopy facilities, however in addition to this, there is a requirement for appropriate software packages to drive these facilities.

The above specifies the requirements of the system, let us now examine in practical terms how a commercial "user friendly system" operates. The Apple Lisa and Xerox Star are acknowledged, commercially available, "user friendly systems"[13]. These systems have been developed in an ergonomically structured manner such that information is input in a desk top manner, i.e. the screen mimicks a desk top. The user decides which facility is required by manipulating items on the screen using a "mouse", rolling it around a surface and clicking one or more switches when the corresponding cursor on the screen is positioned over the desired facility. The basic operations of these two systems can be learned in 'under half an hour'[13]. It is important that the non-computer expert can easily use the system, conversely the regular user of the system should not find the system irritating to use because of unnecessary prompts. It is this balance that these systems have achieved.[13] The facilities are increasingly available on very low cost computer systems, e.g. the Acorn BBC computer and AMX-Mouse.

3.   IMPLEMENTATION OF A CAD-RA PACKAGE

At present the reliability analyst obtains information about the system/plant to be assessed, carries out the research required during problem definition and then draws up one or more reliability assessment diagrams. These diagrams are then examined qualitatively and quantitatively. Finally they are used in the finished report. Thus the drawing of the reliability assessment diagram is an important issue, and a time consuming one if it is done by hand. On average the same diagram is drawn three or more times (see Footnote 1). The ITREE code developed by Impell Corporation, (Footnote 3) tries to overcome this problem by allowing the user to crudely map-out a pseudo fault tree on a IBM-PC. However in our view this adds to the complexity of the problem since it is another level of examination diagram. At present the analyst uses one or a combination of diagrams ranging from Markov diagrams (Fig. 1), block diagrams (Fig. 2), Event Trees (Fig. 3), Fault Trees (Fig. 4) to Piping and Instrumentation (P and I) diagrams and electrical circuit diagrams. It would be easier if the number of diagrams could be reduced, that is an eventual aim but at present the authors feel that the implemention of a CAD-RA system is best served by mimicking the hand-drawn diagrams.

The long term aim would be to capture as much as possible of the system/plant information directly from the designer's CAD facilities, and so further assist the problem definition phase of assessment.

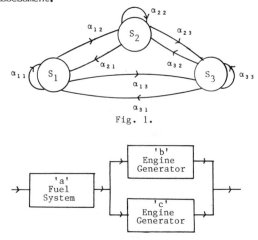

Fig. 1.

Fig. 2.   Reliability Block Diagram for Parallel Engine Generators

---

2.   If a measure of producibility is a requirement, further databanks will need to be accessed.
3.   Impell Corporation, Genesis Centre, Garrett Field, Warrington, U.K.

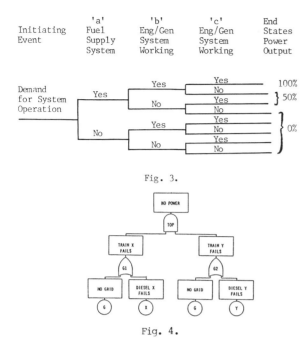

Initiating Event	'a' Fuel Supply System	'b' Eng/Gen System Working	'c' Eng/Gen System Working	End States Power Output

Fig. 3.

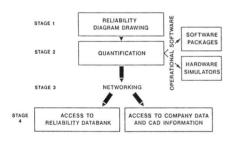

Fig. 4.

The development of a package/system to draw the required diagram using the user-friendly facilities described in Section 2 would be a useful way of demonstrating the benefits CAD can bring to reliability assessment. The next step is to use the available reliability assessment packages to quantify these computer based reliability diagrams when and if required. This would however involve the usage of appropriate data. The system would be complete if the data was accessible from the computer terminal. This requires the organisation of information from data banks which in turn requires communication facilities which implies network facilities. Once network facilities are available then the possibility of using CAD-RA throughout the reliability assessment process is a possibility.

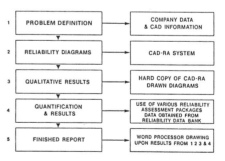

Fig. 5. CAD-RA Specifications

Therefore, the first and very important element of a CAD-RA system is the development of "user friendly" graphics facilities. The system must be capable of drawing and rotating all the reliability assessment diagrams mentioned above and the industrial standard "P and I" and electrical circuit diagrams. The input of these diagrams should be via a "mouse and desk-top system". The facility to pan and zoom is essential, since the reliability diagrams can be extensive, also a tidy up facility must be available (akin to justification and layout of text on Word Processors, and minimisation of track lengths/crossovers in printed circuit layout). Thus, allowing diagrams to be input in a convenient manner but displayed in a "report-standard" tidy manner. Such a system could be implemented on a stand-alone system.

The next stage in the development of a CAD-RA system is the "bolting on" of the quantitative assessment packages. These packages should receive as their input the reliability diagrams. This process will require operational software for which the system user is required to play no part except in selecting the appropriate analysis method and/or package. The selection or inputting of data associated with the reliability diagrams should be as before, via a "mouse and desk-top system". Again this extension could be implemented on a stand-alone system. If, however, CAD-RA is to be used throughout the reliability assessment process a network system must be used such that data associated with the reliability assessment diagrams can be accessed and used. Secondly, CAD diagrams and information about the system/plant to be assessed can also be assessed to aid the analyst in the initial time consuming problem definition stage. Finally, the diagrams and results from the quantitative assessment are also accessible for Word Processing and final report writing.

The above suggestions consider the mechanisation and integration of the traditional tools of the reliability assessor. Slowly, new tools such as ESCAF[10] and START1[11] are beginning to appear. These are hardware simulators, using digital technology, akin to the old analogue computers. ESCAF is an analytical tool and START1 an iterative tool based on the Monte-Carlo simulation technique. Monte-Carlo simulation provides many benefits for the reliability assessor[8], however it currently has serious limitations[14]. START1 holds out the possibility of overcoming these limitations and as such the hardware simulator could become an important feature of the CAD-RA system. ESCAF is a commercially available fast quantitative assessment system and therefore is of importance because of its usage commercially.

The use of hardware simulators in CAD-RA systems is conceptually easy to overcome since they become networked processors capable of communicating with the host system. The diagram being "down-loaded" to them for assessment with solutions being returned. The START1 system could readily be incorporated in this manner. However, ESCAF would require major modifications before such a development were attempted since at present its system model input is via a "wire patch-panel" and not a software package. As before, the hardware simulators should be tied into the host computers via operational software which is transparent to the user.

Fig. 6. CAD-RA Package

4. OTHER SYSTEM FEATURES

To fulfil the CAD-RA requirements specified in Sections 2 and 3 a number of system features must be available in any hardware/software system purchased. The prerequisite system features of a CAD-RA system are:

(i) **Multi-tasking;** It is essential that the various functions required within the CAD-RA system should be available instantaneously. These facilities should then be accessible using a "desk-top" philosophy as mentioned in Section 3. This should be implemented using such "user friendly" methods as overlays, pull down menus, split screens and possibly multi-terminals as used in some CAD systems.

(ii) **Decoupling;** Some functions within the CAD-RA system are useful to Reliability Assessors in a 'stand along mode', e.g. graphics and word processing. It is thus essential that these functions can be isolated for independent usage as and when required.

(iii) **Interconnections;** It has been emphasised in Sections 2 and 3 that the communications facility is of major importance to the CAD-RA system. The OSI (Open System Interconnection) standard is being adopted by many Information Technology (IT) manufacturers to ease the interconnection of various pieces of IT equipment. A minimal requirement of the CAD-RA system is that it meets the OSI specification.

(iv) **Interaction;** The graphics terminal to be used by a CAD-RA system should be a bit-mapped high resolution, raster scan colour monitor with its own processing power. Such a monitor provides good quality pictures with fast operation at reasonable cost. The input to the screen must be via a mouse or light pen or touch sensitive screen or other "user friendly" method. In addition there is a requirement for a standard keyboard.

With such facilities the CAD-RA system would be comparable and equivalent to software engineers use of Integrated Production Software Environments (IPSE) and following the trend in CAD and thus create the same environment and support for Reliability Assessors as for Designers.

5.   CURRENT DEVELOPMENTS

Work is underway at the Systems Reliability Service to implement parts of the "user-friendly" CAD-RA. One approach is the mouse-driver construction of Fault Trees, with annotation, using a micro-computer running under MS-DOS. The tree is constructed by selecting conventional fault tree symbols from a list of symbols on the screen by positioning an icon with the mouse. Having pressed a button the symbol is selected as the current symbol and by moving the mouse can be positioned on the screen. A further press of the button fixes the location of the symbol. Interconnecting lines can then be drawn and the tree annotated. The total fault tree spreads over many screens, with only one screen being current at a time. The current screen has a border overlap with adjacent screens, and the user can move to the left, right, upwards or downwards adjacent screens following inter-connections via fault tree symbols located at the border. The graphic representation of the fault tree is automatically transformed into the input data and commands for a standard calculation package, and the results can be viewed on screen.

A second approach uses a colour graphics terminal and the positioning of block diagram reliability symbols by x, y coordinates and linking the blocks by keyboard input of the block reference/mnemonic. This package is linked to the SRS package ALMONA, which calculates reliability and availability after Boolean operations on the network specified in the block diagram.

This work clearly shows that achievement of a CAD-RA is now feasible, and only a matter of time before it becomes the tool of the reliability analyst.

6.   CONCLUSIONS

The paper has drawn together information from ergonomists concerning "user-friendly" systems and reliability analysts concerning the requirements of CAD-RA. The paper specifies the interpretation of "user-friendly" systems in Section 2 and examines the major attributes of the commercial "user friendly" systems, the Xerox Star and Apple Lisa. Section 3 specifies how CAD-RA can be used to benefit the reliability analyst in all phases of assessment from research through qualitative assessment to quantitative assessment to final report writing (see Fig. 6). Section 3 also specifies logistically how a CAD-RA system can be profitably implemented in an evolutionary fashion. Implementation starts with a system capable of drawing reliability assessment diagrams for qualitative assessment. When appropriate communications facilities are available the quantification stage and the research stage can be incorporated into the CAD-RA facility. Finally, the report writing stage becomes a formality for incorporation into the CAD-RA facility once all other stages of reliability assessment have been incorporated, since it requires only the additional word processing capability. Section 4 as suggested in reference (3) specifies the system features required to meet the needs of the CAD-RA package.

7.   REFERENCES

(1)   Featherstone, A. M., and Daniels, B. K. (1984). Computational Methods of Operational Reliability for CAD. Proceedings of EUROCON '84, Brighton, September 1984.

(2)   Kogon, R., Keppel, E. and Krupp, D. (1976). Applications Development by End Users in Interactive Systems. Proceedings of the 6th Informatik Symposium, Bad Hamburg, September 1976.

(3)   Meadows, A. J., Gordon, M. and Singleton, A. (1982). Dictionary of new information technology. Kogan Page, London.

(4)   Stevens, G.C. (1983). User-friendly computer systems? A critical Examination of the Concept. Behaviour and Information Technology, Vol. 2, No. 1, pp. 3-16.

(5)   Randall, W. R. (1978). Fault Tree Analysis Program FTAP. Operations Research Report, University of California, Berkley, March.

(6)   Brock, P. (1977). The Reliability Analysis of Logical Networks by the Computer Program ALMONA. NCSR-R14, UKAEA, Culcheth, November.

(7)   Vesely, W. E., and Narum, R. E. (1970). PREP and KITT - Computer Codes for the Automatic Evaluation of a Fault. IN-1349, August.

(8)   Featherstone, A. M., and Daniels, B.K. (1984). Simulation for Reliability and Availability Assessment. Proceedings of the 4th International Conference on

Reliability and Maintainability, Lannion, France, May.

(9)   Rothbart, G. B., Fullwood, R. R. and
       Bailey, P.G. (1981). Experiments with
       Stochastic Systems (ERMA). Proceedings of
       the Annual Reliability and Maintainability
       Symposium, January.

(10)   Laviron, A., Carnino, A. and Manaranche, J.
       C. (1982). ESCAF – A New and Cheap System
       for Complete Reliability Analysis and
       Computation. IEEE Trans. on Reliability,
       pp. 74-81, October.

(11)   Deans, N.D., and Mann, D.P. (1982). The
       Development of a New Hardware Reliability
       Simulation. Proceedings of 7th Advances in
       Reliability Technology Symposium, Bradford,
       April.

(12)   Taylor, J. R. (1982). An Algorithm for
       Fault Tree Construction. IEEE Trans. on
       Reliability, Vol. R31, No. 2, June.

(13)   WHICH Computer. (1983), August.

(14)   Hammersley, J. M. and Handscombe, D.C.
       (1964). Monte Carlo Methods. Methuen and
       Co. Ltd., London.

REAL-TIME SYSTEMS WITH HIGHLY RELIABLE STORAGE MEDIA: A CASE STUDY

M. La Manna

Selenia S.p.A., Via S. Maria 83, Pisa, Italy

Abstract. This paper describes a system with highly reliable storage (Stable Storage) implemented on MARA (Modular Architecture for Real-Time Applications).
Stable storage is an ideal storage medium, with no failure modes which must be dealt by its clients. The behaviour of stable storage can be emulated by duplicating physical devices and managing duplication in a suitable way.
In MARA stable storage has been implemented, with regard to disk files, on the disk driver which runs on the parallel interface board.
The implemented mechanisms offer to the user a very highly reliable and continuously available storage medium for disk files, with a very high mean time between failures.

Keywords. Multiprocessing systems; reliability theory; system failure and recovery; computer interfaces; computer maintenance.

INTRODUCTION

In the systems which require high availability, suitable tools must be provided which permit to maintain the integrity and the consistency of the data-base also after a crash of the computer or of the storage medium containing part of the data-base.

The methodologies used to achieve this requirement are based on the use of atomic transactions in order to support the crash of the computer, and stable storage in order to support the crash of the storage medium.

In this paper the guidelines of the implementation of stable storage on MARA are described.

Stable storage is an ideal storage medium, on which atomic operations of "stable read" and "stable write" are defined, with the following features:

a) if an error occurs during the execution of an operation, either the operation will be correctly completed or the operation will not performed at all (i.e. a stable read will not return any read data, a stable write will not perform any update);

b) if no error occurs, the operation will be correctly completed.

Stable storage can be implemented at different levels in the operating system. The choice of the level derives from a compromise between the efficiency and the degree of fault-tolerance required. From the implementation of stable storage at a high level derive low efficiency and high degree of fault-tolerance.

In the context of this implementation on MARA, stable storage has been implemented at the disk driver level, so as to guarantee high efficiency and to maintain a discrete level of fault-tolerance.

THE PHYSICAL MODEL

The physical model is constituted by a processing module connected to a pair of disks (Fig. 1).

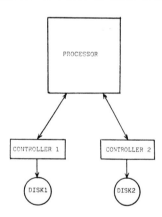

Fig. 1. The physical model

Dealing with operations on disks, two classes of events may occur:

1) desired events, which consist in the correct behaviour of the system with regard to its response to the requests;

2) undesired events, which consist in the wrong behaviour of the system.

The undesired events can be of two types:

a) errors (expected events), which consist in the foreseen and detected wrong behaviour;

b) disasters (unexpected events), which consist in the unforeseen or undetected wrong behaviour.

The proposed mechanisms ensure the integrity and consistency of the data-base in case of errors but not of disasters. An error corresponds to a detected malfunction on a physical disk. All other malfunctions are considered disasters.

A detected malfunction can be caused by a transitory or by a permanent fault. In the case of a permanent fault, the whole disk is considered as crashed.

The states of both disks (good/crashed) are continuously known by the processing module and stored in a data structure called Disk Control Record.

The Disk Control Record is updated after a fault has been detected on one disk and after one disk has been recovered.

STABLE STORAGE ALGORITHMS

Stable storage has been implemented by introducing the following operations on disks:
a) Stable-read;
b) Stable-write;
c) Disk-recovery.

All these operations has been conceived in order to give to the user the illusion of working with disks never affected by faults. In fact such operations are visible at low level by the system and eventually by a local operator (in the case of Disk-recovery), but are structured in such a manner to appear as normal operations of read and write by the point of view of the application programs.

Stable read

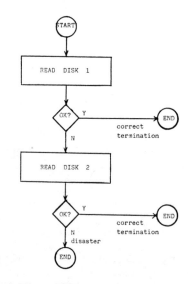

Fig. 2. Stable-read

The Stable-read operation (Fig. 2) consists in a read operation on one disk and eventually also on the other disk if the result of the first read operation has not been correctly completed. The Stable-read operation gives back to the user the read date and a termination state, which can be:
- correct termination;
- disaster.

The correct termination occurs if at least one of

the two read operations has terminated correctly. If the first read operation has terminated correctly, the second read operation will not be executed.

If the first read operation has been completed with a wrong termination as a consequence of an error detected on the disk, the disk is designated as unavailable and the system enters a degraded state. The unavailability of the wrong disk is recorded in the Disk Control Record. The wrong disk is logically isolated from the system and can be demounted and substituted without influencing the behaviour of the rest of the system. The application programs will continue to run, working on one disk only.

The degraded state will last until the wrong disk will have not been substituted and recovered.

The disaster occurs when both the read operations have terminated uncorrectly.

Stable write

The Stable-write operation (Fig. 3) consists in two write operations performed sequentially on both disks.

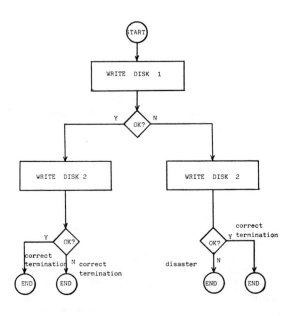

Fig. 3. Stable-write

The Stable-write operation gives back to the user a termination state, which can be:
- correct termination;
- disaster.

The correct termination occurs if both write operations have terminated correctly.

If at least one of the two operations has not terminated correctly, the system enters a degraded state, as in the case examined before. The unavailability of the wrong disk is recorded in the Disk Control Record. Until the system will remain in the degraded state, every Stable-write operation will be performed only on the available disk.

The disaster occurs when both the write operations have terminated uncorrectly.

Disk-recovery

Fig. 4. Disk-recovery

The Disk-recovery operation (Fig. 4) is automatically issued after a disk has been repaired or substituted and has the effect of restoring the contents of the disk by transferring on it the contents of the other disk. The Disk-recovery operation is performed in parallel with the normal operations on disks; so there is no moment at which the application must be suspended or delayed.

This feature permits the correct continuation of user applications and the total transparency to the user of the recovery operation.

THE DISK DRIVER

The disk driver runs on a PPI board (Parallel Processing Interface with DMA capabilities and two physical channels to interface disk controllers) and controls up to 16 physical disks connected on 4 subchannels (SUBC1-SUBC4) organized as two pairs each connected to a channel (channel 1 and 2). Each pair of subchannels is constituted of two sets of wires connected in parallel to the same channel and selectable by means of a "Select" signal. Each subchannel is connected to a controller, which drives up to four disks (Fig. 5).The disk driver has been designed as a single process, which communicates with the application processes and with the I/O system through an input queue to accept requests and an output queue to send answers. The disk process executes first of all an initialization phase and then an infinite loop. During the first phase, the driver process receives some informations from the I/O System in order to initialize its data structures.

In the loop (Fig. 6), the driver process becomes a FIFO driven process, i.e. it continuously checks its input FIFO queue to find service requests. At every time, it unqueues the requests from the input queue and decodes the type of request. The requests directed to the peripheral unit (PUs) are inqueued into the PU queues and then executed.

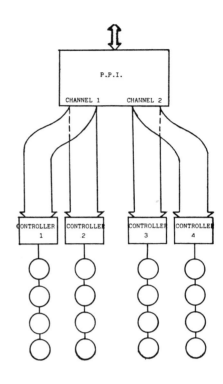

Fig. 5. Organization of the peripheral System

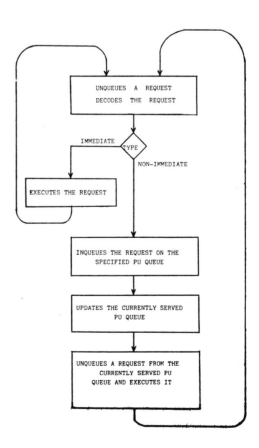

Fig. 6. Driver Loop

If the request is of the type "immediate", e.g. the activate of a disk, the driver process performs the operation, sends back the answer and goes on to find other requests.

If the request is of the type "non-immediate", e.g. a read, write, etc., it examines the request and inqueues the request into the private queue of the addressed PU.

After having inqueued the request, the driver process passes to serve the first request contained in the private queue of the actually served PU and then updates the number of the served PU. In this manner the driver process can serve one PU at a time in correspondence of each instance of the loop.

After having serviced a request, the driver process sends the answer through the output FIFO queue.

STABLE STORAGE IMPLEMENTATION

The transparency of the disk duplication to the user is implemented by making visible to the user only the PUs of the channel 1 (totally 8 PUs), and by masking the PUs of the channel 2. When for example an application program issues a request for activating the PU numbered n (n=1-8), the driver will activate the PU numbered n and the PU numbered (n+8) belonging to the other channel. In effect, the user works on 8 stable PUs which correspond to 8 pairs of physical PUs. To each stable PU a Disk Control Record is associated in the driver memory.

The operations of the "non-immediate" type can be classified into updating (write, seek-write, etc.), and non-updating operations (seek, read, seek-read).

The non-updating operations are performed only on one PU and are executed in conformity with the philosophy of the "stable-read" operation (Fig. 7).

The updating operations are performed on both PUs and are executed in conformity with the philosophy of the "stable write" operation (Fig. 8).

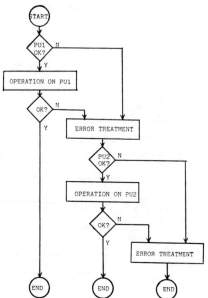

Fig. 7. Non-updating operations

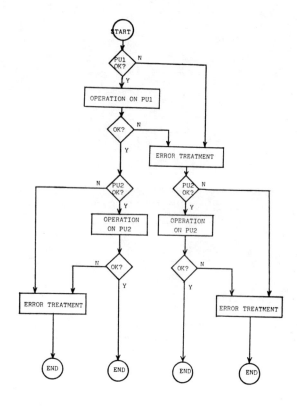

Fig. 8. Updating operations

As a consequence of the faults eventually detected on disks by the driver process while performing operations, each of the 8 stable PUs may be in four different states (Fig. 9):

- normal, which corresponds to the absence of faults on both disks;
- prerecovery, which occurs after discovering a faulty disk, so that only one disk is operative;
- recovery, which occurs after the reentry of the faulty disk and lasts until the contents of the disk have not been completely restored;
- disaster, which occurs when both disks are recognized faulty. In this case the stable PU must be completely reinitialized and the old data will be lost.

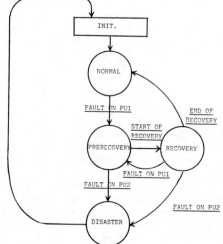

Fig. 9. States of a stable disk

CONCLUSION

The use of the stable storage methodology highly improves the reliability of the storage media. For the presented model, in the hypotesis of a physical disk's MTBF (mean time between failures) of 4.000 hours and MTTR (mean time to repair) of 40 hours, the stable disk's MTBF will be about 50 times 4.000 hours, i.e. more than 20 years.

The implementation of stable storage at the driver level does not affect considerably the efficiency of disk operations, because only updating operations cause an additional overhead. In effect, updating operations are generally only 20% of the total and very often seekwrite operations occur where the time requested is mainly due to the seek (because it implies a mechanical movement of the disk head) than to the write. Moreover the two seek operations on a disk pair can be easily overlapped.

It has to be pointed out that the introduction of physical disk pairs can ulteriorly enhance reliability. In fact, a parallel action of scrubbing can be performed, which consists in the comparison of the contents of the two disks, sector by sector, with the consequent detection and correction of soft errors, i.e. errors due to transitory faults or surface demagnetization. In this manner, only the errors caused by permanent damage of the disk surface (hard errors) will contribute to the MTBF of a physical disk. So the improvement in the total MTBF can be even much greater than the one evaluated before.

REFERENCES

Ciompi, P., M. La Manna, C. Lissoni, I.R. Martin, L. Simoncini, (1983). A highly available multimicroprocessor system for real-time applications. Proc. of SAFECOMP-83, Cambridge, pp. 247-253.

Ciompi, P., M. La Manna, C. Lissoni, L. Simoncini, (1983). A redundant distributed system supporting atomic transactions for real-time control. Proc. of Real-Time Systems Symposium, Arlington, pp. 258-267.

Lampson, B.W., H.E. Sturgis, (1976). Crash recovery in a distributed data storage system. Xerox Palo Alto Research Center Report.

Martin, I.R. (1981). MARA: an overview of the civil implementation. Selenia Internal Report.

REQUIREMENTS AND DESIGN FOR A DISTRIBUTED COMPUTERIZED SYSTEM FOR SAFETY AND CONTROL APPLICATIONS

S. Bagnasco, F. Manzo and F. Piazza

Ansaldo S.p.A./Div. NIRA, Via dei Pescatori, 35, Genoa, Italy

Abstract. The major functions and architectures of Computer Based Protection and Control Systems for Nuclear Power Plants are designed nowadays taking into account the following basic ideas:

. defense in depth. That is independency, redundancy and diversity. To provide several levels of defense so that failures in equipments and mistakes by people will be covered;

. distributability, modularity and flexibility. To cut down the construction costs, provide significant installation time saving and reduce spare part inventory;

. fault tolerance, self diagnosis and graceful degradation. To face faults, errors and other anomalous or unexpected behaviours and give practically one hundred percent availability.

The functions and the architectures presented in the paper, related to the development of distributed microcomputer based Protection and Control Systems for application to Nuclear Power Plants, are especially tailored for the Italian plants. The project, which is under the responsibility of WESTINGHOUSE, has the participation of various Italian organisations, led by ANSALDO S.p.A./Div. NIRA.

Keywords. Safety Systems; Microprocessors; Computer Architecture; Industrial Control.

Acknowledgements. Major contributors to the system architectures were G. Morrison, R. J. Weisner, W. Ghrist and G. W. Remley.

INTRODUCTION

The basic objectives of Nuclear Power Plants are to supply electrical energy under optimum economic conditions to the power distribution network on demand as safety and reliably as it is possible with present day technology. Operative experience on Nuclear Power Generating Plants and, in particular, the results of the TMI accidents studies, have shown the necessity to have a high system integration level in the automation of the plant, in order to generate a safe and efficient plant control in normal operating conditions as well as in emergency occurrences.

In January 1984, ANSALDO S.p.A./Div. NIRA Italian supplier of Nuclear Plants - and WESTINGHOUSE/WRD, agreed to develop an Integrated Protection and Control System (IPCS) prototype based on microprocessor technology taking advantage of WESTINGHOUSE experience. Functional requirements, typical of Italian Nuclear Plant Reference Project, are considered as specific input to the entire IPCS development program.

The defense in depth philosophy is applied: the IPCS consists of two completely separated and independent systems:

. the Integrated Protection System (IPS), that senses the plant parameters meaningful for safety status and provides the necessary actuating signals to shut down the reactor and actuate dedicated engineered safety features (ESF), in order to prevent an accident or to mitigate its effects to acceptable limits;
. the Integrated Control System (ICS), that provides - in normal operating conditions - for automatic and manual controls of the Rod Control System, the Reactor Coolant System, the Chemical and Volume Control System, the Feedwater Control System, the Steam Dump System and other less relevant systems.

At the present time, the development program is at the end of the requirements phase. The architectures described in the paper are under review and can be affected by changes in the near future.

GOALS AND DESIGN REQUIREMENTS

The high demands on Nuclear Power plant reliability and availability require high levels of quality in the system structural design. Moreover, the Protection System is designed to meet the requirements stated by the applied regulations, codes and standards such as testability, single failure avoidance, common mode failure avoidance and operability under design events. Good engineering practice has suggested that testability feature and single failure avoidance criteria should also be applied to the control system design. Flexibility, modularity, plant performances optimization, minimization of maintenance and test effort, easier installation and system integration are typical goals of the 80's technology. The IPCS is designed to achieve these goals. This is accomplished by implementing in a distributed microprocessor based architecture the following design requirements: fault tolerance, fault detection, separation, majority voting (with bypass), and independence, as shown in Table 1.

Fault Tolerance

The key ingredient in all fault tolerance techniques is redundancy.
IPS uses different kind of redundancy techniques.

Redundancy at sensor level. Four channel sets in parallel are used to measure the same physical variable. Two out of four voting logic with bypass is applied to the redundant signals.

Redundancy at system actuation level. Four separate electrical trains of ESF actuation equipments are provided for component actuation. This redundancy is a direct consequence of actuated equipments redundancy itself.

Redundancy at component actuation level. Two out of three majority voting logic is applied to actuate the on-off components.

Redundancy at man-machine interface. Redundancy is applied at man-machine interface level. Two multiplexing units to interface the operator commands and display signals are employed for each electrical train.

The ICS will derive certain of its inputs from signals which are present in the IPS.

This assures that the plant will be controlled by the same measurements with which it is protected. Moreover, the ICS acquires some redundant signals by itself. Two out of three majority logic is applied to them.

The active redundancy concept by hardware replication is extensively applied to the ICS. In particular, all the controllers driving modulating equipments are redundant, incorporating into the ICS fault detection and fault recovery capability. The selection between the redundant subsystems is made using standby replacement.

Two out of three majority logic is applied to actuate on-off components. Graceful degradation capability is implemented in the ICS. For example, since the ICS handles both the automatic and manual controls, when a sensor is out of order, eventually jeopardizing the plant performances, the subsystem, in connection with the sensor, can revert itself to manual mode.

Another way to implement fault tolerance capability is offered by the principle of diversity. Functional diversity is applied in the IPS: different physical parameters are used as initiating criteria for the same protective action. Different parameters are processed in different subsystems.

Fault Detection

The availability of the plant is improved by application of fault detection techniques. Two different facilities are provided: automatic test - test sequences are automatically initiated - and self diagnostics - on line testing - capabilities.

Bypass Capability

The bypass capability allows the IPS to perform the test sequence without system reconfiguration. The majority voting automatically reverts itself from two out of four to two out of three and - under multiple bypass requests - from two out of three to one out of two.

Separation and Independence

Electrical separation is applied by the extensive use of optical isolation devices and fiber optic connections in both the IPS and the ICS.

Physical separation is achieved in the IPS by installing the four instrument channel sets in different fire zones. Complete independence among the reactor trip, the ESF actuation and the control functions is maintained.

IPS SYSTEM OVERVIEW

The plant protection system provides actuating signals to the reactor trip breakers and to the Engineered Safety Features equipment in the event of an accident. The Integrated Protection System comprises the cabinets, electronics and other associated equipments that provide these protective functions. The scope of the IPS encompasses the sensor input circuitry and the manual actuation switches and their input circuitry through to the reactor trip switchgear and the power switching devices which control the plant safety equipment. This equipment includes motor control centers for motor operated valve control, pilot solenoids for air operated valve control and circuit breakers for large motor/pump control.

Figure 1 is a block diagram of the IPS. As this figure shows, the IPS consists of several major groups of equipment:
  - Integrated Protection Cabinets (IPCs)
  - Engineered Safety Features Actuation Cabinets (ESFACs)
  - Protection Logic Cabinets (PLCs)
  - Logic Bus
  - Control Board Multiplexers (CB MUXs)

The IPS is divided into four individual channel sets (I,II,III,IV) which are physically and electrically separated from each other. Each channel set contains sensor and manual inputs, signal conditioning, reactor trip and system-level ESF logic. Each channel set is implemented in an Integrated Protection Cabinet which is composed of several subsystems.

The IPS also contains four electrical trains (A,B,C,D) of ESF actuation equipment. Each ESF train is implemented with a single ESFAC and a group of PLCs. Each ESF train receives input from all four channel sets.

There are three methods employed by the IPS to communicate data among the various cabinets and subsystems of the IPS and to communicate data from the IPS to other external systems: serial data links, data buses and parallel I/O circuits.

Serial Data Links

  - Communication between the IPS and other systems: The Integrated Protection System provides data to several other system in the plant including the Integrated Control System (ICS), the Plant Computer (PC) and the Plant Monitoring System (PMS). This data is transmitted in a simplex, serial fashion via fiber optic data links. The use of fiber optic data links for this application maintains electrical separation between the IPS and external systems. The use of simplex data links prevents feedback error transmission.

  - Communication between various cabinets within the IPS: Simplex, serial fiber optic data links.

  - Communication between subsystems within a cabinet: Simplex, electrical data links.

Data Buses

  - High speed data highway communication network is utilized to connect each ESFAC to its associated Protection Logic Cabinets and the Main Control Board Multiplexers (MCB MUXs). This network, the Logic Bus, consists of two optical data highways.

  - Serial interconnect bus is utilized to connect the PLC logic computers to the input/output interface. The network consists of three of these serial interconnect buses for each PLC. The information in each bus is used to perform a two-out-of-three logic at equipment actuation level.

Parallel I/O

  - Each susbsystem contains some hardwired parallel I/O capability for reading switch positions, driving interface devices etc. In order to preserve the electrical independence between subsystems, the digital I/O circuitry is optically buffered.

INTEGRATED PROTECTION CABINETS

Four identical Integration Protection Cabinets (IPCs) exist within the IPS. Each cabinet is associated with one channel of IPS equipment. The four IPCs provide for the Reactor Trip and Engineered Safety Features redundancy in the IPS.

There are two Reactor Trip (RT) Subsystem in each IPC. The RT functions are divided between the two RT Subsystems to provide functional diversity for accident protection. The primary functions of each of these subsystems are to process inputs and provide reactor trip signals (logic output of the comparison between a plant parameter and its corresponding safety setpoint) to the Trip Logic Subsystems.

Two Engineered Safety Features (ESF) Subsystems are present in each IPC. Their primary function is to process inputs, calculate ESF partial trips and provide this information to the ESFACs. The ESF functions are divided among the two ESF subsystems in the same manner that the RT functions are divided into the two RT Subsystems. That is, the two ESF Subsystems provide diverse ESF actuations.

The Trip Logic Subsystems are composed of the following major parts:

- Global Trip Subsystem
- Trip Enable Subsystem
- Dynamic Trip Bus

The Global Trip and the Trip Enable Subsystems collect the reactor partial trips and bypass status of the individual reactor trip functions in their own channel set and transmit this data to the redundant channel sets. These subsystems also receive the reactor partial trips and bypass status from each of the other three channel sets. The Global Trip Subsystem uses this information to compute the channel set reactor trip request on the basis of the status of the other channel sets, the Trip Enable Subsystem looks for the confirmation of a reactor trip request generated in its own channel set.

The valid requests are sent to the Dynamic Trip bus where, at hardware level, the channel set reactor trip signal is actuated deenergizing the undervoltage trip attachment on each of the two RT breakers associated with that channel set.

The Communication subsystem provides a central point in the IPC for data acquisition, storage and transmission. This subsystem is connected via data electrical data links to all of the other subsystems and provides a communication interface to external systems.

All of these external system interfaces are accomplished via fiber optic data links for isolation purposes.

The Automatic Tester Subsystem provides a means of testing the operability of the IPC. It is connected via electrical data links to all of the other subsystems in its channel set. The Automatic Tester simulates inputs (via analog, digital and data link test injection), monitors logic states and calculations (via data link from each subsystem) and data links emanating from its IPC. This allows the Automatic Tester Subsystem to completely test the functions of all the subsystems in its IPC.

To the extent possible and practical, the subsystems are electrically and physically independent of each other. Each subsystem has its own power supply. Each subsystem which requires raw sensor data contains its own analog to digital conversion capability.

Subsystems which require inputs from the same sensor must be connected together. However, this sensor sharing among subsystems is accomplished ahead of the signal conditioning modules in each of the affected subsystems. This arrangement minimizes the possibility of a failure in one subsystem resulting in a failure in another subsystem.

ENGINEERED SAFETY FEATURES ACTUATION CABINET

The main functions performed are:

- Receive ESF bistable trip and bypass signals from all four IPCs and perform on them the two-out-of-four voting;

- perform system-level ESF logic and provide the system-level actuation outputs to the Protection Logic Cabinets via the logic Bus.

Two ESF Actuation Subsystems exist in each ESFAC. They are redundant computer systems and both transmit system-level commands to the PCL over the corresponding logic Bus. The voting in each redundant ESF Actuation Subsystem is done in two voting computers on an ESF basis.

The functional diversity provided by the two ESF subsystems in the IPCs is therefore maintained through the two-out-of-four voting in the ESFACs.

The Automatic Tester/Data Acquisition Subsystem (AT/DA) is the third subsystem in the ESFACs. This subsystem functions as a central data collection point for the ESFAC. Each of the other two subsystems are connected to the AT/DA Subsystem via a serial data link. The AT/DA subsystem also controls fiber optic data links from the ESFAC to external systems. It functions as an ESFAC tester in much the same way as the Automatic Tester Subsystem functions in the IPC. Each redundant ESF Actuation Subsystem is tested individually. One half of the ESFAC can function normally while the other half is being tested. This arrangement precludes sacrificing availability in order to provide testability.

INTEGRATED LOGIC SYSTEM

The Integrated Logic System (ILS) is composed of the following equipment:

- Four Logic Buses (one per ESF train)
- Four redundant Main Control Board Multiplexers (one per ESF train)
- Four redundant Emergency Control Board Multiplexers (one per ESF train)
- Four sets of Protection Logic Cabinets (one per ESF train)

Logic Buses

The Logic Buses provide the communication interface between the ESFACs, the MCB MUXs and the PLCs. Each bus connects only the equipment (ESFAC, Mcb mux and PCLs) in the same electrical train. It is composed of two data highways utilizing fiber optic cable as transmission medium. One of the highways connects together one of the redundant ESF Actuation Subsystems in that train's ESFAC, one of the redundant halves of the MCB MUX in that train and every PLC in that train.

Control Board Multiplexers

The MCB/ECB MUXs provide for redundant transmission of componentlevel manual actuation signals from the Main and Emergency Control Boards to the PLCs and for reception of component status information from the PLCs for display on the Main and Emergency Control Boards.
Each MCB MUX and each ECB MUX contains two redundant halves or subsystems. The MCB MUX is connected via a Logic Bus to the ESFAC and the PLCs in its train.

The ECB MUX is connected to its train's PLCs via redundant, electrical, serial data links. The ECBMUXs utilize simplex, serial data links, while the MCB MUXs utilize data highways. The ECB communication is accmplished via electrical signal, while the MCB's via optical signals. These differences between the control board multiplexers provide functional and hardware diversity for the manual control function of plant components.

Protection Logic Cabinets

Two redundant functional logic subsystems (FLSs) are housed within each PLCs. Each of them has its own computer bus which contains two Functional Logic Processor (FLPs). The plant component I/O modules (2/3 voted and contact inputs) are connected to the FLPs on the two computer buses via three independent, medium-speed, serial interconnect buses (I/O buses). Two of the three I/O buses are directly controlled by two logic processors, one of each computer bus. The third I/O bus is controlled by the pair of logic processor connected by the parallel I/O communication lines. Only one of these two logic processors controls the I/O modules over the bus at any given time. The other processor is used as a back-up and is capable of taking over control of the highway when failure of the active processor is detected. All four logic processors are sent to the I/O modules via the I/O buses. The I/O modules perform two out of three voting on the signals from the logic processors to determine the status of their outputs which control the plant components.
A portable terminal device may be connected to the maintenance CPU in order to monitor the operation of the logic CPUs and to permit to request individual power outputs to be energized or de-energized when in local maintenance mode.
It is also useful for testing the external wiring and actuators during installation even if the control room and/or the ICs are not yet functional.

ICS SYSTEM OVERVIEW

The ICS provides for control of the plant in normal operating (non-emergency) conditions. It includes the equipments from the process sensor input circuitry through to the power switching devices or modulating signal outputs. Modulating outputs include valve positioners, pump speed controllers, the rod position controller and the main turbine-generator load controller.

Non-modulating devices include motor starters for motor-operated valves, breakers for heaters and for motor operated valves.

Figure 2 is a block diagram of the ICS. As this figure shows, the ICS consists of several major groups of equipment:

- Integrated Control Cabinets (ICCs)
- Process and Logic Buses
- Control Logic Cabinets (CLCs)
- Control Board Multiplexers (CM MUXs)

The ICS:

- automates all control functions: xenon control, power distribution control, boron systems control;
- automates selected operating strategies;
- improves operator/dispatcher interfaces;
- provides load regulation/frequency control.

PROCESS AND LOGIC BUSES

The various subsystems communicate among themselves over two high speed data buses, the process bus and the logic bus, each consisting of a redundant pair of highways. Partial cross-coupling of control subsystems to the highways enhances the redundancy of the system. Where cross coupling is used it provides a connection from each of a pair of redundant controllers to each of a pair of redundant highways. The process bus distributes input information from the signal selector, status and alarm information and other data communication among the control cabinet subsystems. It also passes input and feedback (display) data between the control subsystems and the control board operator interface modules (OIMs) associated with modulated components. The logic bus passes automatic and manual actuation demands from the control board and the control subsystems to the control logic cabinets. It passes status feedback from the control logic cabinets to the control board for display and to the control subsystems for control, diagnostics and remote communication.

INTEGRATED CONTROL CABINETS

The subsystems contained within the ICCs can be grouped into three functional categories:

- input processing: signal selector along with the signal selector tester;

- control calculation and outputs: the major subsystems which perform control algorithms for modulating control: the power control, the power optimization, the feedwater control, the group 1 and the group 2 subsystems;
- status outputs. This is the monitoring interface subsystem.

Signal Selector (SS)

The redundant SS subsystems provide the ICS with the ability to derive certain of its inputs from the IPS. In order to do this certain measures must be taken to ensure the independence of the ICS and IPS. The SS has the ability to select those protection system signals that are representative of the actual status of the plant and to reject those signals which are in error. Each SS receives from each IPC on a simplex serial data link via fiber optical cable and provides validated data to one of the redundant highways of the process bus. The redundancy protects against a failure and provides the capability to remove one of the selectors from service.

Signal Selector Tester (SST)

The SST provides for periodic testing of the two signal selector subsystems in the ICC. The SST transmits simulated IPC data link messages to the signal selector under test injecting them into the data link receiver circuits after the optical data has been converted to electrical form. Moreover, it monitors the output of the SS being tested by examining data that the SS is transmitting on the process bus. The tester sends information to the other ICC in order to allow the controllers to ignore process values coming from a SS under test.

Control Calculation and Outputs

These subsystems are the actual controlling subsystems that provide outputs to modulating control devices and system level logic control signals to the CLC's. Each of these subsystems is redundant. the distribution of control functions among these subsystems is itemized as follows:

- Power Control Subsystem (PCS): this subsystem automatically regulates reactor power by controlling boron concentration, rod position (by interface to the Rod Control System), and turbine load (by interface to the Turbine Control System).

- Feedwater Control Subsystem (FWCS): Control of the Feedwater Control Valves, Bypass Valves and Feedwater Pump Speed is provided by this subsystem.

- Control Group Number 1 (CG1): This subsystem provides several control functions: among them are pressurizer Pressure Control, Pressurizer level Control, Boron Thermal Regeneration Control System (BTRS) and the Equipment Floor & Chemical Drain Collection System (EFDCS).

- Control Group Number 2 (CG2): This subsystem contains the Steam Dump Control, which controls the steam dum valves to regulate reactor loading during transients. It also contains the Chemical & Volume Control System (CVCS), Main Steam & Feedwater miscellaneous control (MSFS) and the Sept Fuel Pool Control System (SFPCS).

Each of these subsystems is redundant. Hardware and software functions built into each subsystem will detect a failure of one of the subsysems of a pair and will automatically transfer control of the outputs to the non-failed system.

Switches located on the subsystem card frame front panel permit manual transfer of control selection. When a subsystem is not in control, it is in stand-by status and it will execute tracking algorithms which places it in a state capable of assuming control without upset.
All the subsystems interface both the buses.

Power Optimization Subsystem (OPT)

The Power Optimization Subsystem provides adjustments to various parameters within the Power Control Subsystem to permit an optimization of the control algorithms being implemented. Operator input is needed for the selection of the desired operating mode and for the entering of needed data, such as anticipated plant load requirements. The Power Optimization Subsystem also provides communications with the Remote Dispatch System. This includes sending plant status information needed for dispatch calculations and receiving plant load demand requests to be passed to the Turbine Control System. Load demand requests are output to the Turbine Control System by the Power Control Subsystem.

Operator data input and display are provided by a keyboard and display device in the control board. Plant operating status is sent to a Remote Dispatch Center and turbine load demand requirements are received from the same center via serial data link.

Monitoring Interface Subsystem (MIS)

All information in the control system used by the plant computer and by the plant alarm and display system(s) is transmitted by the MIS. There are two redundant subsystems to prevent the loss of all alarm and displays originating by the ICS.

CONTROL LOGIC CABINETS

The CLCs are quite similar to the PLCs, but they interface with the ECR. The CLCs interface the logic bus and field contact inputs.

CONTROL BOARD MULTIPLEXERS

The Main Control Board Multiplexer Subsystems serve to concentrate the information passing between the Operator Interface Modules (OIM's) in the control room and the Integrated Control Cabinets (ICC's) or the Control Logic Cabinets. There are two multiplexers:

- The manual/Auto OIM Multiplexer provides communication with the OIM's for modulating control.

- The Logic OIM Multiplexer provides communication with the OIM's associated with non-modulating components.

REFERENCES

WESTINGHOUSE E.C.   Bypass logic for the WESTINGHOUSE Integrated Protection System. WCAP-8897

WESTINGHOUSE E.C.   Axial Power Distribution Monitoring Using Four-Section Ex-Core Detectors. WCAP-9105

WESTINGHOUSE E.C.   WESTINGHOUSE Model 414 Control System Signal Selection Device. WCAP-8899

GALLAGHER J.M.   FISHER J. (1982). IAEA Guidelines and IEC Recommendations for Design of Nuclear Power Plant Control and Instrumentation Systems. IAWA-SM-265

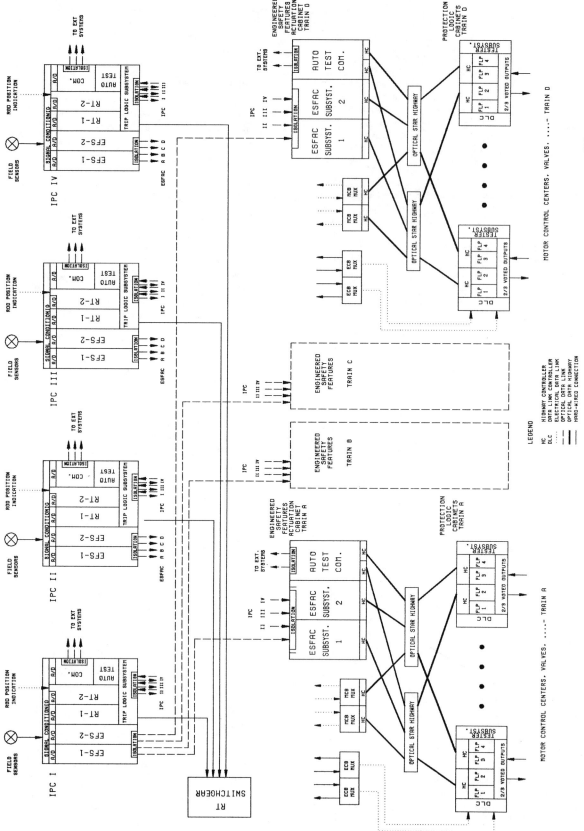

FIG. 1 - IPS ARCHITECTURE

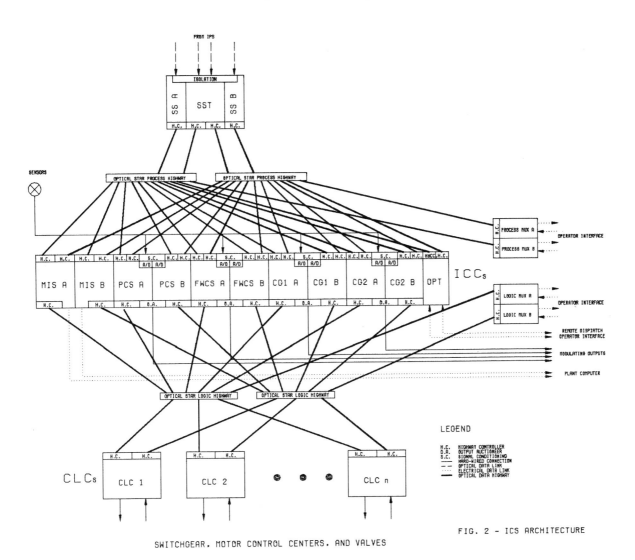

FIG. 2 - ICS ARCHITECTURE

SWITCHGEAR, MOTOR CONTROL CENTERS, AND VALVES

LEGEND :

P = PROTECTION SYSTEM
C = CONTROL SYSTEM

	REDUNDANCY	FUNCTIONAL DIVERSITY	FAULT DETECTION	SEPARATION	DISTRIBUTED ARCHITECTURE	BYPASS CAPABILITY	DIGITAL TECHNOLOGY	INDEPENDENCE
MAXIMUM RELIABILITY	C/P	P	C/P	C/P	C/P		C/P	C/P
TESTABILITY	C/P					P		
PLANT AVAILABILITY	C/P		C/P			P	C	
SINGLE FAILURE AVOIDANCE	C/P			C/P	C/P			C/P
COMMON MODE FAILURE AVOIDANCE		P			P			
OPERABILITY UNDER DESIGN BASIS EVENTS	P			P				P
FLEXIBILITY & MODULARITY					C/P		C/P	
PLANT PERFORMANCES OPTIMIZATION							C/P	
MINIMIZE MAINTENANCE & TEST EFFORT			C/P			P	C/P	
EASIER INSTALLATION					C/P		C/P	
SYSTEM INTEGRATION							C/P	

Table 1-IPCS GOALS AND DESIGN REQUIREMENTS

DESIGN OF A SELF-CHECKING MICROPROCESSOR FOR REAL-TIME APPLICATIONS

A. Osseiran*, M. Nicolaidis*, J. P. Schoellkopf,* B. Courtois*, D. Bied-Charreton** and B. Le Trung**

*TIM3 Laboratory, IMAG-INPG, 46, Avenue Félix Viallet, 38031 Grenoble cedex, France
**Institut de Recherche des Transports, 2, Avenue du Général Malleret-Joinville, 94114 Arcueil cedex, France

ABSTRACT

This paper deals with the design of a microprocessor dedicated to safety applications and more particularly to Automatic Train Control. This microprocessor is self-checking i.e. able to detect its own errors. Its name is COBRA for COntroller with Built in self-checking for Real-time Applications.

In the design of this circuit, low-level fault hypotheses for the N-MOS technology are considered. In this case redundant faults, i.e. undetectable faults, generally exist in any design and thus fault detecting capabilities must be provided for sequences of faults. The functional circuits will be Strongly Fault Secure [SMI 78] and the checkers will be Strongly Code Disjoint [NIC 84-2].

COBRA is a micropressor-type device, its data path processes independently 19 different signals : date out external events, measure frequencies, and supervise 14 level inputs (binary values). 7 independent outputs could be binary values, or clocks, for 3 of them. The data path communicates with an external PROM, used as program storage for COBRA. This PROM is addressed with 14 bits, multiplexed over the 8-bit address/data internal bus of the data path. It contains also one serial I/O, a 64 byte RAM, and 3 independent 14 bits counters. An 8 bit ALU could be used for arithmetical or logical operations. A set of 42 instructions processes all these operations.

1. INTRODUCTION

Safety is of prime concern in the field of ground transportation systems, particularly in the design of Automatic Train Operation equipment.

Such a system is generally separated in two channels :
* the driving channel which drives the train and the safety of which is of no concern
* the Automatic Train Protection channel which activates the emergency brake in case of over-driving or failures.

The use of a conventional microprocessor for the ATP channel is a heavy solution, generally demanding duplication and matching. Tests must be periodically performed to detect latent failures. The coverage of such tests is never very well known.

For these reasons, a Self checking microprocessor is of great interest. In a Self-Checking circuit, the functional blocks process with coded data and are designed in such a manner that any error gives way to a noncode word. Checkers are associated to these functional blocks in order to gives an error signal when they receive at their input a non code word.

This technique has been introduced by Carter (1968) and formally defined by [AND 71]. It has given birth to large developments, function of code and failures hypotheses.

Index terms : VLSI Design, Self-Checking circuits, Strongly Fault Secure Network, Strongly Code Disjoint Checkers.

2. PRINCIPLES OF THE DESIGN OF SELF-CHECKING CIRCUITS

2.1. Foreword

2.1.1. The on-line testing of this circuit is continuous ; it is achieved simultaneously with the application program and uses the same data.

2.1.2. Fig. 1 represents the general structure of the basic cell of a self-checking circuit. The functional circuit block maps encoded inputs into encoded outputs and the checker checks encoded outputs and delivers error indication signals if any.

This network must achieve the Totally-Self-Checking Goal i.e. the first erroneous output due to a fault must cause an error indication at the outputs of the checker.

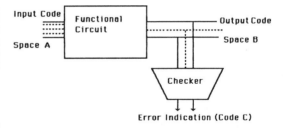

Fig 1 – The Basic Cell

2.2. Fault Hypotheses

2.2.1 Low-level fault hypothesis

Recently, it has been shown that the classical stuck-at logical fault model is not sufficient to represent all failures that can occur in integrated circuits [GAL 80].

This is the reason why it is necessary to use fault models representing real failures occuring in integrated circuits which are referred to as low level fault hypothesis.

3 classes of fault hypothesis for the N-MOS technology have been proposed by [COU 81]. In the design of COBRA, class 1 will be used ; it includes :
- MOS stuck-on and stuck-open
- failed contact or precontact
- cuts of lines : aluminium, diffusion, polysilicon
- 1 short between an aluminium line and the physically nearest one.
- 1 short between a diffusion line and the physically nearest one.

2.2.2. The problem of redundant faults

When using such low-level fault hypothesis, redundant faults, i.e. undetectable faults, generally exist in any design. (For example, a short between power lines).

The properties of the functional block and of the checker must take into account these redundant faults. They are to be defined in regards of sequence of faults.

2.3 Basic definitions

The following definitions are due to [AND 71] :

<u>Definition</u> : A circuit is self-testing if, for every fault from a prescribed set, the circuit produces a noncode output for at least one code input.

<u>Definition</u> : A circuit is fault secure if, for every fault from a prescribed set, the circuit never produces an incorrect code output for code inputs.

<u>Definition</u> : A circuit is totally self-checking if it is both self-testing and fault secure.

Totally Self-Checking circuits are very desirable for use in self-checking design but these properties can no longer be used in the case of low-level fault hypotheses because of the loss of self-testing property.

2.4. Widening these definitions : SFS Functional Blocks and SCD checkers

2.4.1. The following is taken from [SMI 78]. We consider multiple-input, multiple-output combinational logic network G. If a network G has r primary input lines, then the 2^r binary vectors of length r form the input space X of G. The output space Y is similarly defined to be the set of 2^q, where G has q primary outputs. During normal, i. e. failure free, operation G receives only a subset of X called the input code space A and produces a subset of Y called the output code space B. Members of a code space are called code words. under faults, noncode words may be produced (See fig. 2).

The output code space of the checker is denoted C ; all outputs which are out of C are error indications .

Let C_f be the class of fault -hypothesis used for the design and F the set of all possible faults f.

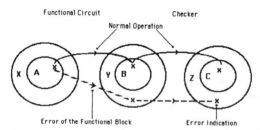

Fig. 2 - Operations of the Basic Cell : SFS Functional Block +SCD checker

2.4.2. Strongly Fault Secure Circuits

Strongly Fault Secure circuits have been introduced by Smith and Metze [SMI 78], to overcome the difficulty presented by circuits that are not Totally Self-Checking because of undetectable faults .

<u>Definition</u> : A functional circuit is Strongly Fault Secure for the class C_f of fault hypothesis if for all sequences of faults f_i belonging to C_f which can occur :
  - either the function of the circuit is not modified
  - or every erroneous output is a noncode word and there is at least one input code -word that results in a noncode output word .

2.4.3. Strongly Code Disjoint Checkers

Strongly Code Disjoint Checkers have been defined by [NIC 84-2]

<u>Definiton</u> : A network is code disjoint if it always maps code inputs into code outputs and noncode inputs into noncode outputs .

It is evident that a checker must be code disjoint since it must produce an error indication when the output of the functional block is a noncode word ; but the code disjoint property is not sufficient for a checker associated to a SFS circuit since the fault sequences within the checker must also produce an error indication in case of the loss of the code-disjunction property . Moreover the fault secure property is not really necessary for a checker.

These two remarks led to the definition of Strongly Code Disjoint checkers which are the necessary companions of SFS circuits.

<u>Definition</u> : A checker is Strongly Code Disjoint for the class C_f of fault hypothesis if it is code disjoint and if for all sequences of faults f_i belonging to C_f which can occur :
  - either the checker is still code disjoint (redundancy)
  - or there is at least one input code word that results in a non code word output i. e. an error indication .

2.5. The Totally Self-Checking Goal

2.5.1. The Hypothesis H2

After the occurrence of a fault in the functional block, a sufficient time elapses so that all code inputs A are applied before a second fault occurs in the functional block or a fault occurs in the checker . After the occurence of a fault in the checker, a sufficient time elapses so that all code inputs B occur before a second fault occurs in the functional block or a fault occurs in the checker .

2.5.2. The following proposition can then be demonstrated[NIC 84-1]
<u>Theorem</u> : Assuming hypothesis H2, a system composed of :
  - a Strongly Fault Secure circuit
  - and a Strongly Code Disjoint Checker
achieves the Totally Self-Checking (i.e. the first erroneous output of the functional circuit will cause an error indication at the output of the checker).

Remark : it is shown in [JAN 84] that the TSC Goal can also be achieved with a weaker hypothesis if the checker has stronger properties .

2.6. General notions about the design of SFS circuits and SCD checkers

For the class 1 of fault hypotheses, layout rules have been derived for the design of SFS functional blocks where output code space will detect single [NIC 85-1], unidirectional and multiple errors [NIC 84-2] .

These errors may be checked respectively by :
  - single parity codes
  - m-out-of-n or Berger codes
  - duplication or double-rail codes

No general layout rules are necessary for the design of checkers since on the contrary of functional blocks, they are designed for one, and only one, function. Thus it is sufficient to know one good design respecting the assumptions, for each type of code .

3 - DESIGN OF COBRA

This device is a single chip processor for specific applications, mainly in ground transportation systems.

The top-down methodology [SCH 77] has been used for the design of COBRA, since the main requirements of transportation system controls, are to measure speed, and to supervise some parameters variations, e.g. related to position, direction, and speed level, etc...

All the functional blocks of the data path are coded each with its appropriate checking structure in order to guarantee the SFS properties. In case of any detected fault during the system operating cycle, the device will indicate it and impose the emergency brake.

3.1 - Inputs/Outputs

COBRA has two kinds of I/O relative to the parameters to measure:
- speed is generally measured using a toothed wheel transforming it directly into frequency. A second way to measure speed is to count equally separated pulses sent by the railway; this way is also a frequency measurement.
- direction, station presence detecting, and vehicles moving modes, are all represented as logical levels, e.g., "zero" for perturbed moving mode, and "one" for normal mode.

Thus, COBRA has specific Frequency and Level Inputs which have to consider these parameters and to measure them independently.

3.1.1 - Level Inputs

A special instructions subset is attached to the Level inputs structure in order to fetch, load, transfer one bit data, and to do logical operations with one input and with the one-bit accumulator of the Logic Unit specific to the Level inputs structure. Figure 3 shows the part of the data path related to the Level inputs structure all with the appropriate self-checking structure: checkers, parity coding, and the structure duplication for the double-rail checking.

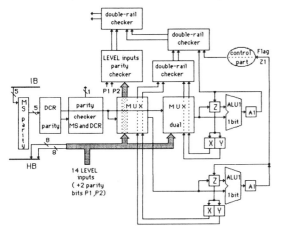

Figure 3 - Level Input self-checking structure

MS contains the word used by the decoder DCR, which selects one input of the MUX and sends it for treatment in ALU1 or loads it in Z. Special instructions load Z contents into X or Y which are considered as inputs by MUX (same as the 14 inputs). The whole structure is duplicated and coded with the double-rail code, to be then sent into the double-rail checkers structure.

The 14 inputs are coded with the parity code. Each one of the 2 parity bits codes 7 inputs. The parity functions are created before the input pads with external parity generators, and they are checked after the MUX in the inputs parity checkers.

3.1.2 - Frequency inputs

The frequency inputs of COBRA are considered as interruption inputs with priority order. They are especially provided to determine a frequency threshold by comparing a fixed value (by the program) with a period measured by a self incrementing register. The emergency brake is imposed when the measured value is higher than the fixed threshold values which correspond to an exeeding of the speed limit in the case of speed measurement.

An interruption is requested each time a frequency input receives a rising edge from an external sensing device, e.g., the toothed wheel for the speed measurement. An interruption subroutine compares the contents of the self-incrementing register CR to the fixed value contained in the corresponding register H (Figure 4).

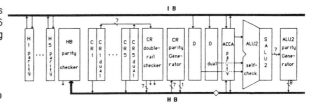

Figure 4 - Self-checking Frequency inputs structure.

If no rising edge arrives to the concerned Frequency input, CR continue its incrementation until it reaches the value of 11...1, and will keep it until the following rising edge, where CR starts its incrementation again for a new cycle. The frequency range measurable with this structure is programmable, and could be different for each register. The target is to cover frequencies ranging from a few Hz to almost 1 KHz, which is reasonable for transportation systems.

3.1.3 - Level/Frequency Outputs

One instruction could be used to activate one of the 7 possible outputs, selected with the instruction operand. It would be possible to use any output pad as a Level output ("1" or "0"), or in an other case, either one, two or three output pads as Frequency outputs. In this case, a fixed frequency value is sent by COBRA for external use. An output register "OR", is used for the programming of the outputs configuration with the ACO (Activate Output) instruction operand.

The output structure is duplicated for double-rail checking (see figure 5).

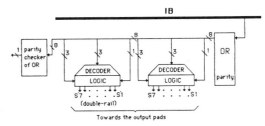

Figure 5 - Outputs activating structure

The double-rail checkers must be placed after the output data reading to be sure that executed operations are the right ones.

3.2 - External PROM communications with COBRA

The external PROM is addressed with 14 bits over the 8 bits bus (7 bits of data coded with the 8th parity bit). Thus the memory map could reach 128 pages of 128 bytes, addressable with two I/O ports, which are selectable with two Address Latch Enable (ALE High and ALE Low) sent by COBRA, for choosing the page and the byte.

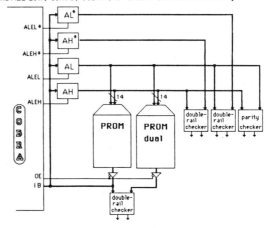

Figure 6 - COBRA/PROM communication self-checking structure.

This communication structure must be duplicated (double-rail checking) in order to guarantee the Totally Self Checking Goal (see figure 6).

The PROM and the dual PROM contain complementary bytes program, thus double-rail checking is direct.

However, this structure can be strongly improved. In fact, a simpler structure can be used, with only one Address Latch Enable pad (duplicated), for the Higher address word. This solution would be very probably the implemented structure for COBRA, and probably discussed in a next paper.

3.3 - Serial I/O

Serial communication between two COBRA devices are necessary in transportation systems, often between a train on board system and the ground sensing devices system using the electromagnetic waves.

A serial transmission instruction SERT transfers a 7 bit-word from an accumulator register ACCA into a transfer register TR, and then to the serial I/O pad, over the shift register, SR. The reception is requested by an interruption request, which is the lowest priority in the interrupts priority encoding.

A special PLA manages the transmission and the reception operations independently of the main program execution. The words are double-rail coded, so a 14 bit-word transmitted contains a 7 bit-word of useful information. The other 7 bit-word is the complementary information needed for the checking of the transmission (see figure 7).

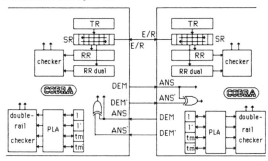

Figure 7 - Serial I/O self-checking structure.

Special Flags (1, tm) indicate to the PLA if the device is ready to receive (or to send) a message and if the transmission conditions are respected. Two special pads, DEM and ANS (duplicated for self-checking), are used for the transmission and the reception request. The "sender" uses DEM to request for a transmission authorization. The "receiver" indicates the acceptance using ANS. Two algorithmes, contained in the PLA, manage the processing and the checking of the serial communications (request conflicts, clocks synchronization, etc...).

The serial communication parameters are fixed, e.g., a7 bit-word, with one even parity bit, 62500 bits/second, two stop bits, and one start bit.

3.4 - Self-checking RAM

COBRA's 64 bytes RAM are coded with the parity code, and checked in the Internal Bus, IB, parity checker. But the RAM select register RS, and the RAM decoder RAMDEC are checked with a special structure (see figure 8).

In order to reduce the decoder's checker dimensions, the RAM would be divided into 8 blocks of 16 x 4 bits each.

One of 16 columns is selected with the 4 -> 16 decoder. One of 4 rows is selected in each block with two address bits. Thus, IB can read (or write) an 8 bits word. The 4 bits of the column address are recreated and checked (double-rail) after the column selection. The 2 bits of the row address are directly checked in a double-rail checker. Then the parity bit of the 6 address bits are recreated and compared with the parity bit contained in RS, for its own check.

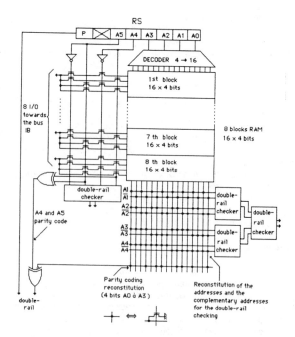

Figure 8 - Self-checking RAM structure.

3.5 - 14 bit- counters

Three 14 bit-counters are available in the data path for use as timers. Three priority levelled interruptions indicate to the main program the end of a counting. Each counter is called with an instruction, and loaded with the contents of the instruction operand (14 bits maximum).

Linear Feedback Shift Registers are used for these functions. Basic cells are Master-Slave Flip flops, used in a 14 bit-shift register. Exclusive OR gates are then used to complete this structure and to obtain then a self-checking (parity coded) LFSR (see figure 9).

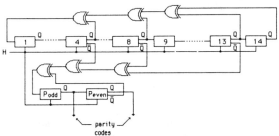

Figure 9 - Self-checking 14 bit-counter (LFSR).

The instruction operands are loaded in a special order, e.g., first the odd cells (cell 1, 3, ..., 13) and then the even ones (2, 4, ..., 14) are loaded with the value to count, in order to avoid the undetected shorts between two consecutive cells. Two cells P_{odd}, and P_{even} contain the parity codes of the counter value when working.

3.6 - Self-checking ALU

The ALU used in COBRA for both general and special purposes, is a new structure proposed by [NIC 85-2]. This self-checking ALU shows the results directly coded for double-rail checking. Its inputs must be duplicated and complemented (see figure 10).

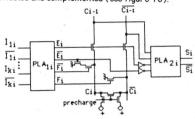

Figure 10 - Self-checking bit-slice ALU to be used in COBRA.

Figure 10 shows two PLAs of the ALU, which could be substitued with the logical gates usually used in a such structure.

ALU is a 7 bit-operator. A parity generator calculates the parity of the 7 ALU outputs. The result is then over 8 bits, compatible with the bus IB, ready for parity checking. The outputs of ALU and their complements are checked in double-rail checkers.

3.7. Data path assembling and checking

Most of the data path cells are designed to be gathered in a bit slice structure. CAD tools for design, assembling, and connecting cells, are used for COBRA design [SCH 83],[JAM 85], thus, design errors are highly limited, and the SFS rules would be then more easy to be considered.

The two buses used in COBRA's data path, IB, and HB are checked in a parity checker, then the parity coded informations using these buses are checked.

The other registers used in the data path, e.g., Stack Pointer, Program Counters(High and Low), and Address Low register, are parity coded, and checked in the bus parity checker. The Code Condition Register is double-rail coded. Are also using double-rail code :
- The RESET commands (duplicated pads).
- The clocks inputs (disjoint from the input pads over most of the device until the frequncy output pads, where it's possible to check for shorts or slidings).

3.8. Self-checking Control Part

The choice of COBRA's Control Part was oriented by [OBR 83], to the timing generator structure with one PLA for instructions decoding(called properties PLA in the following), and another PLA for commands generation.

Figure 11 shows the structure of the Control Part to be used in COBRA.

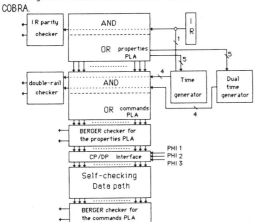

Figure 11-Self-checking Control Part

The properties PLA has to extract properties from the instruction code. A property could be defined as a common characteristic of one or more instructions groups. The target is to cover most of the operations with few properties. This can be achieved if the repetitive characteristics in some instructions (elementary transfers) are grouped together.

The commands on the data path use properties as conditions. Thus the commands PLA recognizes :
- Algorithm state (phase in each sequence)
- properties

This gives equations of timing/property combination :

$$C_j = T_i . P_i$$

C_j : command

T_i : time

P_i : property

T_i is given by the timing generator, P_i by the properties PLA, and C_j is the command given by the commands PLA.

The self checking of the Control Part is made with BERGER code for the PLA, double-rail code for the timing generators, and parity code for the instructions register checking. In all these cases the checkers are placed after the next functional block, in order to be sure that data crossing this block has no fault.

The masks of the Control Part are obtained directly from the instructions description in a special language, IRENE [MAR 83], and using CAD tools,like MACSIM,and PAOLA [CHU 83].

4 . CONCLUSION

This paper has described the design of a self-checking device, specific to the monitoring of automatic security systems, and more particularly,in the Automatic Train Protection channel. This study is a circuit feasibility , and it is expected to have a prototype device available September 1985, (it uses 5v, 2.5 µ NMOS technology with single level metal), after which a more adapted device will be designed and built (probably with CMOS technology).

REFERENCES

[AND 71]   ANDERSON D.A. , Design of self-checking digital network using coding techniques . Coordinated Science Laboratory, report R/527 University of Illinois, Urbana, September 1971.

[CHU 83]   CHUQUILLANQUI S. and al. ,A VLSI Topological Optimization Strategy Applied to PLA Design .
Proc. of the IEEE Intrnational Conference on Computer-Aided Design , Santa Clara, California, USA, September 1983, pp. 184- 189.

[COU 81]   COURTOIS B., VLSI 81, Conference . Edinburgh . August 1981
Academic Press. 1981.

[GAL 80]   GALIAY J. , CROUZET Y., and VERGNIAULT M.,
Physical versus logical fault models in MOS LSI circuits : impaction on their testability .
IEEE Trans. on comput. , vol. C 29 , pp 527-531, June 1980.

[JAM 85]   JAMIER R. , and JERRAYA A. A., APOLLON: a data path compiler . IEEE circuits and devices magazine. To appear 1985.

[JAN 84]   JANSCH I. , and COURTOIS B. , SCD checkers, cellular checkers and multi-checkers structures.
IMAG/University of Grenoble. Report N° 476 . 1984.

[MAR 83]   MARINE S., ANCEAU F., and JAHIDI K., IRENE : un langage de description de circuits intégrés logiques.
IMAG/University of Grenoble. Report N° 356 . 1983.

[NIC 84- 1] NICOLAIDIS M. , and COURTOIS B. ,Design of self-checking N-MOS (H-MOS)integrated circuits.
NATO-AGARD Conference Proceedings N° 361. Design for tactical avionics maitainability. Brussels 7-10 May 1984.

[NIC 84-2] NICOLAIDIS M., JANSCH I., and COURTOIS B. . Strongly Code Disjoint checkers. FTCS 14, KISSIMMEE, June 20-22, 1984.

[NIC 85- 1] NICOLAIDIS M., and COURTOIS B., Layout rules for the of self-checking circuits. To appear in VLSI 85 . Tokyo - Japan . August 1985 .

[NIC 85-2] NICOLAIDIS M.,Evaluation of a self-checking version of the 68000 microprocessor.
IMAG/University of Grenoble. Report N° 506 . 1985.

[OBR 83]   OBREBSKA M., Algorithm transformations improving control part implementation.
IEEE, ICCD'83 : VLSI in computers, p.307, October 1983.

[SCH 77]   SCHOELLKOPF J.P., MACHINE PASC-HLL: Definition d'une architecture pipe-line pour une unité centrale adaptée au langage PASCAL.
Thesis , University of Grenoble. June 28 1977.

[SCH 83]   LUBRICK : A silicon assembler on its application to Data Path , design for FISC. VLSI 83 - North Holland .p 435.

[SMI 78]   SMITH J.E., and METZE G. , Strongly Fault Secure logic networks.
IEEE Trans. on Comput. , vol C 27 ; pp 491-499,June 1978.

FAULT HANDLING CAPABILITIES IN BUS ARCHITECTURES

M. Pauker

Philips CTI, Fontenay-aux-Roses, France

Abstract : Multiprocessor systems with multiple bus architecture provide for hardware
fault tolerance. Several high speed 32 bit parallel bus protocols built-in error
handling features are analyzed : emergency lines, error signalling, information
redundancy, recovery and reconfiguration resources.
Multiple bus, multiple redundance systems, recovery strategies and serial buses usage
as diagnostic and recovery tools are emphasized.

Keywords : Computer architecture. System failure and recovery. Bus protocol.
Multiprocessor.

1. INTRODUCTION

Fault tolerance (FT) is the ability of a system to
continue to perform tasks after fault occuren-
ce.This implies : fault detection, fault location,
fault containment to prevent propagation and fault
recovery.
The aims are continuous operation or short
down-time.

The fault tolerance key is the redundancy.The
degree of FT varies with the degree of used redundancy :
- additional information (space redundancy), like
  Error Correcting Codes or Parity bits, to
control Memory contents and data paths
integrity,
- additional hardware, based on physical replication,
- additional software (time redundancy) used by
  diagnostic and recovery programs.

Multiprocessors based on multiple bus architectures, with built-in fault handling capabilities
have hardware resources for error detection and
isolation, hardware duplication and system
reconfiguration.

The complexity of FT systems is one order higher
than single processor systems.

The two areas of FT computers, on line transaction
processing and embedded real-time computers, were
roughly oriented to two types of architectures :

- loosely coupled multiple processors with inten-
  sive FT software,
- tightly coupled multiprocessors based on
  N-modular hardware redundancy.

The conventional transaction oriented systems as
IBM, DEC, Perkin-Elmer, Prime offer loosely
coupled solutions with attached processors.
The replicated model is a completely stand alone
system. Also automatic recovery software is not
fully transparent for the users.

The new multiprocessor FT systems are mostly based
on multiple bus architecture, often using 680X0
microprocessors.

Several such systems are providing UNIX compatibility using proprietary kernels for multiprocessor
environment (Auragen, Tolerant, Sequoia, Parallel). Others propose SNA high level compatibility
(Tandem, Stratus).

IBM is now entering in this field of N-modular
hardware redundancy with the IBM system /88, models 4576-20, 40, 60 based on Stratus /32
processors and operating system.

Due to shorter downtime requirements, to maintenance cost increasing and to improvement of
microprocessors power, many fault tolerant
features are expected as market general leaning.

2. FAULT HANDLING FEATURES OF SEVERAL 32BIT HIGH SPEED PARALLEL BUSES

An attempt is made to summarize diagnostic and
recovery tools implemented in several bus
protocols.

The examined buses and bus families are :
FASTBUS, VMEBUS, MULTIBUS II, NUBUS and some
features of the new coming DEC BI.

Most of these buses are manufacturer originated
but are now in international standardisation
process :
FASTBUS is endorsed by NBS and in progress in IEC,
VMEbus Rev. C corresponds to the IEC 821 BUS. IEEE
has four committees dealing with VMEbus (P1014),
MULTIBUS II (P896.2), NUBUS (Pxxx), FASTBUS (P960)

Any bus can be seen as a state machine correlated with the error detection capabilities included
in the respective bus protocol. Error states
request time-out escapes and dedicated bus control
signals. The escape states have to localize the
fault.

Bus actions also request test states for sequential conditions (like leave-out idle state -
unassert controls - assert address -a.s.o.).
Full signal transitions must be reached before
returning to an idle state. Most of the bus lines
must go through complete cycle for each transfer :
unasserted - asserted - released.

At the beginning of the cycles, the unasserted control lines prevent incorrect address or data which are not yet stable.

Generic bus protocol limits the faults to the bus itself :

- master asserting non existent slave address ;
- handshaking line blocking at a faulty value which causes control interaction error ;
- impossibility to recover from an error state making the bus inoperative ;
- false acknowledge causing invalid data, in spite of a normal cycle progress ;
- time-out when a resource request is not released.

2.1. System Wide Emergency Bus Signals

Signals on the bus lines related to power supply failure indicate to every bus element (called board or module or agent or node, in the different bus specifications) that all bus activity must be concentrated upon saving the state before power supply is out of range.

Some of these lines are also used for reset, diagnostic or initialisation sequences.
Some protocols allow any of the bus elements to assert the system failure line or the reset line if a failure is detected during self diagnostic or by other test means.

2.1.1 FASTBUS emergency lines

Three lines are dedicated to reset the boards or to force them in a quiescent state, as an essential precondition before initialisation or diagnostics:

- the Reset Bus line, asserted asynchronously by any Master ;
- the Bus Halted line, asserted by the Arbitration Timing Module to protect against spurious Reset signals after a switch Halt request. This line allows live insertion of modules, inhibiting their responses when Bus Halt is asserted ;
- the Wait line, asserted asynchronously by any device in order to extend response delay. It allows single stepped operation for diagnostic procedures.

All devices receiving Reset Bus asserted and Bus Halt released had to :

- disable bus signals assertion, except Arbitration Level and Service Request lines. The operation in progress is terminated without completing the handshaking protocol ;
- reply only to Geographical or Broadcast addressing. Logical Address recognition is disabled.

2.1.2. VMEbus emergency lines

Three bus lines used by this bus utility protocol allow system initialisation and diagnostic :

- ACFAIL* is a power failure signal asserted by the power monitor and warning all bus masters to cease in 200 microseconds any bus activity non related to the power failure ;
- SYSRESET* line is asserted by the power monitor or by any board in response to a switch closure.

These two signals guarantee power failure and power restart timings.

- SYSFAIL* line is asserted by any board during self test at system initialisation and released when self test passes. This line can be driven low by any board at any time when it detects a failure.

2.1.3. MULTIBUS II emergency lines

The Central Services Module of the parallel system bus provides four signals controlling the sequences of power up or cold start, initialisation or warm start and powerfail recovery :

DCLOW* signal is prewarning an imminent power failure ;
PROT* signal is the delayed previous signal, used by agents using battery back-up ;
RST* signal is a reset initializing every bus agent ;
RSTNC* signal is driven by agents to extend initialisation time period provided by the Central Services Module (reset-not-completed).

On cold start, PROT* is not activated.
On warm start, only RST* (and RSTNC* if necessary) are activated.
On power failure, the recovery starts on DCLOW* release, when PROT* and RST* are still activated.

2.1.4. NuBus emergency lines

One bus line, RESET/ is dedicated :

- to bus reset by interface initialization, if the signal is asserted for a single clock period, or
- to system reset, at initial power up, asserting this line for more than one clock.

2.1.5. BI emergency lines

Two signal lines, BI AC LO L and BI DC LO L indicates that AC line voltage of a critical bus element, respectively DC voltages, have dropped below safe limits.

Three signal lines are involved in initialisation and diagnostic :

BI RESET L   wire-or'd signal for power-up/initialisation sequence,
BI STF L   enables self test of the bus nodes,
BI BAD L   wire-or'd signal for reporting node's self test failures.

2.2. Error detection signals

During bus transactions, any concurrent detection of :
- an illegal access attempt, or
- a data path parity error, or
- an uncorrectable memory error

activates the bus error mechanism. The current master has then the responsibility to hold the bus, and try to localize and log the error.

The examined buses are mostly managing these exception conditions during the acknowledge part of the transaction by signalling the errors on the status lines. Dedicated Bus Error signal lines are also used for.

2.2.1. FASTBUS error signalling

Two mechanisms are used during slave reply transaction time : time out interrupt and error encoding on three dedicated Slave Status lines SS $\langle 2:0 \rangle$. Their usage is different during Address Time and Data Time.

At Address Time :

Time out - Slave Detects bad parity ;
           - no addressed Device reply.

SS = 1   - Network Busy (other traffic on segment interconnect. Time-out necessary to avoid deadlock).

SS = 2   - Network Failure due to incorrect initialization or changed configuration or address parity error or defective interconnection.

SS = 3   - Network Abort because traffic in opposite direction was encountered.

SS = 6   - Invalid Interconnect Address, rejected by the Slave.

SS = 7   - Invalid Interconnect Address but address information stored.

At Data Time :

Time-Out due to :
           - too short cycle time,
           - Data Acknowledge lost due to a transient,
           - Defective Slave,
           - Address Strobe/Address Acknowledge lock broken.

SS = 1   - Busy Master may try again later.

SS = 6   - Data Error detected by the Slave refusing data.

SS = 7   - Data error detected by the slave but data accepted or asserted, known as erroneous.

The error messages from the Master are handled by a Host who informs system operator and displays diagnostic information.

2.2.2. VMEbus error signalling

A dedicated Bus Error signal line BERR* is used as a timing line in close loop protocol. It is asserted by a Slave or a Bus Timer to indicate an unsuccessful transfer.

This line is driven by the Bus Timer if the Current Master tries to access an address which is not provided.
The BERR* line may be asserted by a slave :

- if the Master tries to write a Read Only location, or
- when a Slave transferring bytes or double bytes is requested to do a quad-byte transfer, or
- when a Slave without unaligned transfer capability is requested to do an unaligned transfer, or
- when a Slave detects an uncorrectable error in the data retrieved from its internal storage.

On the subsystem VMXbus, an equivalent DERR* line is asserted by the selected slave module to indicate an unsuccessful transfer.

2.2.3. MULTIBUS II error signalling

The Parallel System Bus provides two mechanisms for error signalling : part of the System Control field lines during transfer cycles and two signal lines causing exception cycles.

During the reply phase of the transfer cycles, the bit field SC $\langle 5:7 \rangle$ is reporting agent error encoded indication. When this subfield value is :

1, it indicates multiple errors,
2, indicates agent data error,
3, width error (non compatible with replying agent),
5, replying agent unable to continue,
6, Not Acknowledge - replying agent is not able to reply.

Two bus signal lines BUSERR* and TIMOUT*, when asserted, abort and inhibit any transfer cycle forcing the exception cycle. BUSERR* may be asserted by any agent upon parity error detection on Address/Data or System Control lines.
TIMOUT* is asserted by the Central Services Module when the time taken by an agent to respond to a handshake signal on the bus, overpasses 1 millisecond (on the other buses, it is programmable).

The exception cycle is an error reporting tool, with a signal phase during which exception indication is placed on the bus, followed by a recovery phase of a defined duration.

The Local Bus Extension provides exception cycles for address error, when XAERR* signal line is asserted, for data error, when XDERR* signal line is asserted and for continuation error, on boundary crossing. No provision exists for a recovery phase.
To terminate the bus cycle, the agents may recover from exception condition in subsequent bus cycles.

2.2.4. NuBus error signalling

Two Transfer Mode signal lines, TM1/ and TMO/ provide status information to the current bus master, during ACKnowledge cycles. Three encoded values indicate erroneous operation :

- Error, detected during read or write operation.
- Bus TimeOut, on unimplemented address attempt. It occurs also on bus request without bus arbitration reply.
- Try Again Later, indicates that the transfer was not accomplished. No error occured.

2.2.5. BI error signalling

Event codes and status are provided at Master and Slave ports.

The bus protocol incorporates commands and confirmations related to cache Read/Write, Invalidate, Stall confirmation.

2.3. Space redundance on bus information

Several buses provide parity bits or Error Correction Codes on Data/Address/Status lines together with parity validation bit. The self-checking of the data paths where parity can be preserved by parity checking is a fault tolerant space redundancy mechanism for concurrent error detection.

2.3.1. FASTBUS parity lines

Two lines are reserved for parity : one information line PA inserts odd parity for the 32 bit Address or Data lines pattern and another information line Parity Enable PE indicates, when asserted, that odd parity is generated for the AD lines. No guarantee is given that parity check will occur.

2.3.2. MULTIBUS II parity lines

Four Parallel System Bus lines PAR3* through PAR0* ensure data integrity on AD31* through AD0*. Each parity signal generates even parity for one of the 4-byte Address/Data bus. All agents check parity both during the request phase and during the handshake in the reply phase.
Between System Control signals, the line SC9* is used by the agents to provide even parity for SC3* through SC0* during request and reply phases and the line SC8* as parity bit for SC7* to SC4*.

2.3.3. NuBus parity lines

Parity generation is optional on a cycle by cycle basis. The bus signal line SP/ carries even parity for 32 ADx/lines if the line SPV/ is asserted, validating the parity. Parity check is optional.

2.3.4. BI information redundancy

One line BI PO L carries one parity bit ensuring even parity for the sum of the 32 bit transfer lines and the 4 bit multipurpose Command/ Identify/Mark/Status lines.
During Read Status, the replying agent sends ECC information on the 4 multipurpose status lines.

2.4. Recovery/reconfiguration bus resources

Several bus protocols define hardware reconfiguration facilities, from routing path definition in multiple bus architectures up to geographical reallocation of logical addresses. Such higher level protocols ensure fault containment disconnecting faulty element and preventing fault propagation. In the examined bus architectures, a graceful degradation of system performance is due to local alterations by disconnecting faulty path elements.

2.4.1. FASTBUS reconfiguration resources

FASTBUS basic concept is oriented to a bus network. Multiple independent buses called Segments are linked together for passing data via Segment interconnects. The Crate Segment corresponding to system bus backplane conveys 60 communication protocol lines plus other lines plus power supply lines. The Cable segments convey the 60 lines only.

Each address contains information for segment connection. High order group address field contains routing pattern. Any tree or star or ring interconnection can be obtained. Cable segments can bypass between separated segments to allow high traffic. Global broadcast messages are propagated without cross connections (simple tree) using group address zero for route table entries. Low order address bits represent module address field.

First 256 addresses of any segment (Bus) are reserved.
First 32 of them implement geographical addressing.

Five coded pins give device position with "0-s" in the most significant bit positions. Devices compare coded pins with the five low order address bits. Geographical addressing allows automatic procedure of control and information registers initialization which is the main tool in fault recovery to regain system operability.

2.4.2. VMEbus reconfiguration resources

The Parallel system bus protocol provides six Address Modifier lines which allow the Master to pass additional address information. They are decoded on boards in a flexible way by Slaves and Location Monitors. By providing board possibility to recognize different Address Modifier codes or changing their value by Serial Bus communication, board reconfiguration can be achieved. For board isolation by system recovery, provisions must be implemented to by-pass daisy chaining. Dedicated implementations achieve a distributed arbitration using some of the bus grant daisy chains pins. In such cases, the two arbitration mechanisms can be mixed.
The Location Monitor modules are board capabilities for interconnection, reconfiguration or other dedicated functions.

2.4.3. MULTIBUS II reconfiguration resources

An interconect 16 bit address space is specified by two System and Control bits, during the request phase of the transfer cycles. This address space is available on both Parallel buses, System and Local Extension.

Each interconnect address provides 5 bits identifying the Card slot and 9 bits selecting one of the 512-8 bit registers of each agent.
This interconnect space is a system capability for configuration, diagnostic, initialization and board specific functions.
The arbitration lines are used at system initialisation to assign to each agent a unique cardslot identifier which gives a geographical address. This address is latched and used in addressing the interconnect space.

2.4.4. NuBus reconfiguration resources

Four identification signals ID0/ to ID3/ specify physical location of each module. Each card has a board slot space of 16 megabytes with adresses F(ID)xxxxxx (1/16 of upper 256 MB in 4GB).

3. MULTIPLE BUS ARCHITECTURES

Hardware redundancy can be reduced by alternate solutions to failure handling when each processing element can be connected to more than one bus and each bus allows the connection of a subset of processing elements (PE).

Distributed failure handling facilities in each PE allow to observe the operation of the other PE. The faulty board can be disconnected from the backplane bus using a control register to turn off board's bus drivers or can be isolated by the other PE, stopping all interactions with it.

Routing path can be defined to achieve transfers between PE's which are not connected to the same bus. This mechanism is applicable in case of communication failure due to a bus fault or a processor fault. Message path specifies bus to bus transfers, using different combinations of source and destination buses.

3.1. Hardware redundancy

Main strategies are summarized in table 1.

The first TMR system was FTMP (Fault Tolerant Multiprocessor). Up to five buses interconected up to ten modules. Bus selection is ensured by Bus Guardian Unit.
Voting units are the Bus Isolation Units which connect the modules to the redundant buses.

A DR System example is Tandem Non Stop. Two independent interprocessor buses interconnect two to sixteen modules. Every second, every processor sends on the bus a health message and every two seconds each processor checks message reception from all other processors.

Synapse N+1 XBus allows interleaved accesses by two identical and independent buses.
Bus transactions are unidirectional transfers of six types (read request public/private, read response, write modified, write unmodified and write new data). They ensure data coherence of cache multiple copies in tightly coupled distributed systems. The current owner of the address guarantees correctness.
The processors are self dispatching looking up work queues in main memory and assigning themselves to the new task.

Stratus/32 uses eight microprocessors (68000) coupled in pairs of self-checking processors. The backing-up pairs are running concurrently the same programs, two pairs for executive programs and two pairs for user programs. Up to 32 modules are interconnected over a duplexed ring type LAN but are rather stand-alone, normally unable to share resources between processors.

iAPX 432 ensures the Quad Modular Redundancy in silicium. Two pairs, primary and shadow, form two modules, master and checker. Four confinement areas correspond to processor module, memory module, interface module and memory bus and can be isolated, all communications being only over buses. Five different detection mechanisms are implemented for confinement areas : duplication, parity, ECC, time out, and loop back checks for TTL drivers.
A cost-effective alternative solution is to use only one pair of primary modules. The degree of FT is lower, the system is called "self healing". Fault detection is done by hardware, fault isolation is automatic the faulty module shuts itself but the software ensures recovery. The data base is not corrupted.

3.2. Integrity survey

The evaluation of the resultant degree of FT has following qualifiers :
- the system coverage, defined by the probability that a fault of a type in the range for which the system was designed to anticipate is detected and handled ;
- the System reliability, represented by the probability of the system to survive in the interval |to, t| , if it was operational at to ;

Table 1. Summary of hardware redundancy strategies for FT.

Method	Example	Name	Concurrent processing	Checking method	Effect
Passive	Triplication	TMR	Yes	Voting	Prevents data corruption
Active	Duplication	DR	Yes	Comparison	Disagreement message
	Standby	SR	If"hotspare"	Selfcheck	
Hybrid	N - modular with spares	NMR	Yes	Voting and replacement	System maintained until spare pool exhausted
	Quad-processor with quad half-memory	4,2	Yes	Distributed ECC	Tolerate one failing fault isolation area

- the system availability, which is the
  probability that a system is available to perform its functions at the time t ;
- the depth of fault tolerance, defined by the
  number of faults of a particular kind, that the
  system can handle.

4. RECOVERY STRATEGY

Recovery action depends on the impact of the fault
over the system.
Hardware recovery resources are low level,
microcode based.
Software recovery executes a high level control
and decision.
Recovery ranges from firmware microinterrupts up
to stop-and-control switching to a stand-by
resource.
Error recovery routines attempt to recover
processing without switching to the paired
processor. Progressive reinitialisation monitors
the successive states. If the recovery action does
not succeed, emergency recovery procedures
reconfigure the system, proceeding also to a dead-
start diagnostic.
As an example of allocated time for a hardware
recovery, the AT&T/3B2OD objective is a maximum
down time of two minutes/year in Electronic
Switching Systems. Due to other components of the
downtime (operator, unsuccesful recovery routines,
system software) ; only 0.4 minutes/year are
allowed for hardware total downtime.
The forward recovery strategy uses the erroneous
state of the machine and corrects it.
The backward recovery relies on restoring a prior
correct state. It uses the software checkpointing
mechanism, the audit trail techniques (record of
the modifications), the recovery cache mechanisms,
the disk mirroring.
If concurrent processes are running in the system,
the recovery of the damage spread depends upon the
type of concurrence :
- independent, with private activities,
- competing, with shared resources but without
  information flow,
- cooperating, with shared accesses and inter-
  process communications.
In case of quad-redundancy modules of pair and
spare type, like Stratus (or iAPX 432), no
recovery strategy is required. The system follows
operation on the "spare" subsystem. The detected
fault is automatically dialed to a support
center. When the repaired subsystem is returned to
service the running subsystem brings the repaired
system to full synchronism (the repaired memory
subsystem copies the contents of the functioning
memory). The real time response is maintained,
eliminating any checkpoints or rollback due to
refined error confinement areas which validate
operation during normal processing and prevent
error propagation.

5. FAULT TOLERANCE TOOLS PROVIDED BY SERIAL BUSES

The serial buses are major tools covering the four
error handling functions : detection -
localisation - isolation - recovery/configuration.

Serial buses topology follows normal operation
buses. Each node knows its shadow serial bus.
Several FT immediate functions can be executed
without processor intervention on the faulty
board:

- disconnect the faulty interface
- inconditionnal halt
- maintenance operation
- unmaskable interrupt for power failure or boot,
  connected to an address decoder and a register.

Several of the analyzed parallel buses have two
bus lines providing convenient access of any
parallel bus module to the serial bus.
The connectors of the FASTBUS, VMEbus and MULTIBUS
II convey such shadow serial buses but their
functionality and protocols are different.

5.1. FASTBUS Serial Bus

FASTBUS lines Tx and Rx provide connection to the
FASTBUS Serial Network.

5.2. iSSB

The Serial Bus of MULTIBUS II, ensures
interprocessor communications in message address
space. The messages are defined as unsollicited
(interrupt like) and sollicited (data like). The
transfers are write only, in packed mode, in
groups of 4 to 32 bytes. The source and
destination address lengths are 8-bit width.
The iSBB specification is not yet available, two
lines, SDA and SDB, being reserved for.

5.3. VMSbus fault handling

The VMSbus provides a control path complementary
to a parallel system bus to support fault tolerant
systems and to provide transfer capabilities for
distributed information systems. The data flow
allows "read" and "move" functions besides the
message "write" function.

Two kinds of frames are specified, control frames
and data frames. The control frames FT features :
- reinitialize one or more system boards,
- selectively disconnect a failed board,
- provide semaphores,
- implement token passing.

The data frames pass parameters, pointers, data,
up to 32 bytes. Broadcast and group addressing,
group polling, can be used for control or data
operations.
In the frame format, three subframes are dedicated
to the communication safety and reports the
problems to the higher layers of the systems
management :
. The addressed modules can cancel a frame,
  replying in the type field subframe, just after
  the header subframe :
  - if they are not ready to send or receive data,
  - if a requested semaphore was alredy set, or
  - if a token passing module has already the
    token source reset.
  The cancelled frames end immediately.

. The status subframe allows to report problems :
  - data size conflict among several selected Data
    Senders,
  - data size exceeds Data Receiver capacity,
  - in a control frame, no Data Sender Selected.

. The jam subframe (or bit after a frame), is
  asserted on detecting a frame desynchronization
  and 512 one's are sent. This jam subframe
  ensures security and protection against effects
  of signal noise.
  Jam protocol is a resynchronization tool for :
  - new modules insertion in the system ;
  - extended configuration reset, where modules
    are sharing a commun Reset Signal.

VMSbus state diagrams provide error states during protocol execution, in case of missing conditions or unsuccessful tests.

The VMSbus data link groups semaphores or token passing are mechanisms for single bit mutual exclusion or allocation. Another high security tool provided is the signature checking semaphore. The semaphore code is the code assigned to the sharable resource controlled by it, while a requester code is assigned to the higher layer entity requesting the control of the resource, or to a semaphore group sharing the resource.

Token passing groups are an alternate way to the use of semaphores, configured in a ring, with successors defined in the frame. Each group can use the controlled resource after receiving the token frame and before sending to its successor.

6. CONCLUSION

The need for fault tolerance is increasing with larger usage of VLSI. While the number of discrete components is reduced by VLSI, the defect density is greater due to :
- the bigger number of active elements on a single silicon,
- the susceptibility to external interferences due to extremely low VLSI circuit energy levels.

System maintenance and performance improvement will require fault tolerance techniques.
The added cost for fault tolerance, in Commercial systems, must be balanced by :
- service disruptions reducing,
- annual loss of profits due to the downtime of existing systems.
Various communication buses features presented here are cost effective resources for achieving high availability Commercial Systems.

REFERENCES

1. FASTBUS U.S. NIM Committee National Bureau of Standards, WA
2. VMEbus Specification Manual, Rev C
3. VMXbus Specification Manual, Rev B
4. VMSbus Specification Manual, Rev B
5. MULTIBUS II Architecture Specification Handbook Rev C
6. NuBus Specification, 1983, Texas Instr., Irvine, CA
7. T. Anderson & P.A.Lee, Fault Tolerance Principles and Practice, Prentice Hall International 1981
8. R.C. Hansen, R.W. Peterson and N.O.Whittington Fault Detection and Recovery, Bell System Technical Journal, Jan. 1983
9. Omri Serlin, Fault-Tolerant Systems in Commercial Applications, Computer IEEE, August 1984
10. J. Altaber and R. Rausch, A Multiprocessor Bus Architecture for the LEP Control System, Particle Accelerator Conference, Santa Fe, March 1983
11. Th. Krol, The "(4,2)-concept" Fault Tolerant Computer, FTCS 12, 1982
12. Steve Frank, Armond Inselberg, Synapse Tightly coupled multiprocessors : A new Approach to solve old problems, AFIPS Conference Proceedings, Vol. 53, 1984
13. Howard Pollard, Janak Patel, Fault Tolerant Techniques for Control Signals in Bus Communications Protocols, FTCS 14, 1984
14. D.K. Pradhan, Z. Hanquan and M.L. Schlumberger Fault-Tolerant Multibus Architectures for Multiprocessors, FTCS 14, 1984
15. R. Emmerson, M. Mc Gowan, Fault Tolerance Achieved in VLSI, IEEE Micro december 1984.

BROADCAST REMOTE PROCEDURE CALLS
FOR RESILIENT COMPUTATION

H. R. Aschmann

*Brown Boveri Research Center, Computer Science Group, CH-5405 Baden,
Switzerland*

The remote procedure call mechanism is a well suited communication primitive for procedural languages. Is seems to be very attractive to enhance it in order to hide any
issue of replication and crash recovery at the user level. Much efficiency can be gained
if the broadcast facilities of local area networks are exploited.

This paper presents remote procedure calls based on broadcast of messages in a local
area network. They have semantics properties that make them a simple and powerful
tool to implement replicated objects. However not all problems are solved just by using
this communication primitive. The underlying system has to ensure consistency of replicated objects despite crashes with the aid of a checkpointing mechanism which is designed hierarchically: objects communicating with the outside world (think: device
drivers) ensure their consistency within themselves by explicit code for recovery and
checkpointing. Higher level programs based on these objects can be checkpointed and
recovered by the system. The remote procedure call mechanism is then able to mask
server and client crashes, thereby providing high availability of the overall system.

Keywords: Broadcasting, System failure and recovery, Remote procedure calls,
Distributed systems.

1. INTRODUCTION

Distributed system architectures are finding increasing interest for process control applications.
The advantages commonly mentioned are: high reliability and availability, high through-put, ease
of modular expansion and degradation, possibility
to share resources, on-line maintenance, etc.
These potential benefits can only be exploited if
distribution and fault tolerant computing are supported by the system.

Previous work in the area of distributed process
control systems has been done in the MARS project [1]. An important principle of MARS is the
fault detection by timeout mechanisms and treatment of faults left to the programmer. There is
no explicit support of replication of MARS objects.

ARGUS [2] aims at hiding the problems of distribution and consistency in the programming language. It is not very well suited for control
applications, however, since its major goal is consistency and not availability. Replication of objects to increase system availability is possible
but not supported.

AUGUST systems [3] evolved from the SIFT project [6] and belongs to the category of highly reliable and available control computers, based on
triple modular redundancy (TMR) with 2 out of 3
voting. This architecture is well suited for repetitive control algorithms, but it lacks flexibility for
on-line maintenance or inexpensive integration of
secondary applications with no requirements for
high availability.

The Eden [4] and ISIS [5] projects have an ob-
ject-oriented approach in common. Their goal is to
provide high-level support for fault-tolerant computing. Both use remote procedure calls for communication and a checkpointing scheme to achieve
consistency when recovering from crashes. There

are several interesting ideas brought up in these
projects, but there are still important shortcomings
with respect to real-time process control. The Eden
system has a checkpointing scheme which prevents
building replicated objects because stable storage
is on a disk. ISIS in return offers some support
for replication. Here checkpoints are transferred
to the replicas and the remote procedure call
mechanism ensures "exactly once" semantics.

While a variety of approaches to increase reliability
of control systems is available there is still a need
for an architecture that allows for different degrees of redundancy in a homogeneous way. A
distributed system based on a local area network
seems to be well suited for this: it allows modular
configuration of the system with respect to hardware modules and replication of tasks to choose a
desired degree of availability, reliability and performance. The problems of flexible configuration
and replication are of special interest in this
paper. The presented approach is somewhat similar to the ISIS project but refers more specifically
to process control applications based on a local
area network.

For the remainder of this paper we will make the
following assumptions about the system: it consists
of several fail-stop nodes connected by a local
area network for the purpose of controlling and
monitoring an industrial process. Some nodes are
gateways to the process (process interfaces),
others serve as operator interfaces, data base,
print server, and so on (it is possible that several functions reside also in the same physical
node).

2. PROGRAMMING AND COMMUNICATION
CONCEPTS

In the following section the remote procedure call
(RPC) is introduced as an alternative communica-

tion tool to message passing. First the capability to achieve a higher abstraction is shown, leading to the attempt to generalize it for multiple invocations by broadcasting. This idea then proves to be useful where high availability of services is achieved by replication of server tasks. A further topic will be how checkpointing can be automated, if incorporated in a RPC environment.

2.1 Communication Using Broadcast Schemes

There has been only little work done on communication based on the broadcast principle. Algorithms for reliable broadcast in an unreliable environment have been proposed [7, 8]. Building upon an existing broadcast protocol, Gehani [9] shows how distributed programs can be built based upon this communication mechanism. The examples he gives are not very realistic, however. Message passing does not fit very well into a procedural language, flow control is not considered, and no idea is given how failures should be detected or treated. Before further development on his scheme is performed, it cannot be considered for practical applications.

More promising might be the following scheme based on broadcast remote procedure calls. Let us at this point introduce the distinction between "remote procedure CALLS" and "remote procedure INVOCATIONS". The call resembles the traditional procedure call: the calling process is suspended until the procedure returns, maybe with results. The invocation does not suspend the caller, i.e. a fork operation is performed. When the server terminates, it stops without returning any results (there is no process waiting for them). Of course, a server procedure can itself be client of other servers.

About the broadcast protocol we assume that a send operation returns which nodes accepted the message within a timeout period. A message is only accepted if the receiver consumed the previous message (flow control with buffering of at most one message).

A remote procedure call or invocation is initiated by a broadcast call of the client. If no receiver is present (i.e. no server), then the send operation fails immediately, indicating the failure of the call. Otherwise a service procedure is invoked at all servers. There may be different servers, each with a number of replicated versions. If the client expects a result, however, exactly one server is supposed to return it (if it fails, one of its replica). Other servers may handle the same call only as invocation.

The treatment of failures of servers follows the scheme outlined in a previous paper [10] and is described in the following sections. Here we just note that if any process fails to receive a message, it must be considered to be inconsistent. A primary task will not serve a call, a backup will not' be able to recover correctly. The reason why the process failed to receive the message may be that it crashed (its hardware or software), or that there is some kind of congestion. In either case, it does not follow its specifications and must be assumed to have failed (messages do not get lost, congestion is a due to a design error).

2.2 Levels Of Abstraction For Broadcast Communication

At the physical layer we have a hardware protocol supporting broadcast, like for example Ethernet. On a higher layer we may have a protocol based on this which implements a reliable broadcast (if not already supported by the hardware).

From the point of view of a dumb data or event generating source it will be sufficient to broadcast its data in order to invoke any necessary actions to process that data. On a next higher level we have the view of remote procedure invocation servers which activate actions based on the reception of these messages. While the sources do not care about what their messages mean on a higher level of abstraction, the servers do: the procedures which are activated incorporate that knowledge.

A different type of service is given for intelligent clients: they broadcast a request for a remote procedure call service which is treated very similarly to the above described invocation. A server will activate the corresponding procedure and then return a message containing the result parameters. The abstraction we are using here is the access to a remote object by a procedure call.

This allows to apply the ideas of abstract data types on objects which can reside anywhere in a network. It is relatively simple to implement such a scheme as long as aspects of fault-tolerance are ignored. Crashes need some treatment, however, and an improvement of system availability by replicating objects in the network is often necessary. It is therefore relatively straightforward to enhance the remote procedure call abstraction by including also the capabilities to handle replication and crashes.

In an environment of replicated objects certain semantical classes of RPCs are of particular interest: the "at least once" and the "exactly once" case. The basic idea is to have several servers for some RPC and let one server be the coordinator (ISIS terminology). The other servers are called cohorts and are ready to promote a new coordinator if the previous one failed.

The replication onto other nodes implies the problem of keeping several versions of the same object consistent.

Again a new level of abstraction can be defined which hides the replication to a client, or even to the servers themselves. This abstraction is the point we want to focus on in this paper.

2.3 Checkpointing and Recovery Scheme

2.3.3 Model of Computation

To talk about the semantics of checkpointing and recovery we need a model of computation: a task is a sequence of actions which are virtually atomic and may be I/O operations, internal operations (e.g. a simple procedure call) or a remote procedure call. A sequence of such actions can be interrupted by a checkpoint. The checkpoint saves the internal state of the task onto secure storage for recovery after a crash.

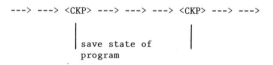

Fig. 2.1:   The flow of a program: a sequence of actions and checkpoints

The effect to the checkpointed program by a checkpointing operation is a no-operation.

Actions are categorized according to repeatability and interference:

Class 1: repeatable (idempotent) actions which are free of interference with other actions,i.e. A1 → A1 == A1 (A1 followed by A1 has the same effect as A1), and A1 → A2 == A2 → A1

Class 2: actions that are repeatable by themselves but interfere with other actions, i.e. A1 → A1 = A1, but NOT: A1 → A2 == A2 → A1 or: (A1 → A2) → (A1 → A2) == A1 → A2.

Class 3: non repeatable actions, i.e. NOT: A1 → A1 == A1. Interference is still possible, but not of special interest.

Let us consider the simple recovery scheme that restores the state of a program to its last checkpoint and resumes execution from there. This implies that all actions done by the crashed task after its last checkpoint must be repeated by the recovered task.

There are two scopes to distinguish: one is the local scope, where the effects of actions are contained within the task. We do not worry about these actions, since they are easily undone by switching to the backup whose state is still given by the last checkpoint.

Actions with a global scope interact with other tasks or devices. Here class 2 and 3 actions need attention not to interfer with each other.

There is no problem with class 1 actions, but there can be only one class 2 action before the next checkpoint is performed. Actions of class 3 make the scheme impossible - a dedicated recovery procedure will have to deal with this.

In the global scope, only I/O operations and remote procedure calls are of interest. Since both types of operations are handled by the operating (and run time) system, it is easy to automatize checkpointing. Class 3 actions can be avoided by taking care while writing I/O drivers and remote procedures (or implementing the exactly-once semantics for remote procedure calls).

I/O operations and particularly remote calls can be also of class 1, so it might be interesting to classify these actions on behalf of the checkpointing system to improve efficiency (by omitting unnecessary checkpoints).

2.3.2 Classification Of Context Saving Methods

There are several checkpointing mechanisms for context saving which are relevant to our approach. They are:

- "absolute complete": all variables and registers are saved when a checkpoint is performed. Also pointers are saved, therefore the address space must be invariant.

- "absolute partial": only selected parts of the variables and registers are saved (e.g. the ones that changed since last time)

- "incremental": a log of performed actions is maintained, so a recovering task can follow this log to recover.

- "eavesdropping": a backup executes in parallel, suppressing any outputs.

The remote procedure call mechanism is well suited for the incremental checkpointing mechanism (this will be outlined in more detail in a later publication).

2.4 Classification Of Remote Procedure Call Semantics

Remote procedure calls (RPCs) resemble closely normal procedure calls (with some restrictions due to the separate address space and different processor). There is a communication protocol between the client (the process issuing the call) and the server (the process executing the call) which transfers call parameters, invokes the server procedure, and returns the results. Depending e.g. on whether there is more than one server, an RPC protocol can have different semantical properties:

- at most once (or maybe): There is only one service request which is probably answered. Implementation usually with non-replicated servers.

- at least once: The call is re-issued until an answer comes back. Replication of servers improves probability of execution, no precautions are taken against duplication of a call.

- exactly once: replicated servers (or servers re-animated after crash) assure very probable execution with precautions against duplication

Practical issues at the client site are:

- When a client crashes, it may re-issue a remote call again. There may still be the orphan call pending, and the call is duplicated. Should the second call be suppressed and the results of the first call be used? Should the client or the server be notified? Or should the call just be redone?

- A call may not be answered within an expected time interval due to congestion or the crash of the server - should we specify a timeout with every call? What actions should be taken on timeout?

- There may currently be no server available - should the call be aborted, or should the server be requested, thereby delaying the client until the call can be executed?

- Do we expect a reply from the server or is it just a remote invocation?

- With respect to the server it must be specified whether calls should be serviced sequentially or a new process should be created to serve a class of calls (i.e. one process for all calls, one process for a class of calls, one process per call, a limited number of processes for all calls).

- Duplicated calls can be treated in different ways by the server: they can be executed anyway, they can be suppressed (the client may wait for an answer), a special reply can be given indicating that the call has been received more than once, or the result of the first call can be returned (this requires results to be retained by the server - see ISIS [5]).

For a more formal classification we choose some degrees of freedom to combine them and analyze the combinations. This is: replication and checkpointing strategy of server and client, invocation versus call, and whether backup servers execute calls or not.

First a look at the replication and checkpointing issue: the diagram below shows what semantics the RPC has depending on whether checkpointing is used.

112   H. R. Aschmann

```
                         SERVER
checkpointing:    no                yes

           no    "maybe"         "at least once"
CLIENT
        · yes   "at most once"   "exactly  once"
```

We are probably not interested very much in the
cases described on the left side of the diagram,
therefore checkpointing of the server is necessary.
As further degree of freedom we introduce RPI/
RPC distinction. The following figures shall illustrate with some examples how messages are passed and how the flow of control works.

Explanation of symbols:

◇   send (broadcast)
◈   atomic send/checkpoint operation
◆   change of state due to reception of
         message or checkpoint
──→R▷   last checkpoint serves as starting point
         for execution
✕   crash
┈┈┈┈   task is blocked (e.g. waiting for a
         message)
────   task is suspended

▨▨▨▨   task is running

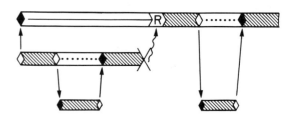

Figure 2.5: Client crash, "at least once" RPC

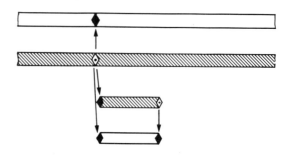

Figure 2.6: Normal operation, "exactly once"
            RPI

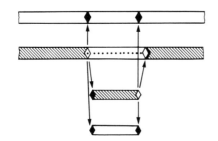

Figure 2.2: Normal operation, "exactly once"
             RPC

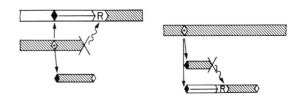

Figure 2.7: Client and server crash,
            "exactly once" RPI

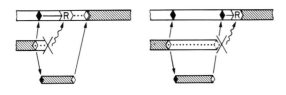

Figure 2.3: Client crash, "exactly once" RPC

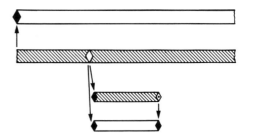

Figure 2.8: Normal operation,
            "at least once" RPI

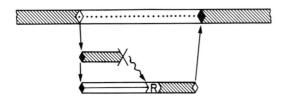

Figure 2.4: Server crash, "exactly once" RPC

The crash of a server in the "at least once" case
is identical to the "exactly once" in figure 2.4.

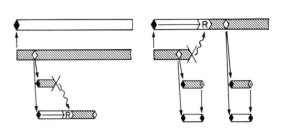

Figure 2.9: Server and client crash,
             "at least once" RPI

At last we note that backup servers may or may not execute the service procedure of a call. It may be more efficient to do some calculations at the backups, too, instead of checkpointing the results of the main server. Of course, the service procedure must not contain any actions that interfere with each other.

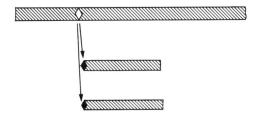

Figure 2.10: Normal operation, "at least once" RPI (Services executed at backup, too)

The diagram below gives an overview where certain combinations are of interest.

	strict execution (only at main)	backup execution
at least once *	RPC,RPI: only if computations are more expensive than a checkpoint	RPC: combined update/inquiry
		RPI: update
exactly once	RPC: difficult cases, action not idempotent	RPC,RPI: only if locally but not globally idempotent (unlikely)
	RPI: id. (unlikely)	

* need idempotent servers!

Notes:

- execution of services at the backup task is reasonable if the service itself does not use RPCs itself. Typically an RPI could be used to update a process measurand in a data base.

- "exactly once" costs more effort because the client needs special checkpoints when issuing a call or getting the answer.

2.5 Recovery of Broadcast Remote Procedure Calls

If the client fails after an invocation, the servers complete the call as they would anyway. The recovering client sets up at its last checkpoint, and depending on the strategy, the call is reissued or the results of the original call are used (i.e. the answer message of the server, saved e.g. by the backup). If duplication must be avoided, then atomicity of the actions of calling and performing a checkpoint right after that must be achieved. This can be achieved by using the same message for both, or using the message for the call to establish the checkpoint which was transferred before.

Another interesting approach treats RPC messages like logical incremental checkpoints. A recovering backup task - which will have to do the same RPC calls again - already has a log of sent and received messages which it will use to replace its own intended send and receive operations. This approach will be discussed in more detail in a subsequent publication.

If a server coordinator fails, a cohort will complete the call (see [9]). A failing cohort needs no treatment. If the coordinator completes regularly, it broadcasts a message (also for remote invocations), which is used by the cohorts to determine when they need no longer remember the invocation.

3. UNDERLYING MECHANISMS FOR FAULT-TOLERANCE

3.1 Node Crash Detection

A full coverage of hardware failure detection is not possible by software but only with extra hardware. For the sake of simplicity of software we assume fail-stop processors, i.e. a faulty processor will not disturb its environment but be quiet.

Node crash detection is thus easily implemented: periodic polling of all processors yields the set of functioning processors, and those missing in the set since the last poll are the ones that just failed.

3.2 Primary/Backup Coordination

The primary task is sometimes called "coordinator", the backup tasks "cohorts". Both kinds of tasks run the same code, but the functionality is somewhat different: cohorts have restricted functionality until they become coordinator. Only the primary task performs checkpoints, while the backups gather checkpoint information. This information is distributed via the network and serves for recovery when the primary task fails.

There may be other restrictions to the functionality of the backup tasks depending on the application. It may not be desirable to do all the work at the backup tasks, too, it may even not be correct to do it. This is the case when I/O operations are to be performed on a shared device, for example. Non-destructive read operations or remote procedure call services which do not involve I/O, on the other hand, can well be performed by all tasks, thereby avoiding the necessity to communicate the read values via checkpoints.

3.3 I/O Handlers

The problems encountered with class 3 I/O operations (see 2.3.1) are dealt with in a special software layer, the I/O handler. A typical handler provides the interface to a sharable device. It provides a high level interface to the device driver of the operating system, assuring consistent control of the device despite of crashes. Obviously it is necessary for an I/O handler to be distributed onto primary and backup tasks and performing its own checkpointing. Additionally to normal applications it controls its checkpoints itself, and activates a dedicated recovery procedure at the location of the new primary after a crash. During normal operation it is responsible to initiate checkpoints on behalf of the application according to a service request.

To summarize the properties of the I/O handlers: they know about the state of shared devices and their recovery, and they know which I/O operations of the application imply a checkpoint. Otherwise they just translate I/O requests of the application into device driver requests of the operating system.

3.4 Checkpointing and Recovery Facilities

There are several methods for efficient checkpointing. One optimization criterion is the amount of information to be transferred, another the time lag to switch from the primary to the backup, or the complexity of the information assembly and disassembly algorithms. In order to reduce the amount of checkpoint data it is useful to know something about the semantics of the data to reduce the scope of data in question, and it is useful to know whether the data has changed since the last checkpoint. A "dirty bit" as used in virtual memory systems can be a solution to the latter problem, but semantical issues need knowledge of the application.

The concept of dividing the state data into context segments allows to reduce the amount of data to be checkpointed. The segments are chosen to match logical data clusters that are mutually independent. An example: the data representing the state of two peripheral devices can easily be separated into two segments, and only the appropriate I/O handlers need to know about them. In a data base system, updating of data does not mean that the whole data base has to be checkpointed, but only the appropriate segment (which includes all data changed by the transaction).

This method seems to be the most attractive solution as long as no special purpose hardware supports checkpointing. Such hardware would monitor write operations and transfer only data that have been changed when a checkpoint is performed.

The recovery mechanism goes through two phases: first I/O handlers are recovered by explicitly calling their recovery procedures, then the context of the last checkpoint is set up and computation resumes. These operations are scheduled by the recovery manager which is a part of the run time system or the operating system.

3.5 Life Phases of a Task

When a task is started, it does some first initializations and determines whether there is already a primary for this task. If there is not, a cold start procedure is executed before full functionality is achieved (right path in figure 2). Otherwise the task will enter a learning phase where it gets a full copy of the context data of the primary. Then it continues observing checkpoints to be ready for immediate recovery of the failing primary. When this happens, a backup task is determined to recover and become the new primary.

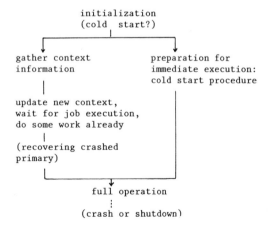

Fig. 3.1: Life Phases

The transitions of the states shown in figure 3.1 are controlled by the recovery manager. It determines during initialization whether the task is a primary or backup, and initiates recovery by the backup when required. The recovery manager is a distributed protocol which is part of all applications.

The algorithm to determine whether a task is a backup and when it must replace the primary is implemented in a resource manager (see [10]). The backups compete for a virtual resource which is always hold by the primary. If this one crashes, it is freed and the backup with highest priority gets it.

4. CONCLUSIONS

Let us briefly state again the principal ideas of the previous chapters: the remote procedure call fits well into a procedural language for interprocess communication. The semantics of broadcast messages can be brought into a context with the invocation of remote procedures, or on a even higher level of abstraction, with the access to a remote object (representing an abstract data type).

While this is about the point of view of the system engineer looking at the communication structure, there is another point of view concerned with fault-tolerance. The replication of objects creates the problem of consistency among different versions. The remote procedure call can here be used as a vehicle to abstract from these issues.

The notion of logical checkpointing brought up in this paper deserves still some more attention. It seems that physical checkpointing as it is traditionally done is not ideally suited for a distributed system, but rather in a closely coupled multiprocessor only.

The critical point why to abolish physical checkpointing is not so much the amount of data to be transferred, but the impossibility to revise a running program, e.g. to correct a bug or extend its functionality.

5. REFERENCES

[1] H. Kopetz, F. Lohnert, W. Merker, G. Pauthner, "An Architecture for a Maintainable Real Time System (MARS)", Report Nr. 82-1, Technische Universitaet Berlin, 1982

[2] B. Liskov, "The Argus Language and System", lecture notes, Advanced Course on Distributed Systems, Munich, 1984

[3] John H. Wensley, "Fault-Tolerant Systems Can Prevent Timing Problems", Computer Design, November 1982, pp. 211-220

[4] G. Almes, A. Black, E. Lazowska, J. Noe, "The Eden System: A Technical Review", University of Washington, Department of Computer Science, Technical Report 83-10-05, October 1983

[5] Kenneth P. Birman, Thomas A. Joseph, "Low Cost Management of Replicated Data in Fault-Tolerant Distributed Systems", Cornell University, Department of Computer Science, Technical Report 84-644

[6] P. Michael Melliar-Smith and Richard L. Schwartz, "Formal Specification and Mechanical Verification of SIFT", IEEE Transactions on Computers, Vol. C-31, No. 7, July 1982

[7] F. B. Schneider, "Broadcast: A Paradigm for Distributed Programs", Dep. Comput. Sci., Cornell Univ., Ithaca, NY, Techn. Rep. 80-440.

[8] Jo-Mei Chang, N. F. Maxemchuk, "Reliable Broadcast Protocols", ACM Transactions on Computer Systems, Vol. 2, No. 3, August 1984, pp. 251-273.

[9] Narain H. Gehani, "Broadcasting Sequential Processes (BSP)", IEEE Transactions on Software Engineering, Vol. SE-10, No. 4, July 1984

[10] H. R. Aschmann, "Recovery in a Distributed Process Control System Based on a Local Area Network", Report Nr. KLR 84-218 C, Brown Boveri Research Center, CH-5405 Baden

STABLE PATHS FOR AN EFFICIENT RECOVERY IN REAL-TIME DISTRIBUTED SYSTEMS

P. Mancini*, P. Ciompi** and L. Simoncini**

*SELENIA S.p.A., Pisa, Italy
**IEI-CNR, Pisa, Italy

Abstract. This paper deals with the problem of communication in a distributed system, composed by nodes connected in a local area network. The system must continue its operation in the event of a node crash. In the system, agent functions cooperate and request services to server functions through message passing. The ability of server functions to provide continuous service, in presence of a node crash in a real-time and highly available environment, is obtained with the replication of the server functions in two different nodes (Master and Stand-by). A solution which allows a stable communication between agent and server functions is presented. This solution allows a role switching between the Master and the Stand-by without any loss of messages or need of retry of messages; this role switching is fully transparent to the agent functions.

Keywords. Local area network; distributed system; real-time; fault tolerance.

INTRODUCTION

A distributed system on a local area network, which should provide an available and prompt service, must be characterized by the ability of continuous service, even in presence of a node crash. The service must continue in the most efficient way, and the crash must be transparent to the user.

The most important issues to be addressed for the design of such a system are:

- the structuring and the management of the redundancy of the physical nodes, of the critical resources and of their managers;

- the structuring of the recovery after a crash, to be performed in an efficient way to minimize the down-time of the system;

- the transparency of the redundancy to the application, to allow an easier programming.

These three issues are seldom jointly addressed in existing distributed systems. The distributed systems like XEROX (Metcalfe, 1976; Lampson, 1976; Lampson, 1979; Cambridge Ring (Wilkes, 1979; Dion, 1980) and CNET (Lijtmaer, 1983) deal with a node crash as the loss of all the resources of the node, and continuous operation is not guaranteed. Systems like LOCUS (Popek, 1983; Walker, 1983) provide features for object replication, but are not designed to serve real-time applications.

The solution outlined in this paper is based on the distinction between server functions, which must provide a service, and agent functions, which request these services. Different redundancy schemes are used for these different functions.

The server functions, which are considered critical for the system, are duplicated on a suitable duplicated physical support. Duplication is managed in stable way to prevent disruptive effects due to a crash. The agent functions may be structured in atomic transactions which allow an efficient recovery in case of their failing.

Even if this structuring may satisfy the previously said requirements, a careful design of the communication and synchronization among functions must be considered to obtain the most efficient behavior in case of a system crash.

In the next sections, the M.A.R.A. distributed system is described and the proposed solution for implementing stable communication and stable server functions is discussed.

THE M.A.R.A. DISTRIBUTED SYSTEM

Physical Configuration

The testbed for the implementation described in the paper is a local network of M.A.R.A. nodes. M.A.R.A. (Modular Architecture for Real-time Applications) is a multiprocessor architecture developed by Selenia S.p.A. for real-time applications in the process control field (Martin, 1981; Ciompi, 1983a and 1983b).

Each M.A.R.A. node (see figure) consists of a set of up to 16 microcomputers, memories and peripheral units connected by a nodal bus. Each microcomputer has also

117

a local bus on which memories and I/O
resources are connected. The error detection is implemented by means of additional
control hardware to monitor the correct
functioning of the node and by periodic on
line diagnostic procedures.

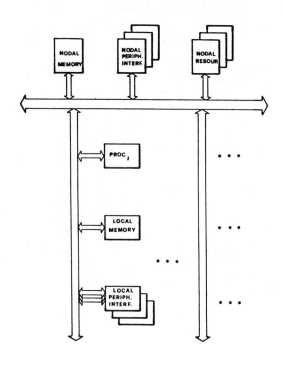

The control hardware, in the case of the
memory modules, allows the automatic
correction of single memory errors, the
detection of double errors, and the automatic correction of soft errors.

Diagnostic procedures are used to detect
errors not covered by the control
hardware. These procedures are performed
partly on line with a period chosen by the
application designer and partly off line.

Each processor of the node indicates to
the external hardware whether the processor itself is able to perform its duty, by
means of a special signal called the processor availability. A node is available
when

When a particular processor becomes not
available, all other processors receive an
error interrupt and can evaluate whether
to remain available or to commit suicide
in order to make the whole node not available. With these mechanisms each node may
be considered either available or crashed.

The distributed system, considered in this
paper, is a local network of M.A.R.A.
nodes. The nodes connected to the network
may have two different configurations:
single M.A.R.A. nodes or M.A.R.A. nodes in
a duplex configuration. In this latter,
one node acts as the Master node and the
other as the Stand-by node. If the Master
crashes, its operations will be continued
by the Stand-by node after a role switching. The role switching inside the duplex
configuration of the M.A.R.A. nodes is a
mechanism to make the crash transparent to
the other nodes in the network. After the

crash of one of the nodes in the duplex
configuration, the availability of the
system is degraded and a suitable strategy
for the repair, the reinsertion and the
conditioning of the crashed node is needed. The role switching may be executed
periodically as an aid to the error detection. In this case periodic diagnostics
may be performed on the switched node.

If the role switching has to be performed
in a transparent way to the system, the
Stand-by node must have, at every instant,
an updated and consistent copy of the
state of the Master. A warm Stand-by is
used to allow a non-deterministic computation of the server functions on the Master
and Stand-by nodes. The Stand-by does not
perform any useful computation for the application; the Master node must take care
of suitable actions which determine the
updating of the state of the Stand-by.
There is no point to point dedicated connection between the Master and the Stand-
by node; they are connected to the network
as any node in it.

Software Environment

The M.A.R.A. software is based on the concept of function. A function is a protected environment for program execution.
Functions are organized hierarchically
into a set of privileged levels. A function is made of a set of processes, which
operates on a set of objects (memory segments, etc.). Processes interact to accomplish a specified service. In other
words, a function implements a virtual
multiprocessor node. The interaction of
the processes in a function is based on
several kernel mechanisms (locks, semaphores, mailboxes, etc.). The communication between functions is based on interface procedure calls or through message
passing. Interface procedure calls are
the mechanism by which a function of an
upper privileged level offers a service to
a lower privileged level function. Two or
more generic functions communicate through
message passing by the use of paths. A
path is a private communication channel
between the two functions which required
to the kernel the need to communicate. A
path is therefore the implementation of a
bidirectional point to point communication
between two virtual nodes. A path is implemented with two queues, one for each of
the partner functions; a function, to send
a message, uses a buffer which is queued
on the queue of the partner. The management of the paths is performed by a kernel
component, called Path Manager which provides the user with a set of procedures
for using the paths, which constitutes an
asynchronous interface. The Path Manager
is in charge of transferring and queueing
message buffers to the proper queues. If
the communicating functions are allocated
on the same physical node, no physical
data transfer is performed; instead, the
Path Manager changes the access rights to
the buffer, assigning them to the destination function, which subsequently assigns
back the buffer to the source function.
If the communicating functions are allocated on different nodes, the message has
to be transferred through the network.
The diversity of the communication mechanism is transparent to the application
functions, being resolved inside the
mechanism itself. A function which need

to communicate with another allocated on a different node, actually communicates with the Networking Communication function on its node. This latter, by sending the message on the network, communicates with the Networking Communication function on the destination node; finally, this delivers the message to the destination function. The two Path Managers in the two partner nodes are involved, since in each node a communication between two functions is performed.

Paths may be:

- towards path server functions;

- paths of the pipe type.

A path server function declares, when it is initialized, its ability to perform a specified service to the system. Any function, which needs that service, must be connected to the path server function; after the connection is granted, such a path is used by the client-file model. When a function declares itself as a path server, it notifies its name and the queue, to be used by any agent function, to the system and to the Path Manager of the node.

The pipe type is a more general type of path: it is instantiated between two generic functions which have both required the connection.

Even if the interface, which is available to the system for the use of the two types of paths, is different, the underlying communication mechanism is the same. The Path Manager is in charge to maintain the necessary informations related to the existing paths and to the paths whose instantiation is not completed, for both path types.

STABLE PATH SERVER FUNCTIONS

As previously outlined, the duplex configuration is perceived by the system as a high available single node. The aim of our work has been to provide a stable support to the communications between functions allocated to different nodes in the local network, particularly between agent functions and path server functions. A path server function has to provide a highly available service and therefore it must be made stable to the crash of a node.

The implementation of a path server function is based on the duplex configuration. The path server function, PSF, is duplicated: one copy, the PSF_M (Master Path Server Function), is allocated on the Master node and the other copy, the PSF_S (Stand-by Path Server Function), on the Stand-by node. The PSF_M performs all the activities of the PSF: it receives the service requests from the agent functions, it provides the requested service and it sends back the answer messages; the PSF_S function is not active, that is it does not perform the activities of the PSF, but it is able to take over the role of Master if and when it is needed. The role switching between the nodes implies the role switching of the path server functions allocated on those nodes. This role switching must be transparent to the agent functions, which have to perceive this event as a delay in the delivery of the answer messages.

The agent function A does not know the existence of the two instances PSF_M and PSF_S; consequently, A knows a unique logical name. A sends a unique message with a service request to the PSF; this message must be received by the PSF_M and the PSF_S. Such a communication must be atomic, that is the message either arrives to both PSF_M and PSF_S or to none of them, if both are active. In this way, the crash of one of the nodes does not determine inconsistencies between the PSF_M and the PSF_S with the consequent loss of transparency. This atomicity insures that the message is stable: each message is present on both the Master and the Stand-by node and the crash of the Master does not determine the loss of the messages not yet serviced.

The communication is based on a reliable multicast protocol, which insures that every message, sent on the network is received correctly by the destination nodes. The choice of a multicast protocol is directly supported by the system physical structure, that must make easy the broadcast of messages. The communication control is distributed since each node has to recognize itself as destination of any message in transit in the network. Both the replicated nodes where the PSF_M and the PSF_S are allocated must recognize themselves as a destination of the message sent by the agent function. Therefore, it is necessary that the interface of each node is able to accept messages in which the destination name is a logical one, not bounded by the name of the physical node.

The stability of the path server functions insures the continuous service which can be provided in the event of the crash of one of the nodes supporting them.

The crash of one node and the consequent role switching is to be made transparent to the function A, that is the crash of PSF_M should not determine any change of activity (roll-back, etc.) in A, but it should be perceived as a delay on the response time of the path server function. At this aim, the PSF_S must have an updated consistent state which should be used to initialize it in case of the role switching. The state of a path server function is composed by the set of the private objects of the function (e.g. if the path server function is the File Management System, its private objects are the files), the contents of its queue, that is the set of all the messages received by the path server function but not yet serviced, and possibly a set of temporary objects, like locks, semaphores, etc.

The outline of the operation of the PSF_M is:

- to read a message from its queue;

- to service the request without sending the answer messages;

- to send to the PSF_S the changes it has to perform to its state to get consistent to the PSF_M state;

- to send the proper answer messages to the agent function.

The particular sequencing of these operations guarantees the impossibility that the agent function may receive double answer messages from the PSF_M and the PSF_S in case of the crash of the PSF_M.

In case of a crash during the first phase or before servicing the request, the message, containing it, is present on the queues of both the PSF_M and the PSF_S. If the PSF_M is servicing the request without sending any answer to the agent function, only its state is changing, while the state of the PSF_S is unchanged: the crash of the PSF_M in this phase has no consequences since the service is provided again by the previous PSF_S (which switches to the new PSF_M).

The state update of the PSF_S must be atomic (if such communication comprehends more than one message from the PSF_M, the PSF_S will update its state after having received all the messages). To update the state, the private objects of the path server function and of the message queue must be updated; the message corresponding to the delivered service must be removed from the message queue. It is necessary to insure that the answer messages will be delivered to the agent function, if we want that the service is atomic. The PSF_M sends to the PSF_S these answer messages together with the state update. If a crash of the PSF_M happens before than the PSF_M has sent these answer messages, they will sent by the PSF_S after it recognizes the crash. The interface of the Stand-by node towards the network should be able to detect the fact that the answer has been sent to the agent function. The name of the agent function is known to the PSF_S since it is contained in the message delivered by the PSF_M.

The delivery of the state update of the PSF_S is performed with the same protocol which is used for the delivery of the service request from the agent function; it is needed that the destination names, in the communication between the two functions PSF_M and PSF_S, must identify univocally the other function to avoid a loss of performance on the interface. The logic name, known by the agent functions, is used only by them, while the logic names of the PSF_M and the PSF_S, used for communicating between them, depend on the role of the functions.

The network interface of the nodes in a duplex configuration has to be able to recognize the messages towards functions allocated on the node, and towards a dynamically variable set of functions external to the node.

The nodes in the system, to provide high availability, need to be easily replaced and conditioned after repair, to reconstitute a duplex configuration. This operation implies:

- recovery to a correct state of the communication structures;

- recovery of a correct state of the objects and of the messages of the path server function; to this aim, a complete copy of all the objects of the Master node is needed;

- reinsertion and conditioning of the node in the Stand-by role.

These operations must be executed with no interruption of the normal functioning of the Master node, to make the reinsertion operation transparent to the agent function and to maintain a good response time. Solutions, which are based on message removal or backward recovery of agent functions, are not usable. The Master node must recreate on the Stand-by node the communication structure and send the updates which may be happened, such as the creation of new paths, the transfer of all the messages which are present in the mailboxes, etc. Finally, the Master node must communicate to the Stand-by the termination of this operation.

CONCLUSIONS

In this paper we have provided a discussion of a possible implementation of a distributed system in local area network, which should exhibit high availability. The problem of critical resources has been considered and a protocol for managing a redundant configuration has been proposed. In a Master/Stand-by duplex approach, the path server functions are duplicated and this organization is in charge of the continuous managing of the resources. A useful support to an efficient role switching has been identified in the stability of the messages on both instances of the path server function. The transparency to the agent functions has been provided by the service request protocol which does not distinguish between the two replicated instances of the path server function. The implementation of this solution is underway on a testbed, composed by two M.A.R.A. nodes, each with two processors, and connected on an Ethernet local area network.

REFERENCES

Ciompi, P., M. La Manna, C. Lissoni, I. R. Martin, and L. Simoncini (1983a). A highly available multimicroprocessor system for real-time applications. Proc. of SAFECOMP-83, Cambridge.

Ciompi, P., M. La Manna, C. Lissoni, and L. Simoncini (1983b). A redundant system supporting atomic

transactions for real-time applications. Real-Time System Symposium,
Arlington.

Dion, J. (1980). The Cambridge file
server. Op Sys Rev, 14(4), 26-35.

Lampson, B. W., and H. E. Sturgis (1976).
Design of a distributed file system.
Xerox Palo Alto Research Center Re-
port.

Lampson, B. W., and H. E. Sturgis (1979).
Crash recovery in a distributed data
storage system. Xerox Palo Alto
Research Center Report.

Lijtmaer N. (1983). The first one hundred
Cnet abstracts. Progetto Finalizza-
to Informatica, C.N.R., Progetto P1
Cnet, Report n.101. ETS/PISA.

Martin, I. R. (1981). MARA: an overview of
the civil implementation. Selenia
Internal Report.

Metcalfe, R. M., and D. R. Boggs (1976).
Ethernet distributed packet switch-
ing for local computer networks.
CACM, 19(7), 395-404.

Popek, G. J., G. Thiel, and C. S. Kline
(1983). Recovery of replicated
storage in distributed systems.
UCLA Computer Science Technical Report.

Walker B. J., G. J. Popek, R. M. English,
C. Kline, and G. Thiel (1983). The
LOCUS distributed operating system.
Proc. of the Ninth Symposium on
Operating Systems Principles, Bret-
ton Woods, NH.

Wilkes, M. V., and D. J. Wheeler (1979).
The Cambridge Digital communications
ring. Proc Local Area Communications Network Symp. Boston, May
1979, Nat. Bur. Standards Special
Publication.

FUZZY BASED SAFETY SYSTEM AS A PART
OF COMPUTER CONTROL SOFTWARE

P. Vaija*, K. Keskinen*, M. Järveläinen* and M. Dohnal**

*Laboratory of Chemical Engineering, Helsinki University of Technology, Espoo,
Finland
**Department of Chemical Engineering, Technical University of Brno, Brno,
Czechoslovakia

Abstract. Fuzzy simulation is used to develop a closed loop for a process - safety
action system. The dynamics of the process are specified either by a conventional or a
fuzzy dynamic model. The fuzzy decision making algorithm recommends some safety
actions, if necessary. By this action the dynamics of the process can be modified.

Keywords. Fuzzy diagnosis, artificial intelligence, chemical industry, control
engineering computer application, failure detection, safety system.

INTRODUCTION

The important goal of a control system is to
guarantee the safety of the process. When the
process under study is complex and it is difficult
to measure, the existing methods for analysis of the
safety of the process seems to have some defects.
A promising approach seems to be an optimal
combination of subjective and objective or
partially subjective algorithms (Vaija and co-
workers, 1985). The main goal of this paper is to
demonstrate how a fuzzy based diagnostic
algorithm can be integrated into control software.

ELEMENTS OF FUZZY MATHEMATICS

Fuzzy mathematics is a branch of mathematics which
has reach a level permitting practical
applications. However, for the purpose of
diagnosis of chemical processes it has not been
used so far. The following introduction to the
fuzzy set theory is addressed in particular to
readers who would like to explore in more detail
the opportunities which it offers. Those who want
to acquire a systematic knowledge of fuzzy
mathematics are advised to consult e.g. (Dubois
and Prade, 1980).

The basic element of the fuzzy mathematics is the
fuzzy set. An element can belong to the fuzzy set
partially. Let

$$U = \{ x \}$$

denote a conventional set. Then a fuzzy set A in
universe U is a set of ordered pairs

$$A = \{ (x, m_A(x)) \}, \quad x \in U \qquad (1)$$

where $m_A(x)$ is the grade of membership of x in A.

$$0 \leq m_A(x) \leq 1 \qquad (2)$$

According to Dohnal (1984) simple fuzzy
implication has the following general form:

$$\text{if A then B} \qquad (3)$$

Where A and B are fuzzy sets in the universes U_A
and U_B. The one dimensional fuzzy implication (3)
is the fuzzy set in the universe $U_A \times U_B$. The

grade of membership function of this fuzzy
set is given by the following formula:

$$m_{A \times B}(x,y) = \min_{x \in U_A, y \in U_B} (m_A(x), m_B(y)) \qquad (4)$$

A fuzzy composition using one implication (3)
is a rule which assigns to the fuzzy set A´ a
fuzzy set B´ with the following grade of
membership

$$m_{B´}(y) = \max_{x \in U_A} (\min(m_{A´}(x), m_{A \times B}(x,y))) \qquad (5)$$

A multidimensional and multivariable problem
can be determined by a set of fuzzy implications:

$$\begin{aligned}
&\text{if } A_{1,1} \text{ and } A_{1,2} \ . \ . \ \text{and } A_{1,n} \text{ then } B_1 \text{ or} \\
&\text{if } A_{2,1} \text{ and } A_{2,2} \ . \ . \ \text{and } A_{2,n} \text{ then } B_2 \text{ or} \\
&. \\
&. \qquad\qquad\qquad\qquad\qquad\qquad\qquad (6) \\
&. \\
&\text{if } A_{m,1} \text{ and } A_{m,2} \ . \ . \ \text{and } A_{m,n} \text{ them } B_m
\end{aligned}$$

Where the fuzzy set $A_{i,j}$ represents a value
of the j-th independent variable in the i-th
conditional statement. The fuzzy set B_i
represents the corresponding value of the
dependent variable. The evaluating algorithm
of a multidimensional and multivariable set
(6) is based on the formula (5).

The fuzzy decision making algorithm can be
interpreted as an evaluation of the latter
case. The only difference is that the fuzzy
sets Bs are not fuzzy sets but discrete
alternatives. The fuzzy diagnosis is actually
a decision problem.

In the diagnostic algorithm, the relationship
between symptoms in the process variables and the
corresponding failures is specified as a set of
conditional statements of the general form:

$$\begin{aligned}
&\text{if } S_{i,1} \text{ and } S_{i,2} \ . \ . \ \text{and } S_{i,n} \text{ then } F_i \qquad (7) \\
&i = 1, \ . \ . \ . \ m
\end{aligned}$$

where $S_{i,j}$ is the fuzzy value of the j-th symptom
in the i-th statement.

F_is are the corresponding failures. The diagnosis
of an unknown failure $F_i´$ causing the set of

symptoms $S'_{i,j}$ is made by evaluating the grade of membership for this failure.

FUZZY BASED SAFETY ACTION SYSTEM

The safety action system works as a supervisor for the control system. This is reasonable because the time interval in computer control systems for checking the safety of the process is usually much longer than the interval for control.

The fuzzy safety action system forms a closed loop with the process through the controller. The results of the prediction of the state of the process made by conventional or fuzzy dynamic models are fed to the fuzzy safety action system. On the basis of the prediction the safety action system recommends some safety actions to be carried out, if necessary.

As an example of the set of fuzzy diagnostic heuristics, the following LDPE reactor is studied. The LDPE polymerization reaction is highly exothermic and a very rapid one. There is a danger of a thermal runaway reaction and an axtinction. The designed, safe operating temperatures vary between $140^{\circ}-300^{\circ}C$. Normally the reactor is controlled by a PI-controller which manipulates the initiator feed rate.

The state of the reactor depends on the temperature in the reactor and its rate of change. So the conditional statements (6) in the safety action system have the following form:

$$\text{if } T_i \text{ and } \Delta T/\Delta \text{ then } SA_i \qquad (8)$$

where T_i is the temperature at the time moment Δi and $\Delta T = T_i - T_{i-1}$. SA_i represents the corresponding safety action.

Some examples of these conditional statements are given in Table 1. The linguistic values of temperature and its rate of change are given in Tables 2 and 3. As safety actions the following operations are used:

```
N    = no safety actions i.e. normal set values
       for initiator feed rate
IP1  = reset initiator feed rate to    56
IP2  =   "        "        "   "   "   41
IP3  =   "        "        "   "   "   32
IN1  =   "        "        "   "   "   106
IN2  =   "        "        "   "   "   135
IN3  =   "        "        "   "   "   188
SD   = shut down the process i.e. close
       initiator feed, stop compressors and
       purge the reactor content
```

In Table 4 five temperatures of the reactor and their rates of change are given. These are tested against the knowledge of the state of the process given with the conditional statements (8) in the safety system. Results of the diagnosis are given in Table 5. The results are interpreted so that the safety action which has the highest grade of membership ought to be carried out (Vaija and co-workers, 1985).

FUZZY BASED SAFETY SYSTEM AS A PART
OF COMPUTER CONTROL SOFTWARE

Several years ago diagnostic procedures were studied separately from control problems e.g. turbocompressors were checked at regular time intervals independently of their control systems. The rapid development of microelectronics makes it possible to include a diagnostic algorithm in a control algorithm as a standard and integrated part of it.

The state of the process which is under control is checked against the fuzzy diagnostic algorithm as is shown in Fig. 1. There are two principal alternatives. The simplest one is to check the present situation which is specified by process output / see Fig. 1/. The second way is to use a predictor / see Fig. 2/.

There is not enough experience to make any recommendations on which of the alternatives to use. It just seems probable that the predictor system will have similar disadvantages as feed-forward control of complex processes with long timedelays, highly nonlinear behaviour and which are difficult to measure.

As long as diagnostic systems have to be tested, development of a model of the process is inevitable. The fuzzy predictor is another reason for the development of suitable specification of the process behaviour.

FUZZY MODEL OF UNSTEADY STATE BEHAVIOUR

There is a long tradition in the use of differential equations in the development of models for processes. Different sophisticated algorithms are applied to identify values of different constants. However, in reality it is very difficult to use these methods if measurements are of poor quality. As typical examples of such processes, the cement kiln and bioreactors can be given. Unfortunately, safety systems are urgently needed for such types of processes.

In order to be able to test a safety system, as a kind of formal method specification, unsteady state simulation is needed. Therefore an attempt has been made to apply fuzzy mathematics to predict the behaviour of a process. There are two possible approaches to the development of such a model. The first one is to use primary data directly. The second one is based on statements which come from the human operator. The direct use of primary data i.e. time records is a very simple and efficient method. In Fig. 3 there is an example of a time-dependent temperature record. The sampling period is Δ. The temperature in the time moment Δi is T_i. This temperature is considered as a fuzzy set. Its grade of membership function is given in Fig. 4. For diagnostic purposes the following is supposed

$$\begin{aligned} b &= c \\ a &= b(1-\varepsilon) \\ d &= b(1+\varepsilon) \end{aligned} \qquad (9)$$

where ε is the relative measurement error of the temperature. The accuracy of measurements determines the fuzziness. The crucial problem of the direct application of the primary data is the choice of history length which is sufficiently long to allow the prediction of the temperature change during Δ time units forward and sufficiently short to be acceptable for fuzzy evaluation of the safety action model.

The set of fuzzy conditional statements which are used to specify the dynamic behaviour of the process has the following general form:

$$\text{if } T_i \text{ and } T_{i-1} \ldots \text{ and } T_{i-s} \text{ then } T_{i+1} \qquad (10)$$

where all values of Ts are fuzzy sets specified by (9). s is the acceptable number of steps backwards ("the history"). For real problems, more than one variable X is needed to predict the value of the dependent variable. Therefore the following general formula is needed:

if X_i^1 and X_{i-1}^1 . . and $X_{i-s_{r,t}}^1$ and

X_i^j and X_{i-1}^j . . and $X_{i-s_{r,t}}^j$ then X_{i+1}^t (11)

where X_i^j is the value of the j-th variable in the time moment Δi. $s_{d,t}$ is the legth of the history of the d-th variable needed for the prediction of the value of the t-th variable. The statement (11) is a fuzzy conditional statement. It is possible to create a set of such statements based on direct time records of all variables. The number of statements in such a set is equal to the number of samples taken during identification procedure. Such an approach has been used for identification of a laboratory fermentor where three variables and eight sampling intervals as a history for all variables have been considered.

The second approach is based on heuristics which come from an experienced operator who knows the process very well. Such an intuitive approach seems to be suprisingly efficient e.g. wood drying, fermentation, polymerization.

The safest way to a relatively realiable model of dynamic behaviour is to combine the set of conditional statements (11) with the operator´s heuristics. The fuzzy simulation can test operator´s heuristics against primary data to discover all inconsistencies. In this article, the operator´s heuristics are chosen as a basis for the description of dynamic behaviour because it requires certain skill which can be demonstrated just by an example.

TEST EXAMPLE

As a test example, a LDPE reactor is chosen. Its mathematical model has been studied by Martini and Georgakis (1984). This model has been used as an example of a conventional model. NESTE company kindly provided an operator´s heuristics which have been used in development of the fuzzy model. The results reached by both models were very similar.

In Fig. 5, there is a time record of the reactor temperature and of the initiator feed rate. The initiator feed rate is chosen to be manipulated. The diagnostic algorithm described above is used to check the temperature every tenth part of the residence time. In Fig. 5, up to the time point A no dangerous situations were identified. Because of certain disturbances in the time interval AB, the fuzzy diagnostic algorithm identified a dangerous situation and recommended resetting initiator feed rate (for details, see example of fuzzy diagnostic algorithm). In this way the controller is activated. As a consequence of the controller activity, the temperature in the reactor went down to an acceptable level.

CONCLUSION

Expert systems, and indirectly artificial intelligence, are gradually being incorporated into control sysetms to guarantee that dangerous situations will be recognised in good time. However, this development requires the solution of the following problems:
- development of a flexible fuzzy oriented expert system
- development of user friendly interface which guarantees that the experience of operators can be transformed into fuzzy conditional statements without detailed knowledge of fuzzy mathematics
- integration of safety action as a part of

synthesis algorithms for multidimensional control The advantage of the fuzzy model which seems to be the most important one, is that dangerous situations can be detected before any catastrophe and one can try to normalize the process with some safety actions before shutting it down. This can be done because the fuzzy system compares continuously the values of process variables with their normal values.

ACKNOWLEDGEMENT

The authors would like to thank EURECHA for the control simulator TACS (Vajda, 1984) which is used in this study together with our own computer software.

LIST OF SYMBOLS

$m_A(x)$ = grade of membership of x in A
T = T_r/T_{ref}
T_r = temperature of reactor, K
T_{ref} = reference temperature, K
I = I^*/I_{ref}
I^* = initiator feed rate, mol/LT
I_{ref} = reference initiator feed rate, mol/LT
t = t^*/τ
t^* = time, s
τ = residence time, s
TP1-13 = positive deviation of temperature
TN0-4 = negative deviation of temperature
DP1-5 = positive rate of change of temperature
DN0-4 = negative rate of change of temperature
IP1-3 = manipulated set values of I
IN1-3 = manipulated set values of I
SD = shut down the process
N = no safety action

REFERENCES

Dohnal, M. (1984). Fuzzy methodology of chemical engineering models, 8th CHISA congress, Praque.
Dubois, D. and H. Prade (1980). Fuzzy Sets and Systems, Academic Press, New York.
Martini, L., and C. Georgakis (9184). Low-Density Polyethylene Vessel Reactors, Part I and II, AIChE Journal, 30.
Vaija, P., Turunen, I., Järveläinen, M., and M. Dohnal (1985). Fuzzy strategy for failure detection and safety control of complex processes, to be published in Microelectronics and Reliability.
Vajda, S. (1984). TACS- A Teaching Aid for Control Studies, Manual, EURECHA, Budapest.

TABLE 1 Conditional Statements for Safety
Action system

| no | indenpendent variables | | dependent variable |
	T2	ΔT2/ Δt	safety action
1	TP3	DP5	SA
2	TP2	DP4	IP1
3	TP6	DP3	IP1
4	TP7	DP2	IP2
5	TP9	DP1	IP3
6	TP2	DN0	N
7	TP4	DN1	N
8	TN2	DN2	IN2
9	TP5	DN3	N
.			
.			
.			
164			

TABLE 2 Linguistic Values and their Membership
Functions for Temperatures

| ling. values | grade of membership function | | | |
	a	b	c	d
TP13	1.245	1.255	10.0	10.0
TP12	1.225	1.234	1.245	1.255
TP11	1.205	1.215	1.225	1.235
TP10	1.185	1.195	1.205	1.215
TP9	1.165	1.175	1.185	1.195
TP8	1.145	1.155	1.165	1.175
TP7	1.125	1.135	1.145	1.155
TP6	1.105	1.115	1.125	1.135
TP5	1.085	1.095	1.105	1.115
TP4	1.065	1.075	1.085	1.095
TP3	1.045	1.055	1.065	1.075
TP2	1.025	1.035	1.045	1.055
TP1	1.005	1.015	1.025	1.035
TN0	0.998	1.000	1.005	1.015
TN1	0.994	0.994	0.998	1.000
TN2	0.945	0.951	0.994	0.994
TN3	0.912	0.915	0.925	0.935
TN4	0.000	0.000	0.912	0.915

TABLE 3 Linguistic Values and their Membership
Functions for Rates of Change of the
Temperature

| ling. values | grade of membership function | | | |
	a	b	c	d
DP5	0.195	0.205	1.000	1.000
DP4	0.145	0.155	0.195	0.205
DP3	0.095	0.105	0.145	0.155
DP2	0.045	0.055	0.095	0.105
DP1	0.000	0.005	0.045	0.055
DN0	-0.005	0.000	0.000	0.005
DN1	-0.035	-0.030	-0.005	0.000
DN2	-0.065	-0.060	-0.035	-0.030
DN3	-1.000	-1.000	-0.065	-0.060

TABLE 4 Temperature and its Rate of Change
in Examples as Presented in Fig. 3

| variable | | example | | | | |
		EX1	EX2	EX3	EX4	EX5
T	a	1.018	1.170	0.095	1.132	1.067
	b	1.021	1.173	0.096	1.134	1.071
	c	1.021	1.173	0.096	1.134	1.071
	d	1.024	1.175	0.097	1.136	1.073
ΔT/ Δt	a	0.053	0.040	-0.037	0.104	0.143
	b	0.055	0.043	-0.036	0.106	0.145
	c	0.055	0.043	-0.036	0.106	0.145
	d	0.058	0.046	-0.034	0.108	0.147

TABLE 5 Results of Test Examples

| safety action | example | | | | |
	EX1	EX2	EX3	EX4	EX5
N	1.00	0.38	0.00	0.08	0.57
IP1	0.00	0.00	0.00	0.25	0.67
IP2	0.00	0.08	0.00	0.08	0.00
IP3	0.00	0.83	0.00	0.00	0.00
IN1	0.00	0.00	0.00	0.00	0.00
IN2	0.00	0.00	0.00	0.00	0.00
IN3	0.00	0.00	1.00	0.00	0.00
SD	0.00	0.08	0.00	0.92	0.17

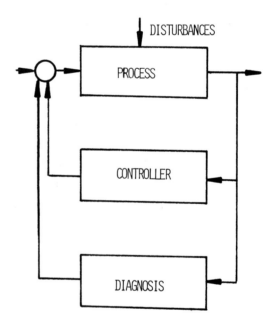

Fig. 1. Process control with safety diagnosis
using output values of process variables.

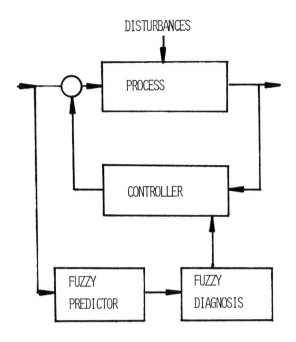

Fig. 2. Process control with safety diagnosis using predictor.

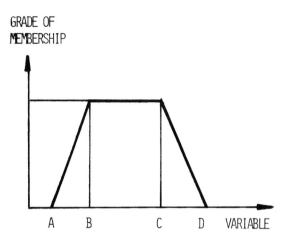

Fig. 4. Grade of membership function.

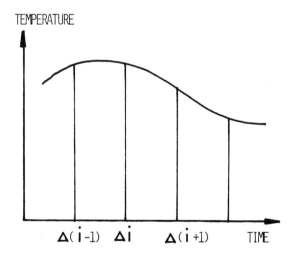

Fig. 3. The time record of temperature.

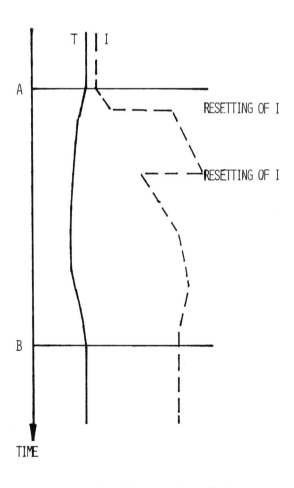

Fig. 5. An example of the operation of the controller - safety action system. In the LDPE reactor the initiator feed rate I is manipulated.

MODELLING THE EFFECT OF TRANSIENT FAULTS IN FAULT TOLERANT COMPUTER SYSTEMS

Y. W. Yak*, K. E. Forward** and T. S. Dillon**

*Chisholm Institute of Technology
**Monash University

Abstract. The Bounded Set Approach to reliability modelling is extended to the case of transient faults in Fault Tolerant Systems. An arbitrary arrival time distribution is assumed for transient faults rather than a constant rate. The method has been automated and results of several studies are given.

Keywords. Computer Evaluation, Modelling, Reliability Theory, Computer Organization.

1.   INTRODUCTION

The bounded set approach [1, 2, 3, 4] to modelling the reliability of systems is usually restricted to systems where each module's failure characteristics are independent of the other modules in the system. In fault tolerant computer systems the co-operating nature of the modules and the required redundancy of such systems means that the failure characteristics of an individual module are dependent on the properties of many other modules. This interdependence of the modules has meant that decompositional approaches such as the bounded set have not been used to model such systems. The Markov State Transition Approach (MSTA) provides for first stage dependencies and for that reason has become the traditional approach to these problems [5, 6, 7, 8]. Recently we have described extensions to the bounded set approach which permit the inclusion of intermodular dependencies of the type which occur in fault tolerant systems [2, 3, 4]. As the decomposition methods provide reliabilities as a function of time as well as the parameters and form of the failure characteristics, they permit the solution of reliability problems by direct substitution and do not require the solution of simultaneous differential or integral equations as in the Markov method. For this reason, the solution to cases where the failure rates are a function of time are more easily computed by the bounded set approach as we have shown in [4]. Here we extend the method to considerations of transient faults in fault tolerant computer systems where the bounded set method is found to be a better means of solution, since the arrival rates of such faults is not exponentially distributed and hence it is not possible to easily provide mathematically tractable solutions by the MSTA.

2.   BOUNDED SET METHOD

The method has been described in detail in [2, 3, 4] but for those readers not yet familiar with these papers a very brief introduction to the method is included here.

Let us consider a system, for the purposes of explanation, in which a module can be in one of three states namely (a) working; (b) failed but with a covered failure; (c) failed - uncovered failure.

The N modules are arranged in an N-tuple, with their order being determined by the system

designers perception of their criticality to the functioning of the system.

The total collection of states is now systematically decomposed into sets of operating states and sets of non-operating states such that

(a)   the sets of states obtained during the decomposition are non-overlapping;
(b)   upper and lower bounds on a set are developed to allow classification into operational or non-operational sets of states;
(c)   any sets that cannot be classified into either sets of non-operational or sets of operational states are further expanded. Such expansion continues until all child sets can be classified.

This decomposition process is illustrated in Fig. 1 for a system with two active modules operating in duplex with one spare.

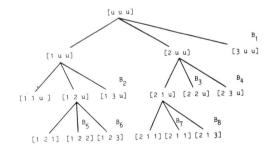

The power of the method derives from the fact that one only needs to consider transitions between these sets of operational states and sets of failed states which greatly reduces the number of states involved in the calculations, as the number of such sets is usually far less than the total number of states. Since the sets are non-overlapping the requisite reliability parameters can readily be computed for Fault Tolerant Systems [2, 3, 4], in the case of permanent faults.

In this paper, we describe extensions of the method to model transient faults, together with applications to example systems.

3.   TRANSIENT FAULT

Transient faults constitute a major proportion of
all hardware faults that can arise in a fault
tolerant system. All previous attempts to model
transient faults analytically have been based on a
Markov model. This assumes that the transient
fault arrival rate is a constant. Several studies
reveal that the arrival rate of transient faults
is not a constant but decreases with time [9], and
hence such an assumption is not valid. This non-
constant nature of transient fault arrival rate is
a major problem. Existing techniques of performance modelling can only handle special cases of
non-constant transition rates which does not
include the case where all the failure rates are
non-constant. The non-constant fault arrival rate
problem is further compounded by a more subtle
problem created by the fact that a transient fault
leaves the hardware undamaged after its occurence.
If the system can successfully recognise the
transient fault, the module will not be switched
out of the system. This is unlike the case of a
permanent faults where the affected module will be
switched out of the system if recovery is
successful.

While existing techniques cannot handle non-
constant failure rates effectively, the ability of
the bounded set approach to handle closed systems
that have modules with non-exponential distributions has already been demonstrated. This
technique could therefore be extended to
incorporate the transient fault process.

4.   SYSTEM RECOVERY PROCESS

Before proceeding to incorporate transient faults,
it is necessary to understand how transient faults
will affect the system. Transient faults leave
the hardware undamaged after their occurrence. A
recovery procedure which is designed specifically
to combat only permanent faults would be extremely
wasteful, as it would discard a module that had a
transient fault even though it is fully functional. Furthermore, because transient faults occur
more frequently, than permanent faults, the system
will run out of spares very quickly. Therefore,
any effective recovery procedure must possess the
capability to distinguish between transient and
permanent faults. As the system has no way of
telling whether a detected fault is transient or
permanent, the transient fault recovery process
will be initiated first, followed by the permanent
fault recovery process. If the fault is positive-
ly identified as transient, the system recovers
without discarding the affected module. If this
is not possible, then the permanent fault recovery
process is initiated in an attempt to identify the
faulty module. Once identified, as a permanent
fault, the system recovers by discarding the
affected module. The system may also fail during
the recovery process for a variety of reasons such
as the corruption of insufficiently protected
critical information.

Ng and Avizienis [10] have proposed a model for
the transient fault recovery process. In their
analysis, it was assumed that the transient fault
arrival rate is a constant. In addition, 3 parameters were introduced to account for the three
possible outcomes of the transient recovery
process. They are as follows:

C_T = Transient Coverage
  = Pr Transient recovery is successful | fault
    occurs
L_T = Transient Leakage
  = Pr Fault is treated as permanent | fault
    occurs

F_T = System Failure Factor
    Pr System fails | fault occurs

Note that all these parameters were defined to be
conditional on the occurrence of all faults,
transient or permanent. Data collected [9] on
transient faults has indicated that the transient
fault arrival rate is not a constant but decreasing with time. The permanent faults arrive at a
constant rate while the rate for transients
varies. Hence the two types of faults must be
represented.

We will therefore re-analyse the model relaxing
the assumption that the transient fault rate is a
constant and redefine the 3 parameters to be
conditional on the occurrence of transient faults
only i.e.

C_T = Transient Coverage
  = Pr Transient recovery is successful |
    transient fault occurs
L_T = Transient Leakage
  = Pr Fault is treated as permanent |
    transient fault occurs
F_T = System Failure Factor
  = Pr System fails | transient fault occurs

Note that $C_T + L_T + F_T = 1$.

The case of a permanent fault from which the
system fails to recover because it attempted a
transient fault recovery is modelled by the
coverage factor, C_a.

5.   TRANSIENT FAULTS ONLY

We will first model a system subjected to transient faults only. In this section we will derive
the failure characteristics of such a system. The
following assumptions are made in the analysis:

(a) The arrival time of transient faults in each
     module is independent and follows the
     distribution $F_t(t)$.
(b) Transient faults affect only the active mod-
     ules and have no effect on the spare modules.

As we have described in the preceding section, on
the arrival of a transient fault, there are three
possible outcomes of the system transient recovery
process.

(a) System successfully recovers from the
     transient fault without discarding the
     affected module with probability, C_T.
(b) A transient fault is treated as a permanent
     fault with probability, L_T.
(c) The system fails during transient recovery
     with probability, F_T.

When a transient fault is treated as permanent,
there is still a further probability of $(1-C_a)$
that the permanent fault recovery process may be
unable to recover from the transient fault and
probability, C_a that the transient fault is
successfully recovered from during the permanent
fault recovery process by discarding the affected
module. Therefore, when a transient fault occurs,
a fraction of the faults given by $C_a L_T$ will be
treated as covered permanent faults, another
fraction $(1-C_a)L_T + F_T$ will be treated as
uncovered faults and the remainder C_T will be
successfully recovered during the transient
recovery stage. This is illustrated in Fig. 2.

As we are interested in the effect of transient
faults on the reliability of the system, we can
for all practical purposes assume that the
recovery process is instantaneous and merge state
1 with state 1a to give the 3 state model as shown

in Fig. 3. Let us first derive $p_t(t)$, $q_t(t)$ and $r_t(t)$, the probability that the active module is in state 1, 2, and 3 respectively in the 3-state model. The expanded state diagram of an active module being subjected to transient faults only is shown in Fig. 4. There are many working states denoted by W_i since every occurrence of a transient fault is a regenerative point, and

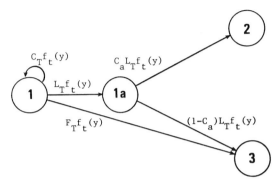

Fig. 2a. System Response to a Transient Fault

successful recovery of the transient fault will bring the system to another working state similar to the previous working state, except that the

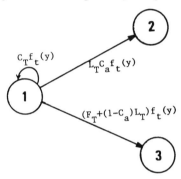

Fig. 3. System Response to a Transient Fault – Merged State Diagram

time is reset to the origin. Unsuccessful recovery will either lead to the fault being treated as a covered permanent fault or will cause a system failure. State 1 of Fig. 2 is the sum of all the working states in Fig. 4, i.e.

$$p_t(t) = \sum_{i=1}^{\infty} Pr(W_i) \tag{1}$$

$$q_t(t) = C_a(L_T/(L_T+F_T))(1-p_t(t)) \tag{2}$$

$$r_t(t) = 1 - p_t(t) - q_t(t) \tag{3}$$

Let the time between arrival of transient faults be X_k where X_1, X_2 ... are identically and independently distributed with distribution $F_t(t)$. Then

$$p_t(s) = \overline{F}_t(s) + C_T\overline{F}_t(s)f_t(s)$$
$$+ C_T^2\overline{F}_t(s)f_t(s)f_t(s) + \ldots$$
$$= \frac{\overline{F}_t(s)}{1 - C_Tf_t(s)} \tag{4}$$

where $F(s)$ denotes the Laplace transform of $F(t)$.

$q_t(t)$ and $r_T(t)$ can be obtained from Eqn. (2) and (3) respectively. Equation (4) can easily be evaluated numerically and efficiently for any $F_t(t)$ using the Fast Fourier transform technique. $p_t(t)$ in the time domain can similarly be obtained by a numerical inversion using the Fast Fourier transform technique.

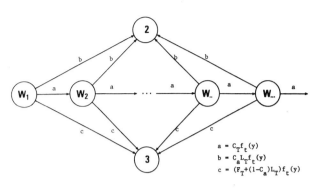

Fig. 4. System Response to a Transient Fault – Expanded State Diagram

6.   INCORPORATION OF PERMANENT AND TRANSIENT FAULT

Having derived the expression of $p_t(t)$, $q_t(t)$ and $r_t(t)$ for a module subjected to transient faults only, we can now extend it to incorporate the effect of both permanent and transient faults. An active module is now subjected to permanent faults with a constant arrival rate, λ, and transient faults following a distribution, $F_t(t)$. Let $p_p(t)$, $q_p(t)$ and $r_p(t)$ be the probability that the module is in state 1, 2 and 3 respectively considering permanent faults only. Then

$$p_p(t) = e^{-\lambda t} \tag{5}$$

$$q_p(t) = C_a(1-e^{-\lambda t}) \tag{6}$$

$$r_p(t) = (1-C_a)(1-e^{-\lambda t}) \tag{7}$$

Let $p_a(t)$, $q_a(t)$ and $r_a(t)$ denote the probability that the active module is in state 1, 2 and 3 respectively considering both transient and permanent faults. Then

$$p_a(t) = p_t(t)p_p(t) \tag{8}$$

$$q_a(t) = p_p(t)q_t(t) + p_t(t)q_p(t) + q_t(t)q_p(t) \tag{9}$$

$$r_a(t) = 1 - p_a(t) - q_a(t) \tag{10}$$

Therefore for an active module, $p_a(t)$, $q_a(t)$ and $r_a(t)$ can be derived for any given transient fault arrival time distribution and permanent fault rate. Note that the permanent fault rate need not be a constant but can follow any arbitrary distribution. This will be reflected in $p_p(t)$. As a transient fault is assumed to affect only the active module, the probabilities that a module, in the spare mode, is in state 1, $p_s(t)$, state 2, $q_s(t)$ and state 3, $r_s(t)$ are given by

$$p_s(t) = e^{-\lambda't} \tag{11}$$

$$q_s(t) = C_s(1-e^{-\lambda't}) \tag{12}$$

$$r_s(t) = (1-C_s)(1-e^{-\lambda't}) \tag{13}$$

where λ' and C_s are the failure rate and fault coverage of the module in the spare mode. Knowing $p_a(t)$, $q_a(t)$, $r_a(t)$, $p_s(t)$, $q_s(t)$ and $r_s(t)$, the failure characteristics of the system can be obtained as explained in references [2, 3, 4].

7.   SAMPLE SYSTEM STUDIES

Let us now study the performance of a fault

tolerant system taking transient faults into
account. In order to do this, we will use results
obtained by McConnel et al. [10] from data
collected on transient faults in digital computer
systems. The results indicate that transient
faults follow a decreasing fault rate and fit the
Weibull distribution well. The Weibull density
function is of the form

$$f(t) = \alpha \lambda t^{\alpha-1} e^{-\lambda t^{\alpha}} \qquad (14)$$

with the mean, μ, given by the expression

$$\mu = \lambda^{-1/\alpha} \Gamma(1 + \frac{1}{\alpha}) \qquad (15)$$

where Γ( ) denotes the gamma function.

The values of α obtained from those studies for
three architectures of computer systems range from
0.4 to 0.9. We will use the value of α and λ
obtained for the C.vmp [11, 12] for the sole
purpose of illustration of the application of the
bounded set technique to incorporate transient
faults in a closed fault tolerant system. For the
C.vmp, the maximum likelihood estimate of α is
0.654 and λ is 0.0629. This gives a mean rate of
1.616×10^{-2}/hr.

Since permanent faults, as several studies [13, 9]
have revealed, only constitute about 10% of all
faults, we will use a permanent fault arrival rate
of 1×10^{-3}/hr which is about 1/10 of the transient fault arrival rate. The failure characteristics of the system can be obtained as explained in
Ref. [4]. The parameters for the fault tolerant
system are summarised as follows:

Number of active modules: 2
Permanent failure rate : 1×1^{-3}/hr
Permanent fault coverage: 0.95
Transient λ: 0.0629
Transient α: 0.654
Transient coverage : 1, 0.99, 0.95
Transient leakage factor: variable
Number of spare modules: 3
Permanent failure rate: 1×10^{-6}/hr
Permanent fault coverage: 0.99

The result for the studies are shown in Fig. 5 for
C_T = 0.95, 0.99 and 1. For C_T = 0.95 and 0.99,
two cases are shown, one with F_T = 0 and the other
with L_T = 0 marking the upper and lower bound for
the probability of system failure for each instant
of C_T. For comparison purposes, the result for
permanent faults only is also given. This
corresponds to C_T = 1, i.e. transient faults have
no effect on the system.

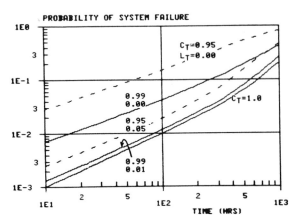

Fig. 5. Studies on Transient Faults
(Note $C_T + F_T + L_T = 1$)

The result indicates that even when 99% of the
transient faults are successfully recovered from

(C_T = 0.99), transient fault can be a major cause
of system failure if L_T is low compared to F_T. In
general, the effect of transient faults on the
system will depend on several factors such as the
number of active modules, active module coverage
etc. and it is difficult to give any conclusion
based only on C_T, L_T and F_T alone.

8.   CONCLUSIONS

We have previously demonstrated that the bounded
set approach has the ability to model a wide class
of closed fault tolerant systems, and it can be
applied to the modelling of a system consisting of
modules with embedded TMR submodules and a system
where the modules can have any arbitrary failure
time distribution, F(t). The extension of the
method to modelling transient faults with
arbitrary arrival time distribution was given in
the present paper. Using this approach, system
modelling can be easily automated and the results
of studies, which were obtained using such a
computer program, have been reported on.

9.   ACKNOWLEDGEMENT

The authors would like to thank the General
Manager of Telecom Australia and The Australian
Research Grants Scheme for financial support for
the work reported in this paper. The authors
would also like to acknowledge the numerous useful
discussions we had with several members of the
Telecom Research Laboratory Staff.

10.   REFERENCES

[1] Cheong, H.K., T.S. Dillon, "A bounded set
     theoretical approach to reliability modell-
     ing and calculations for composite gener-
     ation-transmission systems including systems
     with unconventional energy sources", Int.
     Journal of Electrical Power and Energy
     Systems, Vol. 1, No. 2, pp. 95-106, 1979.

[2] Yak, Y.W., T.S. Dillon, K.E. Forward, "A new
     approach to the modelling of closed fault
     tolerant computer systems", Proc. Int.
     Workshop Modelling and Performance
     Evaluation of Parallel Systems, Grenoble,
     Dec., 1984, France, pp 230-249.

[3] Yak, Y.W., T.S. Dillon, K.E. Forward, "A
     bounded set approach to the evaluation of
     reliability of fault tolerant systems, Part
     I: Methodology, powered spares", Accepted
     for publication, Proc. IEE, Part E, 1985

[4] Yak, Y.W., T.S. Dillon, K.E. Forward, "A
     bounded set approach to the evaluation of
     reliability of fault tolerant systems, Part
     II: Unpowered spares, non constant failure
     rate, aggregatable systems", Accepted for
     publication, Proc. IEE, Part E, 1985.

[5] Costes, A., J.E. Doucet, C. Landrault, J.C.
     Laprie, "SURF: A dependability evaluation
     of complex fault tolerant systems", Proc. of
     the 11th Int. Symposium on Fault Tolerant
     Computing, pp. 72-78, June, 1981.

[6] Makam, S.V., A. Avizienis, "Modelling and
     analysis of periodically renewed closed
     fault tolerant systems", Proc. of the 11th
     Int. Symp. on Fault Tolerant Computer, pp.
     134-141, June, 1981.

[7] Yak, Y.W., T.S. Dillon, K.E. Forward,
     "Incorporation of recovery and repair time
     in the reliability modelling of fault
     tolerant systems", IEE/IFAC SAFECOMP',
     Cambridge U.K., pp. 45-52, Sept., 1983.

[8]   Yak, Y.W., T.S. Dillon, K.E. Forward, "The
       effect of imperfect periodic maintenance on
       fault tolerant computer systems", Proc. of
       the 14th Int. Conf. on Fault Tolerant
       Computing, Florida, U.S.A., pp. 66-70, 20th-
       22nd June, 1984.

[9].   McConnel, S.R., D.P. Siewiorek, M.M. Tsao,
       "The measurement and analysis of transient
       errors in digital computer systems", Proc.
       of the 9th Int. Symp. on Fault Tolerant
       Computing, pp. 67-70, June, 1979.

[10]   Ng, Y.W., A. Avizienis, "A unified reliabil-
       ity model for fault tolerance computers",
       IEEE Transactions on Computers, Vol. C-29,
       No. 11, pp. 1022-1011, 1980.

SPECIFICATION AND DESIGN OF RELIABLE SYSTEMS IN TERMS OF UNRELIABLE COMPONENTS

J. Górski

Institute of Informatics, Technical University of Gdańsk, Gdańsk, Poland

Abstract . The paper addresses the problem of designing reliable systems out of unreliable components. The system and its components are specified as modules, using state function temporal logic specifications. Faulty (but tolerable) behaviours are specified by means of spontaneous inputs and nondeterministic post-conditions. Global restrictions on possible behaviours are expressed using temporal logic. Individual specifications of modules can be incorporated by the stucture specification to form the abstract design of a higher level (system) module.

Keywords . Specification; reliability; design; fault-tolerance; temporal logic.

INTRODUCTION

Formal specification techniques intend to express requirements on system behaviour. A widely aplied model for system behaviour is the set of sequences that can result from execution. Specification techniques encode requirements on system behaviour in two basic ways: by encoding within the state or by restricting possible sequences of states. A variety of specification approaches can be identified based upon this state versus history encoding (Schwartz, Meliar-Smith, 1982). According to this classification at one end we have the state machine specifications where the only description of history allowed is a set of possible successor states from a given state. At the other end are event specifications where the state component simply defines whether a given (possibly parametrized) event occurs. The specification is a set of predicates on the event history. A duality exists between information encoded in terms of state and in terms of previous history. Given a set of (possibly infinite) sequences of finite states as an underlying model and a language capable of expressing arbitrary first-order properties of sequences, one can eliminate any state information in favor of properties of the history or can transfer any finitely expressible portion of the history to auxiliary state components.

In this paper we use a module specification technique which is related to the state transition specification methods, i.e. one specifies a collection of state components and possible state changes that can be caused by the module inputs. However, in our approach we can also express liveness properties and this way impose restrictions on state sequences. The liveness properties are expressed as temporal formulas. Within the spectrum of specification methods considered in (Schwartz, Meliar-Smith, 1982), our method can be placed beside the Lamport's mathod (Lamport, 1983). The useability of our technique is illustrated by specification of the stable storage module. Then we discuss the problem of faulty behaviours and introduce extensions which allow for specification of tolerable failures of the module. This is illustrated by specification of the unreliable storage and the lossy transmission line modules. Then the abstract design of a stable storage

in terms of the server and the unreliable storage modules is presented which illustrates the possibility of building hierarchical specifications.

TEMPORAL LOGIC

Temporal logic (Pnueli, 1977) adds operators to the standard logical system to allow reasoning about the future properties of computations. A computation is a sequence of states that could arise during execution, and has the form

$$s_0 \rightarrow s_1 \rightarrow \cdots$$

Informally, the first state in the computation represents the present, and subsequent states represent the future.

The two new operators added to make temporal logic are $\Box$ (henceforth) and $\Diamond$ (eventually). Temporal assertions are built up from state assertions, using the ordinary logical operators and the temporal operators. A state assertion is a boolean valued function of the module (system) state. For a state assertion P, the formula $\Box P$ means "P is true for all states in a computation". The formula $\Diamond P$ means "there is some state in the computation in which P is true". The operators $\Box$ and $\Diamond$ are duals, and the duality is given by the tautology

$$\sim \Box P \equiv \Diamond \sim P \,,$$

which states formally that P is not always true iff it is eventually false. Safety and liveness properties of computations can be expressed using temporal logic. Safety properties can be expressed in terms of a formula of the form $\Box P$ or $Q \supset \Box P$. A formula of the first form, if stated for a given set of computations, says that every computation continuously satisfies P. In the second form, the formula says that whenever Q is true, P is immediately realized and will hold continuously throughout the rest of the computation.

Liveness properties are those expressible by temporal formulas using the $\Diamond$ operator. For example, $\Diamond P$ guarantees the occurrence of a state satisfying P, $Q \supset \Diamond P$ guarantees that if Q is true at state s_0 then P will be true at some s_j , $j \geq 0$. As the final example, consider the assertion $\Box (Q \supset \Diamond P)$. It states that if Q ever becomes true, then P will be true at the same time or later. Such an assertion expresses a liveness property which we pronounce "Q leads to P". In the sequel, it will be abbreviated as $Q \leadsto P$.

UNDERLYING MODEL

We assume that a system is defined in terms of modules. For each module, a set of inputs and outputs is defined. The system is composed by connecting outputs to inputs among modules. Outputs and inputs are associated with message types. Only outputs and inputs with matching message types are allowed to be interconnected. Messages are created and destroyed in the system. The system state can be observed by state functions. The following state functions are pre-defined for all systems:

enabledOUT(m) - a predicate; true for a state s iff the message m is created at output OUT, in this state,

inINP(m) - a predicate; true for a state s iff m exists (is processed) in input INP, in this state,

atINP(m) - a predicate; true for a state s iff m arrived at input INP, in this state,

afterINP(m) - a predicate; true for state s iff it is the first state after m has been destroyed in the input INP.

The following dependencies among these predicates always hold

$atINP(m) \supset inINP(m)$,
$afterINP(m) \supset \sim inINP(m)$,
if OUT is connected to INP then
$\qquad enabledOUT(m) \supset atINP(m)$.

The relationship among the predicates is shown in Fig. 1.

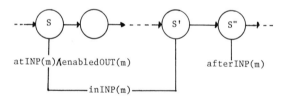

atINP(m)∧enabledOUT(m)   afterINP(m)

―――――― inINP(m) ――――――

Fig. 1. The lifespan of a message m in the system. m is created in state s, exists through states s,...,s′ and is destroyed in s″. It is assumed that OUT is connected to INP.

SPECIFICATIONS

A module specification has the following form:

MODULE modname
PARAMETERS p1:D1, ... , pn:Dn
DOMAINS d1=D1, ... , dm=Dm
INTERFACE
    INPUTS inp1(m1), ... , inpk(mk)
    OUTPUTS out1(m1), ... , outr(mr)
STATE f1:D1, ... , fp:Dp
INITIAL I1, ... , Iq
BEHAVIOUR P1, ... , Ps

PARAMETERS section identifies values that are constant for a particular instant of the specified module. DOMAINS section introduces named domains of values that are refered to throughout the specification. Some standard, pre-defined domains like INTEGER, BOOLEAN are included implicitely. New domains can be constructed using domain constructors like SEQ, SET, MAPPING, ONEOF, STRUCT. In particular, SEQ(D) denotes the domain of sequences of elements of the domain D (including an empty sequence <>). For a given sequence v, v[i] denotes the i-th element of v, v[i .. j] denotes the subsequence of v composed of elements v[i] .. v[j] , LENGTH(v) denotes the number of elements in v. The first element of v is always denoted v[1]. SET(D) denotes the domain of all subsets of D. MAPPING D1 TO D2 denotes a set of all total functions from D1 to D2. ONEOF(D1, ...,Dn) denotes the disjoint union of domains D1, ...,Dn. If $d \in ONEOF(D1,...,Dn)$ then IS_Di(d) is true iff $d \in Di$. STRUCT(n1:D1,...,nm:Dm) denotes the Cartesian product of domains D1,...,Dm with columns named by n1,...,nm . Elements of this domain are denoted (n1=d1,...,nm=dm) or (d1,...,dm) if there is no ambiguity with respect to column names. NUL is a distinguished, singleton domain. ANY stands for any value, the domain resulting from the context.

INTERFACE section specifies inputs and outputs together with the corresponding message domains. If there is no ambiguity, it is allowed that an input and the corresponding output bare the same name. STATE section introduces state functions specific for the module together with their ranges. INITIAL defines a set of initial conditions (predicates). The specification places constraints only on those state sequences for which each Ij holds for the initial state s_0.

BEHAVIOUR section defines a set of properties Pi, i=1,...,s . Each property Pi expresses a constraint on the entire state sequence $s_0 \to s_1 \to \cdots$. The properties specified are safety properties and liveness properties. A safety property asserts that something must never happen. It has the form

(a)   atINP: PRE Q   or (b) INP: PRE V
          POST R   POST W

The interpretation is as follows (the universal quantification over all possible messages is assumed)

(a) if there is a state q such that atINP(m) holds for q then Q must have held for the state r immediately preceding q, and R must be true for all states where inINP(m) holds.

(b) if there is a state s such that afterINP(m) holds for s then V must have held for the state u immediately preceding s, and W must hold for s.

Q is a state predicate refering to the state q. R is a state predicate refering to the states q and r. V is a state predicate refering to the state u. W is a state predicate refering to the states u and s. The reference to states is by state functions f1,...,fp . To distinguish between references to different states in R and W, references to later states are primed. It is also assumed that if a pre-condition is constantly TRUE then it can be omitted in the specification. Assertions of the form (a) refer to a state before the message arrives at the input and also they say what condition should be invariant while the message is being processed by the input. Usually, those requirements can not be satisfied by the module itself and express some constraints imposed on the module 's environment. The property of type (b) specify conditions under which a message can be consumed (destroyed) by the input. Note, that the message can be consumed only once and then disappeares forever. Creation of new messages is specified in W by stateing that enabledOUT(m) holds for the state s. This means that a new message m has been created in the state s and consequently, atINP(m) holds for an input INP, if OUT is connected to INP. The relationship of Q,R,V and W predicates to system state is shown in Fig. 2.

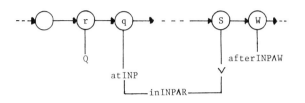

Fig. 2. Interpretation of the safety specification.

An interconnection between two modules is specified by OUT =⇒INP, where OUT and INP can be qualified by module names to avoid ambiguities (an usual dot notation is assumed here). The connection can be one-to-one or one-to-many. If OUT is connected to inputs INP1,...,INPn, and enabledOUT(m) holds for some state s then atINPi(m) holds in s for exactly one i, i.e. the newly created message may not arrive at several inputs. To allow for specification of message destinations the SOURCE(m) state function is defined for each message which returns a name of the module creating the message. Also, we modify the "enabled" predicate to become enabledOUT(m;c), where c is understood to be a module name and is used to choose the destination input among inputs connected to OUT. If there is no ambiguity, c can be omitted.

Safety properties assert that something must never happen but they do not require that anything does ever happen. Liveness properties assert what must occur. They are specified using temporal logic assertions. Usually they have the form Q ⟿ P , which means that for any time at which Q is true, P must be true then or at some later time.

EXAMPLE: STABLE STORE

As an example let us consider a stable store specification. A pictorial representation of the module is given in Fig. 3. and the specification is given in Fig. 4.

DEPOSIT   FETCH

STORE

Fig. 3. Stable store module.

MODULE Store
DOMAINS   Address=
          Data=
INTERFACE
  INPUTS Deposit(at:Address,d:Data)
          Fetch(at:Address)

OUTPUTS   Deposit()
          Fetch(d:Data)
STATE   store: MAPPING Address TO Data
INITIAL   FORALL a∈Address, store[a]=ANY
BEHAVIOUR
1. atDeposit: POST ∼EXISTS m,
       inStore(m)∧ SOURCE(m)=SOURCE

2. Deposit:
   POST ‵store[at]=d ∧ enabledDeposit(;SOURCE)

3. atFetch: POST ∼EXISTS m,
       in Store(m)∧ SOURCE(m)= SOURCE

4. Fetch:
   POST enabledFetch(d=store[at];SOURCE)

5. inDeposit ∧ SOURCE=S ⟿ afterDeposit ∧
       enabledDeposit(;S)

6. inFetch ∧ SOURCE=S ⟿ afterFetch ∧
       enabledFetch(%;S)

Fig. 4. Specification of the module Store.
  inStore(m)≡ inDeposit(m) ∨ inFetch(m).

Properties 1 and 3 assert that each user of the module must deposit or fetch data one after another, i.e. no concurrent calls from the user are allowed (however, concurrent calls from different users are not excluded). These are requirements imposed on the environment of the module. Property 2 states that if a given Deposit request terminates, the new data d is stored at the address at, and an (empty) response message is created at the Deposit output, directed to the client module. Property 4 asserts that if Fetch terminates then an output message with data read from the address at arrives at the Fetch output and is directed to the client module. Any number of modules may be connected to Store. Requests from different modules are served concurrently. Properties 5 and 6 assert that each request will be eventually served. % stands for the unspecified part of the enabled message.

SPECIFYING FAILURE

When attempting to specify failure, the main difficulty encountered is that there is no limit to severity of failure in reality . For instance,while it might be very unlikely, it is possible that all components of the system might fail at once and break the system beyond repair. There is no system which can survive all possible failures – it will tolerate only certain set of failures. Our approach is to make it explicit which failures will be tolerated , an approach similar to that of (Lampson, 1981). We assume that the intolerable failures can be made as rare as necessary, thus permitting an arbitrary high (though not perfect) level of reliability to be achieved. Following this line, we divide the possible behaviours of a real system or component into acceptable and unacceptable behaviours. We assume that unacceptable behaviours never occur. In practice it means that we assume that the unacceptable behaviours can be made arbitrarily unlikely. The acceptable behaviours are further classified as either good (normal) or bad (failing) but tolerable. Notice, that the notion of tolerability or intolerability is a relative one: behaviours are tolerable or intolerable depending if the environment can or can not handle them.

In our approach we assume that failing but tolerable behaviours can be included in the specification. Two basic extensions to our specification technique allow for failure specification.

These are the possibility to use non-deterministic post-conditions in safety properties of type (b), and spontaneous inputs which can be included in the specification. The former extension allow to specify failures which can happen in response to a specific input stimulation. The latter extension is used to specify failures which can happen spontaneously, without strong correlation with the input history. Restrictions on the liveness of the faulty states are specified by temporal logic assertions. While connecting modules to form the system structure, the spontaneous inputs are always left not connected (they specify an internal dynamics of the module). These inputs are considered as being permanently connected to the (invisible) outputs which spontaneously generate messages according to the safety and liveness properties of the module.

EXAMPLE: UNRELIABLE STORE

The specification of the unreliable store module is given in Fig. 5.

MODULE Ustore
DOMAINS   Address=
          Data=
INTERFACE
  INPUTS   Udeposit(ad:Address,dt:Data)
            Ufetch(ad:Address)
  OUTPUTS   Udeposit()
            Ufetch(OK:BOOLEAN,dt:Data)
STATE   store:MAPPING Address TO Data
INITIAL   FORALL a∈Address, store[a]=ANY
BEHAVIOUR
1. atUdeposit: POST ~EXISTS m,
      m≢CURRENT∧ inUstore(m)

2. Udeposit: POST
      EITHER
      `store[ad]=dt ∧ enabledUdeposit(;SOURCE)
      OR
      `store[ad]≠dt ∧ enabledUdeposit(;SOURCE)

3. atUfetch: POST ~EXISTS m,
      m≢ CURRENT ∧ inUstore(m)

4. Ufetch: POST
      EITHER
      enabledUfetch(OK=TRUE,dt=store[ad];SOURCE)
      OR
      enabledUfetch(OK=FALSE,dt=ANY;SOURCE)

5. inUdeposit ∧ SOURCE=S ⤳ afterUdeposit(;S)

6. inUfetch∧ SOURCE=S ⤳ afterUfetch(%;S)

7. □◇(atUfetch ∧ Ufetch.ad=A ∧ SOURCE=S)⤳afterUfetch∧ enabledUfetch(OK=TRUE, dt=store[A];S)

8. □◇(atUdeposit∧ Udeposit.ad=A ∧ Udeposit.dt=D ∧ SOURCE=S)⤳afterUdeposit(;S)∧ store[A]=D

Fig. 5. Specification of the Ustore module.

Properties 1,3 assert that the module is used serially (CURRENT refers to the message bound by the universal quantifier over all messages, implicitly assumed for each property). Property 2 specifies that Udeposit can corrupt data stored at the address ad. Similarly, property 4 states that Ufetch, if completed, returns either OK=TRUE together with data stored at the address ad, or OK=FALSE together with any data. Properties 5,6,7,8 are liveness properties. Properties 5,6 specify that Udeposit and Ufetch input messages must be eventually processed. Property 7 asserts that if Ufetch is requested infinitely often with ad=D then eventually an output message will be returned with uncorrupted data read from the address A. Property 8 states that if Udeposit is requested infinitely often with ad=A and dt=D then eventually D will be stored at A.

EXAMPLE: LOSSY TRANSMISSION LINE

The use of spontaneous inputs is illustrated by a lossy transmission line specification shown in Fig. 6.

MODULE Transmission_line
PARAMETERS max=
DOMAINS element=
INTERFACE
  INPUTS   Transmit(el:element)
            Receive()
  OUTPUTS   Transmit()
            Receive(el:element)
SPONTANEOUS INPUTS Lose()
STATE queue:SEQ(element)
INITIAL queue=
BEHAVIOUR
1. Transmit: PRE LENGTH(queue)<max
   POST `queue=queue•el ∧ enabledTransmit(
          ;SOURCE)

2. Receive: PRE LENGTH(queue)> 0
   POST `queue=queue[2..LENGTH(queue)]∧
      enabledReceive(el=queue[1];SOURCE)

3.Lose: PRE LENGTH(queue)>0
   POST `queue=q, WHERE q≺queue

4. inTransmit∧ SOURCE=S∧ □◇ LENGTH(queue)
   < max ⤳ afterTransmit(;S)

5. inReceive∧ SOURCE=S∧□◇LENGTH(queue)
   >0 ⤳ afterReceive(%;S)

6. □◇ inTransmit∧□◇(atTransmit⊃ Transmit.el=E)
∧□◇ inReceive ⤳ afterReceive∧ enabledReceive(
   el=E;%)

Fig. 6. Specification of the Transmission_line module.

The specification given in Fig. 6. specifies a lossy one-way transmission medium. Up to max data elements can be currently during transmission. Elements are inserted through the Transmit input. In order to receive elements, the Receive input has to be activated. Losing of elements in transmission is specified by introducing the SPONTANEOUS INPUTS section which defines the input Lose. Lose generates messages spontaneously. It can force losing of elements each time the queue is nonempty (≺ in property 3 means "is a proper subsequence of"). Property 4 asserts that the processing of the Transmit request messages is fair, in the sense that if queue is infinitely often nonful then the request is eventually served and the message is put at the end of the queue. Similarly, property 5 states that the Receive request messages will be processed if the queue is infinitely often nonempty. Property 6 states that if a given element E is transmitted infinitely often and there are still attempts to receive elements then E is eventually received.

DESIGNING A STABLE STORE

Aformal design of a system is given by its structure specification. The constructs that describe the design are the system specification, the subsystems specifications, the subsystems interconnection specification and the interface specification. The system and subsystems specifications are given as module specifications, in the form introduced in the previous sections. The subsystem interconnection specification connects outputs to inputs among subsystems. The construct S1.OUT ⟹ S2.INP specifies that the output OUT of S1 is connected to the input INP of S2. Then, if enabledOUT(m;S2) holds for a given state s then atINP(m) also holds for s. The interface specification, given in the form

```
   SYS.INPi = SUB.INPj
 or
   SYS.OUTi = SUB.OUTj
```

specifies that the input INPj of the subsystem SUB is used as the input INPi of the system SYS , or that the output OUTj of SUB is used as the output OUTi of SYS.

In this section we specify the module Server and then define a structure which is the formal design (in terms of subsystems Server and Ustore) of the stable store system specified by the module Store. The specification of the Server module is given in Fig. 7.

```
MODULE Server
DOMAINS
  Data=
  Address=
  PendingW=STRUCT(to:Address,dat:Data,
                  who:Modname)
  PendingR=STRUCT(from:Address,who:
                  Modname)
  Modname=
INTERFACE
  INPUTS  Write(at:Address,d:Data)
          Read(at:Address)
          Uwrite()
          Uread(OK:BOOLEAN,dt:Data)
  OUTPUTS
          Write()
          Read(d:Data)
          Uwrite(ad:Address,dt:Data)
          Uread(ad:Address)
STATE serve:ONEOF(PendingW,PendingR,NIL)
INITIAL IS_NIL(serve)
BEHAVIOUR
1. atWrite: POST ~EXISTS m,
   m≠CURRENT ∧ inServer(m) ∧ SOURCE(m)=
      SOURCE
2. Write: PRE IS_NIL(serve)
   POST 'serve=(at,d,SOURCE) ∧ enabledUwrite(
      ad=at, dt=d)
3.atRead: POST ~EXISTS m,
   m≠CURRENT ∧ inServer(m) ∧ SOURCE(m)=
      SOURCE
4. Read: PRE IS_NIL(serve)
   POST 'serve=(at,SOURCE) ∧ enabledUread(
      ad=at)
5.atUread: ~ IS_NIL(serve)
6. Uread: POST
 IF IS_PendingW(serve) ∧ OK THEN
   IF serve.dat=dt THEN
  IS_NIL('serve) ∧ enabledWrite(;server.who)
   ELSE enabledUwrite(ad=server.to,dt=se rver.dat)
 IF ~OK THEN
   IF IS_PendingW(serve) THEN
    enabledUwrite(ad=server.td,dt=server.dat)
   ELSE enabledUread(ad=server.from)
 IF IS_PendingR(serve) ∧ OK THEN
  IS_NIL(serve) ∧ enabledRead(d=dt;server.who)

7. atUwrite: POST IS_PendingW(serve)
8. Uwrite: POST enabledUread(ad=serve.to)
9. inUwrite ⇝ afterUwrite
10. inUread ⇝ sfterUread
11. inWrite ∧ Write.d=D ∧ Write.at=A ∧ SOURCE=S
 ∧ □◇IS_NIL(serve) ⇝ afterWrite ∧ serve=(A,D,S)
12. inRead ∧ Read.at=A ∧ SOURCE=S ∧
   □◇IS_NIL(serve) ⇝ afterRead ∧ serve=(A,S)
```

Fig. 7. Specification of the Server module.

The meaning of the specification is as follows. Processing of a Write request sets the serve state component according to the parameters of the request message and then repeat Uwrite followed by Uread until the Uread response confirms that the data were stored correctly (OK=TRUE). Processing of a Read request sets the serve state component according to the requesting message and then repeats Uread requests generated at the Uread output until receiving an uncorrupted data (OK=TRUE). The liveness properties 9,10,11,12 specify conditions under which the input messages of Server are eventually processed.

Formal design of the stable storage system is shown in Fig. 8.

```
SYSTEM  Storage
SUBSYSTEMS  Server, Ustore
CONNECTIONS
  Server.Uwrite ⟹ Ustore.Udeposit
  Server.Uread ⟹ Ustore.Ufetch
  Ustore.Udeposit ⟹ Server.Uwrite
  Ustore.Ufetch ⟹ Server.Uread
INTERFACE
  INPUTS
    Store.Deposit = Server.Write
    Store.Fetch = Server.Read
  OUTPUTS
    Store.Deposit = Server.Write
    Store.Fetch = Server.Read
```

　J. Górski

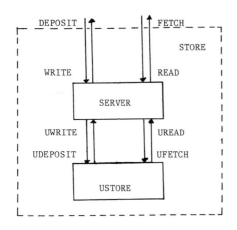

Fig. 8. Formal design of the stable storage.

REFERENCES

Lamport L. (1983). Specifying Concurrent Program Modules. ACM Trans. Program. Lang. Systems, vol. 5, No. 2, 190-222.

Lampson B. (1981). Atomic Transactions. In Distributed Systems: Architecture and Implementation, Lect. Not. Comp. Sci., No. 105, 246-265.

Pnueli A. (1977). The Temporal Logic of Programs. Proc. 18th Symp. Foundations of Computer Science, IEEE, Providence, 46-57.

Schwartz L.R. and P. Meliar-Smith. (1982). From State Machines to Temporal Logic: Specification Methods for Protocol Standards. IEEE Trans. Comm., vol. COM-30, No. 12, 2486-2496.

CONCLUSIONS

We have presented a method of module specification which allows for

- specification of both, safety and liveness properties of the module,
- specification of modules that are used concurrently,
- specification of tolerable failures,
- structural specification.

Module specification describes its possible behaviours by giving a set of properties which have to be satisfied by each individual behaviour (a history of states). The properties impose restrictions either on the possible state transitions resulting from the module's interaction with the environment, or on the whole histories of states. The safety properties can include assumptions about the environment of the module, e.g. properties 1,3 in the specification of Store. In particular, these assumptions can restrict the amount of concurrency exercised with respect to the module.

Spontaneous inputs and nondeterministic postconditions allow for specification of faulty behaviours which can depend on or be independent of the specific input stimulation. The corresponding liveness properties restrict the occurrence of faults in state histories and this way provide a guarantee that the correct behaviours are achievable, at least to the extend which allow to tolerate failures at the higher (system) level.

Structural specifications combine module specifications into a formal design and link the design to the higher level (system) specification. This is this system level where the lower level failures are tolerated. This has been illustrated by a formal design of the stable storage system. Evidently, a verification step is necessary to demonstrate that the design satisfies the specification of the Store module. Such a verification would require a definition of the state functions of Store in terms of the state functions of Ustore and Server and then we would have to show that the properties of the subsystems do not invalidate the properties specified for the whole system. Such a verification technique is currently under development.

RELIABILITY VERSUS SAFETY

M. Mulazzani

Institut für Praktische Informatik, Technical University Vienna, Gusshausstr. 30, Vienna, 1040 Austria

Abstract. This paper discusses the impact of computer based control systems on the reliability and safety of the total real-time system. It deals with applications, where safety is of utmost importance, but reliability is also an important goal. Both aspects are fundamental qualities of real-time systems, their tradeoff is discussed.

Based on a high level view of the system a quantitative model for an analysis of the impact of the computer system on the reliability and safety of the system is presented. This model is applied to different software fault tolerant techniques, the following methods are compared: single version, "2 out of 2"-voting, "2 out of 3"-voting (N-version-programming) and the recovery block technique. The degree of correlation between faults is an important parameter of the model. Finally the impact of a binary output space, which occurs quite often in safety critical real-time systems, is analysed.

Keywords. reliability; safety; models; software fault tolerance; traffic control.

Introduction

Due to the increasing complexity of technological products and due to the decreasing costs of hardware components the application of computer systems in the area of real-time-control has become more important (power switching stations, aerospace systems, nuclear power plants, transportation systems, chemical plants). It is well recognised that the reliability of the computer system is of crucial importance for the success of a system and for the accomplishment of a mission. Research focused on fault-tolerant capabilities[1] to get a high reliability, MTTF (mean time to failure) or availability.

Both in hardware and software the principle of redundancy was used to increase reliability: The SIFT[2,3] and the FTMP[4] project are well known examples for ultra-reliable-systems. Each critical task executes on a triple-modular-redundant hardware system (TMR-system). The results are voted, in SIFT this is done by software whereas FTMP provides hardware voters. This kind of redundancy covers transient and permanent hardware faults, which are the main sources of hardware malfunctions.

In the field of software the situation is different, software fails due to design faults. Two basic techniques have been developed for the toleration of design faults: N-version-programming[5] and the recovery-block-scheme[6] (acceptance test). Both techniques use diverse software, design faults may be discovered (or even tolerated) by the voting algorithm or by the acceptance test.

This paper is the result of an analysis of different system structures for a traffic signaling system. Such a system has to provide high reliability and high safety.

The aspect of safety is important: A fault in the signaling system may immediately cause a crash with great losses of human life (for example: a traffic light showing green in both directions). This work is not restricted to that special application. In the last years computer systems entered many critical application areas (air traffic control systems, systems monitoring patients in hospitals,...), where the safety aspect of the real-time-system is important. This paper accounts for applications, where safety is of utmost importance, but reliability is also an important goal.

Reliability and Safety

In critical applications there are two goals for real-time systems: reliability and safety. On a superficial basis it is sometimes assumed, that a reliable system is automatically a safe system. A detailed analysis[7,8] shows, however, that high reliability, while necessary, is not sufficient to ensure safety. Thus it is important, to distinguish between reliability and safety:

Definition: Reliability
The reliability of a system is the probability of accomplishment of a function under specified environmental conditions and over a specified time.

Reliability is oriented towards the purpose of the system and to the intended action, it is the extent to which a system can be expected to perform the specified task. Reliability requirements are concerned with making a system failure-free.

Definition: Safety
Safety is the probability, that no catastrophic accidents will occur during system operation, over a specified period of time.

Safety looks at the consequences and possible accidents. Safety requirements are concerned with making a system accident-free. It is the task of the safety requirements to guarantee, that the system does not reach a hazardous or unsafe state, where an independent event may cause an accident. Moreover it must be transparent from the safety requirements, what to do, if an event in the environment leads to an unsafe state.

From the point of safety it doesn't matter, if the system does not reach its purpose, as long as the safety requirements are not violated. On the other hand it is possible, that a system is ultra-reliable but unsafe: A system with a formally verified software system where a safety critical situation has not been specified.

Furthermore there may be a tradeoff between reliability and safety: In case of an internal fault it may be necessary to to power down the system in order to guarantee safety, thus reducing the reliability of the system due to safety requirements (for example an internal failure in a nuclear power plant).

There is another difference between safety and reliability: Software has a reliability by its own, it is possible to analyse[9, 10, 11, 12] the reliability of software packages. On the other hand it is meaningless to speak about software safety on its own. For a safety analysis it is necessary to look at the total system, the software must be seen in the context of the particular application.

Reliability and safety are important qualities of real-time systems, which have to be specified, analysed and verified separately, so that an optimal solution for the application may be found. Hardware safety and hardware reliability are both well established techniques, there exist models and procedures to increase the reliability and to eliminate the risk of hazards. Software reliability is beginning to emerge. During the last years qualitative analysis of software safety[7, 8, 13, 14] has been carried out.

It is the aim of this paper, to analyse the effect of software fault tolerant techniques on the safety and reliability of a system.

The Application System

In real-time systems there are two basic subsystems, the control system and the control environment. All subsystems external to the computer based control system will be referred to as the control environment. Since this is a top level view, in this paper the real-time system will be seen as set of cooperating subsystems. So the boundaries of the subsystems can be varied, according to the level of observation.

It is the task of the model, to study the impact of different subsystem parameters on the reliability and safety of the whole system. This effect depends on the partitioning into subsystems. The model is a mapping function from the subsystems into the total system, describing the impact of these subsystems. The mapping is dependent on the boundaries of the analysed subsystems, expressed by characteristic parameters. The reliability and safety of an implemented system is not affected by the variation of the boundaries of the subsystems (different viewpoints, no real change in the system), only the impacts of the different subsystems are changing.

Before this mapping from software characteristics to the system is done in detail, we have to discuss our system development cycle, which is shown in Fig. 1.

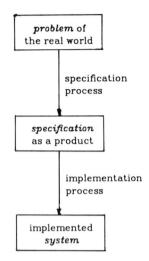

Fig. 1. System Development Cycle

Three phases of the system live cycle are distinguished: Starting with the *problem* to be solved, the analysis of requirements and the abstract formulation of problem (specification process) results in the *specification* of the system. That specification (probably containing errors) is then implemented, resulting in the *system* (the computer system is only one subsystem). The system cycle is described at a very high level. Note, that this model of system evolution can be used at different levels, it describes the subsystem "computer based control system" as well as the sub-subsystem "computer software".

We look at the system from the functional point of view: The control subsystems are assumed to be transaction oriented. Starting with a stimulus (which may be an external or internal event) the new results are calculated from the current state of the system (operational view). The input space I contains all possible situations of the system, including time aspects and environmental conditions. It is important to realize, that in an implemented system each element of the input space occurs according to a statistical density function. If the input space is discrete, each $i \in I$ will occur with probability e_i (with $1 = \sum_{i \in I} e_i$)[15].

Model of the impact of computer based subsystems

This chapter is applicable for a real-time computer system (hardware and software) as well as for software. In the first case the reliability of the virtual machine (hardware, operating system, compiler,...) has to be included into the model parameters. The following chapter will look at the impact of software phenomena in detail.

The safety and the reliability of the system can be influenced by the following three classes of results of the computer system:

intended result:
> The result is the intended one for the problem, not only for the specification. Correct value and timely.

unintended result:
> Incorrect value, or wrong sequencing.

no result:
> No result is obtained due to system crash, an internal error detection mechanism (program exceptions, time-out), or missing a real-time requirement.

This three cases will be denoted by the letters G (good), F (faulty result) and N (no result). According to the operational view of the subsystem, the input-space I of the subsystem can be seen as partitioned into three exclusive sets G, N, F (Fig. 2).

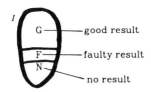

Fig. 2. Partitioning of the Input-Space I

According to the distribution of the inputs for the system (external or internal events) we get the probability W_G for good results, W_F for faulty results, and W_N for no results ($W_G + W_F + W_N = 1$). Based on these probabilities we model the impact of the subsystem on the reliability (R) and safety (S) of the system as follows:

$$Reliability = R_{obs} = 1 - W_N - A \cdot W_F \qquad 0 \le A \le 1$$

The unreliability of the system is caused by obtaining no result, or by obtaining a result, which is recognised by the environment (or the operator) to be wrong. The factor A (external error detection factor) denotes the proportion of faulty results, detected by the environment.

Ideally, all wrong results are recognised in the environment, which is modelled by $A = 1$, yielding to $R_{ideal} = 1 - W_N - W_F$. More realistic, we will have $A < 1$. A wrong status message on the operator console which lasts only for one second has a high probability of not being detected as faulty. The value of A will strongly depend on the application and the environment.

$$Safety = S = 1 - B \cdot W_F - C \cdot W_N$$

The unsafety of a system is caused by faulty results of the subsystem, but on the other hand "no result" may also cause an accident. B and C can be assumed to be dimensionless values ($0 \le B, C \le 1$), according to the probabilities of causing an accident or an unsafe state (where an independent trigger event from the environment causes the accident).

The meaning of the factors B and C is further analysed:

In the case $B \gg C \approx 0$ we have a system were the safety depends on *correct* results. It does not matter for the safety of the system, if there is no result due to internal faults (for some time). For example, in an air-traffic control system, which coordinates the landing of planes, it does not matter if there is no permission for a landing approach, but a wrong permission will be disastrous.

The situation $B \approx C$ will be found in hard real-time systems, "no results" and "faulty results" have an equal effect on safety. Examples for this case are the control of a dynamically unstable aircraft in landing phase or the space-shuttle in re-entrant-phase. This situation will be rare, since in many cases there is enough time to invoke a higher level recovery procedure in case of "no result" (e.g. decision by the operator) or falling back to a lower level of service (e.g. active safety system, emergency shutdown, ...).

Variation of A, B, and C due to design decisions

The impact of a subsystem on the reliability and safety of the system is characterised by the parameters A, B, and C. Whereas W_F and W_N depend on the control system, the parameters A, B and C depend on the control environment, they can be influenced during design time: This starts with the design of the interfaces to the environment and the decision, which part of the problem is to be solved by the computer system, it may end with the implementation of an autonomous safety system, implemented independently from the "main computer system". This method is used in the area of railway signaling (relay based interlocking system), chemical plants (independent overpressure valves), and in many other applications.

The main principle applied is an independent subsystem, which prevents a mishap in case of an error of the computer system. For such a subsystem it is necessary to detect the error. "No result" is easy to detect (watchdog-timer), whereas in the case of "faulty results" the problem of unsafety and fault propagation is severe. This is the reason for the great practical importance of the case $B \gg C \approx 0$ ($C \approx 0$ indicates that the impact of "no result" on the safety of the system is small, due to the fact that the environment detects that error and acts properly). For the same reason the method of safety assertions[14] is used in critical applications. An architecture which is based on self-checking components (e.g. MARS[16]) has an intrinsic advantage from the safety point of view.

Application to fault-tolerant software schemas

The model of the previous chapter will now be used to study the impact of the different techniques for software fault tolerance on the reliability and safety of the total system. Only the basic techniques are discussed:

In the N-version-programming approach n different versions of a program are run, fault-tolerance is achieved by a voting procedure. For the comparison we will look at the "2 out of 3" voting strategy, which is the most commonly used method of N-version-programming (the formulas for the "1 out of 2" and "1 out of 3" techniques are shown in the appendix).

In the recovery-block-schema[6] the result of the primary package is checked by an acceptance-test. In case of rejection by the acceptance test, the results of an alternate software package are checked and submitted to the environment (in case of acceptance). This situation is modelled by an optimistic and a pessimistic model (in regard to safety): The "2 out of 2 (primary software + acceptance test) + 1 (alternate software)" technique, where the results of the alternate software are not checked by the acceptance test, and the "(2 out of 2)²" method, which assumes that there exists a second acceptance-test and these two "2 out of 2" systems are completely independent (no correlation).

These standard methods of fault tolerance are compared with the single version software system ("1 out of 1") and a "2 out of 2" voting system.

For the comparison it is necessary to estimate the probabilities W_G and W_N of the results of the redundant software system. This is done by a simple model:

A single software version may yield to a good result (with probability p), a faulty result (q) or "no result" ($1 - p - q$). For simplicity reasons it is assumed, that all diverse software packages have the same probabilities p and q (will be satisfied, if the programming teams have the same skill). Ideally, the faults of the different software packages should be independent. Unfortunately that is not true in reality, so ε will denote the correlation of the faults of the different software versions. The situation for two software packages is shown in Fig. 3.

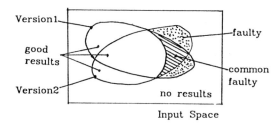

Fig. 3. Partitioning on Input-Space for two Software Versions

In the case of three software versions the parameter δ ($0<\delta<\varepsilon$) denotes the correlation of all three versions failing in the same way. The input-space (for faulty results) in case of three versions is shown in Fig. 4.

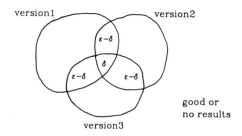

Fig. 4. Partitioning of Input-Space for triple redundant software

A small δ indicates, that there are many different faults, for example due to different specification ambiguities. The case of $\delta\approx\varepsilon$ (high delta) is characteristic for the situation of one specification error.

Experiments, concerned with the measurement of the fault coverage aspects of N-version-programming[17,18] showed, that there is a high correlation of faults, which cannot be ignored. This may be caused by many different reasons: faulty specification, ambiguous or incomplete specification, interpretation faults due to misunderstanding of the problem, and implementation faults. All these possible sources of errors will be modelled properly. Furthermore this simple model is even applicable in the case of diverse specification (ε will be smaller).

For each technique the different probabilities have been analysed. The results are summarised in the appendix, the formulas of some other software redundancy schemas which have not been discussed here, are included in the appendix, too.

Scott[19] modelled the reliability of the previous mentioned techniques for a more general situation. His aim was an analysis of the impact of an imperfect execution environment and of faulty voting procedures. Unfortunately he assumed that the faults of the different versions are independent, so that his models could not be used in the context of this paper.

Discussion of the results

Based on the theoretical analysis of the previous chapter the different redundancy techniques have been studied. The following two figures show a typical situation of the impact of the computer system on the reliability and safety of the system. The special data used for the example are as following: $A = 0.8$ (high detection rate of faulty results by the environment), $B = 1$, $C \approx 0$ (safety endangered only by faulty results), $\delta = 0$, $\varepsilon = 0.1$ (correlation 10 %) and $q = 2/3(1-p)$. The pictures show the safety (Fig. 5) and reliability (Fig. 6) of the systems, depending on parameter p (probability of getting a good result).

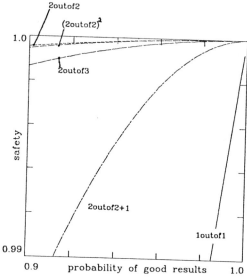

Fig. 5. System Safety versus p (prob. of good results)

As we look at safety, the "2 out of 2"- and the optimistic recovery block method ("(2 out of 2)²"-technique) are a little bit better than the "2 out of 3" technique, the pessimistic recovery block technique ("2 out of 2 + 1") is worse. This indicates, that the second acceptance test in the recovery-block-technique is of great importance for the safety of the system. Note, that in the optimistic model of the recovery-block-technique it is assumed, that there is no correlation between the two acceptance tests. Thus the safety of the recovery-block technique will lie in between those two extrema (optimistic and pessimistic model).

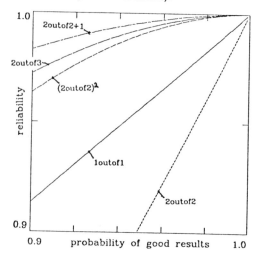

Fig. 6. System Reliability versus p (prob. of good results)

The best reliability characteristic is provided by the recovery-block schema (lies between "2 out of 2 + 1" and "(2 out of 2)²") and the "2 out of 3" approach. The "2 out of 2" technique has a high unreliability, higher than that of the single version system.

The variation of the different parameters showed the following dependencies: An increase of q (probability of faulty results) decreased the safety (due to the correlation of the versions). There are no great changes in the reliability of the system due to variation of the other parameters. Only in the case of increasing C, the results changed: For $C \approx 0$ the safety of the "2 out of 2" technique is best, for $C \gg 0$ the "2 out of 3" method and the recovery block technique are superior (in order for safety).

Impact of Binary Output

In many real-time applications the output of the system is binary ("switch on motor", "ready for takeoff", "power down system (due to safety requirements in case of an internal fault", "activate ejection seat"). As we analyse binary output the situation is completely different: Two faults, even if caused by different sources, are completely correlated ($\varepsilon = 100\%$) because of the binary output space.

As experimentally observed, the reliability is not changed significantly by an increase of ε. Figure 7 shows the safety of the system for binary output. The "2 out of 2" technique is significantly better than the other two methods. All other redundancy techniques are in the danger of two faulty versions outvoting a correct solution, thus they provide a low safety for a system. For the recovery-block-technique only in the optimistic case of no correlation between primary software, secondary software and acceptance tests a high safety is provided.

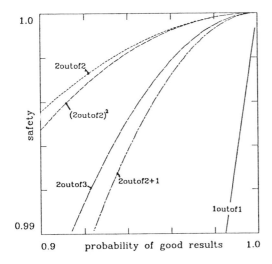

Fig. 7. System Safety for Binary Output Space

In the case of high correlation ε ($\varepsilon > 20\%$) the "2 out of 2" method provides a significantly better safety of the system, at the costs of lower reliability (lower reliability than a single software version). This again demonstrates the tradeoff between reliability and safety: If the reliability aspects are more important or in case that safety is severely endangered by "no results" ($C \gg 0$), the "2 out of 3" technique and the recovery-block schema are to be preferred.

Conclusions

Reliability and safety are important attributes of real-time systems. High reliability, while necessary, is not sufficient to ensure safety[7]. It is important, to distinguish between reliability and safety, the tradeoff between these goals has been discussed.

A model has been presented, which analyses the impact of a subsystem to the reliability and safety of the total system. This model can be seen as a mapping of the internal parameters of a subsystem (probability of good, faulty or no results) into the total system. This mapping function depends on the application and is influenced by design decisions (tasks of the subsystems).

This model is used to analyse different fault-tolerant software schemas. For a low correlation of faults it is shown that for the safety of a system the "2 out of 2"-schema is best, but there is only a small difference to the "2 out of 3" technique and the recovery-block-method. As we look at reliability, the recovery block technique and the "2 out of 3"-technique are best. The reliability of the "2 out of 2" technique is poor, even the single version software will be better. This is a good example for the tradeoff between reliability and safety, the "2 out of 2"-method provides high safety at the costs of low reliability.

The case of a binary output space is of significant importance for safety critical real-time systems. The assumption of an binary output space implies, that all faults are correlated (correlation 100 %). For this case it is shown, that the "2 out of 2"-voting strategy is significantly better for safety reasons. Only in the rare case, that "no result" endangers the safety of a system, the other two methods will be superior.

Acknowledgment

I would like to thank H. Kopetz, N. Theuretzbacher and W. Schwabl for their helpful comments and discussions.

References

1.   A. Avizienis, "Fault-Tolerance: The Survival Attribute of Digital Systems," *Proceedings of the IEEE* **66**(10) pp. 1109-1125 (Oct. 1978).

2.   J. H. Wensley, L. Lamport, J. Goldberg, P. M. Melliar-Smith, and R. E. Shostak, "SIFT: Design and Analysis of a Fault-Tolerant Computer for Aircraft Control," *Proceedings of the IEEE* **66**(10) pp. 1240-1255 (Oct. 1978).

3.   P.M. Melliar-Smith and R. L. Schwartz, "Formal Specification and Mechanical Verification of SIFT: A Fault-Tolerant Flight Control System," *IEEE Transactions on Computers* **C-31**(7) pp. 616-630 (Jul. 1982).

4.   A. L. Hopkins, T. B. Smith, and J. H. Lala, "FTMP - A Highly Reliable Fault-Tolerant Multiprocessor for Aircraft," *Proceedings of the IEEE* **66**(10) pp. 1221-1239 (Oct. 1978).

5.   L. Chen and A. Avizienis, "N-version-programming: A Fault-Tolerant Approach to the Reliability of Software Operation," *8th International Conference on Fault-Tolerant Computing, FTCS-8*, pp. 3-9 (Jun. 1978).

6.   B. Randell, "System Structure for Software Fault Tolerance," *IEEE Transactions on Software Engineering* **SE-1**(2) pp. 220-232 (June 1975).

7.   N. G. Levenson, "Software Safety in computer-Controlled Systems," *IEEE Computer* **17**(2) pp. 48-55 (Feb. 1984).

8. N. G. Levenson, "Software Safety," *ACM SIGSOFT Software Engineering Notes* **7**(2) pp. 21-24 (Apr. 1982).

9. B. Littlewood and J. L. Verrall, "A Bayesian Reliability Growth Model for Software Reliability," *IEEE Symp. Computer Software Reliability 1973*, pp. 70-76 (May 1973).

10. J. D. Musa, "A Theory of Software Reliability and its Application," *IEEE Transactions on Software Engineering* **SE-1**(3) pp. 312-327 (Sep. 1975).

11. B. Littlewood, "Theories of Software Reliability: How good are they and how can they be improved?," *IEEE Transactions on Software Engineering* **SE-6**(5) pp. 489-500 (Sep. 1980).

12. C. V. Ramamoorthy and F. B. Bastani, "Software Reliability - Status and Perspectives," *IEEE Transactions on Software Engineering* **SE-8**(4) pp. 354-371 (Jul. 1982).

13. N. G. Levenson and P. R. Harvey, "Analysing Software Safety," *IEEE Transactions on Software Engineering* **SE-9**(5) pp. 569-579 (Sep. 1983).

14. N. G. Levenson and T. J. Shimeall, "Safety Assertions for Process-Control Systems," *13th International Symposium on Fault-Tolerant Computing FTCS-13*, pp. 236-240 (Jun. 1983).

15. H. Kopetz, *Software Reliability*, Springer, New York (1978).

16. H. Kopetz and W. Merker, "The Architecture of MARS, a MAintainable Real-time System," *Proceedings on fault-tolerant computer systems, FTCS-15*, (June 1985).

17. J. P. Kelly and A. Avizienis, "A Specification-oriented Multi-version Software Experiment," *13th Annual Symposium on Fault-Tolerant Computing FTCS-13*, pp. 120-126 (Jul. 1983).

18. A. Avizienis and J. P. Kelly, "Fault Tolerance by Design Diversity: Concepts and Experiments," *IEEE Computer* **17**(8) pp. 67-80 (Aug. 1984).

19. R. K. Scott, J. W. Gault, and D. F. McAllister, "Modeling fault-tolerant Software Reliability," *Third Symposion on Reliability in distributed Software and Database Systems 1983*, pp. 15-27 (Oct. 1983).

APPENDIX

TABLE 1   System Models

Voting	G (good)	F (faulty)	N (no result)
1 out of 1	p	q	$1 - p - q$
2 out of 2	p^2	εq^2	$1 - p^2 - \varepsilon q^2$
2 out of 2 +1	$p^2 + p(1 - p^2 - \varepsilon q^2)$	$\varepsilon q^2 + q(1 - p^2 - \varepsilon q^2)$	$1 - \approx$
(2 out of 2)^2	$p^2 + p^2(1 - p^2 - \varepsilon q^2)$	$\varepsilon q^2 + \varepsilon q^2(1 - p^2 - \varepsilon q^2)$	$1 - \approx$
2 out of 3	$3p^2 - 2p^3$	$3\varepsilon q^2 - 2\delta q^3$	$1 - \approx$
1 out of 2	$p^2 + 2p(1 - p - q)$	$\varepsilon q^2 + 2q(1 - p - q)$	$1 - \approx$
3 out of 3	p^3	δq^3	$1 - p^3 - \delta q^3$
1 out of 3	$3p^2 - 2p^3 + {} + 3p(1 - p - q)^2$	$3\varepsilon q^2 - 2\delta q^3 + {} + 3q(1 - p - q)^2$	$1 - \approx$

FAULT TOLERANT SOFTWARE TECHNIQUES
FOR A RAILWAY ELECTRONIC
INTERLOCKING DEVICE

I. Ruello and F. Torielli

Esacontrol S.p.A.*, via Hermada, 6, Genova, Italy

Abstract.   Electronic interlocking device for railway stations must be both very reliable and safe; in order to get such qualities special designing techniques are used: this paper concerns those used for the software design.

Software not only has to be developed in accordance with structured programming criteria, but also "fault tolerant", in order to mask effects of hardware faults and software errors.

Techniques selected for this application concern:

- control flow checking
- data protection (structure and value).

The illustrated techniques were analysed first in the literature; then they were applied to a benchmark program and estimated with respect to:

- type of tolerated errors;
- feasibility of implementation;
- software complexity increase.

After that evaluation, techniques and their associated methodologies were chosen.

Keywords. Reliability; fault-tolerant software; software engineering.

* This work was partially sponsored by the Italian National Research Council (C.N.R.)

INTRODUCTION

A railway electronic interlocking system for station traffic control requires an extremely high degree of safety. In such a system, the main requirement is to assure that the overall output is safe, with a high availability degree.

To meet these needs the system must be able to detect and if possible correct errors. This article gives a description of the architecture chosen for this kind of system, a brief outline of fault-tolerant software techniques known in literature and a more detailed description of techniques used in development of the system software.

DESCRIPTION OF THE SYSTEM ARCHITECTURE

The system configuration has been designed evaluating the characteristics and general requirements as well as the properties of the hardware and software techniques used to guarantee appropriate characteristics of reliability, availability and fault-tolerance in a computer based control system.

The hardware chosen is as follows:

- a configuration with triple redundancy of the computers (TMR, Triple Modular Redundancy) for the central unit;

- majority selection of 2 out of 3 of the outputs of the three computers (voting);

- independent acquisition for the three computers, for the inputs from the keyboard and the state information from the field;

- construction of the representation of the state of the process on the panel through comparison of the outputs of the three computers.

The three computers carry out the same functions in parallel and simultaneously produce all outputs.

The programs elaborated by the three computers are different: they are developed, beginning from the functional specification of the software in accordance with different criteria of design and coding such that both the code and the data-base used are different; in this way the possibility of unsafe output caused by program errors or equal disturbances to the three computers is eliminated.

If the programs of the three computers were identical either an error in the program or an equal disturbance to the three computers could provoke the issue of an erroneous output from the voting circuit, in that it came from all three computers.

147

The organization of the programs is based on certain basic concepts common to the three computers. The functions implemented have a fixed sequence and are activated cyclically. The operating system is reduced to an essential kernel necessary to manage the physical resources of the system and the fault-tolerance mechanisms used. The choice of mechanisms has been made, given equivalent performance, following criteria of simplicity of use and low cost of implementation.

STATE OF THE ART

Techniques, noted in literature, of error detection and correction are considered separately.

Error detection

The following measures have been proposed.

A. Functional check: verification that a certain procedure has properly carried out its function by means of:

- repetition of the procedure with a different (and if possible more rapid and safer) algorithm, and comparison of results;

- reasonableness of results;

- conformation of the results to pre-fixed ranges.

B. Data check: the characteristics of the data are:

- structure
- value.

The structure of the data can be made redundant in various ways, according to the structure used: of these the most common in the literature is the linear list for wich additional pointers,identifiers field, node counters have been proposed.

Protection of the value is generally by means of checksums inserted in the data which make it possible to detect errors; to correct these, recourse can be made to reference copies of the database.

To detect errors affecting value, information about the nature of the data such as absolute and relative range limits can be used.

C. Control of the execution sequence

Given a program, the execution flow can be represented by a flow graph (see Fig.3).

Each node in the graph represents a program block terminating in a jump instruction or an instruction which receives the control from two or more points in the program.

The control flow of a program can be affected by various kinds of errors:

- a loop is executed an incorrect or infinite number of times; the occurrence of an infinite loop can be detected introducing time-outs or limits to the number of times the loop can be executed.
- an illegal branch is executed: a branch is illegal when it does not appear in the graph associated to the program. For example in Fig. 3 the branch $V_4 - V_7$ is illegal because there is not a direct transition between these nodes.
The detection of illegal branches can be achieved by passwords to be checked and updated in proper points of the program; the use of passwords requires only the knowledge of the program structure.

- a wrong branch is executed: a branch is wrong when, although it is included in the graph, it does not represent a correct control tranfer given the program inputs.
The detection of wrong branch execution is quite difficult and requires knowing the program structure and its implementation. Mention should be made of the method of illegal and wrong branch detection proposed by Yau and Chen (3).

Error recovery

Basically there are two ways to correct errors present in the state of the system: backward error recovery restores the system to a previous error free state; forward error recovery elaborates a part of the system in an attempt to eliminate errors. The different characteristics of the forms of error recovery are:

1. Backward error recovery:
   - does not depend on system damage evaluation i.e. it does not require the results of such evaluation;
   - is independent of preventive fault analysis;
   - can be applied to any system;
   - can be operated by means of a mechanism available to the system user.

2. Forward error recovery:
   - implies a damage evaluation phase, whose output must be available;
   - gives no coverage from unpredicted errors;
   - must be designed for the particular system;
   - cannot be operated as a mechanism.

To eliminate the effect of unpredicated faults some type of backward error recovery is needed: this means simulating a shift backward in time, bringing the system back to a previous instance; this can be done automatically in various ways

(for a more detailed treatment of this subject see (2)). The instant in time in which the state of the system is saved for subsequent restoration, if the necessity arises, is called recovery point. More than one recovery point may be active at the same time and the state of each must be saved. The operations which must be available are the following:
- establishment of a recovery point (with saving of the state);
- restoration of the state;
- discarding of a recovery point, which makes it possible to no longer consider a previous state.

Saving of the state can be done in different ways:
- at the establishment of a recovery point, the entire state is memorized;
- from the recovery point establishment to its discarding only variations in the state are memorized (9).

CRITERIA OF TECHNIQUE EVALUATION

Some of the above techniques have been submitted to a sample program which was developed so as to have the same characteristics as the final product but with less complexity. This program consisted of a series of modules which carried out operations on a set of state variables.
The operations are of two types:

- verification that a variable has an expected value;
- assignment of a fixed value to a variable.

The techniques were examined in terms of:

- error type;
- ease of implementation;
- increase of SW complexity.

CONTROL OF ACCESS TO DATA

The data used in the program is organised on tables interconnected by means of pointers. As an example a typical structure used is illustrated in Fig.2.

Generally each element in tables is costituted by the following fields:
- information;
- pointer to the lower level related table.

Each table has a password, in consequence each element in the table has:
- password of table identification;
- information;
- pointer to lower level table;
- password of lower level table.

These passwords are used to verify the absence of malfunctions which may be caused by:

- addressing error, caused by either software errors or possible hardware malfunction;
- damage to the data area containing address and password.

Data access routines cannot distinguish among possible error causes, therefore they must signal this event to the higher level for the proper treatment.
This technique has the advantage of easy implementation as access to each element on the table only requires adding the password: the overhead of space introduced has been calculated at around 30%.
The data used is mostly static: to verify their value integrity, checksum will be introduced on blocks of data. The control of the checksums is not be carried out by the program itself but by a control program; it will be carried out periodically once per elaboration cycle.

CONTROL FLOW CHECKING

To verify the correctness of the control flow, the above mentioned method developed by Yau-Chen (3) has been taken into consideration: in this approach a data-base, containing a formal description of the flow graph is used and the paths actually followed at run-time are verified by comparison with the information in the data-base. The method proposed covers a wide range of errors but also has certain drawbacks:
- the test of correctness is virtually as complex as the program itself;
- as the data base has two parts relating respectively to illegal branches and wrong branches the generation of the part related to the wrong braches is fairly heavy; the data-base has, on the whole, large dimensions.

In consequence a simpler technique based on password control has been used. This detects the execution of illegal branches in the program using variables with the function of password. To each node of the program, a list, containing the identifiers of the nodes connected to the node being examined via a legal branch, is associated. For example in the graph, Fig. 3, the list relative to V4 will contain the identifiers of nodes V2 and V3.
In practice, given that each node consists of a block of instructions, simple checking using a password does not give a complete guarantee against flow errors. The approach used consists of the insertion of a check code at the beginning and end of a node and the definition of two passwords:
- the external passwords, common to the whole program, is the means for checking correctness from a subsequent module;
- the internal password, local to the single module, is used to check the correctness of the flow within the module itself.

A generic module will have the following structure:

```
BEGIN

    SET LOCAL PASSWORD

    TEST EXTERNAL PASSWORD

    IF ERROR THEN   SIGNAL ERROR

        ELSE BEGIN


                    . . . . . . . . . . . .

                SET EXTERNAL PASSWORD

                TEST LOCAL PASSWORD

                IF ERROR THEN SIGNAL    ERROR

            END;

END
```

The execution of illegal branches is detected by means of this technique; wrong branches are not detected, but their occurence is quite unlikely, for the redundancies in the data.

BEHAVIOR OF THE SYSTEM IN WRONG STATES

The techniques described have the purpose of detecting errors: each time an error is detected on a TMR computer, the event is signalled by means of a message to the diagnostic terminal; moreover the current cycle is interrupted with consequent disabling of the output for that cycle. The computer must now be taken to a correct state, this can be done by the comparison of the states of the other two and in the case of equivalence such a state is considered correct and therefore used for subsequent elaboration.

Recalling that the configuration and programming of the system are such that errors which are common to, and simultaneous in, the three computers of the TMR are avoided, two equal states can be considered correct.
Where comparison between the states has a negative outcome the whole system is disabled and steps are taken to a general restart.

CONCLUSIONS

The introduction of fault-tolerant software techniques does increase the reliability of the software, but it also risks the introduction of errors.

Thus the whole process of software development must be carried out applying software engineering techniques, taking particular care in the testing phase. These methodologies, together with the described fault-tolerance techniques, play a very important role when dealing with applications requiring high performance in terms of reliability and security.

REFERENCES

(1) Yau, S.S. and Cheung, R.C., "Design of Self-Cheching Software", Proc. 1975 Int. Conf. on Reliable Software, April 1975, pp.450-457

(2) Anderson, T. and Lee, P.A., "Fault Tolerance: principles and practice", Prentice-hall, London, 1981

(3) Yau, S.S. and Chen, F.C. "An Approach to Concurrent Control Flow Checking", IEEE Trans. on Software Engineering, March 1980

(4) Taylor, D.J., Morgan, D.E. and Blanck. J.P. "Redundancy in Data Structures: improving Software Fault Tolerance", IEEE Trans on Software Eng., Nov. 1980

(5) Taylor D.J. Morgan, D.E. and Blanck. J.P. "Redundancy in Data Structures: some theoretical results" IEEE Trans. on Software Engineering, Nov. 1980

(6) Black, J.P. Morgan D.E. and Taylor, D.J. " A case Study in fault Tolerant Software" Software Practice and Experiences, vol II, 1981

(7) Anderson, T and Kerr, R. "Recovery blocks in action", Proc and int. Conf. Software ing., Oct. 1976, pp. 447-457

(8) Randell, B., "System structure for Software Fault Tolerance" IEEE Trans. On Software Eng. June 1975, pp. 220-232

(9) Lee, P.I., Ghani, N. and Heron, K., "A recovery cache for the PDP-11"., IEEE Trans on Computers, C-29 (6), pp. 546-549, June 198

(10) Lee, P.A., "A reconsideration of the Recovery Block Scheme", Computer Journal, 21 (4), pp. 306-310, Nov. 1978

(11) Horning, J.J. Laver H.C., Melliar-Smith, P.M. Randell, B., "A program Structure for Error Detection and Recovery", in Proc. Conf. Operating Systems, IRIA, Apr.1974, pp. 177-193.

(12) Shrivastava, , "Sequential Pascal with Recovery Blocks", Software Practice and Experience, vol. 8, pp. 177-185, 1978.

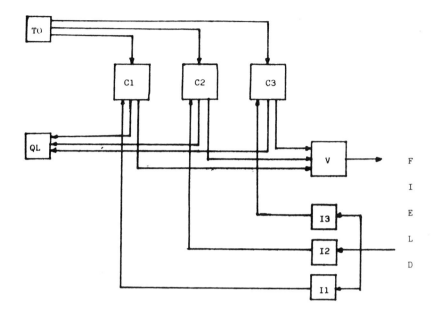

Fig. 1

TO   : keyboard
QL   : panel
C1,C2,C3   : TMR computers
V   : voter, majority selector of 2 out of 3 of the
              outputs of the computers
I1,I2,I3   : systems for the acquisition of the state of the
              field

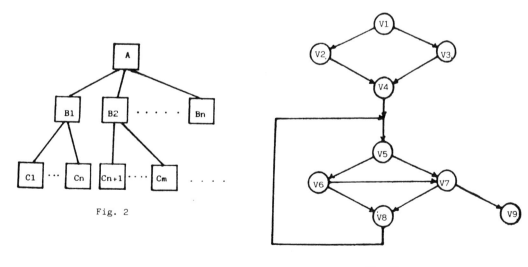

Fig. 2

Fig. 3

PROJECT ON DIVERSE SOFTWARE — AN EXPERIMENT IN SOFTWARE RELIABILITY

P. Bishop*, D. Esp*, M. Barnes**, P. Humphreys**, G. Dahll***,
J. Lahti† and S. Yoshimura††

*Central Electricity Research Laboratories, Kelvin Avenue, Leatherhead, Surrey, UK
**Safety and Reliability Directorate, UKAEA, Wigshaw Lane, Culcheth, Warrington,
UK
***OECD Halden Reactor Project, Os Alle 13, N-1750 Halden, Norway
†Technical Research Centre of Finland, Otakaari 7, SF-02150 Espoo, Finland
††Nippon Atomic Industry Group Co, Ukishima-cho, Kawasaki-city, 210 Japan

Abstract. The Project on Diverse Software (PODS) is an experiment which has attempted to quantify the impact of a number of commonly used software development techniques on software reliability. The main objectives of the project were to:

- Provide a measure of the merits of using diverse software.
- Evaluate the formal specification language X.
- Compare the time and effort expended using high- and low-level languages and using formal and informal specification techniques.
- Compare the reliability of software written in high- and low-level languages.
- Evaluate testing methodologies.
- Observe the software development process.

This paper describes the experimental design, organisation and documentation of the project and presents an analysis of the results. Some of the major conclusions of the experiment are that:

- Diverse implementation was effective in revealing faults not discovered by normal development methods. Testing diverse programs 'back-to-back' is a powerful method for discovering residual faults.
- The functional specification contained the most persistent program faults and was the only source of common mode failure. Better methods of establishing the customer requirements are needed.
- Assembler programming required about twice as much coding effort and generated about 4 times as many coding faults as the equivalent Fortran program, but the number of residual faults was about the same.
- Current 'best practice' software development methods are effective in removing implementation faults.

Keywords. Software diversity, software reliability, programming languages, specification languages, software faults, fault classification, reactor protection, PODS.

INTRODUCTION

The Project on Diverse Software (PODS, Barnes 1985) is a collaborative experiment which has attempted to provide a quantitative basis for assessing the effect of some commonly used implementation methods on software reliability. The experiment was part of the Halden Reactor Project Research programme, and the participants were : the UKAEA Safety and Reliability Directorate (SRD), the CEGB Central Electricity Research Laboratory (CERL), the OECD Halden Reactor Project (HRP) and the Technical Research Centre of Finland (VTT). The main objectives of the project were to:

1. Provide a measure of the merits of using diverse software.
2. Evaluate the formal specification language X.
3. Compare the time and effort expended using high- and low-level languages and formal and informal specification techniques.
4. Compare the reliability of software written in high- and low-level languages.
5. Evaluate testing methodologies.
6. Observe the software development process.

EXPERIMENTAL PROCEDURE

In order to fulfil the objectives, the experiment was designed according to the following scenario. Three programs were to be developed, each capable of implementing an identical function, namely a reactor over-power protection (trip) system specified by a customer. The three programs would be run within an environment where each of their equivalent outputs were voted on, by a 2-out-of-3 majority voting process. The majority output values were to be used to control operator indicators and initiate reactor power level control and trip processes. SRD was to act as 'customer' while CERL, HRP and VTT each took the role of software 'manufacturer' for one of the three programs. The trip system specified was a realistic one, incorporating the following functions:-

- Power level calculation from analogue inputs
- 'Calibration' from operator thumbwheel switches
- Primary and Secondary Trip Logic.
- Test Mode
- ROM integrity check
- Diagnostic indications
- Initialisation on request.

Each team was to implement this trip program using different combinations of programming language (FORTRAN and assembler) and specification methods (X and informal), so that the effect of each could be assessed. Diversity was also introduced into the specification of the reactor power algorithm. The various modes of implementation are summarised below.

Team	Program Language	Main Algorithm	Spec. Method
CERL	Fortran	Polynomial	Informal
HRP	Assembler	Table	X
VTT	Fortran	Table	X

All participants maintained records of the amount of effort, in man-hours, expended in each of the project phases. This was to permit the comparison of effort involved in using high and low level programming languages (objective 3).

All faults and program or document changes were recorded on specially designed forms for subsequent analysis. A fault classification scheme was devised so that faults could be attributed to their root causes, and the influence of specification and programming languages identified (contributing to objectives 2, 4, 5 and 6).

Project Structure

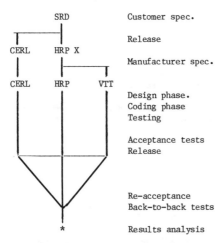

PODS was organised into phases, as shown above. In the first phase, SRD produced a customer specification (PODSPEC). Next, in the manufacturer specification phase, CERL and the HRP X specification language team each produced a manufacturer specification, based on PODSPEC. At the end of that phase, the HRP specification (written in X) was supplied to both HRP and VTT programming teams.

Each team then followed its own software development procedure, consisting basically of design, code and acceptance testing phases. During this period, no communication took place between the teams. This was to enable the fault detecting effectiveness of the specification language X and the informal specification used by CERL to be compared. However, each team reported faults in the customer specification to SRD. At the end of acceptance testing, common specification faults were exchanged between the teams by SRD.

Each of the three programs was then declared a release version and taken to the installation site at Halden. There they were incorporated into the special test harness (MOTH) for the back-to-back testing. In this phase, the programs were run in parallel using 665,288 test cases to detect and characterise remaining program faults (objective 1). Finally, in the results analysis phase, all the information collected in each phase was analysed from the viewpoint of the project objectives.

PROJECT MANAGEMENT

SRD carried out overall project management. They produced a PODS project control document which defined the project objectives, resources, responsibilities, phases and timescales. It also required that each team produced their software under controlled conditions by specifying a structured development approach, quality assurance procedures, and forms for recording time and effort. A Pert Network was used to record planned and actual start and finish dates for all major PODS activities. A companion "Quality Assurance and Development Guidelines" document specified the development requirements in more detail. Each development team had to produce the following set of documents during development:-

- Local Project Control Plan.
- Local Quality Assurance Plan.
- Description of work done in each phase.
- Quality Assurance applied to each phase.
- Design document.
- Description of Design Methodology.
- Man-hour, and fault report forms

An independent quality assurance auditor was nominated at each site, who reported formally to SRD to verify that the software development conformed to the project standards agreed for the site.

Project management meetings were held at regular intervals to assess progress, and to plan subsequent phases of the project.

SYSTEM IMPLEMENTATION

Specification

In the customer specification phase SRD produced an informal customer's specification (PODSPEC). HRP and VTT collaborated to derive an equivalent specification written in their own formal specification language, X (Dahll and Lahti 1983), while CERL produced an informal manufacturer specification The three teams then followed independent paths of analysis and fault reporting to SRD. SRD maintained three different contexts when dealing with the three teams. Faults found by one team were not communicated to the other teams. The production of the manufacturers' specification proved to be rather time-consuming since all the faults and the subsequent changes had to be formally documented. This process was complicated by the fact that three different versions of PODSPEC had to be maintained by SRD.

The X specification was produced by members of the HRP team and VTT performed the quality control checks. A number of different quality checks were applied to check for internal consistency and compatability with the customer specification. A software tool called SPEX was being developed to support X, but it was not fully developed, so some of the checks were performed manually.

CERL did not use a particular specification language, but it did attempt to produce a concise and unambiguous interpretation the customer specification. The customer specification was analysed using group inspections and was re-formulated using Boolean logic definitions and state transition diagrams. Some parts of the customer specification were discarded since they were considered to be implementation details.

Software Production

All teams subsequently produced their programs based on these specifications. 'Good practice' (Myers, 1976) methods were used by all teams This involved documentation and inspection at each stage of development. All teams used a top-down design approach where a complete software design was produced and inspected before detailed design and coding commenced.

The various techniques employed are summarised below:

Activity	CERL	HRP	VTT
Design	Yourdan-Constantine	Nassi-Schneidermann diagrams	Flow-charts
	Pseudo-code	Pseudo-code	Pseudo-code
Coding	FORTRAN 77	Assembler	FORTRAN 77
Test	Module test	Module test	Module test
	System tests	System tests	System tests
	Symbolic debug		Symbolic debug
QA	Inspections	Inspections	Inspections

ACCEPTANCE TESTING

SRD Acceptance test data

SRD specified its acceptance test as a sequence of 672 sets of inputs and expected outputs. The format of the acceptance test data file was defined at an early stage of the project, as part of the back-to-back test harness specification (MOTHSPEC). The test cases were structured, concentrating in turn on different functional aspects of the trip system.

Testing

The CERL and VTT teams had to pass the acceptance tests in two stages: local testing at the development site and remote testing at the target site (Halden). Local acceptance test harnesses were constructed by the teams to apply the SRD acceptance tests to their programs. The test harness programs accepted test data from a file and made calls to the trip system subroutine under test and reported any disagreements with the expected results. When a program fault was discovered, the fault was recorded, then the program was corrected and re-tested from the beginning. This process was intended to continue until no more faults were discovered. In practice there were minor faults in the test data that were only resolved with SRD when the CERL and VTT programs were re-accepted at Halden.

BACK-TO-BACK TEST PHASE

By this time, all three programs had passed the customer acceptance tests on the Halden computer, and the three programs were ready for back-to-back testing. The MOTH test was designed to apply common input data to all three trip programs and then check the calculated output values. Program faults were revealed through discrepancies between the outputs of the three programs.

MOTH test harness

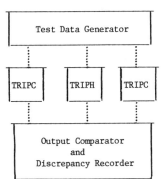

Back-to-Back test strategy

The test philosophy for back-to-back testing was developed by the HRP back-to-back test implementation team. The tests were designed to be as comprehensive as possible, and comprised a series of systematic checks designed to uncover particular types of fault, and checks employing pseudo-random input data. The test data values were derived using a variety of different techniques:

- Equivalence partitioning was used to divide the input domain into a finite number of equivalence classes. Test data was designed to cover as many valid equivalence classes as possible, to maximise the effectiveness of a finite number of tests. Invalid equivalence classes (which relate to faulty input data) were designed to be tested one at a time to avoid masking effects.

- Boundary value analysis was used to derive test cases at the boundaries of input and output equivalence classes.

- Decision Tables were used to take into account possible combinations of input conditions, output conditions and internal program states.

On the basis of these analyses, a series of test cases were designed to test the function of the main trip algorithm, together with additional test cases to check the ancilliary functions of ROM corruption checks and re-calibration. The total number of test cases was 2470.

In addition a series of test cases were designed which selected input values using a pseudo-random data generator. The test cases comprised the following distributions:

- Uniform over the input domain
- Gaussian over the input domain
- Rectangular over domain boundaries
- Gaussian over domain boundaries

The total series of tests comprised 665,288 test cases.

Testing Procedure

A formal manual procedure was designed for back-to-back testing. When a discrepancy occurred between the programs, testing automatically halted. A group diagnosis of the causes of the discrepancy was made, with SRD making the final judgement. The faults were recorded on a computer file, and the programmers completed change notices for the program modifications. The modified programs were tested against the SRD acceptance test data and, if successful, the three programs were again tested back-to-back.

Estimation of Failure Rate

After all the above tests had been completed, further back-to-back test runs were performed in order to establish consistent relative failure rates for each individual fault. In these test runs, uniformly distributed random input data was used throughout. It should be noted that this distribution is not representative of normal operating conditions, but it was capable of activating every known fault. Failure rates for each fault were calculated from incremental changes in overall failure rate, after considering known fault interactions.

Seeded Fault Tests

To assess the effectiveness of the test data employed, faults were deliberately seeded into one the trip programs (TRIPH), and then tested back-to-back with the remaining programs using the same sequence of tests employed in back-to-back testing.

PROGRAM CHARACTERISTICS

The characteristics of the programs produced by each team are summarized below. It can be seen that the VTT program has the simplest structure and the smallest amount of additional comment:-

Team	Modules	Code Lines		Total Lines
CERL	35	859	Fortran	3235
HRP	27	1906	Assembler	3407
VTT	17	477	Fortran	797

The structure of each program is summarized below using the structure metrics of Gilb (1977):-

Team	Nodes	Av Depth	Max Depth	Width
CERL	19	4	4	14
HRP	27	3	5	16
VTT	20	2	3	14

It can be seen that there is considerable diversity in the software structures used by each team, even though HRP and VTT were working from a common X specification.

PROJECT EFFORT

The amount of effort expended on mainstream activities is shown below:

Man-Hours Expended				
Activity	SRD	CERL	HRP	VTT
Proj. Management	546	213	246	170
Customer spec.	280			
Manufac. spec.+ QA		441	138	43
Design + QA		200	185	110
Code + QA		62	196	110
Testing		75	96	45
Acceptance	86	82	64	45
Back-to-back tests	264	50	180	119
MOTH development	72	–	120	–
Test data dev.	60	–	238	–
Total	1453	1123	1463	642

It should be noted that HRP and VTT collaborated in the production of the X specification (VTT performed the quality assurance). So the combined time of 181 hours should be used for comparison with CERL.

ANALYSIS OF FAULTS

The fault records of each team were analysed and the following tables summarise some of the major results.

Faults Reported

Fault Created in:	CERL	HRP	VTT
Customer spec.	68	43	11
Manufacturer spec.	53	42	56
Design spec.	19	26	3
Implementation	26	87	5
Acceptance mod.	6	0	0
Back-to-back mod.	1	0	1
Test data	1	0	0
Support software	2	0	0
Total	176	198	76

Note that the customer specification faults were actually created by SRD. To compare the faults created by each team during development, the specification faults should be subtracted.

Fault Causes

Cause	CERL	HRP	VTT
Clerical	20	44	15
Human	144	146	28
Tools	2	8	32
Other	10	15	0
Total	176	198	76

Detection Methods

Detection Method	Faults Found		
	CERL	HRP	VTT
Inspection	26	101	28
Walkthrough	14	8	1
Individual checks	81	19	27
Translation	4	33	1
Test	47	25	17
Other	4	12	–
Total	176	198	76

Fault Persistence

A large proportion of the faults generated were discovered during the same phase. This can partly be attributed to the quality assurance programme employed during development. It can be seen that the most persistent faults are in the customer specification.

Faults Created in Phase:	Team	Faults Discovered in Phase:				
		Mspec	Design	Impl	Accept	B/B
Customer spec.	CERL	52	0	0	14	2
	HRP	35	2	0	3	3~
	VTT	–	–	2	6	3~
Manufact spec.	CERL	38	6	6	3	0
	HRP	28	7	4	3	0
	VTT	–	20	37	0	1
Design	CERL		14	4	1	0
	HRP		22	3	1	0
	VTT		0	0	0	0
Implementation	CERL			23	2	0
	HRP			84	3	0
	VTT			2	3	0
Acceptance	CERL				6	0
	HRP				3	0
	VTT				0	0
Back to Back	CERL					1
	HRP					0
	VTT					1

~ Two faults were common to HRP and VTT

Approximately 90 different faults were detected in the customer specification. These included 'cosmetic' faults and obvious ambiguities that did not cause any subsequent faults.

ANALYSIS OF SOFTWARE DIVERSITY

Residual Faults

The faults discovered during back-to-back testing correspond to the in-service operation of the trip system. The assessment of the benefit of diversity is based on an analysis of the residual faults discovered in this phase.

Seven different residual faults were found, 6 were caused by PODSPEC faults and one related to the X specification. Two more faults were accidentally introduced while making corrections, as a result of incorrect on-the-spot designing. There were no faults that could be traced back to implementation. The faults are summarized below:

Fault	Team	Description	Cause
1 ·	V	error flag logic	Ambiguous spec
* 2	H	error flag logic	Ambiguous spec
3	C	error flag logic	Ambiguous spec
4	C	correction to 3	Forgetting
* 5	C	trip limit calc	Ambiguous spec
* 6	V,H	Power calculation	Incorrect spec
7	V,H	sec trip logic	Incorrect spec
8	V	power calculation	Ambiguous X spec
9	V	bad correction	Oversight

The common mode faults (faults 6 and 7) would win a majority vote and cause overall system failure. Faults 1 and 2 were mutually exclusive and the other faults were independent, so all the remaining faults could only produce failure on a single channel and the system would have behaved correctly.

The program faults marked with an asterisk have been classified as dangerous. A safe failure occurs when a trip or alarm signal is operated unnecessarily, while a dangerous failure occurs when a trip or indicator flag is not operated under circumstances that demand it should be operated, or when the calculated power level is spuriously low.

Failure Rates of The Faults

The failure rates derived from the extended back to back test using uniform pseudo-random data, are shown below. This shows the probability of failure per test-case, and gives an indication of the fraction of the total input domain that is capable of activating the fault. The failure rate for system version 8 (which contained only fault 8) is an estimate based on the number of test cycles to failure in the main part of back-to-back testing. Unlike the other faults, it was not discovered by the pseudo-random test data as the number of test cycles employed was too small to reveal a fault with such a low failure probability. The final failure rate figure of 0.0000015 is calculated assuming that the very next test would have resulted in failure.

Program Versions	Maj. Vote	CERL	HRP	VTT
C1,H1,V1	.0008	.01	.25	.0018
C1,H1,V2	.0008	.01	.25	.0008
C1,H2,V2	.0008	.01	.0008	.0008
C2,H2,V2	.0008	.70	.0008	.0008
C3,H2,V2	.0008	.0006	.0008	.0008
C4,H2,V2	.0008	.0000015	.0008	.0008
C4,H3,V3	.00009	.0000015	.00009	.0001
C4,H4,V4	.0000015	.0000015	.0000015	.0000066
C4,H4,V5	.0000015	.0000015	.0000015	.106
C4,H4,V6	.0000015	.0000015	.0000015	.0000015

The two common mode faults (6 and 7) have a combined failure rate of .0008. These faults cannot be excluded by majority voting. The remaining faults are all diverse so that, although the total failure rate of all the faults in version (C1, H1, V1) is around 0.26, the failure rate after majority voting is only 0.0008. The majority vote failure rate stays at this 'plateau' level until faults 6 and 7 are removed.

To check the sensitivity of the failure rate to the distribution of test values over the input domain, further back-to-back measurements were made on System C1,H1,V1 using three different types of back-to-back test data:

Test		Failure Rate		
Type	Test cases	CERL	HRP	VTT
Systematic	2472	.043	.53	.023
Uniform	65000	.010	.25	.002
Gaussian	65000	.002	.069	.088

These results highlight the fact that it is only possible to assess the reliability of software for a specific mode of use. Recent (unconfirmed) measurements show that all test sequences with a uniform random distribution yield very similar failure rates. This indicates that a probabilistic input distribution may be an adequate way of representing the mode of use. However further measurements would be needed validate this observation.

TEST DATA EFFECTIVENESS

The test data was also used to locate 30 seeded faults in TRIPH by comparing the outputs with the TRIPC and TRIPH programs. The test data was applied in the normal back-to-back test sequence. When a fault was detected, the program was corrected and the tests were repeated from beginning. The results are summarised below:

Test Data	Faults Found
Acceptance	22
B-B Systematic	1
B-B Uniform Rand.	2

An analysis of the remaining 5 faults showed that they could not have been found by testing. One fault, for example, was in defensive code which should never be executed, while another fault affected part of a constant that was not used.

It is clear that the acceptance test data is quite efficient at detecting faults, while the back-to-back tests found all the remaining detectable faults. It would be interesting to examine whether back-to-back testing with random data could have revealed all the faults without the need to define acceptance test data. This analysis has yet to be done.

ANALYSIS OF PROGRAM LANGUAGE

Number of Faults

Only specification-related faults persisted beyond development and acceptance testing for any of the teams. This shows that 'good' practice methods can remove a high percentage of implementation faults. The reliabilities of the post-acceptance programs depended only on faults that could be traced back to specification.

However, the effectiveness of local and acceptance testing can be attributed to the lack of complexity in the system, enabling fairly exhaustive testing to be carried out. In general such testing may not always be possible, in which case the greater the number of errors made in coding, the greater the probability that some will persist into the final product. So the numbers of faults created in coding and development testing phases have been examined for each of the three teams:

Team	Language	Faults	Lines/Fault
CERL	Fortran	25	34
HRP	Assembler	87	22
VTT	Fortran	5	95

The faults found in the CERL and HRP programs are fully documented, while the information on the VTT development faults is less satisfactory. It would seem that the use of a high level language reduced the number of coding faults by at least a factor of 4. This is consistent with other observations that there will be one fault in every 30 lines of code written, regardless of the programming language.

Programming Effort

For the purposes of this analysis, programming is defined as coding plus development testing (both module and integration). Other activities such as manufacturer's specification and local test harness production are not included, as they are not equivalent between the teams.

Man-Hours in Programming

Activity	CERL Fortran	HRP Assemb.	VTT Fortran
Coding	58	150	74
Code QA	4	46	36
Dev. Testing	75	96	45
Total	137	292	155

It would appear that the HRP assembler program took about twice as long to write as the equivalent FORTRAN programs. It should be noted however that coding and testing was a small fraction of the total effort of each team.

Language Faults

No faults were discovered in the VAX VMS Fortran compilers used by CERL and VTT for local development. One commonly expected declaration check was absent from the pre-release NORD assembler used by HRP. In addition two faults were discovered in a pre-release version of NORD Fortran used by CERL during re-acceptance.

IMPACT OF SPECIFICATION TECHNIQUES

Experimental Difficulties

The trip system requirements are relatively simple. It was not complex enough to exercise more than a small part of the X specification facilities. In addition it was difficult to eliminate the spirit of competition between the teams, so that although CERL did not use a special language, the customer specification was analysed in great depth to locate potential problems. CERL also tried to raise the customer specification to a higher level of abstraction using state transition diagrams. In this respect the experiment was not entirely successful because CERL were not informal enough.

The X Specification Language

X enables the organisation of a system to be specified in detail, all the component parts and their interactions are specified. Using a computer-aided tool SPEX a wide variety of consistency checks and analyses could be made. Only one fault in the X specification persisted into the back-to-back test phase and this was due the use of free text (which is permitted in X) rather than a rigorous mathematical definition. This compares well with the 6 faults remaining in the customer specification. HRP also used X as a software design aid and, as such, it was quite successful. It was easy to translate the X specification into a program.

CERL Specification Approach

The PODSPEC described the primary and secondary trip logic using terms similar to a conventional sequential programming language (e.g. if condition then trip), resulting in ambiguities and coding type faults in the specification. In the CERL manufacturer specification, trip logic was re-formulated using boolean logic and state machine diagrams. As a consequence a number of apparently unnecessary states were found in the PODSPEC primary and secondary trip logic. These problems were reported but never properly resolved. The unnecessary states were removed from the CERL specification. This gave rise to a CERL test 'failure' in the primary trip logic during acceptance testing and discrepancies in back-to-back testing. However on analysis it was agreed that the initial PODSPEC was erroneous, so that the HRP and VTT programs both contained a common mode fault in the secondary trip.

Summary

The two methods appear to be complementary, The re-formulation of the customer requirements in more abstract terms such as boolean logic and state machines (Minsky 1967), showed up potential faults in the customers statement of requirements, while the X specification helped to ensure that the software specification was internally consistent and complete. While the CERL specification did not suffer from any major internal inconsistencies, these could have occurred in a more complex specification.

CONCLUSIONS

- Diverse implementation was effective in revealing faults not discovered by normal development methods. Testing diverse programs 'back-to-back' is a powerful method for discovering residual faults.

- The functional specification contained the most persistent program faults and was the only source of common mode failure. Better methods of establishing the customer requirements are needed.

- Assembler programming required about twice as much coding effort as an equivalent Fortran program.

- Assembler programming generated about 4 times the number of coding faults compared with the same function written in Fortran.

- The assembler and Fortran programs contained about the same number of residual faults when they were released for acceptance testing.

- Current 'best practice' software development methods are effective in removing implementation faults.

REFERENCES

Barnes, M., et al, 1985, "PODS - The Project on Diverse Software", OECD Halden Reactor Report HPR-323.

Dahll, G. and Lahti, J., 1983, "The Specification System X-SPEX", IFAC Conference "Safety of Computer Control Systems", Cambridge, UK, pp 111-118.

Gilb, T., 1977, "Software Metrics", Winthrop Inc., ISBN 0-87626-855-6.

Minsky, M.L., 1967, "Computation: Finite and Infinite Machines", Prentice Hall.

Myers, G.J., 1976, "Software Reliability Principles and Practices", Wiley, ISBN 0-471-62765-8.

Nassi, I., Schneidermann, B., 1973, Sigplan Notices (ACM) 8, 8.

Yourdan, E., Constantine, L., 1975, "Structured Design", Yourdan Inc.

CORRELATED FAILURES IN MULTI-VERSION SOFTWARE[1]

J. C. Knight* and N. G. Leveson**

**Computer Science Department, University of Virginia, Charlottesville,
Virginia 22903, USA*
***Information & Computer Science Department, University of California, Irvine,
California 92717, USA*

Abstract. N-version programming has been proposed as a method of incorporating fault tolerance into software by independently preparing multiple versions of a program and voting on the results. This method depends for its reliability improvement on the assumption that programs that have been developed independently will fail independently. In this paper an experiment is described in which the fundamental axiom is tested. A total of twenty seven versions of a program were prepared independently from the same specification at two universities and then subjected to one million input test cases. The results of the tests revealed that the programs were individually extremely reliable but that the number of tests in which more than one program failed was substantially more than expected. The conclusion from this experiment is that independence of failure patterns in separate produced software versions cannot in general be assumed to be true and that analysis of the reliability of n-version programming must include the effect of dependent errors.

Keywords. Multi-version programming, N-version programming, software reliability, fault-tolerant software, design diversity.

INTRODUCTION

Multi-version or N-version programming (Chen and Avizienis, 1978) has been proposed as a method of providing fault tolerance in software. The approach requires the separate, independent preparation of multiple (i.e. "N") versions of a piece of software for some application. These versions are executed in parallel in the application environment; each receives identical inputs and each produces its version of the required outputs. The outputs are collected by a voter and, in principle, they should all be the same. In practice there may be some disagreement. If this occurs, the results of the majority (assuming there is one) are assumed to be the correct output, and this is the output used by the system.

Separate development can start at different points in the software development process. Since each version of the software must provide the same functional capability, there must exist some common form of system requirements document. Coordination must also exist if the versions are to provide data to the voter, especially if intermediate data is compared as well as the final output data. Any work that occurs before the separate development begins or which involves coordination between the versions obviously can lead to common faults in the separate versions. Therefore, all design specification must be redundant and independent for the versions to have any chance of avoiding common design faults

(assuming, of course, that one believes that there is some randomness in the process of producing software design errors).[2]

An interesting approach to dual specification was used by Ramamoorthy and colleagues (1981) where two independent specifications were written in a formal specification language and then formal mathematical techniques used to verify consistency between the specifications before the next step in development proceeded. Thus they were able to detect specification faults by using redundancy and then repair them before the separate software versions were produced. Kelly and Avizienis (1983) also used separate specifications for their N-version programming experiment, but the specifications were all written by the same person so independence was syntactic only (three different specification languages were used).

The great benefit that N-version programming is intended to provide is a substantial improvement in reliability. It is assumed in the analysis of the technique that the N different versions will fail *independently*, that is, faults in the different versions occur at random and are unrelated. Thus the probability of two or more versions failing on the same input is very small.

---

[1]This work was sponsored in part by NASA grant number NAG1-242 and by a MICRO grant cofunded by the state of California and Hughes Aircraft Company.

[2]It is interesting to note that, even in mechanical systems where redundancy is an important technique for achieving fault tolerance, common *design* faults are a source of serious problems. An aircraft crashed recently because of a common vibration mode that adversely affected all three parts of a triply redundant system (Bonnett, 1984). Common Failure Mode Analysis is typically used in critical hardware systems along with redundancy in an attempt to determine and minimize common failure modes.

We are concerned that this assumption might be *false*. Our intuition indicates that when solving a difficult intellectual problem (such as writing a computer program), people tend to make the same mistakes (for example, incorrect treatment of boundary conditions) even when they are working independently. Some parts of a problem may be inherently more difficult than others. In the experiment described in this paper, the subjects were asked in a questionnaire to state the parts of the problem that caused them the most difficulty. The responses were surprisingly similar.

If the assumption of independence is not born out in practice for an N-version software system, it would cause the analysis to overestimate the system reliability. Eckhardt and Lee (1985) have shown that even small probabilities of common errors in redundant systems will cause a substantial reduction in reliability. This could be an important practical problem since N-version programming is being used in existing critical systems and is planned for others. For instance, dual programming has been used in the slat and flap control system of the Airbus Industrie A310 aircraft (Martin, 1983). The two programs are executed by different microprocessors operating asynchronously. The outputs of the two microprocessors are compared continuously, and any difference greater than a defined threshold causes the system to disconnect after a preset time delay. On the A310, it is sufficient to know that there has been a failure as backup procedures allow the continued safe flight and landing of the aircraft. Dual programming has also been applied to point switching, signal control, and traffic control in the Gothenburg area by Swedish State Railways (Taylor, 1981). In the latter system, if the two programs show different results, signal lights are switched to red. Dual programming has further been proposed for safety systems in nuclear reactors. Voges, Fetsch, and Gmeiner (1982) have proposed its use in the design of a reactor shutdown system which serves the purpose of detecting cooling disturbances in a fast breeder reactor and initializing automatic shutdown of the reactor in case of possible emergency. Also, both Ramamoorthy and colleagues (1981) and Dahll and Lahti (1980) have proposed elaborate dual development methodologies for the design of nuclear reactor safety systems.

A common argument (Dahll and Lahti, 1980; Gmeiner and Voges, 1980; Ramamoorthy and colleagues, 1981) in favor of dual programming is that testing of safety-critical real-time software can be simplified by producing two versions of the software and executing them on large numbers of test cases without manual or independent verification of the correct output. The output is assumed correct as long as both versions of the programs agree. The argument is made that preparing test data and determining correct output is difficult and expensive for much real-time software. Since it is assumed "unlikely" that two programs will contain identical faults, a large number of test cases can be run in a relatively short time and with a large reduction in effort required for validation of test results.

In addition, it has been argued that each individual version of the software can have lower reliability than would be necessary if only one version were produced. The higher required software reliability is assumed to be obtained through the voting process[3]. The additional cost incurred in the development of multiple software versions would be offset by a reduction in the cost of the validation process. It has even been suggested (Avizienis and Kelly, 1984) that elaborate software development environments and procedures will be unnecessary and that mail-order software could be obtained from hobbyist programmers.

The important point to note is that all of the above arguments in favor of using redundant programming hinge on the basic assumption that the probability of common mode failures (identical incorrect output given the same input) is very low for independently developed software. Therefore, it is important to know whether this assumption is correct.

Several previous experiments have involved N-version programming, but none have focused on the issue of independence. In two (Gmeiner and Voges, 1980; Ramamoorthy and colleagues, 1981) independence was assumed and therefore not tested. In each of these, the two versions developed were assumed to be correct if the two outputs from the test cases agreed and no attempt was made to verify independently the correctness of the output. Thus common errors would not necessarily have been detected. In other experiments, common errors were observed but since independence was not the hypothesis being tested, the design of the experiments make it impossible to draw any statistically valid conclusions. Kelly and Avizienis (1983) report finding 21 related faults. Taylor (1981) reports that one common fault was found in practical tests of the Halden nuclear reactor project and that common faults have been found in about half of the practical redundant European software systems.

In summary, although there is some negative evidence which raises doubts about the independence assumption, there has been no experiment which attempted to study this assumption in a manner in which clear evidence for or against can be drawn. Because the independence assumption is widely accepted and because of the potential importance of the issue in terms of safety, we have carried out a large scale experiment in N-version programming to study this assumption. A "*statistically rigorous*" test of independence was the major goal of the experiment and all of the design decisions that were taken were dominated by this goal.

The experiment and its results are presented in the remainder of this paper. In section two we describe the experiment itself. The results of the tests performed on the various versions are presented in section three, and various issues arising from this experiment are discussed in section four. Our conclusions are presented in section five.

DESCRIPTION OF EXPERIMENT

In graduate and senior level classes in computer science at the University of Virginia (UVA) and the University of California at Irvine (UCI), students were asked to write

---

[3]One might note that even in the hardware Triple Modular Redundancy (TMR) systems, from which the idea of N-version programming arises, overall system reliability is not improved if the individual components are not themselves sufficiently reliable (Anderson and Lee, 1981). In fact, incorporating redundancy into a system can actually reduce overall system reliability due to the increased number of components (Wakerly, 1976).

programs from a single requirements specification. The result was a total of twenty seven programs (nine from UVA and eighteen from UCI) all of which should produce the same output from the same input. Each of these programs was then subjected to one million randomly-generated test cases.

In order to make the experiment realistic, an attempt was made to choose an application that would normally be a candidate for the inclusion of fault tolerance. The problem that was selected for programming is a simple (but realistic) anti-missile system that came originally from an aerospace company. The program is required to read some data that represents radar reflections and, using a collection of conditions, has to decide whether the reflections come from an object that is a threat or otherwise. If the decision is made that the object is a threat, a signal to launch an interceptor has to be generated. The problem is known as the "launch interceptor" problem and the various conditions upon which the decision depends are referred to as "launch interceptor conditions" (LIC's). The conditions are heavily parameterized. For example, one condition asks whether a set of reflections can be contained within a circle of given radius; the radius is a parameter.

The problem has been used in other software engineering experiments (Nagel and Skrivan, 1982; Dunham, 1984). Dunham (1983) used it in a study of software reliability measurement that was carried out at the Research Triangle Institute (RTI). We chose this problem because of its suitability and because we were able to use the lessons learned in the experiment at RTI to modify our own experiment. RTI had prepared a requirements specification and had experienced some difficulties with unexpected ambiguities and similar problems. We were able to rewrite the requirements specification in the light of this experience. Thus the requirements specification had been carefully "debugged" prior to use in this experiment.

The requirements specification was given to the students and they were asked to prepare software to comply with it. No overall software development methodology was imposed on them. They were required to write the program in Pascal and to use only a specified compiler and associated operating system. At UVA these were the University of Hull V-mode Pascal compiler for the Prime computers using PRIMOS, and at UCI these were the Berkeley PC compiler for the VAX 11/750 using UNIX.

The students were given a brief explanation of the goals of the experiment and the principles of N-version programming. The need for independent development was stressed and students were carefully instructed not to discuss the project amongst themselves. However, we did not impose any restriction on their reference sources. Since the application requires some knowledge of geometry, it was expected that the students would consult reference texts and perhaps mathematicians in order to develop the necessary algorithms. We felt that the possibility of two students using the same reference material was no different from two separate organizations using the same reference sources in a commercial development environment.

As would be expected during development, questions arose about the meaning of the requirements. In order to prevent any possibility of information being inadvertently transmitted by an informal verbal response, these few questions were submitted and answered by electronic mail. If a question revealed a general flaw in the specifications, the response was broadcast to all the programmers.

One result of the earlier experiment at RTI was some difficulty with machine precision differences between versions. Although two programs computed what amounted to the same result, different orders of computation yielded minor differences which gave the impression that one or more versions had failed. To prevent this, all programmers in this experiment were supplied with a function to perform comparison of real quantities with limited precision. The programmers were instructed to use this supplied function for all real-number comparisons.

Each student was supplied with fifteen input data sets and the expected outputs for use in debugging. Once a program was debugged using these tests and any other tests the student developed, it was subjected to an acceptance test. The acceptance test was a set of two hundred randomly-generated test cases; a different set of two hundred tests were generated for each program. Different data sets were used for each program to prevent a general "filtering" of common faults by the use of a common acceptance test. An acceptance test was used since it was felt that in a real software production environment potential programs would be submitted to extensive testing and would not be used unless they demonstrated a high level of reliability. Although the data was generated randomly, the test case generator was written for, and tailored to this application. Once a program passed its acceptance test, it was considered complete and was entered into the collection of versions.

The acceptance test that was used represents a realistic amount of validation for this type of software, and resulted in highly reliable programs as is shown below. Each of our test cases represents an "unusual" event seen by the radar. Most of the time the radar echoes will be identical from one scan to the next with only an occasional change due to the entry of an object into the field of view. Producing realistic unusual events to test a production tracking program is clearly an expensive undertaking, and we feel that two hundred such events would indeed be a realistic number and is the equivalent of a very elaborate testing process for production programs of this type.

Once all the versions had passed their acceptance tests, the versions were subjected to the experimental treatment which consisted of simulation of a production environment. A test driver was built which generated random radar reflections and random values for all the parameters in the problem. All twenty seven programs were executed on these test cases, and the determination of success was made by comparing their output with a twenty-eighth version, referred to as the *gold* program. This program was originally written in FORTRAN for the RTI experiment and was rewritten in Pascal for this experiment. As part of the RTI experiment, the gold program has been subjected to several million test cases and we have considerable confidence in its accuracy. It was also subjected to an extensive structured walkthrough at UVA after translation to Pascal.

A gold version was used so that a larger number of test cases could be executed than would be possible if manual checking of the outputs was performed. Naturally, it is possible (but very unlikely) that a common undetected fault existed in all 28 versions, including the gold version. This would have no effect on our final results, however, and any additional undetected common faults would only strengthen our conclusion.

A total of one million tests were run on the twenty seven versions written for this experiment and the gold program. Although testing was not continuous on any of the machines, a total of fifteen computers were used in performing these tests between May and September of 1984; five Primes and a dual processor CDC Cyber 730 at UVA, and seven VAX 11/750's and two CDC Cyber 170's at NASA Langley Research Center.

One million test cases (several hundred hours of computer time per version) corresponds to dealing with one million unusual events during production use. In practice, as noted above, these one million events will be separated by a much larger number of executions for usual events. If the program is executed once per second and unusual events occur every ten minutes, then one million tests correspond to about twenty years of operational use.

EXPERIMENTAL RESULTS

For each test case executed, each program produces a 15 by 15 Boolean array, a 15 element Boolean vector, and a single Boolean launch decision, for a total of 241 results. The program calculates these results from the simulated radar tracking data and various parameters, all of which are randomly generated for each test case. The launch condition is the only true output in this application. The other results are really intermediate although they must be produced since the specifications require them as part of the determination of the launch condition. For the programs written for this experiment, all these results must be supplied to the driver program during testing to allow for error detection. We record *failure* for a particular version on a particular test case if there is *any* discrepancy between the 241 results produced by that version and those produced by the gold program, or the version causes some form of exception (such as negative square root) to be raised during execution of that test case.

The quality of the programs written for this experiment is remarkably high. Table 1 shows the observed failure rates of the twenty seven versions. Of the twenty seven, no failures were recorded by six versions and the remainder were successful on more than 99% of the tests. Twenty three of the twenty seven were successful on more than 99.9% of the tests.

Table 2 shows the number of test cases in which more than one version failed on the same input. We find it surprising that test cases occurred in which eight of the twenty seven versions failed.

Where multiple failure occurred on the same input, it is natural to suspect that the failures occurred in the versions supplied by only one of the universities involved. It might be argued that students at the same university

TABLE 1 - Version Failure Data

Version	Failures	Pr(Success)	Version	Failures	Pr(Success)
1	2	0.999998	15	0	1.000000
2	0	1.000000	16	62	0.999938
3	2297	0.997703	17	269	0.999731
4	0	1.000000	18	115	0.999885
5	0	1.000000	19	264	0.999736
6	1149	0.998851	20	936	0.999064
7	71	0.999929	21	92	0.999908
8	323	0.999677	22	9656	0.990344
9	53	0.999947	23	80	0.999920
10	0	1.000000	24	260	0.999740
11	554	0.999446	25	97	0.999903
12	427	0.999573	26	883	0.999117
13	4	0.999996	27	0	1.000000
14	1368	0.998632			

TABLE 2 - Occurrences of Multiple Failures

Number	Probability	Occurrences
2	0.00055100	551
3	0.00034300	343
4	0.00024200	242
5	0.00007300	73
6	0.00003200	32
7	0.00001200	12
8	0.00000200	2

have a similar background and that this would tend to cause dependencies. However, the exact opposite has been found. Table 3 shows a correlation matrix of common failures between the versions supplied by the two universities. For table 3, and for table 1, versions numbered 1 through 9 came from UVA and versions numbered 10 through 27 came from UCI. A table 3 entry at location i, j shows the number of times versions i and j failed on the same input. In table 3, the rows are labeled with UCI version numbers and the columns with UVA version numbers. Thus, a non-zero table entry show the number of common failures experienced by a UVA version and a UCI version. In the preliminary analysis of common faults, *all* were found to involve versions from both schools.

Since the experiment resulted in millions of pieces of data, it is impossible to reproduce the data in a paper. To give the reader some feel for the amount of common errors, some summary data can be given. Out of the million test cases, there were 16,461 cases of input data which resulted in at least one program failing. This total is somewhat skewed by the fact that one program abended frequently due to attempting to take the square root of a negative number (which had not occurred in the programmer's debugging environment due to subtle differences in the finite precision arithmetic between the debugging and testing computers). Eliminating this particular failure, there were 5871 instances of at least one failure. Of this total, 503 input cases caused more than one program to fail.

Separate versions of a program may fail on the same input even if they fail independently. Indeed, if they did not, their failures would be dependent. We base our probabilistic model for this experiment on the statistical definition of independence:

TABLE 3 - Correlated Failures Between UVA And UCI

		UVA Versions								
		1	2	3	4	5	6	7	8	9
	10	0	0	0	0	0	0	0	0	0
	11	0	0	58	0	0	2	1	58	0
	12	0	0	1	0	0	0	71	1	0
	13	0	0	0	0	0	0	0	0	0
	14	0	0	28	0	0	3	71	26	0
	15	0	0	0	0	0	0	0	0	0
	16	0	0	0	0	0	1	0	0	0
UCI	17	2	0	95	0	0	0	1	29	0
Versions	18	0	0	2	0	0	1	0	0	0
	19	0	0	1	0	0	0	0	1	0
	20	0	0	325	0	0	3	2	323	0
	21	0	0	0	0	0	0	0	0	0
	22	0	0	52	0	0	15	0	36	2
	23	0	0	72	0	0	0	0	71	0
	24	0	0	0	0	0	0	0	0	0
	25	0	0	94	0	0	0	1	94	0
	26	0	0	115	0	0	5	0	110	0
	27	0	0	0	0	0	0	0	0	0

TABLE 4 - Faults Located In Each Version

Version	Faults	Version	Faults
1	1	15	0
2	0	16	2
3	4	17	2
4	0	18	1
5	0	19	1
6	3	20	2
7	1	21	2
8	2	22	3
9	2	23	2
10	0	24	1
11	1	25	3
12	2	26	7
13	1	27	0
14	2		

Two events, A and B, are independent if the conditional probability of A occurring given that B has occurred is the same as the probability of A occurring, and vice versa. That is $pr(A|B) = pr(A)$ and $pr(B|A) = pr(B)$. Intuitively, A and B are independent if knowledge of the occurrence of A in no way influences the occurrence of B, and vice versa.

The null hypothesis that we wish to test is basically that the data satisfies this statistical definition of independence, i.e. that the number of common failures which actually occurred could have resulted by chance. Details of the statistical model can be found in Knight and Leveson (1985). It is enough to say here that the null hypothesis was rejected with a confidence level of 99%. That is, it was determined that the programs did not fail independently.

ANALYSIS OF FAULTS

We define a *fault* to be any instance of program text in any particular version that causes that version to fail when that program text is executed on some test case. The various launch conditions that have to be computed are sometimes similar in their description. If a programmer made the same mistake in implementing two different but similar launch conditions, we record that as two different faults.

A total of forty five faults were detected in the program versions used in this experiment. The numbers of faults found in the individual versions is shown in Table 4. All of these faults have been found and corrected. The corrective code was installed so that it could be selectively enabled and an extensive analysis of the faults has been undertaken (Brilliant, 1985). Many of the faults were unique to individual versions but several occurred in more than version. We will refer to the former as *non-correlated* and the latter as *correlated*. The details of the faults are quite complex and a complete description is beyond the scope of this paper. We include in this section a description of two non-correlated and two corre-

lated faults for illustrative purposes. Recall that all the versions used in this experiment were required to pass two hundred tests as part of the acceptance procedure. The faults described in this section all survived that acceptance procedure.

The non-correlated faults that we describe here will be recognized as commonly occurring. They are subtle and important nonetheless. The first was an omission by the programmer of the assignment of a value to a function for one path through the function. This was not checked by any of the compilers used in this experiment. The result of executing that particular path through the function was that the function returned whatever happened to be at the memory location allocated for the result. The effect was therefore implementation dependent since some implementations always initialize storage. The effect was also time dependent since the result obtained was acceptable on some calls and not on others. In the million test cases, this particular fault caused the version containing it to fail only 607 times.

The second non-correlated fault was the use of the wrong expression to index an array. This occurred in several versions. The required expression was usually a single identifier, and the fault usually consisted of using the wrong identifier. A specific example is the following function call:

sam3pts(x[i], y[i], x[j], y[i], x[k], y[k]);

The wrong index expression has been used for the fourth parameter. The correct function call is:

sam3pts(x[i], y[i], x[j], y[j], x[k], y[k]);

This particular fault caused the associated version to fail 1297 times during the one million tests. We find it surprising that major faults such as this can occur in programs that are doing extensive manipulation of arrays yet cause relatively few failures.

The correlated faults were, in general, far more obscure. The first example involves the comparison of angles. In a number of cases, the specifications require that angles be computed and compared. As with all comparisons of real quantities, the limited precision real comparison function was to be used in these cases. The fault was the assumption that comparison of the *cosines* of angles is equivalent to comparison of the angles. With arbitrary precision this is a correct assumption of course but for this application it is not since finite precision floating point arithmetic was used and the precision was limited further for comparison. Of the twenty seven versions written, four made this incorrect assumption. In borderline cases this assumption was false, and this caused the associated versions to disagree with the gold program. The number of failures attributable to this fault varied from 71 to 206 in the various versions although this particular fault caused more than one version to fail on the same test case on only eight occasions.

This fault cannot be attributed to the specifications. Rather it was caused by a fundamental lack of understanding of numerical analysis. The solution lies in a thorough analytic treatment of the arithmetic of the machine involved, and the algorithms used in the computation of the angles and their cosines.

The second correlated fault example involved an assumption about the angle subtended by three points. Recall that the program is required to process simulated two-dimensional radar data. The data is presented as points in a plane expressed in Euclidean coordinates. The specifications for the problem require the determination of whether three data points (simulated radar echos) lie on a straight line. It is possible to determine this by examining the angle subtended by the three points, regarding one of them as the vertex of the angle. If the angle is zero or the angle is 180 degrees, the points lie on a straight line. Figure 1A shows the general case, and Figures 1B and 1C show the two cases where all three points lie on a straight line. The fault made by more than one programmer is the *omission* of the second case.

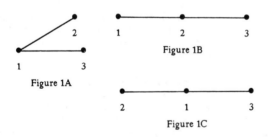

Figure 1A

Figure 1B

Figure 1C

Again, this fault cannot be attributed to the specifications. It was caused by a lack of understanding of geometry. It is not clear how such a fault could be prevented since basically it is attributable to an incomplete case analysis. In fact, although the fundamental fault was the same in more than one version, the effects were different and caused different numbers of failures in the affected versions (StJean, 1985). One version failed 231 times because of this fault and a second only 37 times. However, whenever the second of the two failed, the first did also. The reason for the difference is the interaction between this fault and the overall algorithms used by the different versions.

Further analysis of the faults which occurred is proceeding. However, in summary, it appears that the common faults were of a significantly different type than the individual ones. None of the faults can reasonably be traced back to specification deficiencies but instead appear to be (as hypothesized earlier) more a function of the difficult parts of the problem than random errors made by programmers. That is, the common failure modes appear to arise from features of the application itself and by the fact that it must be run on a finite precision machine rather than by features of the development environment (e.g. programming language, programmer). Although the latter can be varied in separate development environments, the former cannot.

CONCLUSIONS

For the particular problem that was programmed for this experiment, we conclude that the assumption of independence of errors that is fundamental to the analysis of N-version programming *does not hold*. Using a probabilistic model based on independence, our results indicate that the model has to be rejected at the 99% confidence level.

It is important to understand the meaning of this statement. First, it is conditional on the application that we used. The result may or may not extend to other programs, we do not know. Other experiments must be carried out to gather data similar to ours in order to be able to draw general conclusions. However, the result does suggest that the use of N-version programming in safety-critical systems, where failure could endanger human lives for example, should be deferred until further evidence is available. It might be noted that Kelly and Avizienis (1983) in their experiment which involved three-version software got a correct output on only 80% of the test cases.

A second point is that our result does not mean that N-version programming does not work or should never be used. It means that the reliability of an N-version system may not be as high as theory predicts under the assumption of independence. If the implementation issues can be resolved for a particular N-version system, the required reliability might be achieved by using a larger value for N. However, it should be noted that recent work has shown that even a very small probability of coincident errors could require a very large number of versions in order to achieve the types of reliability usually needed for safety-critical systems (Eckhardt and Lee, 1985). For example, using the model developed by Eckhardt and Lee, they state that even given a relatively small probability of dependent errors, it would take seventeen versions from a population whose average failure probability is 2×10^{-4} to produce an N-version system with failure probability less than 10^{-9} rather than the five versions when independence is assumed. Cost will be a consideration here, of course, if it turns out that N must be very large. There is, as yet, no information available on whether it would not be better to produce one version and spend the same amount of resources on other reliability-enhancing procedures such as sophisticated verification and validation procedures (e.g. formal verification) or sophisticated program development environments and techniques.

Based on a preliminary analysis of the faults in the programs, we have found that approximately one half of the total software faults found involved two or more programs. This is surprisingly high and implies that either programmers make a large number of similar faults or, alternatively, that the common faults are more likely to remain after debugging and testing. Several alternative hypotheses are possible and need to be further explored. One is that certain parts of any problem are just more difficult than others and will lead to the same faults by different programmers. Thus the fault distribution is more an artifact of the problem itself than the programmer, and thus is *not* random. Another possible hypothesis is that unique (random) faults tend to be those most likely to be caught by a compiler or by testing. Common faults may reflect inherently difficult semantic aspects of the problem or typical human misconceptions which are not easily detected through standard verification and validation efforts.

A final possibility is that common faults may reflect flaws in the requirements specification document. We do not think this is the case in this experiment since great care went into its preparation and the requirements specification had been debugged through use in an earlier experiment. Furthermore, the particular common faults made in this experiment are quite subtle. In our opinion, none involve ambiguity, inconsistency, or deficiency in the specification.

Given that common faults (as shown by this and other experiments) are possible and perhaps even likely in separately developed multiple versions of a software system, then relying on random chance to get diversity in programs and eliminate design faults may not be effective. However, this does not mean that diversity is not a possible solution to the software fault tolerance problem. What it does imply is that further research on common faults may be useful. Hardware designers do not rely on simple redundancy or independently generated diverse designs to get rid of common design faults. Instead, they use sophisticated techniques to determine common failure modes and systematically alter their designs to attempt to eliminate common failure modes or to minimize their probability. Perhaps we need equivalent techniques for software. Unfortunately, this will not be simple but perhaps a simple solution just does not exist for what is undoubtedly a very difficult problem.

REFERENCES

Anderson, T. and P.A. Lee (1981). *Fault Tolerance: Principles and Practice.* Prentice Hall International, London.

Avizienis, A. and J.P.J. Kelly (1984). Fault tolerance by design diversity: concepts and experiments. *IEEE Computer, 17*, 8.

Bonnett, B. (1984). Software in safety and security critical systems (panel presentation). *COMPCON 84,* Washington D.C. (transcription of the panel session available from Albert W. Friend, ELEX 70343, NAVELEX, Washington, D.C. 20363).

Brilliant, S.S. (1985). Analysis of faults in a multi-version software experiment. M.S. Thesis, University of Virginia, May 1985.

Chen, L. and A. Avizienis (1978). N-version programming: A fault-tolerance approach to reliability of software operation. *Digest of Papers FTCS-8: Eighth Annual International Symposium on Fault Tolerant Computing,* Toulouse, France, pp. 3-9.

Dahll, G. and J. Lahti (1980). An investigation of methods for production and verification of highly reliable software. In L. Lauber (Ed.), *Safety of Computer Control Systems (Proceedings of SAFECOMP '79),* Pergamon Press, London. pp. 89-94.

Eckhardt, D.E. and L.D. Lee (1985) A theoretical basis for the analysis of redundant software subject to coincident errors. NASA Technical Memorandum 86369, NASA Langley Research Center, Hampton, Virginia.

Gmeiner, L. and U. Voges (1980) Software diversity in reactor protection systems: An experiment. *Safety of Computer Control Systems (Proceedings of SAFECOMP '79),* Pergamon Press, London. pp. 75-79.

Kelly, J.P.J. and A. Avizienis (1983) A specification-oriented multi-version software experiment. *Digest of Papers FTCS-13: Thirteenth International Conference on Fault Tolerant Computing.* Milan, Italy, pp. 120-125.

Knight, J.C. and N.G. Leveson (1985). A large scale experiment in n-version programming. *Proceedings of the 15th International Symposium on Fault Tolerant Computing,* Ann Arbor, Michigan.

Martin, D.J. (1983). Dissimilar software in high integrity applications in flight controls. Software for Avionics, AGARD Conference Proceedings, No. 330, pp. 36-1 to 36-9.

Nagel, P.M. and J.A. Skrivan (1982). Software Reliability: Repetitive Run Experimentation and Modeling. prepared for National Aeronautics and Space Administration at Boeing Computer Services Company, Seattle, Washington.

Ramamoorthy, C.V., Y.R. Mok, E.B. Bastani, G.H. Chin, and K. Suzuki (1981). Application of a methodology for the development and validation of reliable process control software. *IEEE Trans. on Software Engineering, SE-7,* 6, 537-555.

St.Jean, L.D. (1985). Testing version independence in multi-version programming. M.S. Thesis, University of Virginia.

J.R. Taylor, J.R. (1981) in Letter from the editor. *ACM Software Engineering Notes, 6,* 1, 1-2.

Voges, U., F. Fetsch, and L. Gmeiner (1982). Use of microprocessors in a safety-oriented reactor shut-down system, In E. Lauber and J. Moltoft (Eds.) *Reliability in Electrical and Electronic Components and Systems,* North-Holland. pp. 493-497.

Wakerly, J.F. (1976). Microcomputer reliability improvement using triple-modular redundancy. *Proceedings of the IEEE, 64,* 6, 889-895.

SOFTWARE FAULT-TOLERANCE AND DESIGN DIVERSITY: PAST EXPERIENCE AND FUTURE EVOLUTION

L. Strigini* and A. Avižienis**

*Istituto di Elaborazione della Informazione, CNR, Pisa, Italy
**Computer Science Department, University of California, Los Angeles, California,
USA

Abstract. Interest in software fault-tolerance (following an interest in fault-tolerance in general, and prompted by the so-called "software crisis") is now exhibited by many institutions.
Though many software fault-tolerance techniques are known, their use is limited by the lack of consistent, flexible methodologies, of support mechanisms in operating systems and of design tools.
In this paper, we discuss the known software fault-tolerance techniques, with particular reference to the two coherent methodologies proposed, Multiple Version Software and Recovery Blocks. We argument that a more general methodology is needed for use in complex software system, and outline how the necessary mechanisms could be included in low-level system software.

Keywords. Computer applications; computer software; fault tolerance; system failure and recovery.

1. INTRODUCTION.

Concurrently with the increasing interest in the reliability of computer systems, a growing concern can be observed about the software component of this problem. This is due to the awareness that present state of the art software is much less dependable than hardware, and that this gap keeps growing along with the size and complexity of systems. The huge costs paid in the effort of making large software systems reliable is one of the components of the so-called "software crisis". A complete research area, namely Software Engineering, has been created by the problem of software reliability.

Up to now, software reliability has been pursued mostly through fault avoidance, i.e. by attempting to ensure that programs are error-free, through the usage of refined techniques for design, validation and test of programs. But it is usually acknowledged that increasing expenses in such techniques beyond some threshold yields decreasing improvements in reliability.

This fact produces a growing interest in software fault-tolerance (SWFT), i.e. design methodologies that: assume some error will appear in the behavior of programs during execution; build into the software enough redundancy (checks and correction procedures, that would be useless if the software always behaved correctly) for it to be able to detect and possibly correct such errors.

The advantages expected from the application of SWFT techniques are: a) higher reliability, for given cost; b) lower cost of testing and debugging (through on-line error detection); c) faster "dentition" of a system, with earlier deployment of a

sufficiently reliable release; d) possibly, higher absolute reliability, regardless of cost (if the aforementioned decreasing returns from expense in fault avoidance imply some asymptotic maximum reliability for any given non-redundant software system); this may be relevant in those applications where the cost of a failure largely outweights the cost of the computer system.

In this paper, we give a brief review of SWFT techniques, attempting to discuss them in a unitary way, and propose a combined integrated usage of these techniques, suitable for a large class of applications, and in particular for process control.

In Section 2, some basic principles of SWFT are discussed; in Section 3, the two most important SWFT methods, namely Multiple Version Software and Recovery Blocks, are recalled and compared; in Section 4, combinations of various techniques are discussed, and in Section 5 a set of mechanisms is proposed supporting such a combination.

2. SWFT AND DESIGN DIVERSITY.

It is our opinion that error correction and detection are always based on some form of design independence or diversity. As previously stated, FT consists in adding redundant components to compensate for errors by basic components (those components that, if always correct, would be sufficient to perform the function required of the system).

In this discussion, we will use the following definitions (Avizienis and Kelly, 1984): a failure is a loss of service perceived at the boundary of the resource; an error is an undesired resource state that exists either at the boundary or at an internal point in the resource; a fault is the identified or hypothesized cause of the error or failure.

Now, it is apparent that for FT to work properly, the means used to detect that a result is erroneous, or to correct it, must not be disabled by the fault that caused the error.

In other words, once a system has been designed such that only a combination of errors by several subsystems can make it produce an error (redundancy), the designer strives to obtain a very low probability for such combinations of errors. The way of obtaining this is to make the several "subfaults" independent of each other, so that their joint probability, given by a product of small numbers, is far smaller than any of their single probabilities. In the case of hardware faults, this usually implies physical separation between the basic and the redundant subsystems. In the case of software faults, i.e. design errors (errors in the design process), this implies separation between the design processes of the two subsystems.

We have thus stated an evaluation criterion for a SWFT methodology: the degree of independence, or diversity, that it allows among the redundant software parts (for the application problem under study). Other evaluation criteria are the drawbacks in development (possibility of adding design faults, increase in development costs; both influenced by ease of use, documentation and management overhead, etc.), the hardware and run-time costs (required redundancy in storage and/or processing power, increased response times), and the effectiveness against hardware faults.

To assess the effectiveness of methodologies for software reliability, it would be desirable to obtain mathematical evaluations of the latter. This is not possible nowadays. Software reliability modelling has proven useful so far in forecasting reliability growth within a single project. But we need to compare the effects on reliability produced by the use of different techniques in large and/or very high reliability systems. We cannot collect statistics on experiments, since large projects are not reproducible in a controlled environment; and very high reliability implies that many years would be required to collect good error statistics. Hence, we need convincing models to describe systems both large and small, and both reliable and unreliable, allowing us to extrapolate experimental results to non-experimentable situations. Such a model is not currently available.

So, the discussion of methodologies for software reliability is necessarily based primarily on anecdotal experience and common sense; some unsupported assumption about the psychology of programming underlies most discussions on these topics, including our own.

3. COMPARISON OF SWFT TECHNIQUES.

Several SWFT methods are now in use or have been proposed. We mention executable assertions, exception handling, Recovery Blocks (RBs), Multiple Version Software (MVS), robust data structures and audit programs. Among these, only MVS and RBs are complete, widely applicable methodologies: our discussion will therefore be centered on them.

Recovery Blocks (Randell, 1975; Anderson and Lee, 1981) combine detection by executable assertions with recovery by backward recovery and retry. A RB is a program block, augmented with a final acceptance test and error treatment action, and zero or more retry program sequences (alternates). Failure of the acceptance test causes the execution state to be rolledback to the beginning of the block and the next available alternate, if any, to be executed. Only if all the alternates fail the system gives up and invokes the error treatment action.

In Multiple Version Software (Avizienis and Chen, 1977; Avizienis and Kelly, 1984), errors are detected by comparing independently computed results and masked by voting on these results; a correct system status is [forward] recovered by feeding back corrected results to the erring programs. MVS is a form of design diversity. This is an extension of the n-modular redundancy technique, (use of several identical systems, voting on their results to mask errors), in which the redundant modules are designed independently of each other, to avoid common design errors. For software, it consists in first generating several different versions of a program (i.e. program modules satisfying the same specifications, and produced independently, by using different programming teams, algorithms, programming languages and compilers), and then running them together: at pre-specified points in the flow of control (usually called cross-check points) the results are compared and combined (by bit-by-bit voting, or more refined algorithms (Avizienis et al., 1985)), to detect errors and to obtain correct data to be output and possibly fed back to the executing versions. Cross-check points are usually implanted at least at outputs from the computing system to the external world (unless voting peripherals are used), and at inter-process communications.

Let us compare the MVS and RBs concepts, as described above, according to the criteria listed in Section 2.

From the point of view of error-detection, RBs present the problem of obtaining acceptance tests with high error coverage, but sufficiently simple to be reliable and cheap. Cases where this is possible are discussed by Hecht (1979). But this is not always the case (for experimental data about the coverage provided by such tests, see for example Anderson (1984), Glass (1980)). Where the acceptance test would be as complicated as the original algorithm, it makes sense to substitute it with a recomputation of the result by an alternate (which can the be performed in parallel, saving time (Kim, 1984)), followed by a simple, comparatively cheap comparison. Sometimes, this will be mandatory, as the assertions to be verified cannot be formulated otherwise than by restating the procedural specification of the problem. We are thus led to employ MVS.

But the concept of diverse computations and comparison has its drawbacks too. Kelly and Avizienis (1983) give some encouraging experimental results for one particular problem (consistently correct outputs from a combination of 3 faulty versions, for example); but is that a typical problem? Independence among different versions may not be easily attainable: there may be problems for which only one algorithm is known, or efficient enough; programmers are likely to have similar backgrounds.
In general, it seems that acceptance tests different from recomputing the result are free from errors arising from algorithmic peculiarities of the solution. On the other hand, they are often just reasonableness checks (detecting only a subset of blatantly incorrect results), while comparison of multiple results supposedly discriminates the correct result from all the incorrect results. Another advantage of comparison is that it can be performed by a module on the result of another (multiple) module, without any knowledge of the internal behavior of that module: e.g., a peripheral driver can check consistency among output requests from multiple versions, no matter what they compute and how.

The coverage provided by error-detection mechanisms directly influences safeness of outputs, latency of faults, recovery. Avoiding unsafe outputs means simply exercising the error detection mechanisms on each single output. An advantage of MVS is that it allows the final validation of results to be closer to the external boundary of the computer system (and possibly in the external world, if voting actuators are used), decreasing the number of nonredundant operations and components that can influence the output. Fault latency is determined by the coverage of fault detection mechanisms together with the frequency of their use. Successful recovery of a correct internal state is important to ensure prolonged fault tolerant operation, since carrying on computation on a corrupted state, even if not directly affecting safety, would allow subsequent errors to accumulate up to the point where the error detection mechanisms can no longer detect them. In both MVS and RBs recovery is possible only for those errors that are detected. Once an error is detected, its correction is automatic in MVS, but will affect only the data items that were found to be erroneous: so the specification must require that all the relevant status information be subjected to comparison. In RBs, a detected error will cause a roll-back, thus eliminating all the errors produced during execution of the current RB; the alternates must not then reproduce (the same or other) errors: effective diversity among the alternates is as important as independence between each alternate and the acceptance test.

The development costs of the two SWFT approaches are produced by the requirement of several versions of the same code. For RBs, it is sometimes assumed that older releases of programs can be used as alternates for a newer, more efficient and presumably less reliable release. Actually, the number of these "free" alternates available grows during the life cycle of the system: it may be that at the first release of the system, when redundancy is most needed, no alternate is available.
MVS is usually described based on at least 3 versions (guaranteeing single-fault masking); actually, variable redundancy in a MVS environment is possible (Farber, 1981; Deswarte et al., 1984), with more redundancy for more critical tasks, as it is in an RB-based system.
So, both approaches require substantial, and comparable, extra programming effort. On the other hand, the use of SWFT should reduce the cost of debugging and testing, as already mentioned. A notable advantage of MVS is its effectiveness in exposing specification ambiguities, that may otherwise go undetected until the wrong software package is successfully released (Kelly and Avizienis, 1983; Gmeiner and Voges, 1979).

Examples of hardware and run-time costs are: watchdog timers, to cope with errors (say, infinite loops), that would cause a program never to call the error detection mechanisms, and protection mechanisms (to avoid that errors in a software module can corrupt the state of other modules in unanticipated ways). Of course, such mechanisms are often required independently from the usage of SWFT, and cannot then be regarded as additional costs.

A problem in applying software redundancy is at which level of modular decomposition it should be applied, i.e. how large a recovery block, or the piece of code between two successive comparisons, should be. Both small and large modules have pros and cons. For example, small modules imply: a) frequent invocations of the error detection mechanisms, resulting in low error latency (but high overhead); b) less computation must be redone in case of roll-back, or less data must be corrected by a vote (but more temporary data need to be saved in checkpoints or voted upon); c) the specifications common to the diverse implementations must be similar to a higher level of detail (instead of specifying just what a large module should do, and which variables must compose the state of the computation outside that module, one needs to specify how the large module is decomposed in smaller modules, what each one does, and how it shall present its results to the acceptance test or comparison): this decreases the independence among the several programming efforts, and supposedly increases the probability of correlated errors.

4. COMPOSITE SCHEMES.

Summarizing, our discussion has shown that the two approaches share a number of basic problems, inherent in the concept of SWFT itself. Their discussion is usually influenced by the consideration of the different environments they have been devised for. The natural environment for the application of MVS is in systems with n-modular hardware redundancy, like SIFT (Wensley et al., 1978), that are able to tolerate hardware faults: by running a different software version on each processor, programming errors can be tolerated as well. The natural environment for recovery blocks seems to be where a cheaper form of SWFT is needed, as time is available for backward error recovery and temporarily unsafe outputs can be tolerated.

Actually, these two methods are but two of the many possible combinations of decisions about the components of fault tolerant software: a list of alternatives, with their relative advantages, might be:

a) error detection (acceptance test vs. comparison): the former can be a more independent test, the latter is usually a more complete test;

b) distribution of executions (parallel vs. sequential): the former is more effective against hardware faults, and makes the redundant system almost as fast as a non-redundant one, thus satisfying stricter real-time requirements; it requires more processors (see c));

c) execution of alternates (unconditional vs. on demand): the former (mandatory in case of parallelism) makes execution time independent from the occurrence of faults; it also requires more processor throughput in absence of faults.

d) error correction (voting vs. rollback): the former is usually faster; it implies unconditional execution of alternates.

We shall now examine other possible combinations. Let us first consider only items a) and d) above.

The combination "comparison + rollback" seems unappealing, as comparison implies that correct results are already available (unless more than one simultaneous errors are expected), making rollback useless. "Assertions + masking", by the same token, would neglect using for detection the alternative results available for masking. But it might be useful, for example, where multiple correct solutions were possible for the same problem: requiring that all versions produce the same result would limit the degree of diversity obtainable; on the other hand, a reasonableness check could be sufficient to detect errors, while real-time considerations might require parallel computation of the diverse results (such an approach is called MVS by Scott et al. (1984) and is called a variation of RBs by Kim (1984)).

We have thus defined a first class of hybrid SWFT schemes, by varying the combination between error detection and correction mechanisms. Another form of hybridization is possible in the detection mechanisms themselves. Let us consider the last example: the reasonableness test included in each version can be based on some kind of consistency with the results of the other versions. Such "consistency checks" exist in the DeDiX system's (Avizienis et al., 1985) "decision function": it is there possible to consider

"consistent" two numerical results that differ by less than an assigned maximum error, or two character strings with some difference in spelling. But more application-specific consistency checks are possible: we could allow two versions updating a data base to produce different sets of update requests, provided the global effects of the two transactions are the same.

Hybrid forms of recovery are possible as well. Consider an application program that maintains a comparatively large computation state (say, a data base), and suppose it is implemented in MVS. Comparing the whole contents of the data bases to guarantee their correctness would be exceedingly expensive. We could then choose to compare only some part of the data (e.g. the last modified items and the responses to queries) or some compressed form thereof (e.g. item counts, lists of initials): a disagreement would not delay the response, but would prompt a more complete verification (e.g., a vote on the complete state, or queries of the majority versions by the minority version).

5. DISCUSSION.

The SWFT techniques known are seldom used systematically; in our opinion, this is mainly due to the lack, in the production environment, of a well-developed, coherent methodology and of proper support mechanisms (i.e., language constructs and corresponding operating system primitives). Without such methodology and standard mechanisms, adding redundancy to application software can lead to unmanageable complexity, as normal and exceptional behaviors are managed together at the same level of visibility in the source programs. Such methodologies and mechanisms cannot be economically developed as part of a single application project: they must be a standard tool available to the development team, and sufficiently general for the needs of many different applications.
MVS and RBs are two proposals for such general methodologies and support mechanisms; but in our view neither is general enough, and we have shown cases in which either is inadequate. So, we think it may be necessary to apply different SWFT methods to different parts of the same application problem. This need arises from two considerations: first, the need to apply safety mechanisms wherever the application allows them to be placed economically (e.g., using cheap and effective acceptance tests even in an MVS system); second, the current trend toward the connection of all the computer based components of control systems into one integrated hardware-software system implies that such a system will include parts with different reliability requirements, and algorithms that cannot all accommodate the application of the same SWFT technique.

A relevant problem is how much of the FT characteristics of a system can be provided by the usage of application-independent mechanisms (that can be included in a kernel or executive and used, in a largely transparent way, by all application software), and how much must depend on the knowledge of the application problem (and therefore be coded into each application program). An important consideration here is that the use of transparent mechanisms, while often useful, must not be rigidly imposed on the application designers: the latter may then be compelled to dispense with them altogether, to avoid their cost.

Due to the nature of process control software, our proposal refers to a process-based environment (Farber, 1981; Banino and Fabre, 1982): the system appears as a set of processes communicating via messages; passive resources can be incapsulated in processes.

Such an environment naturally supports MVS at the task level. This capability we consider to be necessary, due to its easy integration with hardware modular redundancy, real-time fault masking capability and expected high coverage.

RBs can be implemented within each process; if it is intended to allow backward recovery in communicating processes, some automated method for avoiding domino effect (Russell, 1980) must be used: this can be based on compiler-enforced structuring of RBs with respect to interprocess communications and/or on system calls that automatically exchange supplementary information and establish recovery points (Barigazzi and Strigini, 1983; Ciuffoletti, 1984; Kim, 1982; Russell, 1980).

Production of hybrid FT SW would be facilitated by such tools as:

a language that includes executable assertions, and structured hierarchical exception handling;

a set of efficient low-level (operating system kernel and hardware) mechanisms: multi-cast message sending, multiplexed message receiving (to obtain multiple results for comparison) with time-outs (see e.g. Leitner (1984)), process state checkpointing and rollback, possibly comparison and voting procedures (these are simple but costly procedures (Palumbo and Butler, 1983), that may benefit from the use of dedicated hardware; however, the users should be allowed to use their own "custom" voting procedures, i.e to specify their own consistency criteria);

a set of more complex mechanisms (library procedures and system calls); and corresponding language constructs, built upon the preceding ones: recovery blocks, cross-check points, remote and replicated procedure calls (Cooper, 1984),

system configuration tools, allowing the designer to describe manage the redundancy added to the application software (multiple versions or alternates) independently from its basic functional structure: so that redundancy can be varied according to the requirements of each installation and to the varying degree of confidence in each software part.

Within this framework, the addition of redundancy could be organized as follows:

at the task level, a variable-redundancy MVS organization can be realized;

within each task or version, structured exception handling can be provided, including roll-back and retry, i.e.

recovery blocks (the last-resort handler being the output of an exceptional "ignore me" result, that the voting procedures must be able to recognize);

wherever application-specific FT is possible, it can be applied by directly employing part of the low-level mechanisms instead of more complex, costlier mechanisms (suppose for example that a partial differential equation is to be solved over a multi-dimensional grid, by a relaxation method; some function of the grid values is to be fed to a critical output; so, three versions of a task manage a triple grid, voting on their outputs. Multiple demon processes repetitively access one of the tables and solve a step of the relaxation algorithm for one point. If the algorithm used naturally converges despite any single data errors, there is no need to correct the contents of the table by voting. So, MVS can be used with very low overhead, thanks to the properties of the application);

FT utilities can be built for use by the general applications: e.g., file systems can be implemented supporting an "atomic transaction" model (Lampson, 1981; Randell, 1983; Ciompi et al., 1983).

Let us give an example. Consider an application comprising a real-time process, plus a large data base. For reasons of safety and real-time, the process control part must run on triplicated hardware, and is therefore implemented in MVS. Output devices are either voting devices or single devices driven by a software voter. The data base must be duplicated to guarantee data integrity against hardware faults: the two copies are managed by two versions of a task, that are individually protected against local disk failures via robust data structures in the disk files, with periodical auditing (a non-replicated, asynchronous audit process can be used), and against software faults via RB-structuring of update procedures; finally, a combined data base recovery capability is provided, as outlined at the end of Section 4.

6. CONCLUSIONS

SWFT is an important component of computer systems reliability. Though SWFT is used in practice, its full exploitation is hindered by the lack of comprehensive, flexible methodologies that can be embedded in system SW and development tools.

We have discussed the existing techniques, and proposed that they should be combined together to obtain cost effective FT. We have also proposed a general, flexible tool set for building fault-tolerant software: we advocate a conscious approach to the problem, where all the tools are orderly made available before the starting of the work.

Many projects are now in progress for the design of LAN-based distributed systems for process control, usually featuring a process-based operating system. Our proposal fits well in this kind of designs, and takes into account the trend towards wider extension and integration of such systems.

It consists mainly in a slight expansion of the basic primitives of distributed operating system, so as to allow the efficient and flexible implementation of typical SWFT mechanisms.

Our intention has been to discuss a realistic general approach to FT SW design, based on its fundamental principles. Our proposal is therefore a statement of design principles, rather than a design, and an invitation to further discussion and experimentation.

ACKNOWLEDGMENTS

The ideas exposed here are partly based on the experience of the DeDiX project at UCLA, and discussions with all the participants in that experiment were most important for their development.

REFERENCES

Anderson, T. and P.A. Lee (1981). Fault Tolerance: Principles and Practice. Prentice Hall Int., Englewood Cliffs.

Anderson, T. (1984). Can Design Faults be Tolerated?. Fault Tolerant Computing Systems 2nd GI/GMR Conf. Bonn, pp. 426-433.

Avizienis, A. and L. Chen (1977). On the implementation of N-version programming for Software Fault-Tolerance During Execution. Proc. COMPSAC 77, (First IEEE-CS Intern.l Computer Software and Application Conf.), pp. 149-155.

Avizienis, A. and J. P. J. Kelly (1984). Fault-Tolerance by Design Diversity: Concepts and Experiments. Computer, 17, 67-80.

Avizienis, A., P. Gunningberg, J.P.J. Kelly, L. Strigini, P.J. Traverse, K.S. Tso (1985). Software Fault-Tolerance by Design Diversity. DeDiX: A Tool for Experiments. Proc. IFAC Workshop SAFECOMP '85, Como, Italy.

Banino, J.S., J.C. Fabre (1982). Distributed coupled actors: a CHORUS proposal for reliability. Proc. 3rd IEEE Internl. Conf. on Distributed Computing Systems, Miami, Florida.

Barigazzi, G., L. Strigini (1983). Application-transparent setting of Recovery Points. 13th Annual Intern.l Symp. Fault-Tolerant Computing, Milano, Italy.

Ciompi, P., L. Simoncini, M. La Manna, C. Lissoni and I.R. Martin (1983). A highly available multimicroprocessor system for real-time applications. Proc. IFAC Workshop SAFECOMP '83, Cambridge, UK, pp.247-253.

Ciuffoletti, 4A. (1984). Error Recovery in Systems of Communicating Processes. Proc. 7th Intern.l Conf. on Software Engineering, Orlando, Florida, pp. 6-17.

Cooper, E.C. (1984). Circus: A Replicated Procedure Call Facility. Proc. 4th Symp. on Reliability in Distributed Software and Database Systems, Silver Spring, Maryland, pp. 11-24.

Cristian, F. (1982). Exception Handling and Software Fault-Tolerance. IEEE Trans. on Computers, C-31, 531-539.

Deswarte, Y., J.C. Fabre, J.C.Laprie, D. Powell (1984). The SATURNE Project, A Fault-Tolerant and Intrusion-Tolerant Distributed System. LAAS Technical Report, Toulouse.

Farber, G. (1981). Task-Specific Implementation of Fault Tolerance in Process Automation System. Proc. Workshop on Self-diagnosis and Fault-Tolerance, Tubingen, pp.84-102.

Glass, R.L. (1980). A Benefit Analysis of Some Software Reliability Methodologies. ACM SIGSOFT Software Engineering Notes, 5, 26-33.

Gmeiner, L. and U. Voges (1979). Software Diversity in Reactor Protection Systems: An Experiment. IFAC Workshop SAFECOMP '79, Stuttgart, Federal Republic of Germany, May 1979, pp. 73-79.

Hecht, H. (1979). Fault-Tolerant Software. IEEE Trans. on Reliability, R-28, 227-232.

Kelly, J.P.J. and A. Avizienis (1983). A Specification Oriented Multi-Version Software Experiment. Proc. 13th Intern.l Symp. on Fault-Tolerant Computing, Milano, Italy, pp. 121-126.

Kim, K.H. (1982). Approaches to Mechanization of the Conversation Scheme Based on Monitors. IEEE Trans. on Software Engineering, SE-8, 189-197.

Kim, K.H.. (1984). Distributed Execution of Recovery Blocks: an Approach to uniform treatment of Hardware and software faults. Proc. 4th Intern.l Conf. on Distributed Computing Systems, May 1984, pp. 526-532.

Lampson, B. (1981). Atomic Transactions. In Distributed Systems, an Advanced Course. Lecture Notes in Computer Science, Springer Verlag.

Leitner, G. (1984). Stylized Interprocess Communication - A Kernel Primitive for Reliable Distributed Computing. Proc. 4th Symp. on Reliability in Distributed Software and Database Systems, Silver Spring, Maryland, pp. 25-33.

Palumbo, D.L. and R.W. Butler (1983). SIFT - A Preliminary Evaluation. Proc. IEEE/AIAA 5th Digital Avionics Conf., Seattle, Washington, pp. 21.4.1-21.4.6.

Randell, B. (1975). System Structure for Software Fault-Tolerance. IEEE Trans. Software Engineering, SE-1, 220-232.

Randell, B., (1983). Fault Tolerance and System Structuring. University of Newcastle upon Tyne Technical Report Series #183.

Russell, D.L. (1980). State Restoration in Systems of Communicating Processes. IEEE Trans. on Software Engineering, SE-6, 183-194.

Scott, R.K., J.W. Gault, D.F. McAllister, and J. Wiggs (1984). Experimental Validation of Six Fault-Tolerant Software Reliability Models. Proc. 14th IEEE Intern.l Symp. on Fault-Tolerant Computing, Orlando, Florida, pp. 102-107.

Wensley, J.H., L. Lamport, J. Goldberg, M.W. Green, K.N. Levitt, P.M. Melliar-Smith, R.E. Shostak and C.B. Weinstock (1978). SIFT: Design and Analysis of a Fault-Tolerant Computer for Aircraft Control. IEEE Proc., 66, 1240-1255.

SOFTWARE FAULT-TOLERANCE BY DESIGN DIVERSITY DEDIX: A TOOL FOR EXPERIMENTS

A. Avižienis, P. Gunningberg[1], J. P. J. Kelly, R. T. Lyu,
L. Strigini[2], P. J. Traverse[3], K. S. Tso, U. Voges[4]

*UCLA Computer Science Department, University of California, Los Angeles,
CA 90024, USA*

Abstract. A large number of computing systems require very high levels of reliability, availability, or safety. A fault-avoidance approach is not practical in many cases, and is costly and difficult for software, if not impossible. One way of reducing the effects of an error introduced during the design of a program is to use multiple versions of the program, independently designed from a common specification. If these versions are designed by independent programming teams, it is to be expected that a fault in one version will not have the same behavior as any fault in the other versions. Since the errors in the output of the versions will be different and uncorrelated, it is possible to run the versions concurrently, cross-check their results at prespecified points, and mask errors. A DEsign DIversity eXperiments (DEDIX) testbed has been implemented at UCLA to study the influence of common mode errors which can result in a failure of the entire system. The layered design of DEDIX and its decision algorithm are described. The usage of the system and its application in an ongoing experiment are explained.

Key words. Computer Architecture, Reliability Theory, Distributed Parameters Systems, Coding Errors, Fault Tolerance.

INTRODUCTION

A large number of contemporary computing systems intended for process control applications have stringent reliability and availability requirements. This means that they must deliver the output in a timely manner with a high probability of being correct. Such process control computers with high *dependability* goals can be found, for example, in the nuclear and aerospace industries. A simple and efficient way of reaching this dependability goal is to use an *error masking* approach. An error can be masked if the system is provided with enough redundancy: typically, the execution of multiple (N-fold) computations, each computation having the same objective [Avižienis1984]. The output of each computation then is voted on by a more or less sophisticated decision algorithm. The result is either a single output or one output for each computation channel which is within a specified, acceptable tolerance.

In order to allow dependable voting on the output, only a minority of the computation channels may produce an error at a given decision point. This condition is one of the basic assumptions needed for successful voting. Furthermore, if
- the inputs to each computation channel are consistent,
- the outputs are voted upon (in a more or less sophisticated decision function), and
- the probability of having *related errors* is sufficiently low,

then, the output of the system is sufficiently dependable.

These assumptions are usually satisfied. The most troublesome deals with related errors. This assumption is very important, because, if one error appears simultaneously in a majority of channels, any decision function will produce an incorrect result. Therefore, this probability of common mode error has to be kept low.

As long as certain design criteria are obeyed, these related errors are not likely to appear if they are due to internal physical faults (rupture of connection,e. g.), as these faults are likely to have an effect only on one of the channels at a time. External faults are more likely to produce related errors. Ways of dealing with these errors are to have the channels loosely coupled, and to use different technologies for the channels. Then, an external fault will not strike the channels when they are in the same state, and they will not react in the same way. They are thus *distinguishable*.

Another source of related errors are design errors. Indeed, the N copies of faulty software will all be in error at the same time when provided with identical input data. A way to avoid these related errors is to have different versions of the software (and of the entire channels) instead of using simple copies. Thus a key attribute for high dependability systems appears to be *diversity*: diversity in the timing, technology, and design (hardware and software) of the different channels.

Let us define a *cross-check point* (cc-point): to be the voting point at which the different versions exchange their results (cc-vector) for voting. The basic assumption, that only a minority is in error, can then also be expressed as: between two successive cc-points only a minority of the redundant channels are likely to fail, either by producing erroneous output or by failing to deliver their result in time. Errors in the computation will have an effect on

[1] *On leave from Uppsala University, Sweden*
[2] *On leave from IEI-CNR, Pisa, Italy*
[3] *On leave from LAAS, Toulouse, France*
[4] *On leave from KFK, Karlsruhe, F.R. Germany*

this cc-vector and are therefore detectable. The decision algorithm will compare the cc-vectors and will output its result in form of a decision vector.

At UCLA an ongoing research effort was started to investigate design diversity, the problems that can arise, and to estimate the efficiency in dependability improvement by the use of design diversity. The main target is the software, and first results included the definition of the concept of *N-Version Programming*[Chen1978], and some first generation experiments [Kelly1982].

In order to make measurements in a multi version software experiment, a testbed was needed. A basic requirement was to simulate the environments in which design diversity should be used. The Design Diversity Experiments testbed (DEDIX) has thus two aspects: a fault-tolerant computing system, and an experimentation tool. We will develop these two aspects in this paper. The main layout of the DEDIX system will be given and the decision algorithm implemented in DEDIX will be explained more closely. Finally, the use of DEDIX in current experiments will be described. A more complete description of DEDIX can be found in [Avižienis1985].

DEDIX AS A FAULT-TOLERANT COMPUTING SYSTEM

As stated earlier, design diversity will often be used in an environment with high redundancy. Therefore, the testbed has to be a modular, redundant system to allow different experiments. the basic requirements for DEDIX are the following:

> 1. The different versions of the software shall be able to run on different hardware in order to test the influence of errors in the hardware associated with any one version. Version support software, therefore, has to be distributed.
> 2. DEDIX must run on the distributed Locus environment at UCLA [Walker1983], consisting of a network of about 20 VAX 11/750s, and should be portable to other Unix systems.
> 3. A decision algorithm has to be part of the system, which provides different kinds of decision functions for the user like bit-by-bit comparison for identity, and comparison within a specified tolerance.
> 4. The interface for the version programmer has to be simple, and the interface must be independent of the number of actual versions used.

In order to fulfil these requirements, DEDIX was developed as a modular redundant system. Depending on the number of versions and the number of available machines, DEDIX selects appropriate hardware.

DEDIX itself is written in C and makes use of several Locus features, e. g. for setting up the different processes and for linking the processes via pipes. Nevertheless, it should be possible to port DEDIX to a pure Unix system which provides mechanisms for communication between several CPUs.

We use the facilities offered by the UCLA Center for Experimental Computer Science. The machines are linked by an Ethernet local network. We use the Unix software development environment and its inter-process communication features (pipes). Locus allows processes to communicate with each other in the same way whether they are running on the same machine or on different machines. It is thus easy to allocate each computation channel to a different machine.

The decision algorithm implemented will be described in more detail later, as well as the user interface. Both parts are designed to fulfil the above mentioned requirements.

A global view of the DEDIX system supporting N versions is given in Fig. 1. The versions communicate with the different parts of DEDIX, which in turn makes use of the Locus operating system, and the different sites are interconnected with each other via Ethernet.

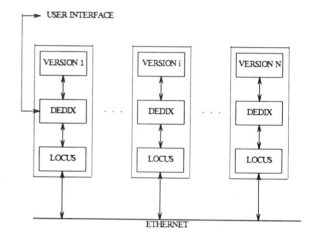

Fig. 1. The N sites of DEDIX

DEDIX: A LAYERED APPROACH

DEDIX is designed as a set of hierarchically structured layers. Each of the sites which are selected for running DEDIX has an identical set of layers and entities, providing services to its version and the external user. These layers, from top to bottom, are:
- the Version Layer,
- the Decision and Executive Layer,
- the Synchronization Layer,
- the Transport Layer.

These layers are implemented as functions, and inside a site, they share some data structures (see Fig. 2).

The Version Layer

This layer contains the application program version. The purpose of this layer is to interface the version with the DEDIX system. The interface function is called the cross-check, or *cc-function* since it is called by the version at each cc-point. Pointers to the results to be corrected are sent as parameters to this function. The cc-function transfers the version representation of results into a cc-vector so that the DEDIX internal representation of a cc-vector is hidden for the version program. If the decision algorithm detects an error in the results of the version, the cc-function writes back the corrected results into the version, therefore masking errors.

To run on DEDIX a version must be instrumented. That is, the version must call DEDIX at each occurrence of a

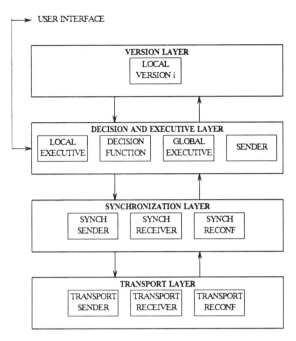

Fig. 2. The layers on one site of DEDIX.

cc-point, and pass its results to generate the corresponding cc-vectors. We will show how this is done in a subsequent section. Currently, the available application languages are C and Pascal. Other languages could be used for the versions, if the interface between this language and C is provided.

The Decision and Executive Layer

This layer receives cc-vectors from the versions, decides on the correct result, determines whether a version is faulty or not, and makes recovery decisions. A corrected cc-vector is forwarded to the version. All exceptions that cannot be handled at lower levels are directed to this layer.

The layer has four entities, a *sender*, a *local executive*, a *decision function*, and a *global executive*. The local executive entity receives requests from the version and responds to the version when a decision has been taken. There are four different types of normal requests: intermediate cc-vector (on a subset of the internal state of the channels), output cc-vector, input, and version termination. All of them are broadcast to the other sites, and run through the decision function to ensure consistency and synchronization. When the version has raised an exception from which it cannot recover, this exception is forwarded to the local executive.

The global executive is activated when the decision function indicates that the result is not unanimous, or when some unrecoverable exception is signaled from the version or some other layer. Such an exception could be disruption of a communication connection. This global executive provides fault diagnosis, reconfiguration, and fault reporting for maintenance purposes. Basically, it has the same functions as the global executive found in SIFT [Melliar-Smith1982].

To ensure that a consistent reconfiguration decision is taken, the global executive at each site must first get a consistent error report. All global executives propose a new configuration that is broadcast to every site and decided upon. The proposed configurations are voted on bit-by-bit which will ensure a consistent view on a new configuration at every correctly working site.

The Synchronization Layer

For each physically distinct site, this layer broadcasts the result from the above executive layer and collects messages with the results ("cc-vector") from all other sites. This layer only accepts messages that are both broadcast within a certain time interval and that will arrive within the same time interval. The collected messages are delivered to the decision function. A new set of results is accepted when every site has confirmed that the messages have been delivered. This layer can establish communication connections between sites.

A protocol was designed to provide the above service. Synchronization of the system is based on the following assumptions:

- correctly working versions produce exactly the same number of cc-vectors,
- correctly working versions have similar execution times, i.e. they will produce results within a specified time-out interval,
- a majority of "missing" messages does not exist at a majority of sites,
- a majority of messages are not delayed more than the specified time-out interval.

Each site has both a sender and a receiver entity in this layer, which communicate with corresponding entities of other sites according to the protocol. The receiver entity collects messages from the senders and it delivers them to the decision function. After the delivery, it sends acknowledgments back to the senders to confirm the delivery. When a sender entity has collected acknowledgements from all the other sites or when it has at least a majority of acknowledgments, it will indicate this to its decision and executive layer. This indication is used by the layer above to restart the version. By using this indication, it is possible to ensure that all sites will start the new set of computations within the specified time interval.

The senders and receivers are designed as communicating extended finite state machines. They respond to events such as commands from the local executive, messages or acknowledgments, and internal time-outs. State variables, i.e. frame sequence numbers, forming predicates on the state transitions are used to discriminate messages and acknowledgments delayed too long in the communication system. The specification and verification of the protocol is described in [Gunningberg1985].

The Transport Layer

This layer controls the communication of messages (containing the results) between the sites. Messages are broadcast to all active sites. The layer makes sure that no message is lost, duplicated, damaged, or misaddressed, and it preserves the ordering of sent messages. A disconnection is reported to the layer above.

Currently, this layer is implemented as a simple loop of

point to point links by UNIX interprocessor pipes. Since this implementation does not allow a site crash, a redundant interconnection structure is under implementation. We are also investigating the use of network-oriented inter-process communication protocol to achieve more transportation efficiency [Cooper1984].

THE DECISION FUNCTION OF DEDIX

The decision function has to recognize whether the versions are in agreement with each other or not. The decision function is used for each cc-point, and each of these decisions is independent of the preceding ones, and based only on the set of cc-vectors that is transmitted by the synchronization layer. An agreement is achieved if at least a majority of versions is considered to be equivalent by the decision algorithm, and this value is used as an output. This value is also communicated to the versions in error, so they can use it for their subsequent computation.

An agreement among cc-vectors means basically that these cc-vectors contain the same information, at the level of abstraction of the user of the versions. This means that the versions (that have been designed by different programmer teams, in different languages, that may run on different machines, ...) may have different ways of representing information. The decision function has thus to extract the meaning of the cc-vectors. A "bit-by-bit" vote can be used for much of the cc-vector since there is only one possible representation of the data. Nevertheless previous experiments have shown that bit-by-bit voting can be too selective and reject semantically equivalent results [Kelly1982].

Therefore, the cc-vectors is subdivided into parts, and a separate decision is possible for each part. The global decision vector is composed of the union of the values of each part. The parts can be classified in the following way:
- "matching class", where a bit-by-bit vote is used (primarily for integers),
- "cosmetic class", where cosmetic errors are allowed (mainly used for character strings),
- "real number class", containing real numbers which are allowed to be slightly different.

Each class is considered separately below.

Matching Decision

This decision is applied on data that must be strictly equal, like binary values or integers. The comparison on equality is done between all cc-vectors.

Cosmetic Decision

Cosmetic errors are defined as errors in character strings like minor misspelling in a word which is to be displayed to the operator. The human would recognise the error and still correctly understand the word or message. If diverse versions are used with a bit-by-bit vote, a "cosmetically faulty" version will be declared faulty, and, according to the reconfiguration policy, could be discarded. If, on the other hand, the decision function can tolerate cosmetic errors, a system using design diversity will not be penalized in comparison to a "classical" fault-tolerant system. A version with cosmetic errors need not be discarded. However a cosmetic error must be distinguished from a fatal error.

As an example consider the integer '9', it can be written as character string '09', '9', or '_9', which would result in disagreement in a bit-by-bit comparison. In contrast, if the word size and the number representation are defined, the comparison of '9' as an integer would result in only one possible representation. Therefore numbers should not be represented as character strings.

For character strings, we have to decide which misspellings to allow. In a study [Pollock1983] misspellings found in several journals have been categorised. As the text of these journals has been processed by computer, the kind of misspellings in them can be expected to be representative of faults entered through a keyboard, and so representative of software. The Study showed that one misspelling occured for every 250 words. More than 90% of these misspellings can be characterized as being
- an omission of one character,
- an insertion of one character,
- a substitution of one character by another one,
- a transposition of two adjacent characters.

Cosmetic errors are tolerated by the cosmetic decision if they are part of the above four cases.

Numeric Decision

For decisions on real numbers, two solutions are proposed: select one representative value or tolerate all values within a given tolerance. In the first case, the representative value has to be defined and its selection algorithm has to be implemented, which will always result in an acceptable solution. In the second case, the results of the different versions are compared with each other to determine whether a majority of them is close enough together within the tolerance. Currently, the first approach is implemented in DEDIX, since we have been able to derive a very simple decision algorithm. This algorithm is summarized in the following.

We assume that an ideal value exists (IDEAL_VALUE), from which an allowed imprecision is defined (δ_-, δ_+), such that a version V_i is assumed to be non faulty, if and only if its response (R_i) is such that:
$$\text{IDEAL\_VALUE} - \delta_- \leq R_i \leq \text{IDEAL\_VALUE} + \delta_+.$$

The key of the algorithm is that it can be proved that, so long as a majority of versions are not faulty, the median of all responses is such that:
$$\text{IDEAL\_VALUE} - \delta_- \leq \text{MEDIAN} \leq \text{IDEAL\_VALUE} + \delta_+.$$

Since taking the median of numbers is very easy to do, we have thus a very simple way to compute a decision value. The most diverging versions can also be detected, as, under the same condition as the preceding property, it can be proved that a version V_i is faulty if
$$\text{MEDIAN} + \delta_- + \delta_+ < R_i$$
or
$$R_i < \text{MEDIAN} - \delta_- - \delta_+.$$

The agreement is reached in the following steps:
- computation of the median of the skews (if the versions use different skews),
- computation of the median of the responses,
- filtration of the versions using the above medians.

An agreement exists if a majority of versions has not been discarded by the filter; the decision value is the median.

DEDIX AS AN EXPERIMENTATION TOOL

Program Interface

In multiple version software the versions of an application program are all written according to the same functional specification. The specification must dictate not only the overall input-output transformation the program has to perform, but also which intermediate results must be compared, and at which points in the execution. The difference between a non-redundant program and the corresponding multiple version software running on DEDIX is minimized for programmers. Figure 3 shows a program written in C and its corresponding instrumented version. The program continues to read the system clock and output the current time until the user stops it.

```
main () {
    char *ctime();
    long clock;
    double f_clock;
    char *ctime_ret;
    char *reply = "y\n                    ";
    static char *s1 = "\tDate is: ";
    static char *s2 = " Do we continue? (y/n) ";
    while (reply[0] == 'Y' || reply[0] == 'y') {
        f_clock = time(0);
        clock = f_clock;
        ctime_ret = ctime(&clock);
        printf ("%s%s%s", s1, ctime_ret, s2);
        scanf ("%s", reply);
    }
    exit (0);
}
```

(a) basic program

```
version () {
    char *ctime();
    long clock;
    double f_clock;
    float f_drift = 2.0;
    char *ctime_ret;
    char *reply = "y\n                    ";
    static char *s1 = "\tDate is: ";
    static char *s2 = " Do we continue? (y/n) ";
    while (reply[0] == 'Y' || reply[0] == 'y') {
        f_clock = time(0);
        ccpoint(1, "%k%e", &f_drift, &f_clock);
        clock = f_clock;
        ctime_ret = ctime(&clock);
        ccoutput(2, "%S%s%S", s1, ctime_ret, s2);
        ccinput(3, "%s", reply);
    }
    return (0);
}
```

(b) instrumented version

Fig. 3. A program for displaying current time.

The differences between the program and the version are as follows:

(1) The name of the main function of the program is changed from main () to version ().

(2) The Cross-check function is called to decide on the clock values of different versions after the system clock is read. The first argument specifies the cc-point id. The second is the format which specifies that the clock value is voted on as a real number with a specified skew.

(3) Instead of using printf function for standard output, the ccoutput function is used which first votes on the output values and then outputs them. %S specifies that the string can tolerate cosmetic error.

(4) Similarly for the input, ccinput is used to input data from the standard input and broadcast it to all the versions.

(5) At the end of the program, *return* is used instead of *exit*.

User Interface

The user interface of DEDIX allows users to debug the system as well as the versions, monitor the operations of the system, apply stimuli to the system, and to collect empirical data during experimentation. A number of commands are available to the user for controlling the execution and defining additional output.

Breakpoint. The *break* command enables the user to set breakpoints. At a breakpoint, DEDIX stops executing and goes into the user interface where the user can enter commands to examine the current system states, examine past execution history, or inject stimuli to the system.

Monitoring. The user can examine the current contents of the message passing through the transport layer by using the *display* command. Since every message is logged, the user may also specify conditions in the *display* command to examine any message logged in the past. The user can also examine the internal system states by using the *show* command, e.g., to examine the breakpoints which have been set, the results of voting, etc.

Stimuli Injection. The user is allowed to inject faults to the system by changing the system states, e.g., the cc-vector, by using the *modify* command.

Statistics Collection. The user interface gathers empirical data and collects statistics of the experiments. Every message passing the transport layer is logged into a file with a time-stamp. This enables the user to do post-execution analysis or even replay the experiment. Statistics like elapsed time, system time, number of cc-points executed, and their results of decision are also collected.

Experiments

Several systems are already using diverse software, e.g. [Anderson1985, Gmeiner1979, Martin1982, Taylor1981]. Nevertheless, it appears (in addition to the fact that some people are not yet convinced of the usefulness of design diversity) that we need to know more about related errors. A primary goal of DEDIX is thus to evaluate these related errors. By using a controlled environment, it will be possible to examine the errors in order to
- trace the related errors,
- know whether the proportion of related errors is important or not,
- know the impact they have on the dependability of the system.

The data so obtained will be used to evaluate the meaning of design diversity and the architecture of future fault-tolerant computers.

Another important goal of DEDIX is the evaluation of specification methods. Indeed, specifications are likely to be the "hard-core" and the choice of a specification method has thus to be carefully evaluated. The number and proportion of related errors is a measure of the efficiency of a specification method. By efficiency, we mean the inherent ability of the method to reduce errors and other ambiguities in the resulting specifications.

What about the cost? It has been claimed that design diversity was too costly to be used. This is obviously not the case when the cost of a failure of the system is important (money or lifes). Without claiming as [Gilb1974] that N-version programming will always reduce programming cost, we consider the advantage of testing the versions in parallel, with DEDIX for example. Indeed, the test data are applied to all versions together, and no reference is needed: the reference is given by the agreeing majority of the versions.

To avoid effecting the execution time of DEDIX, the experimentation analysis is performed off-line. During the execution, files are created with for each occurrence of a cc-point, the cc-vectors of all the versions, the decision vector, and the diverse diagnosis and reconfiguration decision available in DEDIX.

CONCLUSION

Currently, DEDIX is completely implemented and running. The initial number of versions can be 2 or more, and a graceful degradation occurs when a version is rejected as being too often faulty. An experiment is under design, under the management of NASA, with the collaboration of four universities (University of Virginia, University of Illinois, North Carolina State University, and UCLA). After these experiments, some other fault-tolerance techniques will be tried on DEDIX (particularly in the domain of reconfiguration and recovery).

ACKNOWLEDGMENT

The research described in this paper has been supported by the Advanced Computer Science program of the FAA, by NASA contract NAG1-512, and by NSF grant MCS 81-21696.
We thank Jean-Claude Laprie for discussing this paper with us and giving as some valuable remarks.

REFERENCES

Anderson, T., Barrett, P. A., Halliwell, D. N., and Moulding, M. R., "An Evaluation of Software Fault Tolerance in a Practical System," in *Proceedings 15th Internat. Symp. on Fault-Tolerant Computing*, Ann Arbor, MI: 19-21 June 1985.

Avižienis, A. and Kelly, J., "Fault-Tolerance by Design Diversity: Concepts and Experiments," *Computer*, Vol. 17, No. 8, August 1984, pp. 67-80.

Avižienis, A., Gunningberg, P., Kelly, J.P.J., Strigini, L., Traverse, P.J., Tso, K.S., and Voges, U., "The UCLA DEDIX System: A Distributed Testbed for Multiple-Version Software.," in *15th IEEE International Symposium on Fault-Tolerant Computing*, Ann Arbor, Michigan: June 1985.

Chen, L. and Avižienis, A., "N-Version Programming: A Fault-Tolerance Approach to Reliability of Software Operation," in *Proceedings 8th IEEE International Symposium on Fault-Tolerant Computing Systems*, Toulouse, France: June 1978, pp. 3-9.

Cooper, E.C., "A replicated Procedure Call Facility," in *Proceedings 4th Symposium on Reliability in Distributed Software and Database Systems*, Silver Spring, MD: October 1984.

Gilb, T., "Parallel Programming," *Datamation*, October 1974, pp. 160-161.

Gmeiner, L. and Voges, U., "Software Diversity in Reactor Protection Systems: An Experiment," in *Proceedings Safety of Computer Control Systems, IFAC Workshop*, Stuttgart, Federal Republic of Germany: May 1979, pp. 73-79.

Gunningberg, P. and Pehrson, B., "Protocol and Verification of a Synchronization Protocol for Comparison of Results.," in *15th IEEE International Symposium on Fault-Tolerant Computing*, Ann Arbor, Michigan: June 1985.

Kelly, J.P.J., "Specification of Fault-Tolerant Multi-Version Software: Experimental Studies of a Design Diversity Approach," UCLA, Computer Science Department, Los Angeles, California, Tech. Rep. CSD-820927, September 1982.

Martin, D.J., "Dissimilar Software in High Integrity Application in Flight Controls," in *Proceedings AGARD-CPP-330*, September 1982, pp. 36.1-36.13.

Melliar-Smith, P.M. and Schwartz, R.L., "Formal Specification and Mechanical Verification of SIFT: A Fault-Tolerant Flight Control System," *IEEE Transactions on Computers*, Vol. C-31, No. 7, July 1982, pp. 616-630.

Pollock, J.J. and Zamora, A., "Collection and Characterization of Spelling Errors in Scientific and Scholarly Text," *Journal of the American Society for Information Science*, Vol. 34, No. 1, January, 1983, pp. 51-58.

Taylor, R., "Redundant Programming in Europe," *ACM Sigsoft Sen.*, Vol. 6, No. 1, January 1981.

Walker, B.J., Popek, G.J., English, R., Kline, C., and Thiel, G., "The LOCUS Distributed Operating System," in *Proceedings 9th ACM Symposium on Operating System Principles*, Bretton Woods, NH: October 1983, pp. 49-70.

AUTHOR INDEX

SUBJECT INDEX

Architecture, 7, 79, 85, 95, 101, 109, 129, 147, 173
Artificial intelligence, 21, 123

Computer applications, 167
  computer control, 25, 47, 53, 65, 95, 141
  industrial control, 85, 123, 129, 147, 153
  industrial robots, 13
Computer-aided decision making, 21
  artificial intelligence, 21, 123
  computer-aided design, 57, 73
  computer-aided development environment, 31
  operator support system, 25, 47

Design specification, 31, 135, 159
  design techniques, 1, 109, 147, 167
Distributed systems, 1, 7, 109, 117
  concurrent programming, 1
  local area network (LAN), 117
  multiprocessor systems, 79, 85, 101
Diversity, 7, 85, 153, 159, 167, 173
Documentation standards, 39

Fault tolerance, 7, 85, 109, 117, 123, 129, 135, 141, 147, 159, 167, 173
Fuzzy logic, 123

Hardware, 25, 79, 85, 95, 101
  VLSI design, 95

Industrial robots, 13

Maintenance, 79, 101
Man-machine interface, 13, 25, 47, 73
  human-computer interface, 21
  human factors, 25

Programming languages, 153
  coding errors, 153, 173

Reliability, 1, 13, 57, 65, 135, 141, 147
  reliability assessment, 57, 61, 73, 129
  reliability modelling, 21, 57, 129, 141

Reliability (continued)
  reliability theory, 13, 57, 61, 79, 129, 173
  safety assessment, 13, 61, 141
  software reliability, 153, 159
  statistics, 65, 129, 159
Requirements specification, 31, 135
  functional specification, 53
  formal specification languages, 53, 153

Software complexity, 21
Software life cycle, 53
  design and development process, 31, 39
Software reliability, 153, 159
Software tools, 53, 57, 73, 173
System failure and recovery, 79, 101, 109, 167
  failure detection, 85, 123
  fault classification, 153
  self-checking circuit, 95

Temporal logic, 135

Verification and validation, 31, 39, 47, 53
  software testing, 39
  computer testing, 53